Paul Ricoeur

Hermeneutics and the human sciences

Paul Ricoeur
Hermeneutics and the human sciences

Essays on language, action and interpretation

Edited, translated and introduced by
JOHN B. THOMPSON

Cambridge University Press
Cambridge
London   New York   New Rochelle   Melbourne   Sydney
Editions de la Maison des Sciences de l'Homme
Paris

Published by the Press Syndicate of the University of Cambridge
The Pitt Building, Trumpington Street, Cambridge CB2 1RP
32 East 57th Street, New York, NY 10022, USA
296 Beaconsfield Parade, Middle Park, Melbourne 3206, Australia
and
Editions de la Maison des Sciences de l'Homme
54 Boulevard Raspail, 75270 Paris Cedex 06

First published 1981

Printed in The United States of America

British Library Cataloguing in Publication Data

Ricoeur, Paul
Hermeneutics and the human sciences.
1. Hermeneutics
I. Title   II. Thompson, John Brookshire
112   BD241   80-41546

ISBN 0 521 23497 2 hard covers
ISBN 0 521 28002 8 paperback

BD
241
. R484

Contents

Acknowledgements

I began work on this volume while I was a research bye-fellow at Girton College, Cambridge. A grant from the SSRC/CNRS research exchange scheme for social scientists enabled me to spend time in Paris, where most of the translation was done. The volume was completed during the first year of a research fellowship at Jesus College, Cambridge. I wish to thank these institutions for their support.

I have benefited greatly from the comments and criticisms of others. Kathleen McLaughlin, David Pellauer and Michel Audet read all or most of the manuscript and made many valuable remarks. I also received helpful suggestions from David Held, Susanne Kappeler, Mike Barfoot and Alison Hendry. I am grateful to Anthony Giddens for his sound advice at every stage of the project. Above all, I offer my thanks to Paul Ricoeur, who so willingly and generously provided the material which forms this book. Any errors that may remain in the translation are, of course, my own.

All of the essays are reprinted with permission. Details of the original publication are as follows:

'La tâche de l'herméneutique', in *Exegesis: Problèmes de méthode et exercices de lecture*, edited by François Bovon and Grégoire Rouiller (Neuchâtel: Delachaux et Niestlé, 1975), pp. 179–200. An English translation of this essay appeared in *Philosophy Today*, 17 (1973), pp. 112–28.

'Herméneutique et critique des idéologies', in *Démythisation et idéologie*, edited by Enrico Castelli (Paris: Aubier Montaigne, 1973), pp. 25–64.

'Phénoménologie et herméneutique', in *Phänomenologische Forschungen*, vol. 1, edited by Ernst Wolfgang Orth (Freiburg: Karl Alber, 1975), pp. 31–77. A partial translation of this essay appeared in *Noûs*, 9 (1975), pp. 85–102.

'La fonction herméneutique de la distanciation', in *Exegesis: Problèmes de méthode et exercices de lecture*, edited by François Bovon and

Gregoire Rouiller (Neuchâtel: Delachaux et Niestlé, 1975), pp. 201–15. This is a modified version of an essay which appeared in English in *Philosophy Today*, 17 (1973), pp. 129–43.

'Qu'est-ce qu'un texte? expliquer et comprendre', in *Hermeneutik und Dialektik*, vol. 2, edited by Rüdiger Bubner et al. (Tübingen: J.C.B. Mohr, 1970), pp. 181–200. An abridged version of this essay appeared in English on pages 135–50 of David Rasmussen, *Mythic-Symbolic Language and Philosophical Anthropology* (The Hague: Martinus Nijhoff, 1971).

'La métaphore et le problème central de l'herméneutique', *Revue philosophique de Louvain*, 70 (1972), pp. 93–112. English translations of this essay appeared in *New Literary History*, 6 (1974), pp. 95–110; and *Graduate Faculty Philosophy Journal*, 3 (1973–4), pp. 42–58.

'The model of the text: meaningful action considered as a text', *Social Research*, 38 (1971), pp. 529–62.

'Science et idéologie', *Revue philosophique de Louvain*, 72 (1974), pp. 326–56.

'The question of proof in Freud's psychoanalytic writings', *Journal of the American Psychoanalytic Association*, 25 (1977), pp. 835–71.

'La fonction narrative', *Etudes théologiques et religieuses*, 54 (1979), pp. 209–30. A shorter version of this essay appeared in English in *Semeia*, 13 (1978), pp. 177–202.

Cambridge   J. B. T.
May 1980

Editor's introduction

The nature of language and meaning, of action, interpretation and subjectivity, are issues of increasing concern to a wide range of contemporary disciplines. For philosophers, linguists, literary critics and social scientists, the clarification of such issues has become an urgent and inescapable task. In the English-speaking world, however, the pursuit of this task remains hindered by both an institutionalised respect for disciplinary boundaries and a long-standing insularity with regard to Continental traditions of thought. There can be no doubt that the growing familiarity with the work of Paul Ricoeur will help enormously to overcome these obstacles. As one of the leading philosophers in post-war France, Ricoeur has written with originality and authority on an astonishing variety of topics. During the last few years, he has turned his attention more directly to problems of language, entering into a sustained dialogue with the tradition of hermeneutics. The dialogue with this tradition, whose members have focused for centuries on the process of interpretation,[1] forms the backcloth for the contributions contained in this volume.

In order to appreciate fully the significance of Ricoeur's current work, it is necessary to have some perspective on his writings as a whole. My aim in this introduction is to provide such an overall view. I shall begin with a brief synopsis of Ricoeur's career. In the second part, I shall trace the evolution of Ricoeur's thought, from his early project for a philosophy of the will, through his encounters with psychoanalysis and structuralism, to his recent preoccupation with the theory of the text. In the third part, I shall sketch the central themes of Ricoeur's current work. Finally, in the fourth part, I shall summarise some of the main arguments of the essays which appear in this volume. It should be said at the outset that no attempt will be made to give a comprehensive survey of Ricoeur's work. Certain contributions will be emphasised at the expense of others and some of his writings, for example those dealing with educational and theological issues, will largely be left aside.[2] It

1

should also be said that, however important Ricoeur's ideas may be, I do not believe that they are without difficulties; but this is not the place to express my reservations, which I have developed in detail elsewhere.[3] Here my aim is to present a short and thematic exposition of Ricoeur's views, in the hope of facilitating the sympathetic reception of his work in the English-speaking world.

I

Born in Valence in 1913, Ricoeur began his philosophical career at a time when European thought was dominated by the ideas of authors such as Husserl and Heidegger, Jaspers and Marcel. Gabriel Marcel was working in Paris when Ricoeur registered at the Sorbonne as a graduate student in the late 1930s. Marcel had a deep and lasting influence on Ricoeur's thought, directing it towards the formulation of a concrete ontology which would be infused with the themes of freedom, finitude and hope. However, Ricoeur believed that the pursuit of this goal demanded a method more rigorous and systematic than that which Marcel and his disciples employed. Ricoeur discovered the requisite method in the phenomenological writings of Edmund Husserl. As a prisoner in Germany during the Second World War, Ricoeur was allowed to read the work of Husserl, as well as that of Martin Heidegger and Karl Jaspers. He was impressed and attracted by Jaspers's thought, which he found close to Marcel's in many respects. Following the war, Ricoeur and Mikel Dufrenne – a friend and fellow prisoner – published a lengthy sketch of *Karl Jaspers et la philosophie de l'existence* (1947); and in the same year, Ricoeur published his own study of *Gabriel Marcel et Karl Jaspers*. In the early post-war years, Ricoeur also completed a translation of, and commentary upon, Husserl's *Ideen I*, thereby establishing himself as a leading authority on phenomenology.

In 1948 Ricoeur was elected to a chair in the history of philosophy at the University of Strasbourg. Each year he committed himself to read the collected works of one great philosopher, from Plato and Aristotle to Kant, Hegel and Nietzsche. This immersion in the tradition of Western philosophy turned Ricoeur away from the preoccupations of 'existentialism' or 'existential phenomenology', which was then being popularised by Sartre and Merleau-Ponty. For on the one hand, Ricoeur became increasingly concerned with the development of a *reflective* philosophy, a philosophy which seeks to disclose authentic subjectivity through a reflection upon the means whereby existence can be understood. On the other hand, he became more and more convinced that *necessity*, no less than freedom, is an integral aspect of human existence. Ricoeur's ambitious and highly original project on the philosophy of the will expresses this welter of influences on his thought. In the first volume of the project, *Le Volontaire et l'involontaire* (1950) (*Freedom and Nature: The Voluntary and the Involuntary*), Ricoeur employed a phenomenological method to explore the volitional dimension of what Marcel called 'incarnate existence'. The second volume of the philosophy of the will, a volume entitled *Finitude et culpabilité* (*Finitude and Guilt*), was published in 1960 as two separate books: *L'Homme faillible* (*Fallible Man*) and *La Symbolique du mal* (*The Symbolism of Evil*). In these two books, Ricoeur moved away from a strict phenomenological method and pursued the problem of the will into the opaque domain of human fallibility and fault. At the beginning of his project on the philosophy of the will, Ricoeur outlined the task of a third and final volume which would be dedicated to the 'poetics of the will'. He did not, however, undertake this task immediately, embarking instead upon an interrogation of two disciplines which had become a *succès de scandale:* psychoanalysis and structuralism.

Ricoeur was appointed to a chair in general philosophy at the Sorbonne in 1957. The intellectual milieu in Paris was changing rapidly: the ideas of Husserl and Heidegger were being eclipsed by those of Freud and Saussure. Ricoeur did not follow this trend; his inclinations were too distant from the fashions of Paris, his views too deeply rooted in the tradition of phenomenology. Yet Ricoeur could not ignore the change, since psychoanalysis and structuralism offered radical approaches to problems which he had been led to in his work on the philosophy of the will, problems concerning guilt, symbolism and the subject. Ricoeur met the challenge thus presented in a direct and cogent manner. His well-known and justly acclaimed study of Freud, *De l'interprétation: Essai sur Freud* (*Freud and Philosophy: An Essay on Interpretation*), was published in 1965. A collection which includes many of the essays he wrote on psychoanalysis and structuralism was published in 1969 under the title of *Le Conflit des interprétations: Essais d'herméneutique* (*The Conflict of Interpretations: Essays in Hermeneutics*).

In 1966 Ricoeur chose to teach at Nanterre, where he was appointed Dean in March 1969. Following the student occupation of the University in 1970 and the subsequent intervention by the police, Ricoeur resigned as Dean and moved to the University of Louvain. In 1973 he returned to Nanterre, combining his appointment there with a part-time professorship at the University of Chicago. At the same time, he assumed the directorship of the *Centre d'études phénoménologiques et herméneutiques* in Paris. It was during this period that Ricoeur became preoccupied with problems of language and entered more deeply into the dialogue with hermeneutics. His masterly study of metaphor, *La Métaphore vive* (*The Rule of Metaphor*), was published in 1975. He also wrote, and continues to write, many essays on related issues. Such prolificity is amply attested to by Ricoeur's bibliography, which now includes more than a dozen books and several hundred essays. In the next two parts of the introduction, I should like to draw out some of the central themes of this substantial corpus, beginning with the original project for a philosophy of the will.

II

Philosophy of the will
The aim of Ricoeur's philosophy of the will is to reflect upon the affective and volitional dimensions of human existence. This philosophy thus focuses on issues like action and motive, need and desire, pleasure and pain. Ricoeur initially approaches such issues from a phenomenological perspective, that is, from a perspective which attempts to describe the ways in which phenomena appear and to relate these modes of appearance to subjective processes of consciousness. In approaching the dimensions of the will from a phenomenological perspective, Ricoeur distances himself from the work of existentialists, as well as from the position of Husserl himself. For Ricoeur is critical of those authors who plunge too quickly into a vivid portrayal of everyday experience: 'in the early stages at least', he insists, 'phenomenology must be structural'.[4] Yet Ricoeur criticises, with equal force, Husserl's tendency to treat perception as a paradigm of the operations of consciousness. In rejecting this 'logistic prejudice', Ricoeur seeks to develop Husserl's method beyond its idealistic origins, applying it to those regions of human experience which lie on the very boundaries of conscious life.

The first stage of Ricoeur's philosophy of the will is presented in *Freedom and Nature*. In this study, Ricoeur attempts to unfold the basic structures of the will at the level of 'essential possibility', that is, at a level which abstracts from the accidental features of everyday life. What is revealed at this level is that the structures of the will are characterised by a fundamental reciprocity of the voluntary and the involuntary. The dualism of subject and object, of freedom and nature, is not primary, but is rather an attitude which phenomenological description must delve beneath. Through long and intricate analyses, Ricoeur shows how, in the act of willing, consciousness adheres to the elements of involuntary life, and how in turn the elements of involuntary life adhere to the 'I will'. Thus the act of willing involves a decision designating a future action which lies within the agent's power; but the decision is based upon motives, the action is mediated by bodily organs, and the act of willing as a whole is conditioned by character, the unconscious and life, to which the agent must consent. The reintegration of consciousness into body and body into consciousness is not, however, harmonious. The unity of the voluntary and the involuntary is a 'drama', a 'polemic', anticipating a reconciliation which is less a reality than a limiting idea. In the light of this limiting idea, our freedom truly appears for what it is, 'a freedom which is human and *not* divine'.[5]

In *Finitude and Guilt,* the second volume of the philosophy of the will, Ricoeur removes some of the methodological parentheses which restricted his earlier analyses to the level of essential possibility. The first book of this volume, *Fallible Man,* initiates the movement towards that feature of human existence which constitutes the locus of evil. This feature is 'fallibility'; it can be conceived as the line of fault, as the constitutional weakness which gives rise to an interruption or distortion of the basic structures of willing. Hence fallibility is not continuous with the characteristics disclosed in *Freedom and Nature,* wherein 'we sketched', as Ricoeur recalls, 'the undifferentiated keyboard upon which the guilty as well as the innocent man might play'.[6] To grasp hold of this new dimension requires, therefore, a transformation of method. The object of analysis is no longer an essential structure accessible to phenomenological description, but rather an internal aberration that must be approached regressively through reflection on unstable syntheses. Reflection reveals, for example, that the primary passions of possession, power and worth are suspended between a finite pole of pleasure and an infinite pole of happiness, so that each bears the threat of endless pursuit. By means of such reflection, Ricoeur seeks to specify those aspects of human existence which harbour the possibility of evil, thereby preparing the way for an inquiry into the actuality of fault.

The transition from possibility to actuality, from fallibility to fault, is accomplished in *The Symbolism of Evil,* which is the second book of *Finitude and Guilt.* Once again, the movement demands a methodological shift. For the actuality of fault cannot be apprehended directly, in the fullness of experience, but can be approached only through the language in which that experience is expressed. Description of essential structures and reflection on unstable syntheses thus give way to a hermeneutics of symbols and myths. Ricoeur begins his inquiry with the most primitive expressions of the confession of evil, that is, with the 'language of avowal'. This language is thoroughly 'symbolic', in the sense that it speaks of sin or guilt in an indirect and figurative way which calls for interpretation. Although the interpretation of symbols and of the myths constructed from them is not identical with philosophical reflection, nevertheless interpretation paves the way for reflection. For as Ricoeur submits, 'I am convinced that we must think, not *behind* the symbols, but starting from symbols, . . . that they constitute the *revealing* substrate of speech which lives among men. In short, the symbol *gives rise to* thought.'[7] Hermeneutics is thus the route to philosophical reflection, to reflection premised on the assumption that by following the indication of symbolic meaning one will arrive at a deeper understanding of human existence.

Examination of psychoanalysis
The emergence of interpretation as a central moment in the study of the will leads Ricoeur into an examination of psychoanalysis. For if hermeneutics is the route to philosophical reflection, then reflection cannot escape from the conflict of interpretations. As Ricoeur explains at the outset of *Freud and Philosophy*, 'there is no general hermeneutics, no universal canon for exegesis, but only disparate and opposed theories concerning the rules of interpretation. The hermeneutic field . . . is internally at variance with itself.'[8] Thus, according to one view, hermeneutics is construed as the restoration of a meaning addressed to the interpreter in the form of a message. This type of hermeneutics is animated by faith, by a willingness to listen, and it is characterised by a respect for the symbol as a revelation of the sacred. According to another view, however, hermeneutics is regarded as the demystification of a meaning presented to the interpreter in the form of a disguise. This type of hermeneutics is animated by suspicion, by a scepticism towards the given, and it is characterised by a distrust of the symbol as a dissimulation of the real. Ricoeur suggests that it is the latter type of hermeneutics which is practised by Marx, Nietzsche and Freud. All three of these 'masters of suspicion' look upon the contents of consciousness as in some sense 'false'; all three aim to transcend this falsity through a reductive interpretation and critique.

Having situated psychoanalysis within the field of hermeneutics,

Ricoeur undertakes a systematic reading of Freud's work. The reading consists of three basic cycles, each of which isolates a distinctive problematic. The first cycle begins with the 'Project' of 1895, encompasses the interpretation of dreams and neurotic symptoms, and ends in a state of the system which Ricoeur calls the 'first topography': unconscious, preconscious, conscious. In this cycle, the principal concern is with the structure of psychoanalytic discourse, which presents itself as a mixture of statements of force and statements of meaning; and as Ricoeur repeatedly proclaims, 'this mixed discourse is not an equivocal discourse for want of clarification: it grips firmly the very reality we discover when we read Freud and which we can call *the semantics of desire*'. [9] The second cycle of the reading is concerned with the extension of Freud's ideas to the sphere of culture, an extension which reacts back upon the original model and results in the 'second topography' of *ego, id, superego*. Finally, in the third cycle, Ricoeur explores the upheaval effected by the introduction of the death instinct. This instinct completes both the theory of culture and the interpretation of the reality principle, but in so doing it propels Freud into a mythological realm dominated by the figures of Eros, Thanatos and Ananke.

The notion of a semantics of desire provides the parameters for Ricoeur's approach to the epistemological status of psychoanalysis. In reply to those critics who contend that Freud's theory does not satisfy the most elementary criteria of scientificity, and in contrast to those authors who attempt to reformulate the theory in order to accord with these criteria, Ricoeur maintains that all such contentions and reformulations betray the very essence of psychoanalysis. For the latter is not an observational science dealing with the facts of behaviour; rather, it is an interpretative discipline concerned with relations of meaning between representative symbols and primordial instincts. Thus psychoanalytic concepts should be judged, not according to the exigencies of an empirical science, but 'according to their status as conditions of the possibility of analytic experience, insofar as the latter operates in the field of speech'. [10] The recognition of the irreducible role of language and meaning in psychoanalysis brings Ricoeur close to the position of Jacques Lacan and his followers. Ricoeur is critical, however, of the Lacanian attempt to interpret condensation as metaphor and displacement as metonymy. Such an attempt disregards the energetic dimension of psychoanalysis, thus failing to account for the barrier, for the *bar* of repression, which separates ordinary language from the quasi-language of the unconscious. In Ricoeur's view, therefore, neither the behaviourist nor the Lacanian conception does justice to the peculiarity of psychoanalysis as a semantics of desire.

The final phase of Ricoeur's examination of the writings of Freud occurs at the level of philosophical reflection. The question which dominates this phase is twofold: (1) how does the mixed discourse of psychoanalysis enter into a reflective philosophy? and (2) what happens to the subject of reflection when the guile of consciousness is taken seriously? The answer to this question is crystallised in the claim that 'the philosophical place of analytic discourse is defined by the concept of an archaeology of the subject'.[11] This concept concedes the dispossession of immediate consciousness to the advantage of another agency of meaning, namely the emergence of desire. Yet desire is accessible only through the disguises in which it manifests itself; it is only by interpreting the signs of desire that one can capture its emergence, and thus enable reflection to regain the archaic heritage which it has lost. Ricoeur builds upon the implicit teleology displayed by the expansion of reflection, proposing to complement the regressive analysis of Freudianism by a progressive synthesis of the figures of the mind. Indeed, the internal dialectic of archaeology and teleology, of regression and progression, is itself rooted in the overdetermined structure of the authentic symbol. Ricoeur thus concludes his philosophical reflection on Freud with the suggestion that the complex constitution of the symbol contains the key to the resolution of the conflict of interpretations.

Confrontation with structuralism

The growing importance of language in Ricoeur's thought is the stimulus for his critical confrontation with structuralism. The term 'structuralism' refers to an assortment of doctrines which have been prevalent in France since the early 1960s, and which have been associated with such authors as Roland Barthes, Claude Lévi-Strauss and Louis Althusser. The diverse contributions of these and other authors are united by an underlying linguistic model, the presuppositions of which define the limits of the structuralist approach. The model was originally constructed by Saussure, but Ricoeur finds a more trenchant formulation in the work of the Danish linguist Louis Hjelmslev. Drawing upon Hjelmslev's *Prolegomena to a Theory of Language*, Ricoeur summarises the presuppositions of the linguistic model as follows. First, structuralism assumes that language is an object that can be investigated scientifically. Second, structuralism distinguishes between a science of states of the system and a science of changes, and it subordinates the latter to the former. Third, the structuralist model presupposes that in any state of the system there are no absolute terms but only relations of mutual dependence, so that language 'becomes a system of signs defined by their differences alone'.[12] Fourth, structuralism treats the collection of signs as a closed and autonomous system of internal dependencies. It follows from these presuppositions that for structuralism a sign must be defined not in terms of some object for which it stands, but rather in terms of its relation to all other signs of the same level within the system of which it is part.

In the writings of 'structuralist' authors such as Lévi-Strauss, the linguistic model is transposed into other object domains. Lévi-Strauss justifies this transposition with the assumption that the relevant domains are themselves systems of communication and hence comparable to language. Kinship relations, for example, constitute systems of oppositional pairs in which women are circulated between families or clans in a manner analogous to the way in which words are exchanged between individuals. Similarly, myths can be conceived as systems of constituent units or 'mythemes' which are interconnected by laws resembling those of linguistics. In *The Savage Mind*, however, Lévi-Strauss goes well beyond these cautious transpositions and applies the linguistic model to a whole level of thought. The level is that of 'savage thought', of thought, as Ricoeur remarks, 'which orders but which does not think itself'.[13] According to Lévi-Strauss, therefore, savage thought is an 'unconscious' order which can be analysed objectively as a pure system of differences.

Ricoeur develops his critique of structuralism through a reflection on the limits imposed by the presuppositions of the linguistic model. He argues that in founding itself upon these presuppositions, structural linguistics excludes from consideration a number of important phenomena. It excludes, for instance, the act of speaking, not only as an individual performance but as the free creation of new expressions. History is also excluded, for history is more than the passage from one state of a system to another: it is the process whereby human beings produce themselves and their culture through the production of their language. Structuralism excludes, moreover, the primary aim or intention of language, which is to say something about something. Language has both an ideal sense, to say something, and a real reference, to say it about something. In one movement of transcendence language leaps across two thresholds, and thereby takes 'hold of reality and expresses the hold of reality on thought'.[14] The exclusion of such phenomena leads Ricoeur to question the initial presupposition of the linguistic model, namely that language is an object which can be investigated scientifically. For it is too readily forgotten that the object is relative to the theory and method of the structuralist approach. Language is absolutised as an object and structuralism exceeds the limits of its validity, thus occluding the communicative process whereby someone says something to someone about something.

The tendency to overstep the limits of validity of structuralism is characteristic of Lévi-Strauss. Ricoeur attempts to demonstrate such transgressions by arguing, to begin with, that the transition from the linguistic model to the savage mind is accomplished by means of a privileged instance. The examples adduced by Lévi-Strauss are drawn from a particular range of ethnographic material, a range which lends itself with exceptional ease to the reshufflings of the *bricoleur*. However, if one were to draw examples from a different tradition of thought, from the Semitic, pre-Hellenic or Indo-European tradition, it seems unlikely that the examples could be analysed without remainder by the structuralist method; and that remainder, that irreducible residue of meaning, would be the legitimate object of a hermeneutic inquiry. A similar transgression of the limits of validity is evident in the implicit movement, made by Lévi-Strauss and others, from a structuralist science to a structuralist philosophy. Ricoeur maintains that this movement is bound to fail. For structuralism, insofar as it precludes the possibility of self-reflection, can never establish itself as a philosophy. 'An order posited as unconscious can never, to my mind, be more than a stage abstractly separated from an understanding of the self by itself; order in itself is thought located outside itself.'[15] A genuinely reflective philosophy must nevertheless be receptive to the structuralist method, specifying its validity as an abstract and objective moment in the understanding of self and of being. This imperative forms one of the principal guidelines for Ricoeur's recent work on the theory of language and interpretation.

III

Discourse and creativity
The philosophy of the will, the examination of psychoanalysis and the confrontation with structuralism have all raised fundamental questions concerning the nature of language. In response to such questions, Ricoeur seeks to develop a theory of language which would provide the

springboard for a hermeneutic philosophy. The theory is premissed upon a fundamental distinction between system and discourse. Although this distinction is related to the Saussurian dichotomy between *langue* and *parole,* it is more directly indebted to the work of the French linguist Emile Benveniste. According to Benveniste, language is a totality that can be articulated into a series of levels, each of which is characterised by a distinctive and constitutive unit. The transition between these levels is not, however, a continuous one. Whereas the phoneme, the morpheme, the semanteme and so on are all signs defined by their internal and oppositive relations, the sentence is not itself a sign but rather an indeterminate and unlimited creation. The sentence 'is no longer the unit of a language [or system], but of speech or discourse'.[16] The transition to the level of discourse creates the possibility of a genuine semantics of the sentence, as distinct from a semiotics of the sign.

Ricoeur unfolds the features of discourse in terms of an internal dialectic between event and meaning. Discourse has an eventful character, insofar as to speak is to realise an event which immediately disappears. Yet although the utterance of a sentence is an ephemeral phenomenon, nevertheless a sentence may be reidentified as the same on subsequent occasions; in other words, 'if all discourse is realised as an event, all discourse is understood as meaning'.[17] Ricoeur suggests that, on first approximation, the notion of meaning may be analysed into two basic dimensions, comprising both an objective aspect or that which the sentence means, and a subjective aspect or that which the speaker means. In discussing these two dimensions, Ricoeur draws upon the work of philosophers well known in the English-speaking world, most notably the work of J.L. Austin, P.F. Strawson and John R. Searle. Ricoeur further distinguishes, following Frege, between two components of the objective aspect of meaning: the sentence has both an ideal sense and a real reference. It is only at the level of the sentence that language can refer to something, that the closed universe of signs can be related to an extra-linguistic world. The referential relation is thus a crucial characteristic of discourse and one in virtue of which the semiotics of the sign must be regarded as a derivative discipline.

The semantics of discourse sheds light on the primitive processes of creativity and interpretation in ordinary language. The basic condition of creativity is the intrinsic polysemy of words, that is, the feature by which words in natural languages have more than one meaning. The boundaries of polysemy can be defined by a semiotics of the sign, since the potential uses of a word are accumulated and codified in the lexical system. Ricoeur maintains, however, that the actual functioning of polysemy can be grasped only by a semantics of the sentence. For words have meaning only in the nexus of sentences, and sentences are uttered only in particular contexts. Polysemy thus depends on a contextual action which filters out some of the surplus meaning, so that a univocal discourse can be produced from polysemic words. To grasp this filtering effect is to exercise interpretation in its most primordial sense. 'The simplest message conveyed by the means of natural language has to be interpreted because all the words are polysemic and take their actual meaning from the connection with a given context and a given audience against the background of a given situation.'[18] Polysemy, by endowing the word with a surplus of meaning that must be sifted through interpretation, provides the basis for the creative extension of meaning through metaphor.

Ricoeur develops his ideas on metaphor through a detailed analysis of earlier views. In traditional rhetoric, metaphor is regarded as a type of trope, that is, as a means whereby a figurative word is substituted for a literal word on the grounds of an apparent resemblance. Metaphor, so conceived, tells us nothing new; it is merely a decorative device which embellishes a language that is otherwise austere. In an attempt to go beyond this static view, Ricoeur turns to the work of certain Anglo-Saxon authors, such as I.A. Richards, Max Black and Monroe Beardsley. What these authors have shown is that metaphor operates primarily at the level of the sentence rather than that of the word; or more precisely, it operates between these two levels. Metaphor, according to Ricoeur, presupposes the establishment of a tension between two terms in the sentence through the violation of a linguistic code. The metaphorical statement then appears as a reduction of this tension by means of a creative semantic pertinence within the sentence as a whole. Hence Ricoeur suggests that 'metaphor is a semantic innovation that belongs at once to the predicative order (new pertinence) and the lexical order (paradigmatic deviation)'.[19] The emergent meaning can be grasped only through a constructive interpretation which makes sense of the sentence as a whole, building upon and extending the polysemy of the metaphorical terms. The emergence of sense is accompanied by a transformation of the referential dimension, endowing metaphor with its power to redescribe reality. The nature of this transformation, which affects not only metaphor but literary works in general, is clarified by the concept of the text.

Texts and the theory of interpretation

Ricoeur makes the transition from semantics to hermeneutics proper with the formulation of a concept of the text. The text is a work of discourse, and hence in the first instance a *work*. To say that a text is a work is to say that it is a structured totality which cannot be reduced to the sentences whereof it is composed. Such a totality is produced in accordance with a series of rules which define its literary genre, and which transform discourse into a poem, a novel, a play. At the same time as a work belongs to a genre, so too it has a unique configuration which defines its individual style. The production of discourse as a work is thus displayed in its composition, its genre and its style. These categories are categories of production and of labour; 'to impose a form upon material, to submit production to genres, to produce an individual: these are so many ways of treating language as a material to be worked upon and formed'.[20] As a work of discourse, the text preserves the properties of the sentence, but presents them in a new constellation which calls for its own type of interpretation.

In addition to being a work of discourse, the text is a *written* work. Ricoeur emphasises that the text is not merely the inscription of some anterior speech, as if speaking were the oral fount of every written work. On the contrary, speaking and writing are alternative and equally legitimate modes of the realisation of discourse. The realisation of discourse in writing nevertheless involves a series of characteristics which effectively distance the text from the conditions of spoken discourse. Ricoeur encapsulates these characteristics in the key notion of 'distanciation', a notion which displays four principal forms. The first form of distanciation is the surpassing of the event of saying by the meaning of what is said. It is the meaning which is inscribed in writing, and this inscription is rendered possible by the 'intentional exteriorisation' of the speech-act; that is, the constitutive features of the speech-act can be realised in writing by means of various grammatical and syntactic devices. The second form of distanciation concerns the relation between the inscribed expression and the original speaker. Whereas in spoken discourse the intention of the speaking subject and the meaning of what is said frequently overlap, there is no such coincidence in the case of writing. 'What the text signifies no longer coincides with what the author meant; henceforth, textual meaning and psychological meaning have different destinies.'[21] The third form of distanciation introduces a similar discrepancy between the inscribed expression and the original audience. In contrast to spoken discourse, where the hearer is specified by the dialogical relation, written discourse is addressed to an unknown audience and potentially to anyone who can read. The text thus 'decontextualises' itself from its social and historical conditions of production, opening itself to an unlimited series of readings. The fourth and final form of distanciation concerns the emancipation of the text from the limits of ostensive reference. Whereas the reference of spoken discourse is ultimately determined by the shared reality of the speech situation, in the case of writing this shared reality no longer exists. The possibility arises, therefore, that the text has a referential dimension which is of a different order from that of speech, a dimension which is unfolded in the process of interpretation.

The theory of interpretation elaborated by Ricoeur is closely connected to the concept of the text. This connection reveals a shift away from Ricoeur's earlier work, in which interpretation was linked to the complex structure of the authentic symbol. It is no longer the symbol but the text, written discourse as such, which defines the object domain of hermeneutics. Accordingly, the principal features of Ricoeur's theory of interpretation can be derived from the characteristics of written discourse. The first two forms of distanciation – the eclipse of the event of saying by the meaning of what is said and the severance of the latter from the intentions of the speaking subject – imply that the objective meaning of a text is something other than the subjective intentions of its author. From this Ricoeur concludes, in direct opposition to the views of literary critics like E.D. Hirsch, that 'the problem of the right understanding can no longer be solved by a simple return to the alleged intention of the author'.[22] Just as the resolution of the tension established by a metaphor requires the construction of a new sense, so too the meaning of a text must be guessed or construed as a whole. The construal of meaning may indeed result in more than one interpretation of a text, in which case the imminent conflict must be subsumed to a process of argumentation; but this is a process, Ricoeur firmly insists, in which the alleged intentions of the author have no privileged role.

The second two forms of distanciation have equally important consequences for the theory of interpretation. Ricoeur observes that the emancipation of written discourse from the interlocutors and circumstances of the dialogical situation engenders two possible attitudes towards the text. On the one hand, the reader may suspend any judgement concerning the referential dimension of the text, treating the latter as a wholly worldless and self-enclosed entity. On the other hand, the reader may abandon this *epoché* and seek to unfold the non-ostensive references of the text. The first attitude is adopted by the structuralist approach, which attempts to explain the text in terms of its internal relations. Structuralism thereby offers a novel and fruitful type of explanation, a type which comes not from the natural sciences but from the field of language itself. Yet Ricoeur argues, echoing his earlier critique of Lévi-Strauss, that any such explanation presupposes a form of understanding which cannot be reduced to structural analysis. The presupposed form of understanding is the concern of the second attitude that the reader may adopt towards the text. For the reader may seek, not something hidden behind the text, but something disclosed in front of it; not the internal constitution of the text, but that which points towards a possible world. To understand a text at this level is to move from its sense to its reference, from that which it says to that which it says it about. In Ricoeur's theory, therefore, explanation and understanding are no longer contradictory attitudes, as has often been assumed in the history of hermeneutics. On the contrary, with the mediation of structural analysis 'it seems possible to situate explanation and interpretation along a unique *hermeneutical arc* and to integrate the opposed attitudes of explanation and understanding within an overall conception of reading as the recovery of meaning'.[23]

Action and history

Although formulated with respect to texts, Ricoeur's theory of interpretation can be extended to other domains. The extension to the sphere of the social sciences is rendered possible by the claim that action may be regarded as a text, insofar as it may be objectified in a way that embodies the four forms of distanciation. For example, just as the inscription of discourse involves the surpassing of the instance of saying by the meaning of what is said, so too the objectification of action is marked by the eclipse of the event of doing by the significance of what is done. On the basis of such considerations, Ricoeur enters into the methodological debate concerning the relative roles of explanation and understanding in the interpretation of action, a debate which Wilhelm Dilthey, Max Weber and others initiated in the context of the social sciences. For if indeed action may be regarded as a text, then it is plausible to propose that 'the paradigm of reading, which is the counterpart of the paradigm of writing, provides a solution for the methodological paradox of the human sciences'.[24] An action, like a text, is a meaningful entity which must be construed as a whole; and a conflict of interpretations can be resolved only by a process of argumentation and debate, in which the intentions of the agent may be relevant but are not decisive. Moreover, the structuralist mode of analysis can be transposed into the social sphere, providing an explanatory moment which mediates a depth interpretation of action. For Ricoeur contends that human action, no less than literary texts, displays a sense as well as a reference; it possesses an internal structure as well as projecting a possible world, a potential mode of human existence which can be unfolded through the process of interpretation.

The extension of the theory of interpretation to the domain of action is all the more plausible in that action itself is the referent of many texts. Aristotle tells us that tragedy seeks to imitate human action in a poetic way: 'the *mythos* of tragedy – that is, both its fable and its plot – is the *mimesis*, the creative imitation, of human action'.[25] Tragedy does not merely describe action but presents it in a more favourable light, making it appear higher and nobler than it is in reality. The emphasis on the creative character of tragedy points to a further and more profound affinity with action, for the latter too is animated by the creative power of imagination. The role of imagination is evident both on an individual level, where action is projected in accordance with an anticipatory schema, and on a social level, where individuals relate to one another and to their collective tradition through the figures of ideology and utopia. These figures are not mere distortions of social life, but rather are, according to Ricoeur, constitutive of the social bond itself. If utopian thought expresses a critical distance from social reality, such distance is possible only because that reality is first integrated through an ideology which precedes critical reflection and which transmits a collective tradition.

The complex interplay between belonging to a tradition and distancing oneself from it forms the matrix for extending the theory of interpretation to the sphere of history. Historical experience is fundamentally the experience of belonging to a tradition that is received from the past. Yet as Dilthey, Husserl and others have stressed, experience is essentially expressible: it can be externalised in signs that demand to be understood. Thus distanciation is the counterpart of belonging, from which it follows that 'historical experience and writing share the same fate. Historical experience as inscribed is put at a distance, and so history is a science based on traces.'[26] The distanciation of historical experience justifies the incorporation of an explanatory dimension into the discipline of history. One attempt to specify such a dimension was made by Carl Hempel in his classic study of 'The function of general laws in history'. As in his critique of structuralism, Ricoeur does not dismiss Hempel's attempt outright. For Hempel's mistake is not that he searches for an explanatory structure of history, but that he fails to grasp the methodological framework within which the explanatory structure operates. Explanation in history is not an end in itself; it serves to mediate historical understanding which is tied in turn to the narrativity of the historical text. The generalisations or 'explanatory sketches' of the historian thus serve to facilitate the following of stories, especially when the latter process has become interrupted or blocked.

The link between the history of the historians and the interpretation of texts is in no way dissolved by the 'realist intention' of history. There is no doubt that history claims to offer a true representation of past events, and that it typically adduces various kinds of evidence in support of this claim. Yet Ricoeur maintains that, just as *mimesis* endows fiction with a referential relation to the real world of action, so too history has an imaginary aspect. By recognising the values of the past only through their differences from those of the present, history opens up the real towards the possible. As Ricoeur says, 'the "true" histories of the past uncover the buried potentialities of the present'.[27] Indeed, so far from diverging at the level of reference, it is precisely at this level that history and fiction converge upon the fundamental historicity of human experience. Thus the ambiguity of the word 'history', an ambiguity which is even richer in the French word *histoire*, is no accident: retelling the text of the past is part of the reality of the present – part, as Gadamer would say, of the 'effective-historical consciousness'.

Hermeneutics and philosophical reflection

The theory of interpretation, elaborated with respect to texts and then extended to the socio-historical world, reaffirms the connection between hermeneutics and philosophical reflection. In his earlier writings, Ricoeur established this connection by drawing upon the work of the French philosopher Jean Nabert. Closer to Fichte than to Kant, Nabert dissociates reflection from epistemological justification and conceives it instead as the recovery of the effort to exist and the desire to be. However, this effort and this desire cannot be grasped immediately in an act of intellectual intuition; they can only be glimpsed through the mirror of the objects and acts, the symbols and signs, wherein they are disclosed. Hence 'reflection must become interpretation because I cannot grasp the act of existing except in signs scattered in the world'.[28]

Reflection cannot speak from nowhere, for it must always begin by interpreting the cultural products of a specific tradition. Such interpretation makes reflection 'concrete', opening it to the methods and results of all the disciplines concerned with the socio-historical world.

In addition to providing material for philosophical reflection, the humanistic disciplines transform its very nature. For reflection is necessarily self-reflection, and such disciplines raise afresh the question of what 'the self' might signify. Thus psychoanalysis castigates the pretensions of the narcissistic *ego*, leaving behind a wounded and humiliated *cogito*, 'a *cogito* which understands its primordial truth only in and through the avowal of the inadequation, the illusion, the fakery of immediate consciousness'.[29] Freud presents us with the startling discovery that consciousness is not a given but a task, a task to be accomplished through the long and tortuous by-way of a semantics of desire. Similarly the critique of ideology, as formulated by Marx and developed in the writings of the so-called Frankfurt School, proclaims consciousness to be the realm of falsehood. For everyday attitudes are generally distorted representations of reality, concealing and justifying the system of domination. The critique of ideology seeks to unveil these distortions and to engender an authentic consciousness in the minds of the oppressed. So reflection must be linked to hermeneutics not only because existence can only be grasped in its external manifestations, but also because immediate consciousness is an illusion which must be unmasked and overcome through an interpretative critique.

The concept of concrete reflection is further enriched by the theory of interpretation. By subordinating the subjective intentions of the author to the objective meaning of the text, the theory effects an initial displacement of the primacy of the subject. As with psychoanalysis and the critique of ideology, however, this extirpation of the subject as radical origin prepares the way for the reintroduction of subjectivity in a more modest role. For the process of interpretation culminates in an act of appropriation which forms the concluding counterpart of distanciation. To appropriate, Ricoeur explains, 'means "to make one's own" what was initially "alien" ', so that 'interpretation brings together, equalises, renders contemporary and similar'.[30] The act of appropriation does not seek to rejoin the original intentions of the author, but rather to expand the conscious horizons of the reader by actualising the meaning of the text. Although interpretation thus culminates in self-understanding, it cannot be equated with naive subjectivism. Ricoeur emphasises that appropriation is not so much an act of possession as an act of dispossession, in which the awareness of the immediate *ego* is replaced by a self-understanding mediated through the text. Thus interpretation gives rise to reflection because appropriation is bound to the revelatory power of the text, to its power to disclose a possible world.

The culmination of interpretation in an act of appropriation indicates that ontology forms the ultimate horizon of hermeneutics. In endorsing the quest for ontology, Ricoeur reveals his distance from most Anglo-Saxon philosophies of language, as well as his proximity to the work of Heidegger and Gadamer. Like the latter authors, Ricoeur considers hermeneutics to be concerned with the understanding of being and the relations between beings. Nevertheless, Ricoeur wishes to 'resist the temptation to separate *truth*, characteristic of understanding, from the *method* put into operation by disciplines which have sprung from exegesis'.[31] To dissociate method and truth, in the manner proposed by Gadamer, is to disregard the conflict of interpretations within which we perceive the being we seek to understand. It may well follow that the ontology attainable in Ricoeur's account will remain a fragmented and incomplete formulation of being; but this intrinsic fragmentation of the hermeneutical horizon is no basis for renunciation or despair. For it merely attests to the condition of a philosophy which has acknowledged its fundamental finitude.

IV

Studies in the history of hermeneutics

The foregoing remarks provide a philosophical backcloth for the studies collected in this volume. The studies do not purport to reflect this backcloth, to illustrate the evolution of Ricoeur's ideas or to exemplify the scope of his work. Rather, the studies presented here concern a series of problems which are addressed from a single standpoint, that of 'hermeneutics' or more precisely of 'hermeneutic phenomenology'. Although the details of this standpoint have yet to be worked out, Ricoeur demonstrates that it has a great deal to offer to many disciplines of thought. If the essays in this volume focus on issues which are of immediate relevance to the humanistic disciplines, from philosophy and literary criticism to sociology, psychoanalysis and history, this is not because Ricoeur has nothing to say in other spheres. To compile a collection of essays by an author as prolific as Ricoeur requires that the editor adopt a principle of selection; and in the case of this volume the essays have been chosen in order to present a systematic discussion of problems and perspectives in philosophy and the social sciences.

In the first essay of the volume, 'The task of hermeneutics', Ricoeur offers a clear and concise account of the recent history of hermeneutics. He views this history in terms of the interaction between two developments: the movement from a regional to a general hermeneutics, and the transition from epistemology to ontology. The movement of 'deregionalisation' began with the work of the German theologian Friedrich Schleiermacher (1768–1834), and reached its conclusion in the contributions of Wilhelm Dilthey (1833–1911). Writing in the neo-Kantian climate of the late nineteenth century, Dilthey situated the problem of interpretation within the general domain of historical knowledge, for which he sought to elucidate the conditions of possibility. Dilthey's contributions thus remained largely epistemological, and it was not until the work of Martin Heidegger (1889–1976) that the real transition to ontology was made. For Heidegger, understanding is no longer conceived as a way of knowing but as a mode of being, as a fundamental characteristic of our 'being-in-the-world'. Ricoeur maintains, however, that the philosophy of Heidegger as well as that of his eminent student, Hans-Georg Gadamer, fails to resolve the problem of how hermeneutics is to return from ontology to the epistemological questions which have been left behind.

The second essay, 'Hermeneutics and the critique of ideology', continues to explore the hermeneutic tradition. The essay focuses on a debate which took place in Germany a few years ago. The debate was initiated in 1967 with the publication of Jürgen Habermas's *Zur Logik der Sozialwissenschaften*, which contains an incisive critique of Gadamer's *Wahrheit und Methode* (*Truth and Method*), first published in 1960. Gadamer replied to Habermas and a lively debate ensued, each protagonist seeking to curtail the universalistic claims raised by the other. Ricoeur's lengthy study is not only an excellent introduction to this literature: it is also an original and important contribution to the debate. Ricoeur attempts to go beyond a sterile antinomy, a mere juxtaposition of conflicting views, towards a dialogue which would be genuinely constructive. He argues that hermeneutics can no longer treat problems of method as secondary and derivative, as Gadamer tends to do; for we belong to tradition only in and through a distance which implies the possibility of objective analysis and critique. In turn, the critique of ideology can no longer claim to be animated by an interest which is wholly distinct from the governing principle of hermeneutics; for we can criticise the present only in the name of an ideal which acquires its content from the creative appropriation of the past.

'Phenomenology and hermeneutics' is also constructed in the form of a debate, although now the issues are more closely linked to the struggle within Ricoeur's own thought. This essay, which forms something of a landmark in Ricoeur's career, confronts the question of what remains of Husserl's programme in the wake of the upheaval effected by Heidegger and Gadamer. There can be no doubt that the latter authors offer a devastating critique of phenomenology. Yet as Ricoeur convincingly shows, what succumbs to the hermeneutical critique is not phenomenology as such, but rather phenomenology in its most idealistic form, in the form advanced by Husserl himself. Once this form is renounced, the way is prepared for the recognition of a deep and mutual affinity between hermeneutics and phenomenology. On the one hand, hermeneutics shares with phenomenology both the assumption that the question of meaning is primary, and the thesis that the source of meaning is anterior to language. On the other hand, the method of phenomenology is ineluctably interpretative, as Ricoeur shows by a careful analysis of Husserl's texts. The mutual affinity between hermeneutics and phenomenology provides the philosophical basis for Ricoeur's constructive work.

Studies in the theory of interpretation
The studies which appear in Part II present the key ideas of Ricoeur's positive contribution to hermeneutics. All of the essays are concerned with elaborating various aspects of the theory of interpretation. In 'The hermeneutical function of distanciation', Ricoeur begins this task by formulating the concept of the text. As a written work of discourse, the characteristics of the text can be specified, first, in terms of the categories of production; and second, in terms of the relation between speaking and writing. An analysis of the latter relation uncovers the forms of distanciation which constitute the semantic autonomy of the text. By treating the autonomous text as the focal point of hermeneutics, Ricoeur raises the possibility of eluding the alternative between alienating distanciation and participatory belonging. For the text introduces a positive and productive notion of distanciation which is not an obstacle to be overcome, but rather the very condition of historical understanding. Hence for Ricoeur, problems of method are as central as problems of truth.

In 'What is a text? Explanation and understanding', Ricoeur pursues the methodological implications of his reorientation of hermeneutics. Ever since Dilthey, it has been common to contrast 'understanding' with 'explanation', conceptualising the former in psychological terms and expelling the latter altogether from the sphere of the human sciences. Ricoeur regards these tendencies as misleading and seeks to counter them in his theory of textual interpretation. We have seen how, as an objectified and autonomous entity, the text can be submitted to the explanatory methods of structural analysis; but such an analysis does not eliminate the need for understanding, which is mediated and enriched by the structuralist account. Ricoeur offers an illuminating example of this depth-hermeneutical approach through a critique of Lévi-Strauss's analysis of the Oedipus myth. Lévi-Strauss's division of the elements of the myth into four interrelated categories may indeed explain the myth but it does not interpret it, nor does it eliminate the problem of interpretation. For the analysis presupposes a question which it does not pursue, a question concerning the ultimate origin of human life. To recover such a question would be the aim of understanding, which would thus be very different from any psychological notion of empathy.

Some of the connections between the theory of interpretation and the theory of metaphor are examined in 'Metaphor and the central problem of hermeneutics'. The connections are possible because metaphor, like the text, can be analysed within the framework of discourse. The basic unit of metaphors and texts alike is the sentence, even if this unit is maximal in the case of metaphors and minimal in the case of texts. This common ground suggests that the theory of interpretation may be applicable to both entities, and indeed that the problems raised by the interpretation of one may shed light on the interpretation of the other. Ricoeur thus proposes the hypothesis that, from the viewpoint of explanation, the analysis of metaphor is a good guide to the analysis of the text; whereas from the viewpoint of interpretation, the analysis of the text provides the key to the analysis of metaphor. For on the one hand, the necessity of constructing a network of interactions in order to account for the emergence of metaphorical meaning invites us to treat the text as a structured totality whose sense must be constructed as a whole. On the other hand, the appropriation of the world disclosed by the text encourages us to recognise that metaphor too has a referential dimension, a power employed by poetry when it engages in the creative imitation of reality.

The final essay in the second part focuses on the concept of appropriation. This essay, which forms part of a lecture course given by Ricoeur in 1972–3, is published here for the first time. It is important because it represents a systematic attempt to formulate a concept of the subject which would concur with the theory of interpretation. The theory demands not only the initial suspension of the referential relation, but also the initial relinquishment of subjectivity: both subject and object must be submitted to a process of metamorphosis. To explore this process, Ricoeur draws upon Gadamer's analysis of the phenomenon of play. Gadamer shows that play is not so much the activity of the subject as an activity upon the subject, an activity in which the subject 'is played'. Similarly Ricoeur suggests that, in the theory of interpretation, the subject – whether author or reader – is a 'playful figure' of the text. The initial relinquishment of subjectivity is thus the precondition for the ultimate expansion of consciousness under the objective guidance of the text. Understanding is self-understanding, although the return to the self is not the first but the final moment in the theory of interpretation.

Studies in the philosophy of social science

The third part of the volume contains four studies in the philosophy of social science. In the first of these studies, 'The model of the text: meaningful action considered as a text', Ricoeur makes a provocative attempt to extend the theory of interpretation to the field of the social sciences. Ricoeur assumes, along with Max Weber, that the object of these sciences is meaningful action. He then proffers a series of arguments to demonstrate, first, that meaningful action shares the constitutive features of the text; and second, that the methodology of the social sciences is similar to the procedures elaborated for the interpretation of texts. The development of a depth-hermeneutical approach to action suggests a way of overcoming the classical oppositions, such as that between explanation and understanding or between motive and cause, which have plagued the philosophy of social science. The approach also implies that the 'hermeneutical circle' of understanding and self-understanding, of comprehension and commitment, is an ineliminable aspect of social scientific knowledge.

The epistemological problems of the social sciences are discussed at length in 'Science and ideology'. After showing that ideology plays a fundamental role in the integration of social life, Ricoeur turns to the question of the conditions under which a scientific knowledge of ideology would be possible. Such knowledge might be possible if social science were able to satisfy the positivist criteria of scientificity, for example the criteria of generality and falsifiability. It seems clear, however, that theories in the social sciences fall well short of this ideal. Ricoeur willingly allows that the criteria of scientificity for social theory may be quite different from those entailed by the positivist model; but having abandoned this model, we cannot then surreptitiously reintroduce it, in the manner of Althusser and others, in order to institute an 'epistemological break' between science and ideology. The abandonment of the positivist model is at the same time, Ricoeur argues, the rejection of a disjunctive conception of the relation between science and ideology. Henceforth we must acknowledge that there is no privileged place, no Archimedian point, from which a non-ideological knowledge of ideology could be produced. We must recognise instead that the social sciences have a hermeneutical character, from which it follows that all knowledge of the social world is preceded and supported by a relation of belonging – an 'ideological' relation in the primordial sense – upon which we can never fully reflect.

'The question of proof in Freud's psychoanalytic writings' is similarly concerned with problems of epistemology. In this essay, Ricoeur confronts the vexed question of the scientific status of psychoanalysis, a question which had been raised but by no means resolved in *Freud and Philosophy*. Ricoeur's current approach to this question reveals a shift away from his earlier work, where the emphasis was on the structure of psychoanalytic theory. His starting point now is the analytic situation, which determines what counts as a 'fact' in psychoanalysis. The relation between fact and theory is, in addition, much more complicated than that alleged by the traditional empiricist account. These preliminary considerations prepare the way for Ricoeur's suggestion that the type of truth claim raised by psychoanalysis is very different from the notion of truth presupposed by the observational sciences. For the truth claim of psychoanalysis is inseparable from the self-recognition achieved through the process of narration. Nevertheless, the explanatory dimension of psychoanalysis provides means of proof which are not contained in the narrative structure itself. It is in the complex articulation of psychoanalytic theory, the interpretative procedures, the therapeutic treatment and the narrative structure of analytic experience that the means of proof, and hence the criteria of a good psychoanalytic explanation, ultimately consist.

In the final essay of the volume, Ricoeur takes up the theme of narrativity in order to establish a connection between fictional stories and the histories written by historians. The framework for this study is provided by the distinction, by now familiar, between sense and reference. At the level of sense, Ricoeur tries to show that history and fiction share a common structure, that is, a common way of ordering events into a coherent narrative. He defends this thesis through a twofold critique, dealing first with Hempel's argument against the narrative character of history and then examining the attempt by the French structuralist A.J. Greimas to 'dechronologise' the story. At the level of reference, Ricoeur maintains, as we have seen, that whatever differences there may be in the ways that history and fiction relate to reality, nevertheless they both refer to the fundamental historicity of human existence. The referential dimensions of history and fiction 'cross' upon historicity, upon the historical condition of a being which makes and writes history. History and narrativity, narrative and historicity: such are the main axes of the hermeneutical problem in the current writings of Ricoeur.

Conclusion

The essays collected in this volume are part of a philosophical evolution which they both express and continue. As an expression of this evolution, the essays recover and refine many of the ideas which have emerged in the course of Ricoeur's career. The concern with meaning, action and imagination, to mention only a few examples, reveals a deep continuity with his previous work. As in his early writings, so too in these essays: an ontology of human finitude remains the horizon of philosophical reflection. Yet the essays are also a continuation of the evolutionary process in at least two respects. Ricoeur's method is now explicitly hermeneutical, marking a shift away from the phenomenological emphasis of his earlier work. Phenomenology may remain the unsurpassable presupposition of hermeneutics, but it is above all hermeneutics whose presuppositions must be examined. The change in method is closely connected to a displacement of the initial object of investigation. The immediate focus is no longer the intentional objects of subjective processes, or even the symbolic expressions of personal experiences, but rather the whole domain of written discourse, of texts and analogues of texts. The double shift in method and in object reflects the continuing evolution of Ricoeur's work towards the task which draws his thought forward, towards the projected but postponed 'poetics of the will'.

The reader of the essays presented here will discover a philosophy which, in spite of its declared allegiances, is genuinely open. Ricoeur's ideas do not form a closed system. His thought is not constrained by the dictates of an orthodox position or by the boundaries of an established discipline. His work is informed by the contributions of many intellectual traditions, from hermeneutics and phenomenology to analytical philosophy, structuralism and critical theory; and these contributions are moulded into a perspective which is original and unique. The reader will also find that Ricoeur is much more than a 'philosopher', as this term is commonly understood in the English-speaking world. His work is not restricted to a narrow range of logical and linguistic problems, but spills over into a broad spectrum of disciplines. Ricoeur is a philosopher in the classical sense, a thinker who turns his attention to diverse domains and who expresses his views on issues which are of social and political as well as intellectual concern. The reader cannot fail to be impressed by the breadth and the boldness of his thought.

Notes on editing and translating

(1) The essays in this volume differ in minor respects from the form in which they first appeared. With Professor Ricoeur's approval, I have corrected the text at several points. I have also deleted some material in order to reduce repetition. All such deletions are indicated in the text by ellipses in square brackets.

(2) With two exceptions, I have translated or retranslated all of the essays from the original French. The two exceptions are 'The model of the text: meaningful action considered as a text', and 'The question of proof in Freud's psychoanalytic writings'. These two essays were published in English and have never appeared in French. I have made small alterations to these essays in order to minimise repetition and to render terminology consistent throughout the volume.

(3) Most notes and references are placed at the end of the volume. However, when Ricoeur conducts a detailed analysis of a particular work, I have used abbreviations so that the reference may be given directly in the text. In such cases, full bibliographical details and an explanation of the abbreviation appear in the note corresponding to the first citation of the work in each essay.

(4) In the text, the titles of French and German works are given in English when an English translation exists. When Ricoeur quotes from a work for which there exists an English translation, I have included in the notes a reference to the latter in square brackets. I have, wherever possible, used the existing English translation of passages quoted by Ricoeur. However, it was frequently necessary to alter the existing translation in order to render the passage closer to Ricoeur's version. In such cases, the reference to the English translation is followed by the symbol '†'.

(5) The essays contain a variety of German expressions. Since the analysis of these expressions often plays an important role in Ricoeur's argument, I have left them in German. Where the meaning of the expression is not clear from the context, I have added an English equivalent in square brackets.

(6) Ricoeur uses specific terms to translate German expressions. For example, he generally renders *Deutung* as *interprétation* and *Auslegung* as *explicitation,* even though both German expressions are commonly translated as 'interpretation' in English. It is important to preserve Ricoeur's distinction if one is to make sense of his analyses of German texts. Accordingly, I have translated these and related terms as follows.

compréhension (Verständnis) : understanding
explication (Erklärung) : explanation
explicitation (Auslegung) : explication
interprétation (Deutung) : interpretation

Ricoeur translates Gadamer's expression *wirkungsgeschichtliches Bewusstsein* in several ways; I have always followed the French version, so that the expression is rendered variously as 'consciousness of the history of effects', 'consciousness of historical efficacy', 'historical-effective consciousness', etc. Ricoeur changes Gadamer's *Sprachlichkeit* from a noun to an adjective, generally translating it as *le caractère langagier.* The term *langagier* is distinct from *linguistique,* since the former is the adjectival form of 'language' whereas the latter is linked to a particular way of studying language. In order to sustain this distinction, I have translated *langagier* as 'lingual'; this provides a convenient nominal form for Gadamer's original expression: 'linguality'.

I have translated as follows some of the other terms which Ricoeur uses for German expressions.

appartenance (Zugehörigkeit) : belonging
enchaînement (Zusammenhang) : interconnection
remplissement (Ausfüllung) : intentional fulfilment
sciences de l'esprit (Geisteswissenschaften) : human sciences
vécu (Erlebnis) : lived experience
visée (das Vermeinte) : intended meaning

(7) Ricoeur employs two phenomenological terms which deserve comment. 'Noesis' refers to any of the acts of consciousness which remain after the reduction of the world to the sphere of the subject's experience. 'Noema' refers to the intentional object of such an act, that is, to

the 'something' which the subject perceives, imagines, considers, etc., irrespective of whether that something actually exists. Incorporated into the theory of language, the noesis becomes the act of meaning or intending-to-say, and the noema the meaning-content of what is said.

(8) A number of Greek words appear in the essays. Their meaning is usually evident from the context, but there are two which it may be helpful to define in advance. An *aporia* is an insoluble problem, a difficulty with no way out. An *epoché* is a suspension of judgement; it is used by Husserl to describe the act of reduction with which phenomenological analysis begins.

(9) Ricoeur's writings on language present the translator with several problems. One such problem is raised by a series of distinctions stemming from Saussure. Whereas *langue* is the language-system or code, *parole* is the realm of language-use, of the realisation of the system in individual utterances. *Langue* is also distinct from *langage:* the former term designates the object domain of structural linguistics, whereas the latter refers to the totality of language before it has been parcelled into particular object domains. Since these distinctions are blurred by the English words 'speech' and 'language', I have left the French term in square brackets whenever it is essential for comprehension.

Another problem arises from the distinction between *sens* and *signification*. These terms cannot be directly correlated with 'sense', 'meaning', 'signification' or 'significance'; *sens,* for example, has a broader connotation in French than 'sense' has among English-speaking philosophers. I have therefore not translated them in a one-to-one fashion. *Sens* is rendered either as 'sense' or as 'meaning'; but when it is clear from the context that *sens* does not include reference, it is always rendered as 'sense'. I have translated *signification* as 'meaning' or 'signification', and occasionally in non-technical cases as 'significance'; 'signification' is used to emphasise the narrower, logical or linguistic acceptation of *signification*. Both 'meaning' and 'signification' may include reference.

The expressions which I have used for some of the other key terms in Ricoeur's writings are given below.

chose du texte : matter of the text
effectuation : realisation
effet de sens : meaningful effect
énoncé : statement

énonciation : utterance
entente préalable : prior understanding
ludique : playful
monstration : act of showing
propositions de monde : proposed worlds
propositions de sens : proposals of meaning

(10) In discussing ideology, Ricoeur speaks of its function of *dissimulation*. I have generally used the same term in English, since 'dissimulation' means concealing or disguising under a feigned appearance; occasionally, however, I have used the more ordinary expression 'concealment' and its cognates. Ricoeur also speaks of the *critique des idéologies* with *idéologies* in the plural, in order to counter the assumption that there is only one ideology – the ideology of the other – which is in need of critique. However, since the English expression 'critique of ideology' is the customary rendition of the German term *Ideologiekritik*, and since 'critique of ideology' clearly leaves open the possibility that more than one ideology must be criticised, I have preferred this expression to the somewhat clumsier 'critique of ideologies'.

(11) Ricoeur's discussion of Greimas's work poses special difficulties. For Greimas has developed his own terminology for the analysis of narrative, and his work has yet to be translated into English. One of Greimas's central concepts is that of *actant*, which, as Ricoeur explains, refers not to characters as individual subjects but to roles correlated with formalised actions. I have left the term as 'actant' in English, rendering its adjectival form as 'actantial'.

(12) Translating from French into English presents certain choices with respect to the gender of pronouns. To eliminate the masculine bias in such cases would require one to add, for the sake of consistency, the feminine pronoun at every point. This would constitute a substantial alteration of Ricoeur's text, as well as making the English unwieldy. For these reasons, I have allowed the bias to stand.

(13) Ricoeur sometimes exploits the ambiguity of certain words. For example, *sens* means both 'sense' and 'direction'; *jeu* means both 'play' and 'game'; and *histoire* means both 'story' and 'history'. Many such ambiguities and word-plays are unfortunately lost in translation.

(14) I have occasionally left French terms in square brackets when the English equivalent is imprecise. However, this practice has been kept to a minimum so as to avoid cluttering the text.

(15) Throughout the translation, I have tried to be consistent and to stay close to the original French, while at the same time striving for clarity and fluency in English. Whether I have succeeded in transforming a text which reads well in French into one which reads well in English will remain for the reader to judge.

A response by Paul Ricoeur

I should like, in this brief foreword, to express my gratitude to John Thompson for the considerable work which the translation of my essays represents. I am in complete agreement with his choice of terms for rendering French or German expressions that have no equivalents, either in the British philosophical tradition or even in the English language. Of course, there is always a point at which a translation becomes an interpretation; but Thompson has ensured continuity and coherence in his choices. He has thus provided an English translation of my essays which is as readable as it is exact.

I should also like to express my interest in the analysis which he offers, in his substantial introduction, of the development of my work from 1947 until the earliest articles in this collection, none of which date from before 1970. The perspective which he proposes corrects the inverse impression, to which I have a tendency to succumb: that of a certain lack of continuity in my writings. For each work responds to a determinate challenge, and what connects it to its predecessors seems to me to be less the steady development of a unique project than the acknowledgement of a residue left over by the previous work, a residue which gives rise in turn to a new challenge.

The first challenge was that represented by the apparent incapacity of Husserlian phenomenology to deal with volitional experience, since the privilege of theoretical consciousness and perception seemed so much to dominate, to the point of saturating, the descriptive field opened up by the analysis of intentionality; had not Merleau-Ponty as well written a phenomenology of perception? Could one write a phenomenology of the will without abandoning the method of describing the *essential* structures of consciousness? *Freedom and Nature* attempted to respond to this challenge.

However, the residue left by the analysis was considerable. On the one hand, a gap appeared between the intended meaning of freedom of the will and the various limitations attested to by the involuntary – a disproportion which seemed to have no parallel in the sphere of theoretical consciousness, even if one emphasised, more than Merleau-Ponty had done, the gap between the conceptual meaning of language and the corporeal condition of perception. On the other hand, a more disturbing gap appeared between the essential structures of the volitional consciousness – project, motive, the absolute involuntary of character, of unconscious, of life and death – and the historical or empirical condition of the human will, prisoner of the passions and prone to evil. The experience of the evil will seemed to lie on the boundaries of the 'essential' condition of willing.

The first gap still fell within the reflective philosophy conveyed by the French philosopher Jean Nabert and the intentional analysis derived from Husserl. The description of the disproportion between the intended meaning of freedom and the experience of finitude could still be situated within the framework of a phenomenology which is, as it were, dramatised or polemicised, and which opens onto a meditation of a Pascalian kind applied to human fallibility. It is this type of existential phenomenology that one finds at work in *Fallible Man*.

The second gap seemed less amenable to the phenomenological method. The servile condition of the evil will seemed to elude an essential analysis of phenomena. So the only practicable route was that of a detour via the symbols wherein the avowal of the fault was inscribed during the great cultures of which ours is the heir: the primary symbols of stain, guilt and sin; the secondary symbols or myths of tragic blindness, of the fall of the soul, of wandering or decline; the tertiary symbols and rationalisations of the servile will or of original sin. *The Symbolism of Evil* thus marked the turning of Husserlian phenomenology, already extended to the problematic of fallibility, towards a hermeneutics of symbols.

By 'symbols' I understood, at that time, all expressions of double meaning, wherein a primary meaning refers beyond itself to a second meaning which is never given directly. In this regard, Thompson is perfectly right to underline the difference between this initial definition of hermeneutics limited to an interpretation of the hidden meaning of symbols, and the subsequent definition which extends the work of interpretation to all phenomena of a textual order and which focuses less on the notion of hidden meaning than on that of indirect reference. However, the first definition was limited by the very problematic to which it responded, namely the necessity of effecting a detour via symbols in order to account for the specific phenomenon of the evil will.

Once again, it was the residue left by this study of the symbols of evil which was to set reflection in motion. Not only was hermeneutics restricted to the interpretation of phenomena of double meaning, but it sought to actualise the richest and most spiritual meaning of symbols and thus functioned, without explicit critical concern, as a hermeneutics of recollection. This amplifying hermeneutics is opposed in our culture to a demystifying and reductive hermeneutics, stemming more from suspicion than from reminiscence. Psychoanalysis appeared to me as the paradigm of such a hermeneutics. The examination of psychoanalysis was all the more necessary since its interpretation of guilt was diametrically opposed to that which I had offered in *The Symbolism of Evil*. Is guilt not denounced by Freud, if not as always neurotic, at least as arising from the repressive action of cultural norms? *Freud and Philosophy* is the work which attempts to take up this challenge. I thought at first that I would be able to restrict myself to a confrontation with psychoanalysis which was limited to the question of guilt. It quickly became clear that psychoanalytic theory as a whole would have to be confronted, not only with my version of the symbolic function, but also with the reflective philosophy onto which I was grafting the interpretation of symbols. For in my earlier works, the great detour via signs had not called into question the primacy of the subject. I found in Freud not only the counter-pole to hermeneutics conceived as recollection of symbols, but also an incisive critique of the whole reflective tradition to which I continued to link myself through Kant, Husserl and Nabert. The notions of a semantics of desire, of the archaeology and teleology of the subject, thus introduced me to the theme of *The Conflict of Interpretations*, which was to dominate the entire phase of my work prior to the articles gathered together by Thompson.

The field of investigation was to be enlarged and displaced in a new way by the recognition of the *lingual* character which was common to the symbols of my first hermeneutics and to the distorted expressions studied by psychoanalysis. It appeared that the linguistic dimension of all symbolism had not been made the object of a distinct and systematic treatment in my earlier works, in spite of the fact that the detour via symbols had, since *The Symbolism of Evil*, taken the form of a detour of reflection on the self via an investigation of the mediating *signs* of this reflection. It is upon this terrain of the investigation of language that I encountered a new challenge, that of French structuralism, which eliminated any reference to a speaking subject from its analysis of signifying systems. I thus discovered a convergence between the structuralist critique originating from linguistics and the psychoanalytic critique originating from Freud, a convergence in what I called collectively the *semiological challenge*. It was not only the hermeneutics of symbols, but once again its roots in a reflective philosophy, hence in a philosophy of the subject, which was the target of the structuralist and psychoanalytic double attack. In order to respond to this semiological challenge, I took the concept of the *text* as the guiding thread of my research, with the aim of showing that the text is the level at which structural explanation and hermeneutic understanding confront one another. It was then necessary, however, to dissociate the hermeneutical project from the simple interpretation of expressions of double meaning and to expand it to the dimensions of the problem posed by the passage from the structure immanent in every text to its extra-linguistic aim [*visée*] – the aim or reference which I sometimes designate by other related terms: the matter of the text, the world of the text, the being brought to language by the text.

The three articles grouped together in the first part of the present collection take account of the profound methodological revolution demanded by this new definition of hermeneutics. Thompson very wisely chose to open the volume with an essay, 'The task of hermeneutics', which belongs to a series that originally continued with the first essay in the second part, 'The hermeneutical function of distanciation'. Placed at the beginning, 'The task of hermeneutics' acquires introductory value, enabling one to glance backwards over the history of the hermeneutical problem from Schleiermacher to Gadamer. The second essay, dedicated to the debate between Habermas and Gadamer, nicely completes the historical backcloth of my own conception of hermeneutics. Together, these two essays introduce the major essay of this section, 'Phenomenology and hermeneutics'. As Thompson quite rightly says, it is here that I clarify my own debate with phenomenology which I had begun twenty years earlier, in translating Husserl's *Ideas* and in writing *Freedom and Nature*. This essay constitutes in my view the real introduction to my subsequent work. However, it is not so for the reader – particularly for the English-speaking reader – who has not made the same journey as myself from phenomenology to hermeneutics and who, no doubt, has no need to make it in order to enter into the problems of interpretation treated in the second series of essays. Hence Thompson was perfectly right to place this essay at the conclusion of the history of hermeneutics, or rather of the history of my own discovery of post-Heideggerian hermeneutics. This essay also offers an account *après-coup* of the revision of phenomenology and the movement towards hermeneutics which was already discernible in *The Symbolism of Evil.*

The second series of essays gives an idea of the hermeneutics which I practise. Moreover, Thompson has chosen essays which orient hermeneutics more directly towards a debate with the social sciences. If there is a feature which distinguishes me not only from the hermeneutic philosophy of Schleiermacher and Dilthey, but also from that of Heidegger and even Gadamer (despite my great proximity to the work of the latter), it is indeed my concern to avoid the pitfall of an opposition between an 'understanding' which would be reserved for the 'human sciences' and an 'explanation' which would be common to the latter and to the nomological sciences, primarily the physical sciences. The search for a flexible articulation and a continual to and fro between the investigator's personal engagement with the matter of the text, and the disengagement which the objective explanation by causes, laws, functions or structures demands, is the guiding thread of the four essays chosen for the second part.

The first essay, 'The hermeneutical function of distanciation', pursues in a positive epistemological perspective the debate begun in a more historical and polemical way in 'Hermeneutics and the critique of ideology'. For the pair 'distanciation and participatory belonging' is the equivalent, in a language influenced by Gadamer, of the pair 'explanation and understanding', inherited from Dilthey's epistemology. The second essay takes up my earlier discussion of structuralism and continues it within the expanded framework of the theory of the text, seeking to define interpretation as the overarching term of the connections between 'explanation and understanding'. The epistemological status of hermeneutics is thus defined by the very dialectic between these two attitudes, which the Romantic hermeneutics of the nineteenth century tended to contrast and which post-Heideggerian hermeneutics did not succeed in reconciling. The third essay, dedicated to the problem of metaphor, is partially situated in the same framework, while also testifying to a different problematic which I shall raise in conclusion. Apart from taking up the old problem of the symbol within the more sophisticated framework of rhetoric, the theory of metaphor is situated in the problematic of the text insofar as metaphor consists not only in a deviation and extension of the meaning of words, but in a 'bizarre' application of predicates in the context of the sentence, which can be considered as a text in miniature. The fourth essay extends the dialectic of

understanding and explanation, and that of engagement and distanciation, to the very interior of the human subject implicated in the work
of interpretation. This subject appropriates – makes his own – the matter of the text only insofar as he disappropriates himself and the naive,
uncritical, illusory and deceptive understanding which he claims to
have of himself before being instituted as subject by the very texts
which he interprets.

Thompson is right to emphasise that the hermeneutics illustrated by
the four essays of the second part finds its limit in the operative concept
of the text. Although this concept had been introduced with the express
intention of encompassing problematics as diverse as those encountered in *The Symbolism of Evil, Freud and Philosophy* and the essays
brought together under the title of *The Conflict of Interpretations*, nevertheless it retains a restricted scope, insofar as the idea of the text remains linked to that of writing and hence also to the problems posed
by the passage from oral to written discourse. For it is with writing that
the text acquires its semantic autonomy in relation to the speaker, the
original audience and the discursive situation common to the interlocutors. It is also with writing that the problems of reference assume
all their acuteness, when the world of the text is dissociated from the
ostensive references peculiar to oral discourse. However, from the outset the notion of the text incorporated features which freed it partially
from the relation to writing as opposed to oral discourse. Text implies
texture, that is, complexity of composition. Text also implies work, that
is, labour in forming language. Finally, text implies inscription, in a
durable monument of language, of an experience to which it bears tes-
timony. By all of these features, the notion of the text prepares itself for
an analogical extension to phenomena not specifically limited to writing, nor even to discourse.

This analogical extension governs the essays of the third part, which
pertain more directly to Thompson's principal concern, namely the relation between hermeneutics and the social sciences. This concern also
explains why he has chosen the essay entitled 'The model of the text:
meaningful action considered as a text' to introduce this series. For the
basic analogy between text and action is the key to the relation between
the theory of interpretation and the social sciences invoked in the following essays. In turn, the social sciences provide interpretation with
a field much larger than language. If the object of the social sciences is
(directly or indirectly) meaningful action, according to a definition borrowed from the methodological section of Max Weber's *Economy and*

Society, then the analogy between text and action enables the theory of interpretation to be freed from the constraints of discourse and writing and extended to the whole field of the social sciences.

Beginning from this analogy, the contribution of the following essays to the investigation of the relation between the theory of interpretation and the domain of the social sciences becomes clearer. Three samples have been selected by Thompson, because of their link with the investigation of this relation. The question of ideology, already discussed in the context of the debate between Gadamer and Habermas, is reconsidered here from the viewpoint of the interpretation that a social group offers of itself by means of collective representations. The question of the epistemological status of interpretation reappears in the essay on 'The question of proof in Freud's psychoanalytic writings'. In this regard, Thompson is right to stress the difference of approach between this essay and my book on Freud: instead of focusing reflection on Freudian theory – that is, on the metapsychology – as in the period dominated by the conflict of interpretations, this essay deliberately reconnects the work of interpretation to the analytic situation itself and treats the theory as the explanatory phase grafted onto the process of interpretation implied by the analytic situation. Thompson wished to close his selection with a sample of my current research on the narrative function, appearing in the double form of historical and fictional narratives. In a sense, it is the same debate between understanding and explanation which is pursued here; for the capacity to follow a story expresses the irreducible component of understanding in the act of narrating, whereas the investigation of laws in history, and of narrative structures in folktales, plays, novels and fictional literature in general, corresponds to the explanatory phase of the nomological sciences. In this way, my current research on narrativity falls again within the investigation of the role of interpretation in the social sciences.

I shall allow myself, however, to suggest to the reader another way of linking this final essay to those which precede it. My present inquiry into the narrative function supplements from another point of view my earlier work on metaphor, at the level of what Kant calls, in his transcendental philosophy, the productive imagination and the schematism which is the intelligible matrix of it. This is the aspect of the theory of metaphor which I alluded to above. For against the background of the debate between explanation and understanding, the formidable question of creativity stands out. This question always seemed to me to be either too easy or too difficult: too easy, insofar as it invites waffle devoid of rigour; too difficult, as Kant himself said of the schematism which he called 'a mechanism hidden in the depths of the soul, which it is impossible to extricate from nature'. However, if the problem of creativity cannot be approached directly and as a whole, perhaps it can be treated in a lateral and fragmentary fashion. Metaphor constitutes one of these limited approaches, insofar as the productive imagination assumes the form of a *semantic innovation*. The imagination operates here on the verbal level to produce new configurations of meaning, at the cost of extending the polysemy characteristic of natural languages. Another use of the productive imagination can be discerned in the invention of plots whereby the narrator – whether historian or novelist – introduces an intelligible order into a sequence of disparate events and combines together circumstances, goals and hazards.

The same problematic which links my recent work on metaphor to my work in progress on narrativity appears to me now as one of the main themes of my earlier work. Thus, as Thompson himself notes, the analysis of ideology, as well as that of utopia which complements it, falls within the framework of a theory of the *social imaginary*; and psychoanalysis, insofar as it groups together nocturnal dreams, waking dreams, myths and other cultural representations around fantasy, can be considered from the viewpoint of its contribution to the theory of the imaginary. More generally, all symbolism, considered from the point of view of its dynamics, constitutes a vast expression of the *imaginary at its cultural level*. Going back further in my own investigations, I notice that the imagination was already situated, in the period of *Fallible Man*, at the fragile point where the voluntary and the involuntary are articulated and where fallibility insinuates itself into the ontological structure of man. Finally, the constantly postponed project of a 'Poetics of the Will' is that of a general philosophy of the creative imagination, considered in turn on the level of semantic innovation and practical representation, on the individual level, and on the cultural and social level.

So the question is whether it is possible to overcome what I called above a lateral and partial approach to the problem of creativity and to conceive a philosophical anthropology which would deepen into an ontology of finitude. If such a project were to prove feasible, it would be more important than ever to avoid falling back into the ruts of a hermeneutic philosophy which had lost contact with the social sciences. Hence the project of a philosophy of the productive imagination constitutes in no way an alternative to a theory of interpretation concerned to pursue the dialogue with the social sciences. It can only be a deepening of this same theory, but conducted at a level of radicality where the epistemology of the social sciences would rejoin the ontology of human reality.

Part I

Studies in the history of hermeneutics

1. The task of hermeneutics

This essay seeks to describe the state of the hermeneutical problem, such as I receive and perceive it, before offering my own contribution to the debate. In this preliminary discussion, I shall restrict myself to identifying not only the elements of a conviction, but the terms of an unresolved problem. For I wish to lead hermeneutical reflection to the point where it calls, by an internal *aporia*, for an important reorientation which will enable it to enter seriously into discussion with the sciences of the text, from semiology to exegesis.

I shall adopt the following working definition of hermeneutics: hermeneutics is the theory of the operations of understanding in their relation to the interpretation of texts. So the key idea will be the realisation of discourse as a text; and the elaboration of the categories of the text will be the concern of a subsequent study.[1] The way will thereby be prepared for an attempt to resolve the central problem of hermeneutics presented at the end of this essay: namely the opposition, disastrous in my view, between explanation and understanding. The search for a complementarity between these two attitudes, which Romantic hermeneutics tends to dissociate, will thus express on the epistemological plane the hermeneutical reorientation demanded by the notion of the text.

I. From regional hermeneutics to general hermeneutics

The appraisal of hermeneutics which I propose converges towards the formulation of an *aporia*, which is the very *aporia* that has instigated my own research. The presentation which follows is therefore not neutral, in the sense of being free from presuppositions. Indeed, hermeneutics itself puts us on guard against the illusion or pretension of neutrality.

I see the recent history of hermeneutics dominated by two preoccupations. The first tends progressively to enlarge the aim of hermeneutics, in such a way that all *regional* hermeneutics are incorporated into one *general* hermeneutics. But this movement of *deregionalisation* cannot be pressed to the end unless at the same time the properly *epistemological* concerns of hermeneutics – its efforts to achieve a scientific status – are subordinated to *ontological* preoccupations, whereby *understanding* ceases to appear as a simple *mode of knowing* in order to become a *way of being* and a way of relating to beings and to being. The movement of *deregionalisation* is thus accompanied by a movement of *radicalisation*, by which hermeneutics becomes not only *general* but *fundamental*. Let us follow each of these movements in turn.

1. The first locus of interpretation
The first 'locality' which hermeneutics undertakes to lay bare is certainly language, and more particularly written language. It is important to grasp the contours of this locality, since my own enterprise could be seen as an attempt to 're-regionalise' hermeneutics by means of the notion of the text. It is therefore important to be precise about why hermeneutics has a privileged relation to questions of language. We can begin, it seems to me, with a quite remarkable characteristic of natural languages, a characteristic which calls for a work of interpretation at the most elementary and banal level of conversation. This characteristic is polysemy, that is, the feature by which our words have more than one meaning when considered outside of their use in a determinate context. Here I shall not be concerned with the questions of economy that justify the recourse to a lexical code which presents such a singular characteristic. What is important for the present discussion is that the polysemy of words calls forth as its counterpart the selective role of contexts for determining the current value which words assume in a determinate message, addressed by a definite speaker to a hearer placed in a particular situation. Sensitivity to context is the necessary complement and ineluctable counterpart of polysemy. But the use of contexts involves, in turn, an activity of discernment which is exercised in the concrete exchange of messages between interlocutors, and which is modelled on the interplay of question and answer. This activity of discernment is properly called interpretation; it consists in recognising which relatively univocal message the speaker has constructed on the polysemic basis of the common lexicon. To produce a relatively univocal discourse with polysemic words, and to identify this intention of univocity in the reception of messages: such is the first and most elementary work of interpretation.

Within this vast circle of exchanged messages, writing carves out a limited domain which Dilthey, to whom I shall return at length below, calls the expressions of life fixed by writing.[2] These expressions demand a specific work of interpretation, a work which stems precisely from the realisation of discourse as a text. Let us say provisionally that with writing, the conditions of direct interpretation through the interplay of question and answer, hence through dialogue, are no longer fulfilled. Specific techniques are therefore required in order to raise the chain of written signs to discourse and to discern the message through the superimposed codifications peculiar to the realisation of discourse as a text.

2. F. Schleiermacher

The real movement of deregionalisation begins with the attempt to extract a general problem from the activity of interpretation which is each time engaged in different texts. The discernment of this central and unitary problematic is the achievement of *Schleiermacher*. Before him, there was on the one hand a philology of classical texts, principally those of Greco-Latin antiquity, and on the other hand an exegesis of sacred texts, of the Old and New Testaments. In each of these two domains, the work of interpretation varies with the diversity of the texts. A general hermeneutics therefore requires that the interpreter rise above the particular applications and discern the operations which are common to the two great branches of hermeneutics. In order to do that, however, it is necessary to rise above, not only the particularity of texts, but also the particularity of the rules and recipes into which the art of understanding is dispersed. Hermeneutics was born with the attempt to raise exegesis and philology to the level of a *Kunstlehre*, that is, a 'technology' which is not restricted to a mere collection of unconnected operations.

This subordination of the particular rules of exegesis and philology to the general problematic of understanding constituted an inversion fully comparable to that which Kantian philosophy had effected elsewhere, primarily in relation to the natural sciences. In this respect, it could be said that Kantianism constitutes the nearest philosophical horizon of hermeneutics. The general spirit of the *Critique*, as we know, is to reverse the relation between the theory of knowledge and the theory of being; the capacity for knowing must be measured before we confront the nature of being. It is easy to see how, in a Kantian climate, one could form the project of relating the rules of interpretation, not to the diversity of texts and of things said in texts, but to the central operation which unifies the diverse aspects of interpretation. Even if Schleiermacher himself was not conscious of effecting in the exegetical and philological sphere the sort of Copernican revolution carried out by Kant in the philosophy of nature, Dilthey will be perfectly aware of it, writing in the neo-Kantian climate of the late nineteenth century. But it will be necessary first to undertake an extension which had not occurred to Schleiermacher, namely the inclusion of the exegetical and philological sciences within the historical sciences. Only then will hermeneutics appear as a global response to the great lacuna of Kantianism, perceived for the first time by Herder and clearly recognised by Cassirer: that in a critical philosophy, there is no link between physics and ethics.

However, it was not only a question of filling a lacuna in Kantianism; it was also a matter of profoundly revolutionising the Kantian conception of the subject. Because it was restricted to investigating the universal conditions of objectivity in physics and ethics, Kantianism could bring to light only an impersonal mind, bearer of the conditions of possibility of universal judgements. Hermeneutics could not add to Kantianism without taking from Romantic philosophy its most fundamental conviction, that mind is the creative unconscious at work in gifted individuals. Schleiermacher's hermeneutical programme thus carried a double mark: *Romantic* by its appeal to a living relation with the process of creation, *critical* by its wish to elaborate the universally valid rules of understanding. Perhaps hermeneutics is forever marked by this double filiation – Romantic and critical, critical and Romantic. The proposal to struggle against misunderstanding in the name of the famous adage 'there is hermeneutics where there is misunderstanding'[3] is critical; the proposal 'to understand an author as well as and even better than he understands himself'[4] is Romantic.

Similarly it can be seen that, in the notes on hermeneutics which were never transformed into a finished work, Schleiermacher left his descendants with an *aporia* as well as an initial sketch. The problem with which he grappled is that of the relation between two forms of interpretation: 'grammatical' interpretation and 'technical' interpretation. This distinction remained constant throughout his work, but its significance changed over the years. Before Kimmerle's edition,[5] we did not know of the notes from 1804 and the following years. Hence Schleiermacher was credited with a psychological standpoint, even though from the outset the two forms of interpretation were on an equal footing. Grammatical interpretation is based on the characteristics of discourse which are common to a culture; technical interpretation is addressed to the singularity, indeed to the genius, of the writer's message. Now although the two interpretations have equal status, they cannot be practised at the same time. Schleiermacher makes this clear: to consider the common language is to forget the writer; whereas to understand an individual author is to forget his language, which is merely passed over. Either we perceive what is common, or we perceive what is peculiar. The first interpretation is called 'objective', since it is concerned with linguistic characteristics distinct from the author, but also 'negative', since it merely indicates the limits of understanding; its critical value bears only upon errors in the meaning of words. The second interpretation is called 'technical', undoubtedly due to the very project of a *Kunstlehre*, a 'technology'. The proper task of hermeneutics is accomplished in this second interpretation. What must be reached is the subjectivity of the one who speaks, the language being forgotten. Here language becomes an instrument at the service of individuality. This interpretation is called 'positive', because it reaches the act of thought which produced the discourse. Not only does one form of interpretation exclude the other, but each demands distinct talents, as their respective excesses reveal: an excess of the first gives rise to pedantry, an excess of the second to nebulosity.

It is only in the later texts of Schleiermacher that the second interpretation prevails over the first, and that the *divinatory* character of interpretation underlines its psychological character. But even then, psychological interpretation – this term replaces 'technical interpretation' – is never restricted to establishing an affinity with the author. It implies critical motifs in the activity of comparison: an individuality can be grasped only by comparison and contrast. So the second hermeneutics also includes technical and discursive elements. We never directly grasp an individuality, but grasp only its difference from others and from ourselves. The difficulty of reconciling the two hermeneutics is thus complicated by the superimposition of a second pair of opposites, *divination* and *comparison,* upon the first pair, *grammatical* and *technical.* The *Academic Discourses*[6] provide further evidence of this serious obstacle encountered by the founder of modern hermeneutics. Elsewhere I argue that this obstacle can be overcome only by clarifying the relation of the work to the subjectivity of the author and by shifting the interpretative emphasis from the empathic investigation of hidden subjectivities towards the sense and reference of the work itself. But first it is necessary to push the central *aporia* of hermeneutics further by considering the decisive development which Dilthey achieved in subordinating the philological and exegetical problematic to the problematic of history. It is this development, in the sense of a greater *universality*, which prepares the way for the displacement of epistemology towards ontology, in the sense of a greater *radicality*.

3. W. Dilthey

Dilthey is situated at this critical turning point of hermeneutics, where the magnitude of the problem is perceived but where it is still posed in terms of the epistemological debate characteristic of the whole neo-Kantian period.

The necessity of incorporating the regional problem of the interpretation of texts into the broader field of historical knowledge was imposed upon a thinker concerned to account for the great achievement of nineteenth-century Germanic culture, namely the creation of history as a science of the first order. Between Schleiermacher and Dilthey were the great German historians of the nineteenth century: L. Ranke, J.G. Droysen, etc. From then on, the text to be interpreted was reality itself and its *interconnection* (*Zusammenhang*). The question of how to understand a text from the past is preceded by another question: how is an historical interconnection to be conceived? Before the coherence of the text comes the coherence of history, considered as the great document of mankind, as the most fundamental *expression of life*. Dilthey is above all the interpreter of this pact between hermeneutics and history. What is today called 'historicism', in a pejorative sense, expresses in the first instance a fact of culture: the shift of interest from the *chefs-d'oeuvre* of mankind to the historical interconnection which supports them. The discrediting of historicism is a result not only of the obstacles which it itself has created, but also of another cultural change which occurred more recently and which gives priority to system over change, to synchrony over diachrony. The structural tendencies of contemporary literary criticism express both the failure of historicism and the fundamental subversion of its problematic.

At the same time that Dilthey brought to philosophical reflection the great problem of the intelligibility of the historical as such, he was inclined by a second cultural fact to search for the key to a solution, not on the side of ontology, but in the reform of epistemology itself. The second fundamental cultural fact thus alluded to is represented by the rise of positivism as a philosophy, if by that we understand, in very general terms, the demand that the model of all intelligibility be taken from the sort of empirical explanation current in the domain of the natural sciences. Dilthey's epoch was characterised by a total rejection of Hegelianism and an apology for experimental knowledge. Hence it seemed that the only way of rendering justice to historical knowledge was to give it a scientific dimension, comparable to that which the natural sciences had attained. So it was in response to positivism that Dilthey undertook to endow the human sciences with a methodology and an epistemology which would be as respectable as those of the sciences of nature.

On the basis of these two great cultural facts, Dilthey poses his fundamental question: how is historical knowledge possible? or more generally, how are the human sciences possible? This question brings us to the threshold of the great opposition which runs throughout Dilthey's work, the opposition between the *explanation* of nature and the *understanding* of history. The opposition is heavy with consequences for hermeneutics, which is thereby severed from naturalistic explanation and thrown back into the sphere of psychological intuition.

It is in the sphere of psychology that Dilthey searches for the distinctive feature of understanding. Every *human science* – and by that Dilthey means every modality of the knowledge of man which implies an historical relation – presupposes a primordial capacity to transpose oneself into the mental life of others. For in natural knowledge, man grasps only phenomena distinct from himself, the fundamental 'thingness' of which escapes him. In the human order, on the other hand, man knows man; however alien another man may be to us, he is not alien in the sense of an unknowable physical thing. The difference of status between natural things and the mind dictates the difference of status between explanation and understanding. Man is not radically alien to man, because he offers signs of his own existence. To understand these signs is to understand man. This is what the positivist school completely ignores: the difference in principle between the mental world and the physical world. It may be objected that the mind, the spiritual world, is not inevitably the individual; did Hegel's work not attest to a sphere of *objective* spirit, the spirit of institutions and cultures, which could in no way be reduced to a psychological phenomenon? But Dilthey still belongs to the generation of neo-Kantians for whom the pivot of all human sciences is the individual, considered, it is true, in his social relations, but fundamentally singular. It follows that the foundation of the human sciences must be psychology, the science of the individual acting in society and in history. In the last analysis, reciprocal relations, cultural systems, philosophy, art and religion are constructed on this basis. More precisely – and this was another theme of the epoch – it is as activity, as free will, as initiative and enterprise that man seeks to understand himself. Here we recognise the firm intention to turn away from Hegel, to go beyond the Hegelian concept of the popular spirit and thus to rejoin Kant, but at the point where, as we said above, Kant himself had stopped.

The key to the critique of historical knowledge, which was painfully missing in Kantianism, is to be found in the fundamental phenomenon of *interconnection*, by which the life of others can be discerned and identified in its manifestations. Knowledge of others is possible because life produces forms, externalises itself in stable configurations; feelings, evaluations and volitions tend to sediment themselves in a *structured acquisition* [*acquis*] which is offered to others for deciphering. The organised systems which culture produces in the form of literature constitute a secondary layer, built upon this primary phenomenon of the teleological structure of the productions of life. We know how Max Weber, for his part, tries to resolve the same problem with his concept of ideal-types. Both authors come up against the same problem: how are concepts to be formed in the sphere of life, in the sphere of fluctuating experience which is opposed, it seems, to natural regularity? An answer is possible because spiritual life is fixed in structured totalities capable of being understood by another. After 1900, Dilthey relied upon Husserl to give consistency to the notion of interconnection. During the same period, Husserl established that mental life is characterised by intentionality, that is, by the property of intending an identifiable meaning. Mental life itself cannot be grasped, but we can grasp what it intends, the objective and identical correlate in which mental life surpasses itself. This idea of intentionality and of the identical character of the intentional object would thus enable Dilthey to reinforce his concept of mental structure with the Husserlian notion of meaning.

In this new context, what happened to the hermeneutical problem received from Schleiermacher? The passage from understanding, defined primarily in terms of the capacity to transpose oneself into another, to interpretation, in the precise sense of understanding the expressions of life fixed by writing, posed a double problem. On the one hand, hermeneutics completed interpretative psychology by adding to it a supplementary stage; on the other hand, interpretative psychology turned hermeneutics in a psychological direction. That explains why Dilthey retained the psychological side of Schleiermacher's hermeneutics, wherein he recognised his own problem of understanding by transference into another. Considered from the first point of view, hermeneutics comprises something specific; it seeks to reproduce an interconnection, a structured totality, by drawing support from a category of signs which have been fixed by writing or by any other process of inscription equivalent to writing. So it is no longer possible to grasp the mental life of others in its immediate expressions; rather it is necessary to reproduce it, to reconstruct it, by interpreting objectified signs. This *Nachbilden* [reproducing] requires distinct rules, since the expressions are embedded in objects of a peculiar nature. As with Schleiermacher, it is philology – the explanation of texts – which provides the scientific stage of understanding. For both thinkers, the essential role of hermeneutics consists therein: 'to establish theoretically, against the constant intrusion of romantic whim and sceptical subjectivism . . . , the universal validity of interpretation, upon which all certainty in history rests'.[7] Hermeneutics thus constitutes the objectified layer of understanding, thanks to the essential structures of the text.

But the counterpart of a hermeneutical theory founded on psychology is that psychology remains its ultimate justification. The autonomy of the text, which will be at the centre of our own reflections, can only be a provisional and superficial phenomenon. The question of objectivity thus persists in Dilthey's work as a problem which is both ineluctable and insoluble. It is ineluctable because of the claim to respond to positivism by an authentically scientific conception of understanding. Hence Dilthey continued to revise and perfect his concept of *reproduction*, rendering it always more appropriate to the demands of objectification. But the subordination of the hermeneutical problem to the properly psychological problem of the knowledge of others condemned him to search beyond the field of interpretation for the source of all objectification. For Dilthey, objectification begins very early, from the moment of self-interpretation. What I am for myself can only be reached through the objectifications of my own life. Self-knowledge is already an interpretation which is no easier than any other, and indeed probably more difficult, since I understand myself only by means of the signs which I give of my own life and which are returned to me via others. All self-knowledge is mediated through signs and works. That is how Dilthey responded to the *Lebensphilosophie* [philosophy of life] which was so influential in his day. Dilthey shared with the latter the view that life is essentially a creative dynamism; but, in contrast to the philosophy of life, he held that the creative dynamism cannot know itself and can interpret itself only by the detour of signs and works. A fusion was thus effected in Dilthey's work between the concept of dynamism and that of structure: life appears as a dynamism which structures itself. In this way, the later Dilthey tried to generalise the concept of hermeneutics, anchoring it ever more deeply in the teleology of life. Acquired meanings, present values and distant goals constantly structure the dynamic of life, according to the three temporal dimensions of past, present and future. Man learns about himself only through his acts, through the exteriorisation of his life and through the effects it produces on others. He comes to know himself only by the detour of understanding, which is, as always, an interpretation. The only really significant difference between psychological interpretation and exegetical interpretation stems from the fact that the objectifications of life tend to deposit and sediment themselves in a durable acquisition which assumes all the appearances of the Hegelian objective spirit. If I can understand vanished worlds, it is because each society has created its own medium of understanding by creating the social and cultural worlds in which it understands itself. Universal history thus becomes the field of hermeneutics. To understand myself is to make the greatest detour, via the memory which retains what has become meaningful for all mankind. Hermeneutics is the rise of the individual to the knowledge of universal history, the universalisation of the individual.

Dilthey's work, even more than Schleiermacher's, brings to light the central *aporia* of a hermeneutics which subsumes the understanding of texts to the law of understanding another person who expresses himself therein. If the enterprise remains fundamentally psychological, it is because it stipulates as the ultimate aim of interpretation, not *what* a text says, but *who* says it. At the same time, the object of hermeneutics is constantly shifted away from the text, from its sense and its reference, towards the lived experience which is expressed therein. Gadamer has clearly articulated this latent conflict in Dilthey's work (*WM* 205–8; *TM* 192–5): in the last analysis, the conflict is between a philosophy of life, with its profound irrationalism, and a philosophy of meaning, which has the same pretensions as the Hegelian philosophy of objective spirit. Dilthey transformed this difficulty into an axiom: life contains the power to surpass itself through meaning.[8] Or as Gadamer says: 'Life interprets itself. It has itself a hermeneutical structure' (*WM* 213; *TM* 199). But the claim that this hermeneutics of life is history remains incomprehensible. For the passage from psychological to historical understanding assumes that the interconnection of works of life is no longer lived or experienced by anyone. Precisely therein lies its objectivity. Hence we may ask if, in order to grasp the objectifications of life and to treat them as givens, it is not necessary to place speculative idealism at the very roots of life, that is, ultimately to think of life itself as spirit (*Geist*). Otherwise, how can we understand the fact that it is in art, religion and philosophy that life expresses itself most completely by objectifying itself most entirely? Is it not because spirit is most at home here? And is this not to admit that hermeneutics is possible as a reasoned philosophy only by borrowing from the Hegelian concept? It is thus possible to say of life what Hegel said of spirit: at this point, *life grasps life.*

Nevertheless, Dilthey perfectly perceived the crux of the problem: namely that life grasps life only by the mediation of units of meaning which rise above the historical flux. Here Dilthey glimpsed a mode of transcending finitude without absolute knowledge, a mode which is properly interpretative. Thereby he indicated the direction in which historicism could overcome itself, without invoking a triumphant co-incidence with some sort of absolute knowledge. But in order to pursue this discovery, it is necessary to renounce the link between the destiny of hermeneutics and the purely psychological notion of transference into another mental life; the text must be unfolded, no longer towards its author, but towards its immanent sense and towards the world which it opens up and discloses.

II. From epistemology to ontology

After Dilthey the decisive step was not to perfect the epistemology of the human sciences but to question its fundamental postulate, namely that these sciences can compete with the sciences of nature by means of a methodology which would be their own. This presupposition, dominant in Dilthey's work, implies that hermeneutics is one variety of the *theory of knowledge* and that the debate between explanation and understanding can be contained within the limits of the *Methodenstreit* [methodological dispute] dear to the neo-Kantians. The presupposition of hermeneutics construed as epistemology is precisely what Heidegger and Gadamer place in question. Their contribution cannot be regarded, therefore, as a pure and simple prolongation of Dilthey's enterprise; rather it must be seen as an attempt to dig beneath the epistemological enterprise itself, in order to uncover its properly ontological conditions. If the first movement, from regional to general hermeneutics, could be situated under the sign of the Copernican revolution, then the second movement which we are now undertaking must be placed under the auspices of a second Copernican inversion, which would subsume questions of method to the reign of a primordial ontology. So we must not expect that Heidegger or Gadamer will perfect the methodological problematic created by the exegesis of sacred or profane texts, by philology, psychology, the theory of history or the theory of culture. On the contrary, a new question is raised: instead of asking 'how do we know?' it will be asked 'what is the mode of being of that being who exists only in understanding?'

1. M. Heidegger

The question of *Auslegung,* of explication or interpretation, coincides so little with that of exegesis that it is conjoined, in the introduction of *Being and Time,* to the forgotten question of being;[9] what is at issue is the question of the *meaning* of being. But in posing this question, we are guided by the very thing which is sought. From the outset, the theory of knowledge is overturned by an interrogation which precedes it and which concerns the way that a being encounters being, even before it confronts it as an object facing a subject. Even if *Being and Time,* more than Heidegger's later work, places the emphasis on *Dasein,* the *being-there that we are,* this *Dasein* is not a subject for which there is an object, but is rather a being within being. *Dasein* designates the *place* where the question of being arises, the place of manifestation; the centrality of *Dasein* is simply that of a being which understands being. It is part of its structure as being to have an ontological *pre-understanding* of being. Consequently, to display the constitution of *Dasein* is not at all 'to ground by derivation', as in the methodology of the human sciences, but 'to unfold the foundation by clarification' (see *SZ* para. 3). An opposition is thus established between ontological foundation, in the sense just described, and epistemological grounding. It would only be an epistemological question if the problem concerned the concepts which govern the regions of particular objects, the region of nature, of life, of language, of history. Of course, science itself carries out an explication of its fundamental concepts, especially in the case of a 'crisis of foundations'. But the philosophical task of foundation is something different: it seeks to unfold the fundamental concepts which 'determine the prior understanding of the region, providing the basis of all the thematic objects of a science and thereby orientating all positive research' (*SZ* 10; *BT* 30).† What is at stake in philosophical hermeneutics will thus be the 'explication of those beings with regard to their basic state of being' (*SZ* 10; *BT* 30).† This explication will add nothing to the methodology of the human sciences; rather it will dig beneath this methodology in order to lay bare its foundations. Thus in history, 'what is philosophically primary is neither a theory of the concept-formation of historiology nor the theory of historiological knowledge, nor yet the theory of history as the object of historiology; what is primary is rather the interpretation of authentically historical beings as regards their historicity' (*SZ* 10; *BT* 31).† Hermeneutics is not a reflection on the human sciences, but an explication of the ontological ground upon which these sciences can be constructed. Whence the sentence which is crucial for us: hermeneutics thus construed 'contains the roots of what can be called "hermeneutic" only in a derivative sense: the methodology of the human sciences' (*SZ* 38; *BT* 62).†

The first inversion effected by *Being and Time* calls for a second. Dilthey linked the question of understanding to the problem of the other person; how to gain access to another mind was a problem that dominated all of the human sciences, from psychology to history. Now it is remarkable that, in *Being and Time*, the question of understanding is wholly severed from the problem of communication with others. There is indeed a chapter called *Mitsein* – *being-with;* but the question of understanding does not appear in this chapter, as one would expect from a Diltheyan position. The foundations of the ontological problem are sought in the relation of being with the world and not in the relation with another. Understanding, in its primordial sense, is implicated in the relation with my situation, in the fundamental understanding of my position within being. It is not without interest to recall why Dilthey proceeded as he did. He posed the problematic of the human sciences on the basis of a Kantian argument. The knowledge of things runs up against an unknown, the thing itself, whereas in the case of the mind there is no thing-in-itself: we ourselves are what the other is. Knowledge of the mind therefore has an undeniable advantage over the knowledge of nature. Heidegger, who read Nietzsche, no longer has this innocence; he knows that the other, as well as myself, is more unknown to me than any natural phenomenon can be. Here the dissimulation no doubt goes deeper than anywhere else. If there is a region of being where inauthenticity reigns, it is indeed in the relation of each person with every other; hence the chapter on *being-with* is a debate with the 'one', as the centre and privileged place of dissimulation. It is therefore not astonishing that it is by a reflection on *being-in*, rather than *being-with*, that the ontology of understanding may begin; not *being-with* another who would duplicate our subjectivity, but *being-in-the-world*. This shift of the philosophical locus is just as important as the movement from the problem of method towards the problem of being. The question of the *world* takes the place of the question of the *other*. In thereby making understanding *worldly*, Heidegger *de-psychologises* it.

This shift has been completely misunderstood in the so-called existentialist interpretations of Heidegger. The analyses of care, anguish and being-towards-death were taken in the sense of a refined existential psychology, applied to uncommon states of mind. It was not sufficiently recognised that these analyses are part of a meditation on the *worldliness of the world*, and that they seek essentially to shatter the pretension of the knowing subject to set itself up as the measure of objectivity. What must be reaffirmed in place of this pretension is the condition of *inhabiting* the world, a condition which renders situation, understanding and interpretation possible. Hence the theory of understanding must be preceded by the recognition of the relation of entrenchment which anchors the whole linguistic system, including books and texts, in something which is not primordially a phenomenon of articulation in discourse. We must first *find ourselves* (for better or worse), find ourselves *there* and *feel* ourselves (in a certain manner), even before we orientate ourselves. If *Being and Time* thoroughly exploits certain feelings like fear and anguish, it is not in order to 'do existentialism', but rather to disclose, by means of these revelatory experiences, a link to a reality more fundamental than the subject–object relation. In knowledge, we posit objects in front of us; but our feeling of the situation precedes this *vis-à-vis* by placing us in a world.

Thus arises understanding – but not yet as a fact of language, writing or texts. Understanding too must be described initially, not in terms of discourse, but in terms of the 'power-to-be'. The first function of understanding is to orientate us in a situation. So understanding is not concerned with grasping a fact but with apprehending a possibility of being. We must not lose sight of this point when we draw the methodological consequences of this analysis: to understand a text, we shall say, is not to find a lifeless sense which is contained therein, but to unfold the possibility of being indicated by the text. Thus we shall remain faithful to the Heideggerian notion of understanding which is essentially a *projection* or, to speak more dialectically and paradoxically, a *projection* within a prior *being-thrown*. Here again the existentialist tone is deceptive. One small word separates Heidegger from Sartre: *already*. 'The project has nothing to do with a plan of conduct which Dasein would have invented and in accordance with which it would construct its being; insofar as it is Dasein, it has already projected itself and it remains in projection so long as it is' (*SZ* 145; *BT* 185).† What is important here is not the existential moment of responsibility or free choice, but rather the structure of being which underlies the problem of choice. The 'either . . . or' is not primary; it is derived from the structure of the *thrown project*.

The ontological moment which interests the exegete thus appears only in the third position of the triad situation–understanding–interpretation. But before the exegesis of texts comes the exegesis of things. For interpretation is above all an explication, a *development* of understanding which 'does not transform it into something else, but makes it become itself' (*SZ* 148; *BT* 188).† Any return to the theory of knowledge is thus precluded. What is explicated is the *as such* (*als*) which adheres to the articulations of experience; but 'the assertion does not make the "as such" appear, it only gives it an expression' (*SZ* 149; *BT* 190).†

If the Analytic of *Dasein* does not expressly aim at problems of exegesis, nevertheless it gives sense to what may appear as a failure on the epistemological level, reconnecting this apparent failure to an unsurpassable ontological structure. This failure has often been expressed in terms of the *hermeneutical circle*. It has been noted many times that in the human sciences the subject and object are mutually implicated. The subject itself enters into the knowledge of the object; and in turn, the former is determined, in its most subjective character, by the hold which the object has upon it, even before the subject comes to know the object. Thus stated in the terminology of subject and object, the hermeneutical circle cannot but appear as a vicious circle. The function of a fundamental ontology is to disclose the structure which appears as a circle on the methodological plane. It is this structure that Heidegger calls *pre-understanding*. But it would be entirely mistaken if we continued to describe pre-understanding in terms of the theory of knowledge, that is, in the categories of subject and object. The relations of familiarity that we may have, for example, with a world of tools can give us an initial idea of the meaning of 'fore-having', on the basis of which I direct myself towards a new usage of things. This anticipatory character is part of the way of being of every being which understands historically. The following proposition must therefore be understood in terms of the Analytic of *Dasein:* 'the explication of something as this or that is founded essentially upon fore-having, fore-sight, and fore-conception' (*SZ* 150; *BT* 191).† The role of presuppositions in textual exegesis is thus only a particular case of the general law of interpretation. Transposed into the theory of knowledge and measured against the claim of objectivity, pre-understanding receives the pejorative connotation of prejudice. For a fundamental ontology, however, prejudice can be understood only in terms of the anticipatory structure of understanding. The famous hermeneutical circle is henceforth only the shadow, on the methodological plane, of this structure of anticipation. Whoever understands that knows, from now on, that 'what is decisive is not to get out of the circle but to come into it in the right way' (*SZ* 153; *BT* 195).

It will have been noticed that the principal weight of this meditation does not bear upon discourse, even less upon writing. The philosophy of Heidegger – or at least that of *Being and Time* – is so little a philosophy of language that the question of language is introduced only after the questions of situation, understanding and interpretation. Language, at the stage of *Being and Time*, remains a secondary articulation, the articulation of explication in 'assertions' (*Aussage, SZ* para. 33). The derivation of the assertion from understanding and explication prepares us to say that its primary function is not communication to others, nor even the attribution of predicates to logical subjects, but rather 'pointing out', 'showing', 'manifesting' (*SZ* 154; *BT* 196). This supreme function of language merely reflects the derivation of the latter from the ontological structures which precede it. 'The fact that language *now* becomes our theme *for the first time'*, says Heidegger in paragraph 34, 'will indicate that this phenomenon has its roots in the existential constitution of Dasein's disclosedness' (*SZ* 160; *BT* 203); and further on, 'Discourse is the articulation of what understanding is' (*SZ* 161; *BT* 203–4).† It is therefore necessary to situate discourse in the structures of being, rather than situating the latter in discourse: 'Discourse is the "meaningful" articulation of the understandable structure of being-in-the-world' (*SZ* 161; *BT* 204).†

The last remark anticipates the movement to the later philosophy of Heidegger, which will ignore *Dasein* and begin directly with the manifestative power of language. But from *Being and Time* onwards, *saying* (*reden*) appears superior to *speaking* (*sprechen*). 'Saying' designates the existential constitution, whereas 'speaking' indicates the mundane aspect which lapses into the empirical. Hence the first determination of *saying* is not *speaking*, but rather the couple *hearing/keeping silent*. Here again Heidegger goes against our ordinary, and even linguistic, way of giving priority to the process of speaking (locution, interlocution). To understand is to hear. In other words, my first relation to speech is not that I produce it but that I receive it: 'Hearing is constitutive of discourse' (*SZ* 163; *BT* 206).† This priority of hearing marks the fundamental relation of speech to the opening towards the world and towards others. The methodological consequences are considerable: linguistics, semiology and the philosophy of language adhere ineluctably to the level of speech and do not reach the level of saying. In this sense, fundamental philosophy no more ameliorates linguistics than it adds to exegesis. While speaking refers back to the man who speaks, saying refers back to the things said.

At this point, it will no doubt be asked: why not stop here and simply proclaim ourselves Heideggerian? Where is the famous *aporia* previously announced? Have we not eliminated the Diltheyan *aporia* of a theory of understanding, condemned in turn to oppose naturalistic explanation and to rival it in objectivity and scientificity? Have we not overcome it by subordinating epistemology to ontology? In my opinion, the *aporia* is not resolved but merely displaced elsewhere and thereby aggravated. It is no longer between two modalities of knowing *within* epistemology, but it is *between* ontology and epistemology taken as a whole. With Heidegger's philosophy, we are always engaged in going back to the foundations, but we are left incapable of beginning the movement of return which would lead from the fundamental ontology to the properly epistemological question of the status of the human sciences. Now a philosophy which breaks the dialogue with the sciences is no longer addressed to anything but itself. Moreover, it is only along the return route that we could substantiate the claim that questions of exegesis and, in general, of historical critique are *derivative*. So long as this derivation has not been undertaken, the very movement of transcendence towards questions of foundation remains problematic. Have we not learned from Plato that the ascending dialectic is the easiest, and that it is along the path of the descending dialectic that the true philosopher stands out? For me, the question which remains unresolved in Heidegger's work is this: *how can a question of critique in general be accounted for within the framework of a fundamental hermeneutics?* [. . .]

2. H.-G. Gadamer

This *aporia* becomes the central problem of the hermeneutic philosophy of Hans-Georg Gadamer in *Truth and Method*. The Heidelberg philosopher proposes to take up the debate about the human sciences in terms of the Heideggerian ontology, and more precisely in terms of the re-orientation of this ontology in the later works of philosophical poetics. The core experience around which the whole of Gadamer's work is organised, and from which hermeneutics raises its claim to universality, is the scandal constituted, at the level of modern consciousness, by the sort of *alienating distanciation* (*Verfremdung*) which seems to him to be the presupposition of these sciences. For alienation is much more than a feeling or a mood; it is the ontological presupposition which sustains the objective conduct of the human sciences. The methodology of these sciences ineluctably implies, in Gadamer's eyes, a distancing, which in turn expresses the destruction of the primordial relation of belonging (*Zugehörigkeit*) without which there would be no relation to the historical as such. The debate between alienating distanciation and the experience of belonging is pursued by Gadamer through the three spheres into which the hermeneutical experience is divided: the aesthetic sphere, the historical sphere and the sphere of language. In the aesthetic sphere, the experience of being seized by the object precedes and renders possible the critical exercise of judgement for which Kant formulated the theory under the title of the 'judgement of taste'. In the historical sphere, the consciousness of being carried by the traditions which precede me is what makes possible any exercise of an historical methodology at the level of the human and social sciences. Finally, in the sphere of language, which in a certain way cuts across the previous two, any scientific treatment of language as an instrument and every claim to dominate the structure of the texts of our culture by objective techniques are preceded and rendered possible by our co-belonging to the things which the great voices of mankind have said. So one and the same thesis runs throughout the three parts of *Truth and Method*.

The philosophy of Gadamer thus expresses the synthesis of the two movements which we have described above, from regional hermeneutics towards general hermeneutics and from the epistemology of the human sciences towards ontology. The term 'hermeneutic experience' expresses very well this synthetic character. Moreover, Gadamer's work marks, in relation to Heidegger, the beginnings of the movement of return from ontology towards epistemological problems. It is in this light that I shall discuss his contributions here. The very title of the work confronts the Heideggerian concept of truth with the Diltheyan concept of method. The question is to what extent the work deserves to be called *Truth AND Method*, and whether it ought not instead to be entitled *Truth OR Method*. For if Heidegger was able to elude the debate with the human sciences by a sovereign movement of transcendence, Gadamer can only plunge himself into an ever more bitter debate, precisely because he takes Dilthey's question seriously. In this respect, the section dedicated to historical consciousness is most significant. The long historical journey which Gadamer undertakes before presenting his own ideas indicates that hermeneutic philosophy must begin by recapitulating the struggle of Romantic philosophy against the *Aufklärung* [Enlightenment], of Dilthey against positivism, of Heidegger against neo-Kantianism. [. . .]

The welter of influences alternately challenged and assumed terminates in a theory of historical consciousness, which marks the summit of Gadamer's reflection on the foundation of the human sciences. This reflection is placed under the title of *wirkungsgeschichtliches Bewusstsein;* word for word, the *consciousness of the history of effects.* This category no longer pertains to methodology, to historical *inquiry,* but rather to the reflective consciousness of this methodology. It is the consciousness of being exposed to history and to its action, in such a way that this action upon us cannot be objectified, because it is part of the historical phenomenon itself. [. . .]

The concept of historical efficacy provides the backcloth against which I should like to pose my own problem: *how is it possible to introduce a critical instance into a consciousness of belonging which is expressly defined by the rejection of distanciation?* It is possible, in my view, only insofar as historical consciousness seeks not simply to repudiate distanciation but to assume it. Gadamer's hermeneutics contains, in this respect, a series of decisive suggestions which will become the point of departure for my own reflection.

To begin with, in spite of the general opposition between belonging and alienating distanciation, the consciousness of effective history contains within itself an element of *distance.* The history of effects is precisely what occurs under the condition of historical distance. It is the nearness of the remote; or to say the same thing in other words, it is efficacy at a distance. There is thus a paradox of otherness, a tension between proximity and distance, which is essential to historical consciousness.

Another index of the dialectic of participation and distanciation is provided by the concept of the *fusion of horizons (Horizontverschmelzung) (WM* 289ff., 356, 375; *TM* 273ff., 337, 358). For according to Gadamer, if the finite condition of historical knowledge excludes any overview, any final synthesis in the Hegelian manner, nevertheless this finitude does not enclose me in one point of view. Wherever there is a situation, there is an horizon which can be contracted or enlarged. We owe to Gadamer this very fruitful idea that communication at a distance between two differently situated consciousnesses occurs by means of the fusion of their horizons, that is, the intersection of their views on the distant and the open. Once again, an element of distanciation within the near, the far and the open is presupposed. This concept signifies that we live neither within closed horizons, nor within one unique horizon. Insofar as the fusion of horizons excludes the idea of a total and unique knowledge, this concept implies a tension between what is one's own and what is alien, between the near and the far; and hence the play of difference is included in the process of convergence.

Finally, the most precise indication for a less negative interpretation of alienating distanciation is found in the philosophy of language which culminates Gadamer's work. The universal *linguality* of human experience – this word provides a more or less adequate translation of Gadamer's *Sprachlichkeit* – means that my belonging to a tradition or traditions passes through the interpretation of the signs, works and texts in which cultural heritages are inscribed and offer themselves to be deciphered. Of course, the whole of Gadamer's meditation on language is directed against the reduction of the world of signs to instruments which we could manipulate as we like. The entire third part of *Truth and Method* is an impassioned apology for the *dialogue which we are* and for the prior understanding which supports us. But lingual experience exercises its mediating function only because the interlocutors fade away in face of the things said which, as it were, direct the dialogue. Now where is the reign of the thing said over the interlocutors more apparent, if not where *Sprachlichkeit* becomes *Schriftlichkeit*, in other words, where mediation by language becomes mediation by the text? What enables us to communicate at a distance is thus the *matter of the text*, which belongs neither to its author nor to its reader. This last expression, the *matter of the text*, leads me to the threshold of my own reflection.

2. Hermeneutics and the critique of ideology

The debate which is evoked by this title goes well beyond the limits of a discussion about the foundations of the social sciences. It raises the question of what I shall call the fundamental gesture of philosophy. Is this gesture an avowal of the historical conditions to which all human understanding is subsumed under the reign of finitude? Or rather is it, in the last analysis, an act of defiance, a critical gesture, relentlessly repeated and indefinitely turned against 'false consciousness', against the distortions of human communication which conceal the permanent exercise of domination and violence? Such is the philosophical stake of a debate which at first seems tied to the epistemological plane of the human sciences. What is at stake can be expressed in terms of an alternative: either a hermeneutical consciousness or a critical consciousness. But is it really so? Is it not the alternative itself which must be challenged? Is it possible to formulate a hermeneutics which would render justice to the critique of ideology, which would show the necessity of the latter at the very heart of its own concerns? Clearly the stake is considerable. We are not going to risk everything by beginning with terms which are too general and an attitude which is too ambitious. We shall, instead, focus on a contemporary discussion which presents the problem in the form of an alternative. Even if ultimately this alternative must be surpassed, we shall not be in ignorance of the difficulties to be overcome.

The principal protagonists in the debate are, on the side of hermeneutics, Hans-Georg Gadamer; and on the side of critique, Jürgen Habermas. The dossier of their polemic is now public, partially reproduced in the little volume entitled *Hermeneutik und Ideologiekritik*.[1] It is from this dossier that I shall extract the lines of force which characterise the conflict between hermeneutics and the critical theory of ideology. I shall take the assessment of *tradition* by each of these philosophies as the touchstone of the debate. In contrast to the positive assessment by hermeneutics, the theory of ideology adopts a suspicious approach, seeing tradition as merely the systematically distorted expression of communication under unacknowledged conditions of violence. The choice of this touchstone has the advantage of bringing to the fore a confrontation which bears upon the 'claim to universality' of hermeneutics. For the critique of ideology is of interest insofar as it is a non-hermeneutical discipline, situated outside the sphere of competence of a science or philosophy of interpretation, and marking the fundamental limit of the latter.

In the first part of this essay, I shall restrict myself to presenting the contents of the dossier. I shall do so in terms of a simple alternative: either hermeneutics or the critique of ideology. I shall reserve for the second part a more personal reflection, centred on the following two questions: (1) Can hermeneutic philosophy account for the legitimate demand of the critique of ideology, and if so at what price? Must it sacrifice its claim to universality and undertake a profound reformulation of its programme and its project? (2) On what condition is the critique of ideology possible? Can it, in the last analysis, be detached from hermeneutic presuppositions?

I hasten to say that no plan of annexation, no syncretism, will preside over this debate. I readily admit, along with Gadamer, that each of the two theories speaks from a different place; but I hope to show that each can recognise the other's claim to universality in a way which marks the place of one in the structure of the other.

I. The alternative

1. Gadamer: The hermeneutics of tradition

We may go directly to the critical point – the *Brennpunkt* – which Habermas attacks in his *Logik der Sozialwissenschaften*, namely the conception of historical consciousness and the provocative rehabilitation of the three connected concepts of prejudice, authority and tradition. This text is by no means secondary or marginal. It goes directly to the central experience or, as I have just said, to the place from which this hermeneutics speaks and upon which it raises its claim to universality. This experience is the scandal constituted, on the level of modern consciousness, by the sort of *alienating distanciation – Verfremdung –* which is not merely a feeling or a mood, but rather the ontological presupposition which sustains the objective conduct of the human sciences. The methodology of these sciences ineluctably implies an assumption of distance; and this, in turn, presupposes the destruction of the primordial relation of belonging – *Zugehörigkeit* – without which there would be no relation to the historical as such. The debate between alienating distanciation and the experience of belonging is pursued by Gadamer through the three spheres into which the hermeneutical experience is divided: the aesthetic sphere, the historical sphere and the sphere of language. [. . .] So although we shall focus on the second part, it must be remembered that in a sense the debate is already played out in the aesthetic sphere, just as it only culminates in the lingual experience whereby aesthetic consciousness and historical consciousness are brought to discourse. The theory of historical consciousness is therefore an epitome of the work as a whole and a microcosm of the great debate.

At the same time that hermeneutic philosophy declares the amplitude of its aim, so too it announces the locality of its point of departure. Gadamer speaks from a place which is determined by the history of attempts to resolve the problem of the foundation of the human sciences, attempts first undertaken in German Romanticism, then in Dilthey's work, and finally in terms of Heidegger's ontology. This is readily acknowledged by Gadamer himself, even when he proclaims the universality of the hermeneutical dimension. For the universality is not abstract; it is, for each investigator, centred on a dominant problematic, a privileged experience. 'My own attempt', he writes at the outset of 'Rhetorik, Hermeneutik und Ideologiekritik', 'is linked to the revival of the heritage of German Romanticism by Dilthey, insofar as he takes the theory of the human sciences as his theme, placing it on a new and broader foundation; the experience of art, together with the experience of contemporaneousness which is peculiar to it, provides the riposte to the historical distanciation of the human sciences.'[2] Thus hermeneutics has an aim which precedes and surpasses any science, an aim testified to by 'the universal linguality of behaviour relative to the world';[3] but the universality of the aim is the counterpart to the narrowness of the initial experience in which it is rooted. The fact that the localised nature of the initial experience is emphasised, as well as the claim to universality, is therefore not irrelevant to the debate with the proponents of the critique of ideology. It would have been equally possible to begin, not with historical consciousness as such, but rather with the interpretation of texts in the experience of reading, as the hermeneutics of Schleiermacher shows. In choosing this somewhat different point of departure, as I myself shall do in the second part of the essay, the problem of distanciation can be given a more positive significance than Gadamer suggests. Gadamer has specifically dismissed as less important a reflection on 'being for the text' (*Sein zum Texte*), which he seems to reduce to a deliberation on the problem of translation, itself set up as a model of the linguality of human behaviour towards the world. However, it is to this reflection that I shall return in the second part, in the hope of deriving therefrom an orientation of thought which is less subordinated to the problematic of tradition and more receptive to the critique of ideology.

By taking historical consciousness and the question of the conditions of possibility of the human sciences as the axis of reflection, Gadamer inevitably turned hermeneutic philosophy towards the rehabilitation of prejudice and the defence of tradition and authority, placing this philosophy in a conflictual relation to any critique of ideology. At the same time the conflict itself, in spite of the modern terminology, was returned to its original formulation, as expressed in the struggle between the spirit of Romanticism and that of the *Aufklärung* [Enlightenment]. The conflict had to take the form of a repetition of the same struggle along the course of an obligatory route, beginning with Romanticism, passing through the epistemological stage of the human sciences with Dilthey, and undergoing the ontological transposition of Heidegger. In adopting the privileged experience of historical consciousness, Gadamer adopted also a certain philosophical route which, ineluctably, he had to reiterate.

The struggle between Romanticism and the Enlightenment is the source of our own problem and the milieu in which the opposition between two fundamental philosophical attitudes took shape: on one side, the *Aufklärung* and its struggle against prejudices; on the other, Romanticism and its nostalgia for the past. The problem is whether the modern conflict between the critique of ideology according to the Frankfurt School and the hermeneutics of Gadamer marks any progress in this debate.

So far as Gadamer is concerned, his declared intention is perfectly clear: the pitfalls of Romanticism must be avoided. The second part of *Truth and Method*, which culminates in the famous theory of 'consciousness exposed to the effects of history' (*wirkungsgeschichtliches Bewusstsein*), contains a sharp attack on Romantic philosophy for having merely reversed the terms of the argument, without displacing the problematic itself and without changing the terrain of the debate. For 'prejudice', in the double sense of precipitation (to judge too quickly) and predisposition (to follow custom or authority), is the category *par excellence* of the *Aufklärung*. Prejudice is what must be put aside in order to think, in order to dare to think – according to the famous adage *sapere aude* – so that one may reach the age of adulthood or *Mündigkeit*. To recover a less univocally negative sense of the word 'prejudice' (which has become virtually synonymous with unfounded or false judgement), and to restore the ambivalence that the Latin word *praejudicium* had in the juridical tradition prior to the Enlightenment, it would be necessary to question the presuppositions of a philosophy which opposes reason to prejudice. These are, in fact, the very presuppositions of a critical philosophy; it is for a philosophy of judgement – and a critical philosophy is a philosophy of judgement – that prejudice is a predominantly negative category. What must be questioned, therefore, is the primacy of judgement in man's behaviour towards the world; and the only philosophy which sets up judgement as a tribunal is one that makes objectivity, as modelled on the sciences, the measure of knowledge. Judgement and prejudice are dominant categories only in the type of philosophy, stemming from Descartes, which makes methodical consciousness the key of our relation to being and to beings. Hence it is necessary to delve beneath the philosophy of judgement, beneath the problematic of subject and object, in order to effect a rehabilitation of prejudice which is not a simple negation of the spirit of the Enlightenment.

It is here that Romantic philosophy proves to be both a first foundation and a fundamental failure. A first foundation, because it dares to challenge 'the discrediting of prejudice by the *Aufklärung*' (the title of pp. 241–5 in *Truth and Method*); a fundamental failure, because it only inverts the answer without inverting the question. Romanticism wages its war on a terrain defined by the adversary, a terrain on which the role of tradition and authority in the process of interpretation are in dispute. It is on the same terrain, the same ground of inquiry, that the *mythos* is celebrated over the *logos*, that the old is defended against the new, historical Christendom against the modern state, the fraternal community against an administrative socialism, the productive unconscious against a sterile consciousness, the mythical past against a future of rational utopias, the poetic imagination against cold ratiocination. Romantic hermeneutics thus ties its destiny to everything which is associated with the Restoration.

Such is the pitfall which the hermeneutics of historical consciousness seeks to avoid. The question, once again, is whether Gadamer's hermeneutics has really surpassed the Romantic point of departure of hermeneutics, and whether his affirmation that 'the finitude of man's being consists in the fact that firstly he finds himself at the heart of tradition' (*WM* 260; *TM* 244)† escapes from the play of inversions in which he sees philosophical Romanticism, confronting the claims of critical philosophy, ensnared.

In Gadamer's view, it is only with the philosophy of Heidegger that the problematic of prejudice can be reconstituted as, precisely, a problematic. The Diltheyan stage of the problem is, in this respect, not at all decisive. On the contrary, we owe to Dilthey the illusion that the natural sciences and the human sciences are characterised by two scientificities, two methodologies, two epistemologies. Hence, in spite of his debt to Dilthey, Gadamer does not hesitate to write: 'Dilthey was unable to free himself from the traditional theory of knowledge' (*WM* 261; *TM* 245).† Dilthey still begins from self-consciousness; for him, subjectivity remains the ultimate point of reference. The reign of *Erlebnis* [lived experience] is the reign of a primordiality which I am. In this sense, the fundamental is the *Innesein*, the interior, the awareness of self. It is thus against Dilthey, as well as the constantly resurging *Aufklärung*, that Gadamer proclaims: 'the prejudices of the individual, far more than his judgements, constitute the historical reality of his being' (*WM* 261; *TM* 245). The rehabilitation of prejudice, authority and tradition will thus be directed against the reign of subjectivity and interiority, that is, against the criteria of reflection. This anti-reflective polemic will help to give Gadamer's plea the appearance of a return to a pre-critical position. Yet however provoking – not to say provocative – this plea may be, it attests to the resurgence of the historical dimension over the moment of reflection. History precedes me and my reflection; I belong to history before I belong to myself. Dilthey could not understand that, because his revolution remained epistemological and his reflective criterion prevailed over his historical consciousness.

It may be asked nonetheless whether the sharpness of the remarks against Dilthey has the same significance as the attack on Romanticism: is not the fidelity to Dilthey more profound than the critique addressed to him? This would explain why the question of history and historicity, rather than that of the text and exegesis, continues to provide what I shall call, in a manner similar to Gadamer himself, the *primary* experience of hermeneutics. It is perhaps at this level that Gadamer's hermeneutics must be interrogated, that is, at a level where his fidelity to Dilthey is more important than his critique. We shall reserve this question for the second part, restricting ourselves here to following the movement from the critique of Romanticism and Dilthey's epistemology to the properly Heideggerian phase of the problem.

To restore the historical dimension of man requires much more than a simple methodological reform, much more than a mere epistemological legitimation of the idea of a 'human science' in face of demands from the sciences of nature. Only a fundamental upheaval which subordinates the theory of knowledge to ontology can bring out the real sense of the *Vorstruktur des Verstehens* – the forestructure (or structure of anticipation) of understanding – which is the condition for any rehabilitation of prejudice.

We are all familiar with the section of *Being and Time* on understanding (para. 31),[4] where Heidegger, accumulating expressions which exhibit the prefix *vor* (*Vor-habe, Vor-sicht, Vor-griffe*), proceeds to found the hermeneutical circle of the human sciences in a structure of anticipation which is part of the very position of our being within being. Gadamer expresses it well: 'the point of Heidegger's hermeneutical thinking is not so much to prove that there is a circle as to show that this circle possesses an ontologically positive significance' (*WM* 251; *TM* 236). It is worth noting, however, that Gadamer refers not only to paragraph 31, which is still part of 'the fundamental Analytic of *Dasein*' (the title of the first division), but also to paragraph 63, which clearly shifts the problematic of interpretation towards the question of temporality as such; it is no longer just a question of the *Da* [there] of *Dasein* [being-there], but of its 'potentiality-for-being-a-whole' (*Ganzseinskönnen*), which is manifested in the three temporal ecstases of care. Gadamer is right to 'inquire into the consequences which follow for the hermeneutics of the human sciences from the fact that Heidegger derives the circular structure of understanding from the temporality of *Dasein*' (*WM* 251; *TM* 235).† But Heidegger himself did not consider these questions, which would perhaps lead us back in an unexpected way to the critical theme that was allegedly expurgated along with purely epistemological or methodological concerns. If one follows the movement of radicalisation which leads, not only from Dilthey to Heidegger, but from paragraph 31 to paragraph 63 in the very interior of *Being and Time*, then it seems that the privileged experience (if one can still speak in this way) is no longer the history of the historians, but rather the history of the question of the meaning of being in Western metaphysics. So it seems that the hermeneutical situation within which the interpretation unfolds is characterised by the fact that the structure of anticipation, in terms of which we interrogate being, is provided by the history of metaphysics; it is that which takes the place of prejudice. (Later we shall ask ourselves whether the critical relation that Heidegger establishes with respect to this tradition does not also involve a certain rehabilitation of the critique of prejudices.) Heidegger thus effects a fundamental displacement of the problem of prejudice: prejudice – *Vormeinung* – is part of the structure of anticipation (see *SZ* 150; *BT* 190). Here the example of textual exegesis is more than a particular case; it is a development, in the photographic sense of the term. Heidegger may well call philological interpretation a 'derivative mode' (*SZ* 152; *BT* 194), but it remains the touchstone. It is there that we can perceive the necessity of drawing back from the vicious circle in which philological interpretation turns, insofar as it understands itself in terms of a model of scientificity borrowed from the exact sciences, to the non-vicious circle formed by the anticipatory structure of the very being which we are.

However, Heidegger is not interested in the movement of return from the structure of anticipation which constitutes us to the hermeneutic circle in its properly methodological aspects. This is unfortunate, since it is on the return route that hermeneutics is likely to encounter critique, in particular the critique of ideology. Hence our own interrogation of Heidegger and Gadamer will begin from the difficulties raised by the movement of return, upon which the idea that philological interpretation is a 'derivative mode of understanding' can alone be legitimated. Insofar as this derivation has not been attempted, it has still not been shown that the fore-structure itself is fundamental. For nothing is fundamental, so long as something else has not been derived from it.

It is on this threefold basis – Romantic, Diltheyan, Heideggerian – that *Gadamer's distinctive contribution to the problematic* must be placed. In this respect, Gadamer's text is like a palimpsest, in which it is always possible to distinguish, as in the thickness of overlaid transparencies, a Romantic layer, a Diltheyan layer and a Heideggerian layer, and which may thus be read at each of these levels. Each level, in turn, is reflected in the views which Gadamer currently espouses as his own. As his adversaries have clearly seen, Gadamer's distinctive contribution concerns, first, the link which he establishes, purely phenomenologically as it were, between prejudice, tradition and authority; second, the ontological interpretation of this sequence in terms of the concept of *wirkungsgeschichtliches Bewusstsein,* which I shall translate as 'consciousness exposed to the effects of history' or 'consciousness of historical efficacy'; and third, the epistemological or 'meta-critical' consequence, as Gadamer calls it in his *Kleine Schriften*, that an exhaustive critique of prejudice – and hence of ideology – is impossible, since there is no zero point from which it could proceed.

Let us consider each of these three points in turn: the phenomenology of prejudice, tradition and authority; the ontology of consciousness exposed to the effects of history; and the critique of critique.

Gadamer's attempt to rehabilitate prejudice, tradition and authority is not without a provocative aim. The analysis is 'phenomenological' in the sense that it seeks to extract from these three phenomena an essence which the *Aufklärung*, with its pejorative appraisal, has obscured. For Gadamer, prejudice is not the opposite pole of a reason without presupposition; it is a component of understanding, linked to the finite historical character of the human being. It is false to maintain that there are only unfounded prejudices, since there are, in the juridical sense, pre-judgements which may or may not be subsequently grounded, and even 'legitimate prejudices'. So even if prejudices by precipitation are more difficult to rehabilitate, prejudices by predisposition have a profound significance which is missed by analyses conducted from a purely critical standpoint. Yet the prejudice against prejudice is rooted at a deeper level, namely in a prejudice against authority, which is identified too quickly with domination and violence. The concept of authority brings us to the heart of the debate with the critique of ideology. Let us recall that this concept is also at the centre of Max Weber's political sociology: the state is the institution *par excellence* which rests on a belief in the legitimacy of its authority and its right to use violence in the last instance. Now for Gadamer, the analysis of this concept has suffered, since the time of the *Aufklärung*, from a confusion between domination, authority and violence. It is here that the analysis of essence is crucial. The *Aufklärung* posits a necessary connection between authority and blind obedience:

But this is not the essence of authority. It is true that it is primarily persons that have authority; but the authority of persons is based ultimately, not on the subjection and abdication of reason, but on acceptance and recognition – recognition, namely, that the other is superior to oneself in judgement and insight and that for this reason his judgement takes precedence, i.e., it has priority over one's own. This is connected with the fact that authority cannot actually be bestowed, but is acquired and must be acquired, if someone is to lay claim to it. It rests on consideration and hence on an act of reason itself which, aware of its own limitations, accepts that others have better understanding. Authority in this sense, properly understood, has nothing to do with blind obedience to a command. Indeed, authority has nothing to do with obedience; it rests on recognition. (*WM* 264; *TM* 248)†

Thus the key concept is recognition (*Anerkennung*), which is substituted for the notion of obedience. We may note in passing that this concept implies a certain critical moment: 'The recognition of authority', says Gadamer further on, 'is always connected with the idea that what authority states is not irrational and arbitrary, but can be accepted in principle. This is the essence of the authority claimed by the teacher, the superior, the expert' (*WM* 264; *TM* 249).† This critical moment offers the possibility of articulating the phenomenology of authority onto the critique of ideology.

However, this is not the aspect that Gadamer ultimately underlines. In spite of his earlier critique, it is to a theme of German Romanticism that Gadamer returns, linking *authority* to *tradition*. That which has authority is tradition. When he comes to this equation, Gadamer speaks in Romantic terms:

there is one form of authority that romanticism has defended with particular ardour: tradition. That which has been sanctioned by tradition and custom has an authority that is nameless, and our finite historical being is determined by the fact that always the authority of what has been transmitted – and not only what is clearly grounded – has power (*Gewalt*) over our attitudes and behaviour. All education depends on this . . . [Customs and traditions] are freely taken over, but by no means created by a free insight or justified by themselves. This is precisely what we call tradition: the ground of their validity. And in fact we owe to romanticism this correction of the enlightenment, that tradition has a justification that is outside the arguments of reason and in large measure determines our attitudes and behaviour. It is even a mark of the superiority of classical ethics over the moral philosophy of the modern period that it justifies the transition of ethics into 'politics', the art of right government, by the indispensability of tradition. In comparison with it, the modern enlightenment is abstract and revolutionary. (*WM* 265; *TM* 249)†

(Notice how the word *Gewalt* [power] is slipped into the text behind *Autorität* [authority], as well as *Herrschaft* [domination] in the expression *Herrschaft von Tradition* (*WM* 265; *TM* 250).)

Gadamer does not want, of course, to fall back into the rut of the irresolvable debate between Romanticism and the Enlightenment. We must be grateful to him for attempting to reconcile, rather than oppose, authority and reason. The real meaning of authority stems from the contribution which it makes to the maturity of free judgement: 'to accept authority' is thus also to pass through the screen of doubt and critique. More fundamentally still, authority is linked to reason insofar as 'tradition is constantly an element of freedom and of history itself' (*WM* 265; *TM* 250). This point is missed if the 'preservation' (*Bewahr-*

ung) of a cultural heritage is confused with the simple conservation of a natural reality. A tradition must be seized, taken up and maintained; hence it demands an act of reason: 'Preservation is as much a freely-chosen action as revolution and renewal' (*WM* 266; *TM* 250).

It may be noted, however, that Gadamer uses the word *Vernunft* (reason) and not *Verstand* (understanding). A dialogue is possible on this basis with Habermas and Karl-Otto Apel, who are also concerned to defend a concept of reason distinct from the technocratic understanding which they see as subservient to a purely technological project. It may well be the case that the Frankfurt School's distinction between communicative action, the work of reason, and instrumental action, the work of technological understanding, can be sustained only by recourse to tradition – or at least to a living cultural tradition, as opposed to a tradition which is politicised and institutionalised. Eric Weil's distinction between the rationale of technology and the reasonableness of politics would be equally relevant here; for Eric Weil as well, what is reasonable emerges only in the course of a dialogue between the spirit of innovation and the spirit of tradition.

The properly 'ontological' interpretation of the sequence – prejudice, authority, tradition – is crystallised, as it were, in the category of *Wirkungsgeschichte* or *wirkungsgeschichtliches Bewusstsein*, which marks the summit of Gadamer's reflection on the foundations of the human sciences.

This category does not pertain to methodology, to historical *Forschung* [inquiry], but rather to the reflective consciousness of this methodology. It is a category of the awareness of history. Later we shall see that certain of Habermas's concepts, such as the regulative idea of unrestricted communication, are situated at the same level of the self-understanding of the social sciences. It is therefore important to analyse the category of the consciousness of historical efficacy with the greatest care. In general terms, it can be characterised as the consciousness of being exposed to history and to its effects, in such a way that this action over us cannot be objectified, for the efficacy belongs to the very meaning of the action as an historical phenomenon. Thus in *Kleine Schriften* we read:

By that I mean, first, that we cannot extricate ourselves from the historical process, so distance ourselves from it that the past becomes an object for us . . . We are always situated in history . . . I mean that our consciousness is determined by a real historical process, in such a way that we are not free to juxtapose ourselves to the past. I mean moreover that we must always become conscious afresh of the action which is thereby exercised over us, in such a way that everything past which we come to experience compels us to take hold of it completely, to assume in some way its truth.[5]

Let us analyse further the massive and global fact whereby consciousness, even before its awakening as such, belongs to and depends on that which affects it. This properly prevenient action, incorporated into awareness, can be articulated at the level of philosophical thought in terms of four themes, which seem to me to converge in the category of the consciousness of historical efficacy.

To begin with, the concept must be placed together and in tension with the notion of *historical distance*. This notion, which Gadamer elaborated in the paragraph preceding the one we quoted, is made into a methodological condition of *Forschung*. Distance is a fact; placing at a distance is a methodological attitude. The history of effects is precisely what occurs under the condition of historical distance. It is the nearness of the remote. Whence the illusion, against which Gadamer struggles, that 'distance' puts an end to our collusion with the past and creates a situation comparable to the objectivity of the natural sciences, on the grounds that a loss of familiarity is a break with the contingent. Against this illusion, it is important to restore the paradox of the 'otherness' of the past. Effective history is efficacy at a distance.

The second theme incorporated in the idea of historical efficacy is this: there is no *overview* which would enable us to grasp in a single glance the totality of effects. Between finitude and absolute knowledge, it is necessary to choose; the concept of effective history belongs to an ontology of finitude. It plays the same role as the 'thrown project' and the 'situation' play in Heidegger's ontology. Historical being is that which never passes into self-knowledge. If there is a corresponding Hegelian concept, it would not be *Wissen* (knowledge), but rather *Substanz*, which Hegel uses whenever it is necessary to speak of the unfathomable depths which come to discourse through the dialectic. To do justice to Hegel, one must retrace the course of *The Phenomenology of Mind*, rather than descend along the path towards absolute knowledge.

The third theme corrects somewhat the preceding point: if there is no overview, neither is there a situation which restricts us absolutely. Wherever there is a situation, there is an *horizon* which may contract or expand. As the visual circle of our existence attests, the landscape is organised into the near, the far and the open. It is the same in historical understanding. At one time it was thought that the concept of horizon could be accounted for by assimilating it to the methodological rule of placing oneself in the other's point of view: the horizon is the horizon of the other. It was thus thought that history had been aligned with the objectivity of the sciences: to adopt the other's point of view while forgetting one's own, is that not objectivity? Yet nothing is more disastrous than this fallacious assimilation. For the text, thus treated as an absolute object, is divested of its claim to tell us something about something. This claim can be sustained only by the idea of a prior understanding concerning the thing itself. Nothing destroys more the very sense of the historical enterprise than this objective distancing, which suspends both the tension of points of view and the claim of tradition to transmit a true speech about what is.

By restoring the dialectic of points of view and the tension between the other and the self, we arrive at the culminating concept of the *fusion of horizons* – our fourth theme. This is a dialectical concept which results from the rejection of two alternatives: objectivism, whereby the objectification of the other is premised on the forgetting of oneself; and absolute knowledge, according to which universal history can be articulated within a single horizon. We exist neither in closed horizons, nor within an horizon that is unique. No horizon is closed, since it is possible to place oneself in another point of view and in another culture. It would be reminiscent of Robinson Crusoe to claim that the other is inaccessible. But no horizon is unique, since the tension between the other and oneself is unsurpassable. Gadamer seems to accept, at one stage, the idea of a single horizon encompassing all points of view, as in the monadology of Leibniz (*WM* 288; *TM* 271). This is, it seems, in order to combat Nietzsche's radical pluralism, which would lead to incommunicability and which would shatter the idea, essential to the philosophy of *logos*, of a 'common understanding concerning the thing'. In this respect, Gadamer's account is similar to Hegel's, insofar as historical comprehension requires a 'common understanding concerning the thing' and hence a unique *logos* of communication; but Gadamer's position is only tangential to that of Hegel, because his Heideggerian ontology of finitude prevents him from transforming this unique horizon into a knowledge. The very word 'horizon' indicates an ultimate repudiation of the idea of a knowledge wherein the fusion of horizons would itself be grasped. The contrast in virtue of which one point of view stands out against the backcloth of others (*Abhebung*) marks the gulf between hermeneutics and any form of Hegelianism.

The unsurpassable concept of the fusion of horizons endows the theory of prejudice with its most peculiar characteristic: prejudice is the horizon of the present, the finitude of what is near in its openness towards the remote. This relation between the self and the other gives the concept of prejudice its final dialectical touch: only insofar as I place myself in the other's point of view do I confront myself with my present horizon, with my prejudices. It is only in the tension between the other and the self, between the text of the past and the point of view of the reader, that prejudice becomes operative and constitutive of historicity.

The epistemological implications of the ontological concept of historical efficacy are easy to discern. They concern the very status of research in the social sciences: that is what Gadamer wanted to show. *Forschung* – inquiry – scientific research does not escape the historical consciousness of those who live and make history. Historical knowledge cannot free itself from the historical condition. It follows that the project of a science free from prejudices is impossible. History poses meaningful questions to the past, pursues meaningful research and attains meaningful results only by beginning from a tradition which interpellates it. The emphasis on the word *Bedeutung* [meaning] leaves no doubt: history as science receives its meanings, at the outset as well as the end of research, from the link which it preserves with a received and recognised tradition. The action of tradition and historical investigation are fused by a bond which no critical consciousness could dissolve without rendering the research itself nonsensical. The history of the historians (*Historie*) can only bring to a higher level of consciousness the very flow of life within history (*Geschichte*): 'Modern historical research itself is not only research, but the transmission of tradition' (*WM* 268; *TM* 253). Man's link to the past precedes and envelops the purely objective treatment of historical facts. It remains to be seen whether the ideal of unlimited and unconstrained communication, which Habermas opposes to the concept of tradition, escapes from Gadamer's argument against the possibility of a complete knowledge of history and, along with it, of history as an object in itself.

Whatever the outcome of this argument against the critique of ideology, hermeneutics ultimately claims to set itself up as a critique of critique, or meta-critique.

Why meta-critique? What is at stake in this term is what Gadamer calls, in the *Kleine Schriften*, 'the universality of the hermeneutical problem'. I see three ways of construing this notion of universality. It may be construed, first, as the claim that hermeneutics has the same scope as science. For universality is first of all a scientific demand, one which concerns our knowledge and our power. Hermeneutics claims to cover the same domain as scientific investigation, founding the latter in an experience of the world which precedes and envelops the knowledge and the power of science. This claim to universality is thus raised on the same ground as the critique which addresses itself to the conditions of possibility of the knowledge of science and its power. So the first universality arises from the very task of hermeneutics: 'to reconnect the objective world of technology, which the sciences place at our disposal and discretion, with those fundamental orders of our being that are neither arbitrary nor manipulable by us, but rather simply demand our respect'.[6] To remove from our discretion what science places at our disposal: such is the first meta-critical task.

It could be said, however, that this universality is still derived. In Gadamer's view, hermeneutics has a peculiar universality which can be attained, paradoxically, only by starting from certain privileged experiences of universal significance. For fear of becoming a *Methodik* [methodology], hermeneutics can raise its claim to universality only from very concrete domains, that is, from regional hermeneutics which must always be 'deregionalised'. In the process of deregionalisation, hermeneutics may encounter a resistance that stems from the very nature of the experiences with which it begins. For these are, *par excellence*, the experiences of *Verfremdung* – alienation – whether it be in the aesthetic, historical or lingual consciousness. The struggle against methodological distanciation transforms hermeneutics into a critique of critique; it must always push the rock of Sisyphus up again, restore the ontological ground that methodology has eroded away. But at the same time, the critique of critique assumes a thesis which will appear very suspect to 'critical' eyes: namely that a *consensus* already exists, which founds the possibility of aesthetic, historical and lingual relations. To Schleiermacher, who defined hermeneutics as the art of overcoming misunderstanding (*Missverständnis*), Gadamer ripostes: 'is it not, in fact, the case that every misunderstanding presupposes a "deep common accord"?'.[7]

This idea of a *tragendes Einverständnis* is absolutely fundamental; the assertion that misunderstanding is supported by a prior understanding is the pre-eminent meta-critical theme. It leads, moreover, to the third concept of universality which may be found in Gadamer's work. The universal element which permits the deregionalisation of hermeneutics is language itself. The accord which supports us is the understanding reached in dialogue – not so much the relaxed face-to-face situation, but the question-answer relation in its most radical form. Here we come across the primitive hermeneutical phenomenon: 'No assertion is possible that cannot be understood as an answer to a question, and assertions can only be understood in this way.'[8] Every hermeneutics thus culminates in the concept of *Sprachlichkeit* or the 'lingual dimension', although 'language' must be construed here, not as the system of languages [*langues*], but as the collection of things said, the summary of the most significant messages, transmitted not only by ordinary language but by all of the eminent languages [*langages*] which have made us what we are.

We shall approach Habermas's critique by asking whether 'the dialogue which we are' is indeed the universal element that allows hermeneutics to be deregionalised, or if instead it constitutes a rather peculiar experience, enveloping both a blindness with respect to the real conditions of human communication, as well as a hope for a communication without restriction and constraint.

2. The critique of ideology: Habermas

I should like now to present the second protagonist of the debate, reduced for the sake of clarity to a simple duel. I shall discuss his *critique of ideology*, considered as an alternative to the *hermeneutics of tradition*, under four successive headings.

(1) Whereas Gadamer borrows the concept of *prejudice* from philosophical Romanticism, reinterpreting it by means of the Heideggerian notion of pre-understanding, Habermas develops a concept of *interest*, which stems from the tradition of Marxism as reinterpreted by Lukács and the Frankfurt School (Horkheimer, Adorno, Marcuse, Apel, etc.).

(2) Whereas Gadamer appeals to the *human sciences*, which are concerned with the contemporary reinterpretation of cultural tradition, Habermas makes recourse to the *critical social sciences*, directly aimed against institutional reifications.

(3) Whereas Gadamer introduces *mis-understanding* as the inner obstacle to understanding, Habermas develops a theory of *ideology*, construed as the systematic distortion of communication by the hidden exercise of force.

(4) Lastly, whereas Gadamer bases the hermeneutic task on an ontology of the 'dialogue which we are', Habermas invokes the *regulative ideal* of an unrestricted and unconstrained communication which does not precede us but guides us from a future point.

I present this very schematic outline of the alternative with the aim of clarification. The debate would be without interest if the two apparently antithetical positions did not share a zone of intersection which, in my view, ought to become the point of departure for a new phase of hermeneutics, a phase which I shall sketch in the second part. But first, let us take up each of the lines of disagreement.

(1) The concept of interest invites us to say a few words about Habermas's relation to Marxism, which is roughly comparable with Gadamer's relation to philosophical Romanticism. The Marxism of Habermas is of a quite specific sort, having little in common with Althusser's and leading to a very different theory of ideology. In *Knowledge and Human Interests,* published in 1968, Marxism is placed inside an archaeology of knowledge which, unlike Foucault's, does not aim to isolate discontinuous structures that could be neither constituted nor manipulated by any subject; on the contrary, it aims to retrace the continuous history of a single problematic, that of reflection, swamped by the rise of objectivism and positivism. The book seeks to reconstruct the 'prehistory of modern positivism', and thereby the history of the dissolution of the critical function, with a goal that could be called apologetic: namely, 'to recover the forgotten experience of reflection'.[9] Placed within the history of the achievements and the failures of reflection, Marxism can only appear as a very ambiguous phenomenon. On the one hand, it is part of the history of critical reflection; it is at one extremity of a line which begins with Kant and passes through Fichte and Hegel. I do not have the time to describe how Habermas sees this series of radicalisations of the reflective task, across the successive stages of the Kantian subject, the Hegelian consciousness and the Fichtean ego, and culminating with the synthesis of man and nature in the activity of production. This way of formulating the filiation of Marxism from the question of critique is very revealing in itself. To conceive of Marxism as a novel solution to the problem of the conditions of possibility of objectivity and the object, to say that 'in materialism labour has the function of synthesis', is to submit Marxism to a properly 'critical' reading, in the Kantian and post-Kantian sense of the word. Hence Habermas says that the critique of political economy has the same role in Marx's work as the logic has in idealism.

Thus placed within the history of critical reflection, Marxism cannot avoid appearing both as the most advanced position of the metacritique, insofar as man the producer takes the place of the transcendental subject and the Hegelian spirit, and as a stage in the history of the forgetting of reflection and the advance of positivism and objectivism.

The defence of man the producer leads to the hypostatisation of one category of action at the expense of all others, namely instrumental action.

In order to understand this critique which claims to be internal to Marxism, it is necessary to introduce the concept of interest. Here I shall follow the 1965 essay, included as an appendix to *Knowledge and Human Interests*, before returning to the latter work.

The concept of interest is opposed to all pretensions of the theoretical subject to situate itself outside the sphere of desire, pretensions that Habermas sees in the work of Plato, Kant, Hegel and Husserl; the task of a critical philosophy is precisely to unmask the interests which underlie the enterprise of knowledge. It is evident that, however different the concept of interest may be from Gadamer's notions of prejudice and tradition, there is a certain family resemblance which will have to be clarified at a later stage. For the moment it will enable us to introduce the concept of ideology, understood as an allegedly disinterested knowledge which serves to conceal an interest under the guise of a rationalisation, in a sense similar to Freud's.

To appreciate Habermas's critique of Marx, it is important to realise that there are several interests, or more precisely a *pluralism* of spheres of interest. Habermas distinguishes three basic interests, each of which governs a sphere of *Forschung* – of inquiry – and hence a group of sciences.

There is, first, the *technical* or *instrumental interest*, which governs the 'empirical-analytic sciences'. It governs these sciences in the sense that the signification of possible empirical statements consists in their technical exploitability: the relevant facts of the empirical sciences are constituted by an *a priori* organisation of our experience within the behavioural system of instrumental action. This thesis, close to the pragmatism of Dewey and Peirce, will be decisive for understanding the functions of what Habermas, following Marcuse, regards as the modern ideology, namely science and technology themselves. The imminent possibility of ideology arises from this correlation between empirical knowledge and the technical interest, which Habermas defines more exactly as 'the cognitive interest in technical control over objectified processes'.[10]

There is, however, a second sphere of interest, which is no longer technical but *practical*, in the Kantian sense of the word. In other writings, Habermas opposes communicative action to instrumental action; it is the same distinction: the practical sphere is the sphere of intersubjective communication. He correlates this sphere with the domain of the 'historical-hermeneutic sciences'. The signification of propositions produced in this domain does not proceed from possible prediction and technical exploitability, but from understanding meaning. This understanding is accomplished through the interpretation of messages exchanged in ordinary language, by means of the interpretation of texts transmitted by tradition, and in virtue of the internalisation of norms which institutionalise social roles. It is evident that here we are closer to Gadamer than to Marx. Closer to Gadamer, for, at the level of communicative action, understanding is subsumed by the interpreter to the conditions of pre-understanding, which in turn is constituted on the basis of the traditional meanings incorporated into the seizure of any new phenomenon. Even the practical emphasis which Habermas gives to the hermeneutical sciences is not fundamentally foreign to Gadamer, insofar as the latter linked the interpretation of what is distant and past to the 'application' (*Anwendung*) here and now. Closer to Gadamer, we are also further from Marx. For the distinction between the two levels of interest, technical interest and practical interest, between the two levels of action, instrumental action and communicative action, between the two levels of science, empirical-analytic science and historical-hermeneutic science, provides the starting point for the internal critique of Marxism (here I return to the main text of *Knowledge and Human Interests*).

The critique claims to be internal in the sense that Habermas discerns in the work of Marx himself the outlines of his own distinction between the two types of interest, action and science. He sees this in the famous distinction between 'forces of production' and 'relations of production', the latter designating the institutional forms in which productive activity is carried out. Marxism in fact rests on the disjunction between force and form. The activity of production should engender one unique self-productive humanity, one unique 'generic essence' of man; but the relations of production split the producing subject into antagonistic classes. Therein Habermas sees the beginnings of his own distinction, in the sense that the phenomena of domination and violence, as well as the ideological dissimulation of these phenomena and the political enterprise of liberation, take place in the sphere of the *relations* of production and not that of the *forces* of production. An awareness of the distinction between instrumental and communicative action is therefore necessary in order to account for the very phenomena which Marx analysed: antagonism, domination, dissimulation, liberation. But such an awareness is precisely what Marxism, in the understanding which it has of its own thought, lacks. In subsuming forces and relations to the same concept of *production*, it precludes the real separation of interests, and hence also of levels of action and spheres of science. In that respect, Marxism belongs explicitly to the history of positivism, to the history of the forgetting of reflection, even though implicitly it is part of the history of the awareness of reifications which affect communication.

(2) We have still not spoken of the third type of interest, which Habermas calls the *interest in emancipation*. He connects this interest with a third type of science, the *critical social sciences*.

Here we touch upon the most important source of disagreement with Gadamer; whereas the latter takes the 'human sciences' as an initial point of reference, Habermas invokes the 'critical social sciences'. This initial choice is heavy with consequences. For the 'human sciences' are close to what Gadamer calls *humaniora*, the humanities; they are essentially sciences of culture, concerned with the renewal of cultural heritage in the historical present. They are thus by nature sciences of tradition – of tradition reinterpreted and reinvented in terms of its implications here and now, but of continuous tradition nonetheless. From the outset, the destiny of Gadamer's hermeneutics is tied to these sciences. They can incorporate a critical moment, but they are inclined by nature to struggle against the alienating distanciation of the aesthetic, historical and lingual consciousness. Consequently, they forbid the elevation of the critical instance above the recognition of authority and above the very tradition reinterpreted. The critical instance can be developed only as a moment subordinated to the consciousness of finitude and of dependence upon the figures of pre-understanding which always precede and envelop it.

The situation is quite different in the critical social sciences. They are critical by constitution; it is this which distinguishes them from the empirical-analytic sciences of the social order, as well as from the historical-hermeneutic sciences described above. The task of the critical social sciences is to discern, beneath the regularities observed by the empirical social sciences, those 'ideologically frozen' relations of dependence which can be transformed only through critique. Thus the critical approach is governed by the interest in emancipation, which Habermas also calls *self-reflection*. This interest provides the frame of reference for critical propositions: self-reflection, he says in the sketch of 1965, frees the subject from dependence on hypostatised powers. It can be seen that this is the very interest which animated the philosophies of the past; it is common to philosophy and the critical social sciences. It is the interest in *Selbständigkeit*, in autonomy, in independence. But ontology concealed this interest, buried it in the ready-made reality of a being which supports us. The interest is active only in the critical instance which unmasks the interests at work in the activities of knowledge, which shows the dependence of the theoretical subject on empirical conditions stemming from institutional constraints and which orients the recognition of these forms of constraint towards emancipation.

The critical instance is thus placed above the hermeneutical consciousness, for it is presented as the enterprise of 'dissolving' the constraints arising not from nature, but from institutions. A gulf therefore divides the hermeneutical project, which puts assumed tradition above judgement, and the critical project, which puts reflection above institutionalised constraint.

(3) We are thus led, step by step, towards the third point of disagreement, which is the focus of our debate. I shall state the point as follows: the concept of ideology plays the same role in a critical social science as the concept of misunderstanding plays in a hermeneutics of tradition. It was Schleiermacher who, before Gadamer, tied hermeneutics to the concept of misunderstanding. There is hermeneutics where there is misunderstanding. But there is hermeneutics because there is the conviction and the confidence that the understanding which precedes and envelops misunderstanding has the means to reintegrate misunderstanding into understanding by the very movement of question and answer on the dialogical model. Misunderstanding is, if I may say so, homogenous with understanding and of the same genre; hence understanding does not appeal to explanatory procedures, which are relegated to the excessive claims of 'methodologism'.

It is otherwise with the concept of ideology. What makes the difference? Here Habermas constantly resorts to the parallel between psychoanalysis and the theory of ideology. The parallel rests on the following criteria.

First trait: in the Frankfurt School and in a tradition that could still be called Marxist in a very general sense, distortion is always related to the repressive action of an authority and therefore to violence. The key concept here is 'censorship', an originally political concept which has returned to the critical social sciences after passing through psychoanalysis. The link between ideology and violence is crucial, for it introduces into the field of reflection dimensions which, without being absent from hermeneutics, are not accentuated by it, namely the dimensions of labour and power. We may say, in a broad Marxist sense, that the phenomena of class domination appear with the emergence of human labour, and that ideology expresses these phenomena in a way that will be explained shortly. In Habermas's terms, the phenomenon of domination takes place in the sphere of communicative action; it is there that language is distorted as regards its conditions of application at the level of communicative competence. Hence a hermeneutics which adheres to the ideality of *Sprachlichkeit* finds its limit in a phenomenon that affects language as such only because the relation between the three dimensions – labour, power and language – is altered.

Second trait: since the distortions of language do not come from the usage of language as such but from its relation to labour and power, these distortions are unrecognisable by the members of the community. This misrecognition is peculiar to the phenomenon of ideology. It can be analysed phenomenologically only by appealing to concepts of a psychoanalytic type: to *illusion* as distinct from error, to *projection* as the constitution of a false transcendence, to *rationalisation* as the subsequent rearrangement of motivations according to the appearance of a rational justification. To say the same thing in the sphere of critical social science, Habermas speaks of 'pseudo-communication' or 'systematically distorted communication', as opposed to mere misunderstanding.

Third trait: if misrecognition is insurmountable by the directly dialogical route, then the dissolution of ideologies must pass through the detour of procedures concerned with explaining and not simply with understanding. These procedures invoke a theoretical apparatus which cannot be derived from any hermeneutics that remains on the level of the spontaneous interpretation of everyday speech. Here again psychoanalysis provides a good model: it is developed at length in the third part of *Knowledge and Human Interests* and in the article entitled 'Der Universalitätsanspruch der Hermeneutik'.[11]

Habermas adopts Alfred Lorenzer's interpretation of psychoanalysis as *Sprachanalyse,* according to which the 'understanding' of meaning is accomplished by the 'reconstruction' of a 'primitive scene', placed in relation with two other 'scenes': the 'symptomatic scene' and the artificial 'scene of transference'. Certainly, psychoanalysis remains in the sphere of understanding, and of an understanding which culminates in the awareness of the subject; hence Habermas calls it a *Tiefenhermeneutik,* a 'depth hermeneutics'. But the understanding of meaning requires the detour of a 'reconstruction' of the processes of 'desymbolisation', which psychoanalysis retraces in the inverse direction along the routes of 'resymbolisation'. So psychoanalysis is not completely external to hermeneutics, since it can still be expressed in terms of desymbolisation and resymbolisation; rather it constitutes a *limit-experience*, in virtue of the explanatory force linked to the 'reconstruction' of the 'primitive scene'. In other words, to 'understand' the *what* of the symptom, it is necessary to 'explain' its *why*. This explanatory phase invokes a theoretical apparatus, which establishes the conditions of possibility of explanation and reconstruction: topographical concepts (the three agencies and the three roles), economic concepts (the defence mechanism, primary and secondary repression, splitting-off), genetic concepts (the famous stages and the successive phases of symbol organisation). As regards the three agencies *ego–id–superego* in particular, Habermas says that they are connected to the sphere of communication by the dialogical process of analysis, through which the patient is led to reflect upon himself. The metapsychology, concludes Habermas, 'can be founded only as meta-hermeneutics'.[12]

Unfortunately, Habermas tells us nothing about the way in which the explanatory and meta-hermeneutical scheme of psychoanalysis could be transposed onto the plane of ideology. It would have to be said, I think, that the distortions of communication which are linked to the social phenomena of domination and violence also constitute phenomena of desymbolisation. Habermas sometimes speaks, very appropriately, of 'excommunication', recalling the Wittgensteinian distinction between public and private language. It would also have to be shown in what sense the understanding of these phenomena requires a reconstruction which would recover certain features of 'scenic' understanding, or indeed of the three 'scenes' as such. In any case, it would be necessary to show that understanding requires an explanatory stage, such that the sense is understood only if the origin of the non-sense is explained. Finally, it would have to be shown how this explanation invokes a theoretical apparatus comparable to the Freudian topography or economics, and that the central concepts of this apparatus could be derived neither from the dialogical experience within the framework of ordinary language, nor from a textual exegesis grafted onto the direct understanding of discourse.

Such are the major characteristics of the concept of ideology: the impact of violence in discourse, a dissimulation whose key eludes consciousness, and the necessity of a detour through the explanation of causes. These three characteristics constitute the ideological phenomenon as a *limit-experience* for hermeneutics. Since hermeneutics can only develop a natural competence, we need a meta-hermeneutics to formulate the theory of the deformations of communicative competence. Critique is this theory of communicative competence, which comprises the art of understanding, the techniques for overcoming misunderstanding and the explanatory science of distortions.

(4) I do not want to end this very schematic presentation of Habermas's thought without saying something about what is perhaps the most profound divergence that separates him from Gadamer.

For Habermas, the principal flaw of Gadamer's account is to have *ontologised* hermeneutics; by that he means its insistence on understanding or accord, as if the *consensus* which precedes us were something constitutive, something given in being. Doesn't Gadamer say that understanding is *Sein* [being] rather than *Bewusstsein* [consciousness]? Does he not speak, with the poet, of the 'dialogue which we are' (*das Gespräch, das Wir sind*)? Doesn't he regard *Sprachlichkeit* as an ontological constitution, as a milieu within which we move? More fundamentally still, does he not anchor the hermeneutics of understanding in an ontology of finitude? Habermas can have nothing but mistrust for what seems to him to be the ontological hypostatisation of a rare experience, namely the experience of being preceded in our most felicitous dialogues by an understanding which supports them. This experience cannot be canonised and made into the paradigm of communicative action. What prevents us from doing so is precisely the ideological phenomenon. If ideology were only an internal obstacle to understanding, a mere misunderstanding which the exercise of question and answer could resolve, then it could be said that 'where there is misunderstanding, there is a prior understanding'.

A critique of ideology must think in terms of anticipation where the hermeneutics of tradition thinks in terms of assumed tradition. In other words, the critique of ideology must posit as a regulative idea, in front of us, what the hermeneutics of tradition conceives as existing at the origin of understanding. It is at this point that the third interest which guides knowledge, the interest in emancipation, comes into play. This interest, as we have seen, animates the critical social sciences, providing a frame of reference for all the meanings constituted in psychoanalysis and the critique of ideology. Self-reflection is the correlative concept of the interest in emancipation. Hence self-reflection cannot be founded on a prior *consensus*, for what is prior is precisely a broken communication. One cannot speak with Gadamer of the common accord which carries understanding without assuming a convergence of traditions that does not exist, without hypostatising a past which is also the place of false consciousness, without ontologising a language which has always only been a distorted 'communicative competence'.

The critique of ideology must be placed, therefore, under the sign of a regulative idea, that of unlimited and unconstrained communication. The Kantian emphasis is evident here; the regulative idea is more what ought to be than what is, more anticipation than recollection. It is this idea which gives meaning to every psychoanalytic or sociological critique. For there is desymbolisation only within the project of resymbolisation, and there is such a project only within the revolutionary perspective of the end of violence. Where the hermeneutics of tradition sought to extract the essence of authority and to connect it to the recognition of superiority, the interest in emancipation leads back towards the eleventh of the *Theses on Feuerbach:* 'the philosophers have only interpreted the world; the point, however, is to change it'. An eschatology of non-violence thus forms the ultimate philosophical horizon of a critique of ideology. This eschatology, close to that of Ernst Bloch, takes the place of the ontology of lingual understanding in a hermeneutics of tradition.

II. Towards a critical hermeneutics

1. Critical reflection on hermeneutics
I should like now to offer my own reflections on the presuppositions of each position and tackle the problems posed in the introduction. These problems, we said, concern the significance of the most fundamental gesture of philosophy. The gesture of hermeneutics is a humble one of acknowledging the historical conditions to which all human understanding is subsumed in the reign of finitude; that of the critique of ideology is a proud gesture of defiance directed against the distortions of human communication. By the first, I place myself in the historical process to which I know that I belong; by the second, I oppose the present state of falsified human communication with the idea of an essentially political freedom of speech, guided by the limiting idea of unrestricted and unconstrained communication.

My aim is not to fuse the hermeneutics of tradition and the critique of ideology in a super-system which would encompass both. As I said at the outset, each speaks from a different place. Nonetheless, each may be asked to recognise the other, not as a position which is foreign and purely hostile, but as one which raises in its own way a legitimate claim.

It is in this spirit that I return to the two questions posed in the introduction: (1) Can hermeneutic philosophy account for the demands of a critique of ideology? and if so, at what price? (2) On what condition is the critique of ideology possible? Can it, in the last analysis, be detached from hermeneutical presuppositions?

The first question challenges the capacity of hermeneutics to account for a critical instance in general. How can there be critique within hermeneutics?

I shall note to begin with that the recognition of a critical instance is a vague desire constantly reiterated, but constantly aborted, within hermeneutics. From Heidegger onwards, hermeneutics is wholly engaged in *going back to the foundations*, a movement which leads from the epistemological question concerning the conditions of possibility of the human sciences to the ontological structure of understanding. It may be asked, however, whether the return route from ontology to epistemology is possible. For it is only along this route that one could confirm the assertion that questions of exegetico-historical critique are 'derivative', and that the hermeneutical circle, in the sense of the exegetes, is 'founded' on the fundamental anticipatory structure of understanding.

Ontological hermeneutics seems incapable, for structural reasons, of unfolding this problematic of return. In the work of Heidegger himself, the question is abandoned as soon as it is asked. Thus in *Being and Time* we read this:

In the circle of understanding . . . is hidden a positive possibility of the most primordial kind of knowing. We genuinely take hold of this possibility only when, in our explication (*Auslegung*), we have understood that our first, last, and constant task is never to allow our fore-having, fore-sight, and fore-conception to be presented to us by fancies (*Einfälle*) and popular conceptions (*Volksbegriffe*), but rather to make the scientific theme secure by working out these anticipations in terms of the things themselves. (*SZ* 153; *BT* 195)†

Here we find, posed in principle, the distinction between an anticipation according to the things themselves and an anticipation springing from fancies (*Einfälle*) and popular conceptions (*Volksbegriffe*); these two terms have a visible link with prejudices by 'precipitation' and by 'predisposition'. But how can this distinction be pursued when one declares, immediately afterwards, that 'the ontological presuppositions of historiological knowledge transcend in principle the idea of rigour held in the most exact sciences' (*SZ* 153; *BT* 195), and thereby eludes the question of the rigour proper to the historical sciences themselves? The concern to anchor the circle more deeply than any epistemology prevents the epistemological question from being raised on ontological ground.

Is that to say that there is not, in the work of Heidegger himself, any development which corresponds to the critical moment of epistemology? Indeed there is, but the development is applied elsewhere. In passing from the Analytic of *Dasein*, which still includes the theory of understanding and interpretation, to the theory of temporality and totality, which includes the second meditation on understanding (para. 63), it seems that all critical effort is spent in the work of *deconstructing metaphysics*. The reason is clear: since hermeneutics has become the hermeneutics of being – of the meaning of being – the anticipatory structure appropriate to the question of the meaning of being is given by the history of metaphysics, which thus takes the place of prejudice. Henceforth, the hermeneutics of being deploys all its critical resources in the debate with classical and medieval substance, with the Cartesian and Kantian *cogito*. The confrontation with the metaphysical tradition of the West takes the place of a critique of prejudices. In other words, from a Heideggerian perspective, the only internal critique that can be conceived as an integral part of the enterprise of disclosure is the deconstruction of metaphysics; and a properly epistemological critique can be resumed only indirectly, insofar as metaphysical residues can be found at work in the sciences which claim to be empirical. But this critique of prejudices which originate in metaphysics cannot take the place of a real confrontation with the human sciences, with their methodology and with their epistemological presuppositions. The obsessive concern with radicality thus blocks the return route from general hermeneutics towards regional hermeneutics: towards philology, history, depth-psychology, etc.

As regards Gadamer, there is no doubt that he has perfectly grasped the urgency of this 'descending dialectic' from the fundamental towards the derived. Thus he proposes, as we noted above, to 'inquire into the consequences which follow for the hermeneutics of the human sciences from the fact that Heidegger derives (*Ableitung*) the circular structure of understanding from the temporality of *Dasein*' (WM 251; TM 235).† It is precisely these 'consequences' which interest us. For it is in the movement of derivation that the link between pre-understanding and prejudice becomes problematic and the question of critique is raised afresh, in the very heart of understanding. Thus Gadamer, speaking of the texts of our culture, repeatedly insists that these texts signify by themselves, that there is a 'matter of the text' which addresses us. But how can the 'matter of the text' be left to speak without confronting the critical question of the way in which pre-understanding and prejudice are mixed?

It seems to me that Gadamer's hermeneutics is prevented from embarking upon this route, not simply because, as with Heidegger, all effort of thought is invested in the radicalisation of the problem of foundation, but because the hermeneutical experience itself discourages the recognition of any critical instance.

The *primary* experience of this hermeneutics, determining the very place from which it raises its claim to universality, involves the refutation of the 'alienating distanciation' – *Verfremdung* – which commands the objectifying attitude of the human sciences. Henceforth the entire work assumes a dichotomous character which is indicated even in the title, *Truth and Method*, wherein the disjunction overrides the conjunction. It is this initial dichotomous situation which, it seems to me, prevents Gadamer from really recognising the critical instance and hence rendering justice to the critique of ideology, which is the modern post-Marxist expression of the critical instance.

My own interrogation proceeds from this observation. Would it not be appropriate to shift the initial locus of the hermeneutical question, to reformulate the question in such a way that a certain dialectic between the experience of belonging and alienating distanciation becomes the mainspring, the key to the inner life, of hermeneutics?

The idea of such a shift in the initial locus of the hermeneutical question is suggested by the history of hermeneutics itself. Throughout this history, the emphasis has always come back to exegesis or philology, that is, to the sort of relation with tradition which is based on the *mediation* of texts, or documents and monuments which have a status comparable to texts. Schleiermacher was exegete of the New Testament and translator of Plato. Dilthey located the specificity of interpretation (*Auslegung*), as contrasted with the direct understanding of the other (*Verstehen*), in the phenomenon of fixation by writing and, more generally, of inscription.

In thus reverting to the problematic of the text, to exegesis and philology, we appear at first sight to restrict the aim and the scope of hermeneutics. However, since any claim to universality is raised from somewhere, we may expect that the restoration of the link between hermeneutics and exegesis will reveal its own universal features which, without really contradicting Gadamer's hermeneutics, will rectify it in a manner decisive for the debate with the critique of ideology.

I should like to sketch four themes which constitute a sort of critical supplementation to the hermeneutics of tradition.

(a) The distanciation in which this hermeneutics tends to see a sort of ontological fall from grace appears as a positive component of being for the text; it characteristically belongs to interpretation, not as its contrary but as its condition. The moment of distanciation is implied by fixation in writing and by all comparable phenomena in the sphere of the transmission of discourse. Writing is not simply a matter of the material fixation of discourse; for fixation is the condition of a much more fundamental phenomenon, that of the autonomy of the text. A threefold autonomy: with respect to the intention of the author; with respect to the cultural situation and all the sociological conditions of the production of the text; and finally, with respect to the original addressee. What the text signifies no longer coincides with what the author meant; verbal meaning and mental meaning have different destinies. This first form of autonomy already implies the possibility that the 'matter of the text' may escape from the author's restricted intentional horizon, and that the world of the text may explode the world of its author. What is true of psychological conditions is also true of sociological conditions, even though he who is prepared to liquidate the author is less prepared to perform the same operation in the sociological sphere. The peculiarity of the literary work, and indeed of the work as such, is nevertheless to transcend its own psycho-sociological conditions of production and thereby to open itself to an unlimited series of readings, themselves situated in socio-cultural contexts which are always different. In short, the work *decontextualises* itself, from the sociological as well as the psychological point of view, and is able to *re-contextualise* itself differently in the act of reading. It follows that the mediation of the text cannot be treated as an extension of the dialogical situation. For in dialogue, the *vis-à-vis* of discourse is given in advance by the setting itself; with writing, the original addressee is transcended. The work itself creates an audience, which potentially includes anyone who can read.

The emancipation of the text constitutes the most fundamental condition for the recognition of a critical instance at the heart of interpretation; for distanciation now belongs to the mediation itself.

In a sense, these remarks only extend what Gadamer himself says, on the one hand, about 'temporal distance' which, as we have seen above, is one aspect of 'consciousness exposed to the efficacy of history'; and on the other hand, about *Schriftlichkeit* which, according to Gadamer himself, adds new features to *Sprachlichkeit*. But at the same time as this analysis extends Gadamer's, it shifts the emphasis somewhat. For the distanciation revealed by writing is already present in discourse itself, which contains the seeds of the distanciation of the *said* from the *saying*, to follow Hegel's famous analysis at the beginning of *The Phenomenology of Mind*: the *saying* vanishes, but the *said* persists. In this respect, writing does not represent a radical revolution in the constitution of discourse, but only accomplishes the latter's profoundest aim.

(b) If hermeneutics is to account for a critical instance in terms of its own premises, then it must satisfy a second condition: it must overcome the ruinous dichotomy, inherited from Dilthey, between 'explanation' and 'understanding'. As is well known, this dichotomy arises from the conviction that any explanatory attitude is borrowed from the methodology of the *natural sciences* and illegitimately extended to the *human sciences*. However, the appearance of semiological models in the field of the text convinces us that all explanation is not naturalistic or causal. The semiological models, applied in particular to the theory of the narrative, are borrowed from the domain of language itself, by extension from units smaller than the sentence to units larger than the sentence (poems, narratives, etc.). Here discourse must be placed under the category, no longer of writing but rather of the work, that is, under a category which pertains to *praxis*, to labour. Discourse is characterised by the fact that it can be produced as a work displaying structure and form. Even more than writing, the production of discourse as a work involves an objectification that enables it to be read in existential conditions which are always new. But in contrast to the simple discourse of conversation, which enters into the spontaneous movement of question and answer, discourse as a work 'takes hold' in structures calling for a description and an explanation that mediate 'understanding'. We are here in a situation similar to that described by Habermas: *reconstruction* is the path of understanding. However, this situation is not peculiar to psychoanalysis and to all that Habermas designates by the term 'depth hermeneutics'; it is the condition of the work in general. So if there is a hermeneutics – and here I oppose those forms of structuralism which would remain at the explanatory level – it must be constituted across the mediation rather than against the current of structural explanation. For it is the task of understanding to bring to discourse what is initially given as structure. It is necessary to have gone as far as possible along the route of objectification, to the point where structural analysis discloses the *depth semantics* of a text, before one can claim to 'understand' the text in terms of the 'matter' which speaks therefrom. The *matter* of the text is not what a naive reading of the text reveals, but what the formal arrangement of the text mediates. If that is so, then truth and method do not constitute a disjunction but rather a dialectical process.

(c) The hermeneutics of texts turns towards the critique of ideology in a third way. It seems to me that the properly hermeneutical moment arises when the interrogation, transgressing the closure of the text, is carried towards what Gadamer himself calls 'the matter of the text', namely the sort of *world* opened up by it. This can be called the *referential* moment, in allusion to the Fregean distinction between sense and reference. The sense of the work is its internal organisation, whereas the reference is the mode of being unfolded in front of the text.

It may be noted in passing that the most decisive break with Romantic hermeneutics is here; what is sought is no longer an intention hidden behind the text, but a world unfolded in front of it. The power of the text to open a dimension of reality implies in principle a recourse against any given reality and thereby the possibility of a critique of the real. It is in poetic discourse that this subversive power is most alive. The strategy of this discourse involves holding two moments in equilibrium: suspending the reference of ordinary language and releasing a second order reference, which is another name for what we have designated above as the world opened up by the work. In the case of poetry, fiction is the path of redescription; or to speak as Aristotle does in the *Poetics*, the creation of a *mythos*, of a 'fable', is the path of *mimesis*, of creative imitation.

Here again we are developing a theme sketched by Gadamer himself, particularly in his magnificent pages on *play*. But in pressing to the end this meditation on the relation between *fiction* and *redescription,* we introduce a critical theme which the hermeneutics of tradition tends to cast beyond its frontiers. The critical theme was nevertheless present in the Heideggerian analysis of understanding. Recall how Heidegger conjoins understanding to the notion of 'the projection of my ownmost possibilities'; this signifies that the mode of being of the world opened up by the text is the mode of the possible, or better of the power-to-be: therein resides the subversive force of the imaginary. The paradox of poetic reference consists precisely in the fact that reality is redescribed only insofar as discourse is raised to fiction.

A hermeneutics of the power-to-be thus turns itself towards a critique of ideology, of which it constitutes the most fundamental possibility. Distanciation, at the same time, emerges at the heart of reference: poetic discourse distances itself from everyday reality, aiming towards being as power-to-be.

(d) In a final way, the hermeneutics of texts indicates the place for a critique of ideology. This final point pertains to the status of subjectivity in interpretation. For if the primary concern of hermeneutics is not to discover an intention hidden behind the text but to unfold a world in front of it, then authentic self-understanding is something which, as Heidegger and Gadamer wish to say, can be instructed by the 'matter of the text'. The relation to the world of the text takes the place of the relation to the subjectivity of the author, and at the same time the problem of the subjectivity of the reader is displaced. To understand is not to project oneself into the text but to expose oneself to it; it is to receive a self enlarged by the appropriation of the proposed worlds which interpretation unfolds. In sum, it is the matter of the text which gives the reader his dimension of subjectivity; understanding is thus no longer a constitution of which the subject possesses the key. Pressing this suggestion to the end, we must say that the subjectivity of the reader is no less held in suspense, no less potentialised, than the very world which the text unfolds. In other words, if fiction is a fundamental dimension of the reference of the text, it is equally a fundamental dimension of the subjectivity of the reader: in reading, I 'unrealise myself'. Reading introduces me to imaginative variations of the *ego*. The metamorphosis of the world in play is also the playful metamorphosis of the *ego*.

In the idea of the 'imaginative variation of the *ego*', I see the most fundamental possibility for a critique of the illusions of the subject. This link could remain hidden or undeveloped in a hermeneutics of tradition which introduced prematurely a concept of appropriation (*Aneignung*) directed against alienating distanciation. However, if distanciation from oneself is not a fault to be combated, but rather the condition of possibility of understanding oneself in front of the text, then appropriation is the dialectical counterpart of distanciation. Thus the critique of ideology can be assumed by a concept of self-understanding which organically implies a critique of the illusions of the subject. Distanciation from oneself demands that the appropriation of the proposed worlds offered by the text passes through the disappropriation of the self. The critique of *false consciousness* can thus become an integral part of hermeneutics, conferring upon the critique of ideology that meta-hermeneutical dimension which Habermas assigns to it.

2. Hermeneutical reflection on critique

I should like now to offer a similar reflection on the critique of ideology, with the aim of assessing the latter's claim to universality. I do not expect this reflection to return the critique of ideology to the fold of hermeneutics, but rather to confirm Gadamer's view that the two 'universalities', that of hermeneutics and that of the critique of ideology, are interpenetrating. The question could also be presented in Habermas's terms: on what conditions can critique be formulated as meta-hermeneutics? I propose to follow the order of the theses in terms of which I sketched Habermas's thought.

(1) I shall begin with the theory of interests which underlies the critique of the ideologies of transcendental phenomenology and positivism. It may be asked what authorises the following theses: that all *Forschung* is governed by an interest which establishes a prejudicial frame of reference for its field of meaning; that there are three such interests (and not one or two or four): namely, the technical interest, the practical interest and the interest in emancipation; that these interests are anchored in the natural history of the human species, but that they mark the emergence of man out of nature, taking form in the spheres of labour, power and language; that in self-reflection, knowledge and interest are one; that the unity of knowledge and interest is attested to in a dialectic which discerns the historical traces of the repression of dialogue and which reconstructs what has been suppressed.

Are these 'theses' empirically justifiable? No, for then they would fall under the yoke of the empirical-analytic sciences which pertain to *one* interest, the technical interest. Are these theses a 'theory', in the sense given to this word by psychoanalysis for example, that is, in the sense of a network of explanatory hypotheses permitting the reconstruction of a primitive scene? No, for then they would become regional theses as in any theory and would again be justified by *one* interest, the interest in emancipation perhaps; and the justification would become circular.

Is it not necessary to recognise henceforth that the disclosure of interests at the roots of knowledge, the hierarchical ordering of interests and their connection to the trilogy of labour–power–language, are dependent upon a philosophical anthropology similar to Heidegger's Analytic of *Dasein*, and more particularly to his hermeneutics of 'care'? If that is so, then these interests are neither observables, nor theoretical entities like the *ego*, the *super-ego* and the *id* in Freud's work, but rather 'existentiales'. Their analysis depends upon hermeneutics, insofar as they are at once 'the closest' and 'the most concealed', so that they must be disclosed in order to be recognised.

The analysis of interests could be called 'meta-hermeneutical', if it is supposed that hermeneutics is primarily a hermeneutics of discourse, indeed an idealism of lingual life. But we have seen that it has nothing to do with this, that the hermeneutics of pre-understanding is fundamentally a hermeneutics of finitude. Hence I am quite willing to say that the critique of ideology raises its claim from a different place than hermeneutics, namely from the place where labour, power and language are intertwined. But the two claims cross on a common ground: the hermeneutics of finitude, which secures *a priori* the correlation between the concept of prejudice and that of ideology.

(2) I should like now to consider afresh the pact which Habermas establishes between critical social science and the interest in emancipation. We have sharply contrasted the positions of the critical social sciences and the historical-hermeneutic sciences, the latter inclining towards recognition of the authority of traditions rather than towards revolutionary action against oppression.

Here the question which hermeneutics addresses to the critique of ideology is this: can you assign the interest in emancipation a status as distinct as you suppose with respect to the interest which animates the historical-hermeneutic sciences? The distinction is asserted so dogmatically that it seems to create a gulf between the interest in emancipation and the ethical interest. But the concrete analyses of Habermas himself belie this dogmatic aim. It is striking that the distortions which psychoanalysis describes and explains are interpreted, at the meta-hermeneutical level where Habermas places them, as distortions of communicative competence. Everything suggests that the distortions relevant to the critique of ideology also operate at this level. Recall how Habermas reinterprets Marxism on the basis of a dialectic between instrumental and communicative action. It is at the heart of communicative action that the institutionalisation of human relations undergoes the reification which renders it unrecognisable to the participants of communication. It follows that all distortions, those which psychoanalysis discovers as well as those which the critique of ideology denounces, are distortions of the communicative capacity of men.

So can the interest in emancipation be treated as a distinct interest?

It seems not, especially if one considers that taken positively as a proper motif and no longer negatively in terms of the reifications which it combats, this interest has no other content than the ideal of unrestricted and unconstrained communication. The interest in emancipation would be quite empty and abstract if it were not situated on the same plane as the historical-hermeneutic sciences, that is, on the plane of communicative action. But if that is so, can a critique of distortions be separated from the communicative experience itself, from the place where it begins, where it is real and where it is exemplary? The task of the hermeneutics of tradition is to remind the critique of ideology that man can project his emancipation and anticipate an unlimited and unconstrained communication only on the basis of the creative reinterpretation of cultural heritage. If we had no experience of communication, however restricted and mutilated it was, how could we wish it to prevail for all men and at all institutional levels of the social nexus? It seems to me that critique can be neither the first instance nor the last. Distortions can be criticised only in the name of a *consensus* which we cannot anticipate merely emptily, in the manner of a regulative idea, unless that idea is exemplified; and one of the very places of exemplification of the ideal of communication is precisely our capacity to overcome cultural distance in the interpretation of works received from the past. He who is unable to reinterpret his past may also be incapable of projecting concretely his interest in emancipation.

(3) I arrive at the third point of disagreement between the hermeneutics of tradition and the critique of ideology. It concerns the abyss which seems to separate simple misunderstanding from pathological or ideological distortion. I shall not reconsider the arguments, already mentioned above, which tend to attenuate the difference between misunderstanding and distortion; a depth-hermeneutics is still a hermeneutics, even if it is called meta-hermeneutical. I should like instead to emphasise an aspect of the theory of ideology which owes nothing to the parallel with psychoanalysis. A large part of Habermas's work is addressed, not to the theory of ideology taken abstractly, but to contemporary ideologies. Now when the theory of ideology is thus developed concretely in terms of a critique of the present, it reveals aspects which call for a concrete – and not simply a theoretical – *rapprochement* between the interest in emancipation and the interest in communication.

For what is, according to Habermas, the dominant ideology of the present day? His answer is close to that of Herbert Marcuse and Jacques Ellul: it is the ideology of science and technology. Here I shall not discuss Habermas's interpretation of advanced capitalism and of developed industrial societies; I shall go straight to the principal characteristic which, in my view, imperiously returns the theory of ideology to the hermeneutical field. In modern industrial society, according to Habermas, the traditional legitimations and basic beliefs once used for the justification of power have been replaced by an ideology of science and technology. The modern state is a state dedicated no longer to representing the interests of an oppressing class, but rather to eliminating the dysfunctions of the industrial system. To justify surplus-value by concealing its mechanism is thus no longer the primary legitimating function of ideology, as it was in the epoch of liberal capitalism described by Marx, quite simply because surplus-value is no longer the principal source of productivity and its appropriation the dominant feature of the system. The dominant feature of the system is the productivity of rationality itself, incorporated into self-regulating systems; what is to be legitimated, therefore, is the maintenance and growth of the system itself. It is precisely for this purpose that the scientific-technological apparatus has become an ideology, that is, a legitimation of the relations of domination and inequality which are necessary for the functioning of the industrial system, but which are concealed beneath all sorts of gratifications provided by the system. The modern ideology thus differs appreciably from that described by Marx, which prevailed only during the short period of liberal capitalism and possessed no universality in time. Nothing now remains of pre-bourgeois ideology, and bourgeois ideology was expressly linked to the camouflaging of domination in the legal institution of the free labour contract.

Granted this description of the modern ideology, what does it signify in terms of interest? It signifies that the sub-system of instrumental action has ceased to be a sub-system, and that its categories have overrun the sphere of communicative action. Therein consists the famous 'rationalisation' of which Max Weber spoke: not only does rationality conquer new domains of instrumental action, but it subjugates the domain of communicative action. Max Weber described this phenomenon in terms of 'disenchantment' and 'secularisation'; Habermas describes it as the obliteration of the difference between the plane of instrumental action, which is also that of labour, and the plane of communicative action, which is also that of agreed norms, symbolic exchanges, personality structures and rational decision-making procedures. In the modern capitalist system, which here seems identical with the industrial system as such, the ancient Greek question of the 'good life' is abolished in favour of the functioning of a manipulated system. The problems of *praxis* linked to communication – in particular the desire to submit important political questions to public discussion and democratic decision – have not disappeared; they persist, but in a repressed form. Precisely because their elimination is not automatic and the need for legitimation remains unfulfilled, there is still the need for an ideology to legitimate the authority that secures the functioning of the system; science and technology today assume this ideological role.

But the question which hermeneutics then addresses to the critique of contemporary ideology is this: granted that ideology today consists in disguising the difference between the normative order of communicative action and bureaucratic conditioning, hence in dissolving the sphere of interaction mediated by language into the structures of instrumental action, how can the interest in emancipation remain anything other than a pious vow, save by embodying it in the reawakening of communicative action itself? And upon what will you concretely support the reawakening of communicative action, if not upon the creative renewal of cultural heritage?

(4) The ineluctable link between the reawakening of political responsibility and the reanimation of traditional sources of communicative action leads me to say a few words, in conclusion, about what appeared to be the most formidable difference between the hermeneutical consciousness and the critical consciousness. The first, we said, is turned towards a *consensus* which precedes us and, in this sense, which exists; the second anticipates a future freedom in the form of a regulative idea which is not a reality but an ideal, the ideal of unrestricted and unconstrained communication.

With this apparent antithesis, we reach the liveliest but perhaps the most futile point in the debate. For in the end, hermeneutics will say, from where do you speak when you appeal to *Selbstreflexion*, if it is not from the place that you yourself have denounced as a non-place, the non-place of the transcendental subject? It is indeed from the basis of a tradition that you speak. This tradition is not perhaps the same as Gadamer's; it is perhaps that of the *Aufklärung*, whereas Gadamer's would be Romanticism. But it is a tradition nonetheless, the tradition of emancipation rather than that of recollection. Critique is also a tradition. I would even say that it plunges into the most impressive tradition, that of liberating acts, of the Exodus and the Resurrection. Perhaps there would be no more interest in emancipation, no more anticipation of freedom, if the Exodus and the Resurrection were effaced from the memory of mankind . . .

If that is so, then nothing is more deceptive than the alleged antinomy between an ontology of prior understanding and an eschatology of freedom. We have encountered these false antinomies elsewhere: as if it were necessary to choose between reminiscence and hope! In theological terms, eschatology is nothing without the recitation of acts of deliverance from the past.

In sketching this dialectic of the recollection of tradition and the anticipation of freedom, I do not want in any way to abolish the difference between hermeneutics and the critique of ideology. Each has a privileged place and, if I may say so, different regional preferences: on the one hand, an attention to cultural heritages, focused most decidedly perhaps on the theory of the text; on the other hand, a theory of institutions and of phenomena of domination, focused on the analysis of reifications and alienations. Insofar as each must always be regionalised in order to endow their claims to universality with a concrete character, their differences must be preserved against any conflationist tendency. But it is the task of philosophical reflection to eliminate deceptive antinomies which would oppose the interest in the reinterpretation of cultural heritages received from the past and the interest in the futuristic projections of a liberated humanity.

The moment these two interests become radically separate, then hermeneutics and critique will themselves be no more than . . . ideologies!

3. Phenomenology and hermeneutics

This study does not aim to be a contribution to the history of phenomenology, to its archaeology, but rather an inquiry into the destiny of phenomenology today. And if I have chosen the general theory of interpretation or hermeneutics as a touchstone, that does not mean either that I would replace an historical monograph by a chapter on the comparative history of modern philosophy. For with hermeneutics as well, I do not wish to proceed as an historian, even as an historian of the present day. Whatever may be the dependence of the following meditation on Heidegger and above all on Gadamer, what is at stake is the possibility of continuing to do philosophy with them and after them – without forgetting Husserl. Thus my essay will seek to be a debate about the ways in which philosophy can still be pursued. [1]

I propose the following two theses for discussion. *First thesis:* what hermeneutics has ruined is not phenomenology but one of its interpretations, namely its *idealistic* interpretation by Husserl himself; accordingly, I shall speak henceforth of Husserlian idealism. I shall take the 'Nachwort' to the *Ideen* [2] as a reference and a guide, submitting its principal theses to the hermeneutical critique. The first part of the essay will thus be purely and simply *antithetical.*

Second thesis: beyond the simple opposition there exists, between phenomenology and hermeneutics, a mutual belonging which it is important to make explicit. This belonging can be recognised from either position. On the one hand, hermeneutics is erected on the basis of phenomenology and thus preserves something of the philosophy from which it nevertheless differs: *phenomenology remains the unsurpassable presupposition of hermeneutics.* On the other hand, phenomenology cannot constitute itself without a *hermeneutical presupposition.* The hermeneutical condition of phenomenology is linked to the role of *Auslegung* [explication] in the fulfilment of its philosophical project.

I. The hermeneutical critique of Husserlian idealism

The first part of this essay seeks to disclose the gap, if not the gulf, which separates the project of hermeneutics from all idealistic expressions of phenomenology. The antithetical position of the two philosophical projects will alone be developed. We shall nevertheless reserve the possibility that phenomenology as such is not wholly exhausted by one of its interpretations, even that of Husserl himself. It is, in my view, Husserlian idealism which succumbs to the hermeneutical critique.

1. The schematic theses of Husserlian idealism

For the purposes of a necessarily schematic discussion, I have taken the 1930 'Nachwort' to the *Ideen* as a typical document of Husserlian idealism. It constitutes, together with the *Cartesian Meditations*, the most advanced expression of this idealism. I have extracted from it the following theses, which I shall subsequently submit to the critique of hermeneutics.

(a) The ideal of scientificity proclaimed by phenomenology is not in continuity with the sciences, their axioms and their foundational enterprise: the 'ultimate justification' which constitutes phenomenology is of a different order (*Hua* v 138ff., 159ff.).

This thesis, which expresses phenomenology's claim to radicality, is asserted in a polemical style; it is the thesis of a combatant philosophy which always has an enemy in view, whether that enemy be objectivism, naturalism, vitalistic philosophy, or anthropology. Phenomenology begins with a radical move that cannot be framed in a demonstrative argument, for whence would it be deduced? Hence the self-assertive style of the claim to radicality, which is attested to only by the denial of what could deny it. The expression *aus letzter Begründung* [ultimate grounding] is most typical in this respect. It recalls the Platonic tradition of the anhypothetical as well as the Kantian tradition of the autonomy of the critical act; it also marks, in the sense of *Rückfrage* [questioning back] (*Hua* v 139), a certain continuity with the questions of principle that the sciences ask of themselves. And yet the process of returning to the foundations is absolutely discontinuous with regard to any foundation internal to a science: for a science of foundations, 'there can be no more obscure and problematic concepts, nor any paradoxes' (*Hua* v 160). That does not mean there have not been *several* 'ways' answering to this unique Idea; the idea of foundation is rather that which secures the equivalence and convergence of the ways (logical, Cartesian, psychological, historico-teleological, etc.). There are 'real beginnings', or rather 'paths towards the beginning', elicited by 'the absolute absence of presuppositions'. It is thus fruitless to inquire into the motivation for such a radical beginning; there is no reason internal to a domain for raising the question of origin. It is in this sense that justification is a *Selbst-Begründung* [self-grounding].

(b) The foundation in principle is of the order of intuition; to found is to see. The 'Nachwort' thereby confirms the priority, asserted by the sixth *Logical Investigation,* of intentional fulfilment as opposed to any philosophy of deduction or construction (*Hua* v 141ff., 143ff.).

✗ The key concept in this respect is that of an *Erfahrungsfeld* [field of experience]. The strangeness of phenomenology lies entirely therein: from the outset, the principle is a 'field' and the first truth an 'experience'. In contrast to all 'speculative constructions', every question of principle is resolved through vision. I just spoke of strangeness: for is it not astonishing that in spite of (and thanks to) the critique of empiricism, experience in the strict empirical sense is surpassed only in an 'experience'? This synonymy of *Erfahrung* signifies that phenomenology is not situated elsewhere, in another world, but rather is concerned with natural experience itself, insofar as the latter is unaware of its meaning. Consequently, however much the emphasis may be placed on the *a priori* character, on the reduction to the *eidos*, on the role of imaginative variations, and even on the notion of 'possibility', it is still and always the character of experience which is underlined (one has only to consider the expression 'intuitive possibilities'; *Hua* v 142).

(c) The place of plenary intuition is subjectivity. All transcendence is doubtful; immanence alone is indubitable.

✗ This is the central thesis of Husserlian idealism. All transcendence is doubtful because it proceeds by *Abschattungen,* by 'sketches' or 'profiles'; because the convergence of these *Abschattungen* is always presumptive; because the presumption can be disappointed by some discordance; and finally, because consciousness can form the hyperbolic hypothesis of a radical discordance of appearances, which is the very hypothesis of the 'destruction of the world'. Immanence is not doubtful, because it is not given by 'profiles' and hence involves nothing presumptive, allowing only the coincidence of reflection with what 'has just' been experienced.

(d) The subjectivity thus promoted to the rank of the transcendental is not empirical consciousness, the object of psychology. Nevertheless, phenomenology and phenomenological psychology are parallel and constitute a 'doublet' which constantly leads to the confusion of the two disciplines, one transcendental and the other empirical. Only the reduction distinguishes and separates them.

Here phenomenology must struggle against a misunderstanding which constantly reappears and which phenomenology itself provokes. For the phenomenological 'field of experience' has a structural analogy with non-reduced experience; the reason for this isomorphism lies in the very nature of intentionality (Brentano had discovered intentionality without being aware of the reduction, and the fifth *Logical Investigation* still defined it in terms that are as compatible with intentional psychology as with phenomenology). Moreover, the reduction proceeds 'from the natural attitude'; transcendental phenomenology thus presupposes, in a certain way, that which it surpasses and which it reiterates as *the same,* although *in another attitude.* So the difference does not consist in descriptive features but in ontological indices, in *Seinsgeltung* [validity of being]; validity *als Reales* must be 'lost',[3] psychological realism must be shattered. Now that would be no small task, if phenomenology is not to be understood as the necessity of losing the world, the body and nature, thereby enclosing itself within an acosmic realm. The paradox is that it is only through this loss that the world is revealed as 'pregiven', the body as 'existing', and nature as 'being' [*étant*]. So the reduction does not take place between me and the world, between the soul and the body, between the spirit and nature, but through the pregiven, the existing and the being, which cease to be self-evident and to be assumed in the blind and opaque *Seinsglaube* [belief in being], becoming instead *meaning: meaning* of the pregiven, *meaning* of the existing, *meaning* of the being. Thus the phenomenological radicality, which severs the transcendental subjectivity from the empirical self, is the same as that radicality which transforms the *Seinsglaube* into the noematic correlate of the noesis. A noetics or no-ology is therefore distinct from a psychology. Their 'content' (*Gehalt*) is the same; but the phenomenological is the psychological 'reduced'. Therein lies the principle of the 'parallelism', or better of the 'correspondence', between the two. Therein lies also the principle of their difference: for a 'conversion' – *the* philosophical conversion – separates them.

(e) The awareness which sustains the work of reflection develops its own ethical implications: reflection is thus the immediately self-responsible act.

The ethical nuance, which the expression *aus letzter Selbstverantwort-*

ung [ultimate self-responsibility] (*Hua* v 139) seems to introduce into the foundational thematic, is not the practical complement of an enterprise which as such would be purely epistemological: the inversion by which reflection tears itself away from the natural attitude is at the same time – in the same breath, so to speak – epistemological and ethical. The philosophical conversion is the supremely autonomous act. What we have called the ethical nuance is thus immediately implied in the foundational act, insofar as the latter can only be self-positing. It is in this sense that it is ultimately self-responsible.

The self-assertive character of the foundation constitutes the philosophical subject as responsible subject. This is the philosophising subject as such.

2. Hermeneutics against Husserlian idealism

It is possible to oppose hermeneutics, thesis by thesis, not perhaps to phenomenology as a whole and as such, but to Husserlian idealism. This 'antithetical' approach is the necessary path to the establishment of a genuinely 'dialectical' relation between the two.

(a) The ideal of scientificity, construed by Husserlian idealism as ultimate justification, encounters its fundamental limit in the ontological condition of understanding.

This ontological condition can be expressed as finitude. This is not, however, the concept that I shall regard as primary; for it designates, in negative terms, an entirely positive condition which would be better expressed by the concept of belonging. The latter directly designates the unsurpassable condition of any enterprise of justification and foundation, namely that it is always preceded by a relation which supports it. Is this a relation to an object? That is precisely what it is not. The aspect of Husserlian idealism which hermeneutics questions first is the way in which the immense and unsurpassable discovery of intentionality is couched in a conceptuality which weakens its scope, namely the conceptuality of the subject–object relation. It is the latter which gives rise to the necessity of searching for something that unifies the meaning of the object and the necessity of founding this unity in a constituting subjectivity. The first declaration of hermeneutics is to say that the problematic of objectivity presupposes a prior relation of inclusion which encompasses the allegedly autonomous subject and the allegedly adverse object. This inclusive or encompassing relation is what I call belonging. The ontological priority of belonging implies that the question of foundation can no longer simply coincide with that of ultimate

justification. Of course, Husserl is the first to underline the discontinuity, instituted by the *epoché*, between the transcendental enterprise
of foundation and the internal work, proper to each science, whereby it
seeks to elaborate its own grounds. Moreover, he always distinguishes
the demand for justification raised by transcendental phenomenology
from the pre-established model of the *mathesis universalis*. In this way,
as we shall see later, he lays down the phenomenological conditions of
hermeneutics. But hermeneutics seeks precisely to radicalise the Husserlian thesis of the discontinuity between transcendental foundation
and epistemological grounding.

For hermeneutics, the problem of ultimate foundation still belongs to
the sphere of objectifying thought, so long as the ideal of scientificity is
not questioned as such. The radicality of such questioning leads from
the idea of scientificity back to the ontological condition of belonging,
whereby he who questions shares in the very thing about which he
questions.

It is the relation of belonging which is subsequently apprehended as
the finitude of knowledge. The negative nuance conveyed by the very
word 'finitude' is introduced into the totally positive relation of belonging – *which is the hermeneutical experience itself* – only because subjectivity has already raised its claim to be the ultimate ground. This claim,
this immoderate pretension, this *hybris* makes the relation of belonging
appear by contrast as finitude.

Belonging is expressed by Heidegger in the language of being-in-the-
world. The two notions are equivalent. The term 'being-in-the-world'
expresses better the primacy of care over the gaze, and the horizonal
character of that to which we are bound. It is indeed being-in-the-
world which precedes reflection. At the same time, the term attests to
the priority of the ontological category of the *Dasein* which we are over
the epistemological and psychological category of the subject which
posits itself. Despite the density of meaning in the expression 'being-
in-the-world', I prefer, following Gadamer, to use the notion of belonging, which immediately raises the problem of the subject–object relation and prepares the way for the subsequent introduction of the concept of distanciation.

(b) The Husserlian demand for the return to intuition is countered by
the necessity for all understanding to be mediated by an interpretation.

There is no doubt that this principle is borrowed from the epistemology of the historical sciences. As such, it belongs to the epistemological
field delimited by Schleiermacher and Dilthey. However, if interpreta-

tion were only an historico-hermeneutical concept, it would remain as regional as the human sciences themselves. But the usage of interpretation in the historico-hermeneutic sciences is only the anchoring point for a universal concept of interpretation which has the same extension as that of understanding and, in the end, as that of belonging. Hence it goes beyond the mere methodology of exegesis and philology, designating the work of explication which adheres to all hermeneutical experience. According to the remark of Heidegger in *Being and Time*, the *Auslegung* is the 'development of understanding' in terms of the structure of the 'as' (*Als*).[4] In thereby effecting the mediation of the 'as', 'explication does not transform understanding into something else, but makes it become itself' (*SZ* 148; *BT* 188).†

The dependence of interpretation on understanding explains why explication as well always precedes reflection and comes before any constitution of the object by a sovereign subject. This antecedence is expressed at the level of explication by the 'structure of anticipation', which prevents explication from ever being a presuppositionless grasp of a pregiven being [*étant*]; explication precedes its object in the mode of the *Vor-habe*, the *Vor-sicht*, the *Vor-Griff*, the *Vor-Meinung* (*SZ* 150; *BT* 191). I shall not comment here on these well-known expressions of Heidegger. What is important to emphasise is that it is not possible to implement the structure of the 'as' without also implementing the structure of anticipation. The notion of 'meaning' obeys this double condition of the *Als* and the *Vor-*: 'Meaning, which is structured by fore-having, fore-sight and fore-conception, forms for any project the horizon in terms of which something can be understood as something' (*SZ* 151; *BT* 193).† Thus the field of interpretation is as vast as that of understanding, which covers all projection of meaning in a situation.

The universality of interpretation is attested to in several ways. The most ordinary application is the use of natural languages in the conversational situation. In contrast to well-formed languages, constructed according to the exigencies of mathematical logic and in which all basic terms are defined in an axiomatic way, the use of natural languages rests on the polysemic value of words. The latter contain a semantic potential which is not exhausted by any particular use, but which must be constantly sifted and determined by the context. It is with this selective function of context that interpretation, in the most primitive sense of the word, is connected. Interpretation is the process by which, in the interplay of question and answer, the interlocutors collectively determine the contextual values which structure their conversation. So before any *Kunstlehre,* which would establish exegesis and philology as an autonomous discipline, there is a spontaneous process of interpretation which is part of the most primitive exercise of understanding in any given situation.

But conversation rests upon a relation which is too limited to cover the whole field of explication. Conversation, i.e. ultimately the dialogical relation, is contained within the limits of a *vis-à-vis* which is a *face-à-face.* The historical connection which encompasses it is singularly more complex. The 'short' intersubjective relation is intertwined, in the interior of the historical connection, with various 'long' intersubjective relations, mediated by diverse social institutions, social roles and collectivities (groups, classes, nations, cultural traditions, etc.). The long intersubjective relations are sustained by an historical tradition, of which dialogue is only a segment. Explication therefore extends much further than dialogue, coinciding with the broadest historical connection.[5]

Mediation by the text, that is, by expressions fixed in writing but also by all the documents and monuments which have a fundamental feature in common with writing, is connected with the use of explication on the scale of the transmission of historical tradition. This common feature, which constitutes the text as a text, is that the meaning contained therein is rendered *autonomous* with respect to the intention of the author, the initial situation of discourse and the original addressee. Intention, situation and original addressee constitute the *Sitz-im-Leben* [site-in-life] of the text. The possibility of multiple interpretations is opened up by a text which is thus freed from its *Sitz-im-Leben.* Beyond the polysemy of words in a conversation is the polysemy of a text which invites multiple readings. This is the moment of interpretation in the technical sense of *textual exegesis.* It is also the moment of the hermeneutical circle between the understanding initiated by the reader and the proposals of meaning offered by the text. The most fundamental condition of the hermeneutical circle lies in the structure of pre-understanding which relates all explication to the understanding which precedes and supports it.

In what sense is the development of all understanding in interpretation opposed to the Husserlian project of *ultimate* foundation? Essentially in the sense that all interpretation places the interpreter *in medias res* and never at the beginning or the end. We suddenly arrive, as it were, in the middle of a conversation which has already begun and in which we try to orientate ourselves in order to be able to contribute to it. Now the ideal of an intuitive foundation is the ideal of an interpretation which, at a certain point, would pass into full vision. This is what Gadamer calls the hypothesis of 'total mediation'. Only a total mediation would be equivalent to an intuition which is both first and final. Idealist phenomenology can therefore sustain its pretension to ultimate foundation only by adopting, in an intuitive rather than a speculative mode, the Hegelian claim to absolute knowledge. But the key hypothesis of hermeneutic philosophy is that interpretation is an open process which no single vision can conclude.

(c) That the place of ultimate foundation is subjectivity, that all transcendence is doubtful and only immanence indubitable – this in turn becomes eminently doubtful, from the moment that the *cogito* as well seems susceptible to the radical critique which phenomenology otherwise applies to all appearances.

The ruses of self-consciousness are more subtle than those of the thing. Recall the doubt which, in Heidegger's work, accompanies the question 'who is *Dasein*?'

Is it then obvious *a priori* that access to Dasein must be gained only by mere reflective awareness of the 'I' of actions? What if this kind of 'giving-itself' on the part of Dasein should lead our existential analytic astray and do so, indeed, in a manner grounded in the Being of Dasein itself? Perhaps when Dasein addresses itself in the way which is closest to itself, it always says 'I am this entity', and in the long run says this loudest when it is 'not' this entity. What if the aforementioned approach, starting with the givenness of the 'I' to Dasein itself, and with a rather patent self-interpretation of Dasein, should lead the existential analytic, as it were, into a pitfall? If that which is accessible by mere 'giving' can be determined, there is presumably an ontological horizon for determining it; but what if this horizon should remain in principle undetermined? (*SZ* 115; *BT* 151)

Here, as elsewhere, I shall not adhere to the letter of Heidegger's philosophy but shall develop it for my own purposes. It is in the *critique of ideology*, as much as and perhaps more than in psychoanalysis, that I would look for documentation of the doubt contained in Heidegger's question 'who is *Dasein*?'. The critique of ideology and psychoanalysis provide us today with the means to complement the critique of the object by a critique of the subject. In Husserl's work, the critique of the object is co-extensive with *Dingkonstitution* [constitution of the thing]; it rests, as we have said, on the presumptive character of schematic synthesis. But Husserl believed that self-knowledge could not be presumptive, because it does not proceed by 'sketches' or 'profiles'. Self-knowledge can, however, be presumptive for other reasons. Insofar as self-knowledge is a dialogue of the soul with itself, and insofar as the dialogue can be systematically distorted by violence and by the intrusion of structures of domination into those of communication, self-knowledge as internalised communication can be as doubtful as knowledge of the object, although for different and quite specific reasons.

Could it be said that, through the reduction, the *ego meditans* of phenomenology escapes from the distortions of empirical self-knowledge? This would be to forget that the Husserlian *ego* is not the Kantian *I think*, whose individuality is at least problematic if not devoid of sense. It is because the *ego* can be and must be reduced to the 'sphere of belonging' – in a different sense, to be sure, of the word 'belonging', which means no longer belonging to the world but belonging to oneself – that it is necessary to found the objectivity of nature and the objectivity of historical communities on intersubjectivity and not on an impersonal subject. Consequently, the distortions of communication directly concern the constitution of the intersubjective network in which a common nature and common historical entities can be formed, entities such as the 'personalities of a higher order' discussed in paragraph 58 of the *Cartesian Meditations*. Egology must take the fundamental distortions of communication into account, in the same way as it considers the illusions of perception in the constitution of the thing.

It seems to me that only a hermeneutics of communication can assume the task of incorporating the critique of ideology into self-understanding.[6] It can do this in two complementary ways. On the one hand, it can demonstrate the insurmountable character of the ideological phenomenon through its meditation on the role of 'pre-understanding' in the apprehension of any cultural object. Hermeneutics has simply to raise this notion of understanding, initially applied to the exegesis of texts, to the level of a general theory of prejudices, which would be coextensive with the historical connection itself. Just as mis-understanding is a fundamental structure of exegesis (Schleiermacher), so too prejudice is a fundamental structure of communication in its social and institutional forms. On the other hand, hermeneutics can demonstrate the necessity of a critique of ideology, even if, in virtue of the very structure of pre-understanding, this critique can never be total. Critique rests on the moment of *distanciation* which belongs to the historical connection as such.

The concept of distanciation is the dialectical counterpart of the notion of belonging, in the sense that we belong to an historical tradition through a relation of distance which oscillates between remoteness and proximity. To interpret is to render near what is far (temporally, geographically, culturally, spiritually). In this respect, mediation by the text is the model of a distanciation which would not be simply alienating, like the *Verfremdung* which Gadamer combats throughout his work (*WM* 11, 80, 156, 364ff.; *TM* 15, 75, 145, 348ff.), but which would be genuinely creative. The text is, *par excellence,* the basis for communication in and through distance.

If that is so, then hermeneutics has the means to account for both the insurmountable character of the ideological phenomenon, and the possibility of beginning, without ever being able to finish, a critique of ideology. Hermeneutics can do this because, in contrast to phenomenological idealism, the subject of which it speaks is always open to the efficacy of history (to make an allusion to Gadamer's famous notion of *wirkungsgeschichtliches Bewusstsein* (*WM* 284; *TM* 267)). Since distanciation is a moment of belonging, the critique of ideology can be incorporated, as an objective and explanatory segment, in the project of enlarging and restoring communication and self-understanding. The extension of understanding through textual exegesis and its constant rectification through the critique of ideology are properly part of the process of *Auslegung.* Textual exegesis and critique of ideology are the two privileged routes along which understanding is developed into interpretation and thus becomes itself.

⁀ (d) A radical way of placing the primacy of subjectivity in question is to take the theory of the text as the hermeneutical axis. Insofar as the meaning of a text is rendered autonomous with respect to the subjective intention of its author, the essential question is not to recover, behind the text, the lost intention, but to unfold, in front of the text, the 'world' which it opens up and discloses.

In other words, the hermeneutical task is to discern the 'matter' of the text (Gadamer) and not the psychology of the author. The matter of the text is to its structure as, in the proposition, the reference is to the sense (Frege). Just as, in the proposition, we are not content with the sense which is its ideal object but inquire further into its reference, that is, into its claim to truth, so too with the text we cannot stop at the immanent structure, at the internal system of dependencies arising from the crossing of the 'codes' which the text employs; we wish moreover to explicate the world which the text projects. In saying that, I am not unaware that an important category of texts which we call *literature* – namely, narrative fiction, drama, poetry – appears to abolish all reference to everyday reality, to the point where language seems destined to supreme dignity, as if glorifying itself at the expense of the referential function of ordinary discourse. But it is precisely insofar as fictional discourse 'suspends' its first order referential function that it releases a second order reference, where the world is manifested no longer as the totality of manipulable objects but as the horizon of our life and our project, in short as *Lebenswelt* [life-world], as being-in-the-world. It is this referential dimension, attaining its full development only with works of fiction and poetry, which raises the fundamental hermeneutical problem. Hermeneutics can be defined no longer as an inquiry into the psychological intentions which are hidden beneath the text, but rather as the explication of the being-in-the-world displayed by the text. What is to be interpreted in the text is a proposed world which I could inhabit and in which I could project my ownmost possibilities. Recalling the principle of distanciation mentioned above, it could be said that the fictional or poetic text not only places the meaning of the text at a *distance* from the intention of the author, but also places the reference of the text at a *distance* from the *world* articulated by everyday language. Reality is, in this way, metamorphosed by means of what I shall call the 'imaginative variations' which literature carries out on the real.

What is the consequence for Husserlian idealism of the hermeneutical focus on the matter of the text? Essentially this: the phenomenology which arose with the discovery of the universal character of intentionality has not remained faithful to its own discovery, namely that the meaning of consciousness lies outside of itself. The idealist theory of the constitution of meaning in consciousness has thus culminated in the hypostasis of subjectivity. The price of this hypostasis is indicated by the above-mentioned difficulties in the 'parallelism' between phenomenology and psychology. Such difficulties attest that phenomenology is always in danger of reducing itself to a transcendental subjectivism. The radical way of putting an end to this constantly recurring confusion is to shift the axis of interpretation from the problem of subjectivity to that of the world. That is what the theory of the text attempts to do, by subordinating the question of the author's intention to that of the matter of the text.

(e) In opposition to the idealist thesis of the ultimate self-responsibility of the mediating subject, hermeneutics proposes to make subjectivity the final, and not the first, category of a theory of understanding.

Subjectivity must be lost as radical origin, if it is to be recovered in a more modest role.

Here again, the theory of the text is a good guide. For it shows that the act of subjectivity is not so much what initiates understanding as what terminates it. This terminal act can be characterised as appropriation (*Zueignung*) (*SZ* 150; *BT* 191). It does not purport, as in Romantic hermeneutics, to rejoin the original subjectivity which would support the meaning of the text. Rather it *responds* to the matter of the text, and hence to the proposals of meaning which the text unfolds. It is thus the counterpart of the distanciation which establishes the autonomy of the text with respect to its author, its situation and its original addressee. It is also the counterpart of that other distanciation by which a new being-in-the-world, projected by the text, is freed from the false evidences of everyday reality. Appropriation is the *response* to this double distanciation which is linked to the matter of the text, as regards its sense and as regards its reference. Thus appropriation can be integrated into the theory of interpretation without surreptitiously reintroducing the primacy of subjectivity which the four preceding theses have destroyed.

That appropriation does not imply the secret return of the sovereign subject can be attested to in the following way: if it remains true that hermeneutics terminates in self-understanding, then the subjectivism of this proposition must be rectified by saying that to understand *oneself* is to understand oneself *in front of the text*. Consequently, what is appropriation from one point of view is disappropriation from another. To appropriate is to make what was alien become one's own. What is appropriated is indeed the matter of the text. But the matter of the text becomes my own only if I disappropriate myself, in order to let the matter of the text be. So I exchange the *me, master* of itself, for the *self, disciple* of the text.

The process could also be expressed as a *distanciation of self from itself* within the interior of appropriation. This distanciation implements all the strategies of suspicion, among which the critique of ideology is a principal modality. Distanciation, in all its forms and figures, constitutes *par excellence* the critical moment in understanding.

This final and radical form of distanciation is the ruin of the *ego*'s pretension to constitute itself as ultimate origin. The *ego* must assume for itself the 'imaginative variations' by which it could *respond* to the 'imaginative variations' on reality that literature and poetry, more than any other form of discourse, engender. It is this style of 'response to . . .' that hermeneutics opposes to the idealism of *ultimate self-respon-sibility*.

II. Towards a hermeneutic phenomenology

The hermeneutical critique of Husserlian idealism is, in my view, only the negative side of a positive research programme which I shall place under the provisional and exploratory title of *hermeneutic phenomenology*. The present essay does not claim to work out – 'to do' – this hermeneutic phenomenology. It seeks only to show its possibility by establishing, on the one hand, that beyond the critique of Husserlian idealism, phenomenology remains the unsurpassable presupposition of hermeneutics; and on the other hand, that phenomenology cannot carry out its programme of *constitution* without constituting itself in the *interpretation* of the experience of the *ego*.

1. The phenomenological presupposition of hermeneutics

(a) The most fundamental phenomenological presupposition of a philosophy of interpretation is that every question concerning any sort of 'being' [*étant*] is a question about the meaning of that 'being'.

Thus, in the first few pages of *Being and Time*, we read that the forgotten question is the question of the *meaning* of being. In that respect, the ontological question is a phenomenological question. It is a hermeneutical problem only insofar as the meaning is concealed, not of course in itself, but by everything which forbids access to it. However, in order to become a hermeneutical problem – a problem about concealed meaning – the central question of phenomenology must be recognised as a question about meaning. Thereby the phenomenological attitude is already placed above the naturalistic-objectivistic attitude. *The choice in favour of meaning is thus the most general presupposition of any hermeneutics.*

It may be objected that hermeneutics is older than phenomenology. Even before the word 'hermeneutics' was restored to dignity by the eighteenth century, there existed a biblical exegesis and a classical philology, both of which had already 'stood up for meaning'. That is indeed true; but hermeneutics becomes a philosophy of interpretation – and not simply a methodology of exegesis and philology – only if, going back to the conditions of possibility of exegesis and philology, going beyond even a general theory of the text, it addresses itself to the lingual condition – the *Sprachlichkeit* – of all experience (*WM* 367ff.; *TM* 345ff.).

This lingual condition has its own presupposition in a general theory of 'meaning'. It must be supposed that experience, in all its fullness (such as Hegel conceived it, as may be seen in Heidegger's famous text on 'Hegel's concept of experience')[7] has an expressibility in principle. Experience can be said, it demands to be said. To bring it to language is not to change it into something else, but, in articulating and developing it, to make it become itself.

Such is the presupposition of 'meaning' which exegesis and philology employ at the level of a certain category of texts, those which have contributed to our historical tradition. Exegesis and philology may well be historically prior to phenomenological awareness, but the latter precedes them in the order of foundation.

It is difficult, admittedly, to formulate this presupposition in a non-idealist language. The break between the phenomenological attitude and the naturalistic attitude – or as we said, the choice in favour of meaning – seems to amount to nothing more than an opting for the consciousness 'in' which meaning occurs. Is it not by 'suspending' all *Seinsglaube* that the dimension of meaning is attained? Is not the *epoché* of being-in-itself therefore presupposed by the choice in favour of meaning? Is not every philosophy of meaning idealist?

These implications, it seems to me, are not at all compelling, neither in fact nor in principle. They are not compelling in fact – I mean from a plainly historical point of view; for if we return from Husserl's *Ideas* and *Cartesian Meditations* to his *Logical Investigations*, we rediscover a state of phenomenology where the notions of expression and meaning, of consciousness and intentionality, of intellectual intuition, are elaborated without the 'reduction' being introduced in its idealist sense. On the contrary, the thesis of intentionality explicitly states that if all meaning is for a consciousness, then no consciousness is self-consciousness before being consciousness *of* something *towards which* it surpasses itself, or as Sartre said in a remarkable article,[8] of something towards which it 'explodes'. That consciousness is outside of itself, that it is *towards meaning* before meaning is for it and, above all, before consciousness is *for itself*: is this not what the central discovery of phenomenology implies? Thus to return to the non-idealist sense of the reduction is to remain faithful to the major discovery of the *Logical Investigations,* namely that the logical notion of signification – such as Frege, for example, had introduced – is carved out of a broader notion of meaning which is coextensive with the concept of intentionality. Hence the right to speak of the 'meaning' of perception, the 'meaning' of imagination, the 'meaning' of the will and so on. This subordination of the logical notion of signification to the universal notion of meaning, under the guidance of the concept of intentionality, in no way implies that a transcendental subjectivity has sovereign mastery of the meaning towards which it orients itself. On the contrary, phenomenology could be drawn in the opposite direction, namely towards the thesis of the priority of meaning over self-consciousness.

(b) Hermeneutics comes back to phenomenology in another way, namely by its recourse to distanciation at the very heart of the experience of belonging. Hermeneutical distanciation is not unrelated to the phenomenological *epoché*, that is, to an *epoché* interpreted in a non-idealist sense as an aspect of the intentional movement of consciousness towards meaning. For all consciousness of meaning involves a moment of distanciation, a distancing from 'lived experience' as purely and simply adhered to. Phenomenology begins when, not content to 'live' or 'relive', we interrupt lived experience in order to signify it. Thus the *epoché* and the meaning-intention [*visée de sens*] are closely linked.

This relation is easy to discern in the case of language. The linguistic sign can *stand for* something only if it is *not* the thing. In this respect, the sign possesses a specific negativity. Everything happens as if, in order to enter the symbolic universe, the speaking subject must have at his disposal an 'empty space' from which the use of signs can begin. The *epoché* is the virtual event, the imaginary act which inaugurates the whole game by which we exchange signs for things and signs for other signs. Phenomenology is like the explicit revival of this virtual event which it raises to the dignity of the act, the philosophical gesture. It renders thematic what was only operative, and thereby makes meaning appear as meaning.

Hermeneutics extends this philosophical gesture into its own domain, which is that of the historical and, more generally, the human sciences. The 'lived experience' which it is concerned to bring to language and raise to meaning is the historical connection, mediated by the transmission of written documents, works, institutions and monuments which render present the historical past. What we have called 'belonging' is nothing other than the adherence to this historical lived experience, what Hegel called the 'substance' of moral life. The 'lived experience' of phenomenology corresponds, on the side of hermeneu-

tics, to consciousness exposed to historical efficacy. Hence hermeneutical distanciation is to belonging as, in phenomenology, the *epoché*
is to lived experience. Hermeneutics similarly begins when, not content
to belong to transmitted tradition, we interrupt the relation of belonging in order to signify it.

This parallel is of considerable importance if indeed hermeneutics
must incorporate a critical moment, a moment of suspicion, from which
the critique of ideology, psychoanalysis, etc., can proceed. The critical
moment can be integrated with the relation of belonging only if distanciation is consubstantial with belonging. Phenomenology shows that
this is possible when it elevates to a philosophical decision the virtual
act of instituting the 'empty space' which enables a subject to signify
his lived experience and his belonging to an historical tradition.

(c) Hermeneutics also shares with phenomenology the thesis of the
derivative character of linguistic meaning.

It is easy, in this respect, to return to the phenomenological roots of
some well-known hermeneutical theses. Beginning with the most recent theses, those of Gadamer, it can be seen that the secondary character of the problematic of language is reflected in the very composition
of *Truth and Method*. Even if it is true that all experience has a 'lingual
dimension' and that this *Sprachlichkeit* imprints and pervades all experience, nevertheless it is not with *Sprachlichkeit* that hermeneutic philosophy must begin. It is necessary to say first what comes to language.
Hence hermeneutic philosophy begins with the experience of art,
which is not necessarily linguistic. Moreover it accentuates, in this experience, the more ontological aspects of the experience of *play* – in the
playful [*ludique*] as well as the theatrical sense of the word (*WM* 97ff.;
TM 91ff.). For it is in the participation of players in a game that we find
the first experience of belonging susceptible of being examined by the
philosopher. And it is in the game that the constitution of the function
of exhibition or presentation (*Darstellung*) can be seen, a function which
doubtlessly summons the linguistic medium, but which in principle
precedes and supports it. Nor is discourse dominant in the second
group of experiences interpreted in *Truth and Method*. Consciousness of
being exposed to the effects of history, which precludes a total reflection on prejudices and precedes any objectification of the past by the
historian, is not reducible to the properly lingual aspects of the transmission of the past. Texts, documents and monuments represent only
one mediation among others, however exemplary it may be for the reasons mentioned above. The interplay of distance and proximity, consti-

tutive of the historical connection, is what comes to language rather than what language produces.

This way of subordinating *Sprachlichkeit* to the experience which comes to language is perfectly faithful to Heidegger's gesture in *Being and Time*. Recall how the Analytic of *Dasein* subordinates the level of the assertion (*Aussage*), which is also that of logical signification, of signification in the strict sense (*Bedeutung*), to the level of discourse (*Rede*); and the latter, according to Heidegger, is 'equiprimordial' with state-of-mind (*Befindlichkeit*) and *understanding* (*Verstehen*) (SZ sec. 34). The logical order is thus preceded by a 'saying' which is interwoven with a 'finding oneself' and an 'understanding'. The level of assertion can therefore claim no autonomy; it refers back to the existential structures constitutive of being-in-the-world.

The reference of the linguistic order back to the structure of experience (which comes to language in the assertion) constitutes, in my view, the most important phenomenological presupposition of hermeneutics.

Since the period of the *Logical Investigations,* a development can be discerned which enables logical signification to be situated within a general theory of intentionality. This development implied the displacement of the intentional model from the logical plane towards the perceptive plane, where our first signifying relation with things is formed. At the same time, phenomenology drew back from the predicative and apophantic level of signification – the level of the *Logical Investigations* – to the properly pre-predicative level, where noematic analysis precedes linguistic inquiry. Thus, in *Ideen* I, Husserl goes so far as to say that the layer of expression is an essentially 'unproductive' layer (*Hua* III sec. 124); and indeed, the analysis of noetic-noematic correlations can be carried very far without linguistic articulation being considered as such. The strategic level proper to phenomenology is therefore the *noema*, with its modifications (presence, memory, fantasy, etc.), its modes of belief (certitude, doubt, supposition, etc.), and its degrees of actuality and potentiality. The constitution of the *complete noema* precedes the properly linguistic plane upon which the functions of denomination, predication, syntactic liaison and so on come to be articulated.

This way of subordinating the linguistic plane to the pre-linguistic level of noematic analysis is, it seems to me, exemplary for hermeneutics. When the latter subordinates lingual experience to the whole of our aesthetic and historical experience, it continues, on the level of the human sciences, the movement initiated by Husserl on the plane of perceptive experience.

(d) The kinship between the pre-predicative of phenomenology and that of hermeneutics is all the closer in that Husserlian phenomenology itself began to develop the phenomenology of perception in the direction of a hermeneutics of historical experience.

It is well known how, on the one hand, Husserl continued to develop the properly *temporal* implications of perceptual experience. He was thus led, by his own analyses, towards the historicity of human experience as a whole. In particular, it became increasingly evident that the presumptive, inadequate, unfinished character which perceptual experience acquires from its temporal structure could be applied step by step to the whole of historical experience. A new model of truth could thus be elicited from the phenomenology of perception and transposed into the domain of the historical-hermeneutic sciences. Such is the consequence that Merleau-Ponty drew from Husserlian phenomenology.

On the other hand, perceptual experience appeared more and more like an artificially isolated segment of a relation to the 'life-world', itself directly endowed with historical and cultural features. Here I shall not emphasise this philosophy of the *Lebenswelt* which characterised the period of the *Crisis,* and which was contemporaneous with Heidegger's Analytic of *Dasein*. It will suffice to say that the return from a nature objectified and mathematicised by Galilean and Newtonian science to the *Lebenswelt* is the very same principle of return which hermeneutics seeks to implement elsewhere, on the plane of the human sciences; for hermeneutics similarly wishes to withdraw from the objectifications and explanations of historical science and sociology to the artistic, historical and lingual experience which precedes and supports these objectifications and explanations. The return to the *Lebenswelt* can more effectively play this paradigmatic role for hermeneutics if the *Lebenswelt* is not confused with some sort of ineffable immediacy and is not identified with the vital and emotional envelope of human experience, but rather is construed as designating the reservoir of meaning, the surplus of sense in living experience, which renders the objectifying and explanatory attitude possible.

These last remarks have already brought us to the point where phenomenology can be the presupposition of hermeneutics only insofar as phenomenology, in turn, incorporates a hermeneutical presupposition.

2. The hermeneutical presupposition of phenomenology

By hermeneutical presupposition, I mean essentially the necessity for phenomenology to conceive of its method as an *Auslegung*, an exegesis, an explication, an interpretation. The demonstration of this necessity will be all the more striking if we address ourselves, not to the texts of the cycle of the *Crisis*, but to the texts of the 'logical' and 'idealist' periods.

(a) *The recourse to 'Auslegung' in the 'Logical Investigations'*. The moment of *Auslegung* in the first *Logical Investigation* is contemporaneous with the effort to bring the 'signification conferring acts' to intuition.[9] The investigation begins with a very firm declaration against the interference of images in the understanding of an expression (in the logical sense of the word). To understand an expression, says Husserl, is something other than to recover the images related to it. Images can 'accompany' and 'illustrate' intellection, but they do not constitute it and they always fall short of it. This radicalism of intellection without images is well known: it is all the more interesting to locate the weaknesses in it.

We shall leave aside the case of fluctuating meanings which Husserl examines at a later stage (*LU* ii/1 77ff.; *LI* i 312ff.). It would provide, however, an important contribution to our inquiry into the hermeneutical presuppositions of phenomenology. In the first series of fluctuating meanings, Husserl places the occasional meanings such as personal pronouns, demonstratives, descriptions introduced by the definite article, etc. These meanings can be determined and actualised only in the light of a context. In order to understand an expression of this type, 'it is essential to orientate actual meaning to the occasion, the speaker and the situation. Only by looking to the actual circumstances of utterance can one definite meaning out of all this mutually connected class be constituted for the hearer' (*LU* ii/1 81; *LI* i 315). It is true that Husserl does not speak here of interpretation, but conceives the actual determination of occasional meanings as an instance of the intersection between the indicative function (*LU* ii/1 83; *LI* i 316) and the signification function. But the functioning of such meanings coincides, almost to the word, with what appeared above as the first intervention of interpretation at the level of ordinary language, in relation to the polysemy of words and the use of contexts in conversation. Nevertheless, it will be more demonstrative for our purpose to indicate the place of interpretation in the treatment of non-occasional meanings to which, Husserl claims, all forms of meaning return.

The elucidation of meanings which have no occasional aspects appeals, in the most striking way, to *Auslegung*. For these meanings, in principle univocal, do not immediately reveal their univocity. They must, in Husserl's terms, be submitted to the work of elucidation (*Aufklärung*). Now this elucidation cannot be completed unless it is sustained by a minimum of intentional fulfilment, that is, unless some 'corresponding' intuition is given (*LU* II/1 71; *LI* I 306). This is the case for meanings which overlap with one another; and here Husserl surprises himself. He introduces the analysis in the form of a question: 'One might here ask: If the meaning of expressions functioning purely symbolically lies in an act-character which distinguishes the understanding grasp of a verbal sign from the grasp of a sign stripped of meaning, why is it that we have recourse to intuition when we want to establish differences of meaning, to expose ambiguities, or to limit shifts in our signification-intention [*intention de signification*]?' (*LU* II/1 70; *LI* I 306).† Thus arises the problem of an expression 'clarified by intuition' (*LU* II/1 71; *LI* I 307). Suddenly the boundary between fluctuating expressions and fixed expressions becomes blurred:

To recognize differences of meaning, such as that between 'moth' and 'elephant', requires no special procedures. But where meanings shade unbrokenly into one another, and unnoticed shifts blur boundaries needed for firm judgement, recourse to intuition constitutes the normal process of elucidation. Where the signification-intention of an expression is fulfilled by divergent intuitions which do not fall under the same concept, the sharp difference in the direction of fulfilment shows up the cleavage of signification-intentions. (*LU* II/1 71–2; *LI* I 307)†

Thus elucidation (or clarification) requires that meaning be submitted to a genuine form of work, in which representations in imagination [*présentifications*] play a role much less contingent than that of the mere 'accompaniments' which alone are allowed, in principle, by Husserl's theory of signification.

It may be said that such elucidation is a long way from what hermeneutics calls interpretation; and of course, Husserl's examples are taken from domains far removed from the historical-hermeneutic sciences. But the *rapprochement* is all the more striking when, in the course of an analysis in the *Logical Investigations*, the concept of *Deutung* – which is indeed interpretation – suddenly appears. This expression appears precisely in order to characterise a phase in the work of the elucidation or clarification of logical meanings. Paragraph 23 of the first *Logical Investigation*, entitled 'Apperception (*Auffassung*) as connected with expression and with intuitive presentation', begins with the following remark: 'The apperception of understanding, in which the meaning of a word becomes effective, is akin, in so far as *any* apperception is in a sense an understanding and an interpretation (*Deutung*), to the divergently carried out "objectifying apperceptions" in which, by way of an experienced sense-complex, the intuitive presentation (perception, imagination, reproduction, etc.) of an object (e.g. an external thing) arises' (*LU* II/1 74; *LI* I 309).† Thus a kinship is suggested at the very place where we have noted a radical difference. The kinship bears precisely upon the interpretation which is already at work in simple perception and which distinguishes the latter from the mere *data* of sensation. The kinship consists in the signifying activity which allows both the logical operation and the perceptual operation to be called *Auffassung*. It seems that the task of clarification can have recourse to a 'corresponding' intuition (mentioned in paragraph 21) only by virtue of this kinship between the two types of *Auffassung*.

A kinship of the same order explains Husserl's use of the term *Vorstellung* – 'representation' – to encompass both the consciousness of generality and the consciousness of singularity, which the second *Logical Investigation* is concerned to distinguish; the two forms of consciousness refer respectively to 'specific representations' and 'singular representations' (*LU* II/2 131, 157; *LI* I 357, 379). For in both cases we are dealing with a *meinen* by which something is 'placed before us' ('it is further clear that the universal, as often as we speak of it, is a thing thought by us') (*LU* II/2 124; *LI* I 352). Hence Husserl does not side with Frege, who severs the links between *Sinn* and *Vorstellung*, keeping the first denomination for logic and sending the second back to psychology. Husserl continues to use the term *Vorstellung* to describe the intended meaning of the specific as well as that of the individual.

Above all, grasping the generic and grasping the individual share a common core, which is the interpreted sensation: 'Sensations, animated by interpretations, present objective determinations in corresponding percepts of things, but they are not themselves these objective determinations. The apparent object, as it appears in the appearance, transcends this appearance as a phenomenon' (*LU* II/2 129; *LI* I 356). Far from being able to maintain a clear distinction between the intended meaning of the specific and that of the individual, Husserl posits what he calls 'a common phenomenal aspect' at the origin of this bifurcation.

There is, of course, a certain common phenomenal aspect in each case. In each case the same concrete thing makes its appearance, and to the extent that it does so, the same sense-contents are given and interpreted in an identical manner, i.e. the same course of actually given sense- and image-contents serves as a basis for the same 'conception' or 'interpretation', in which the appearance of the *object* with the *properties* presented by those contents is constituted for us. But the same appearance sustains different acts in the two cases. (*LU* ii/2 131; *LI* i 339)†

That explains why the same intuitive given may be 'on one occasion directly meant as *that thing there,* on another occasion as *sustaining* a universal' (*LU* ii/2 131; *LI* i 357). 'One and the same sensuous intuition can on one occasion serve as a basis for all these modes of conceiving' (*LU* ii/2 131; *LI* i 357). This interpretative core assures the 'representative' commonality of the two intended meanings and the transition from one 'apprehension' to the other. Thus perception 'represents' because it is already the seat of a work of interpretation; and it is because it represents that it can, in spite of its singularity, serve as a 'support' for specific representations.

Such is the first way in which phenomenology encounters the concept of interpretation. The concept is embedded in the process whereby phenomenology maintains the ideal of logicity, of univocity, which presides over the theory of signification in the *Logical Investigations*. Husserl states this ideal in the following terms:

Clearly, in fact, to say that each subjective expression could be replaced by an objective expression, is no more than to assert the *unbounded range of objective reason*. Everything that is, can be known in itself. Its being is a being definite in content, and documented in such and such 'truths in themselves' . . . (W)hat is objectively quite definite, must permit objective determination, and what permits objective determination, must, ideally speaking, permit expression through wholly determinate word-meanings. To being-in-itself correspond truths-in-themselves, and, to these last, fixed, unambiguous assertions. (*LU* ii/ 1 90; *LI* i 321–2)

Hence fixed meanings and the contents of stable expressions must be substituted for fluctuating meanings and subjective expressions. The task is dictated by the ideal of univocity and governed by the axiom of the *unbounded range of objective reason*. It is precisely the execution of the task of clarification which successively reveals, first, the split between essentially *occasional* meanings and univocal meanings; then the function of *accompaniment* fulfilled by illustrative intuitions; and finally the role of *support* played by perceptual interpretations. Step by step, the inversion of the theory of intuition into the theory of interpretation begins.

   (b) *The recourse to 'Auslegung' in the 'Cartesian Meditations'*. These hermeneutical beginnings could not be developed any further by the *Logical Investigations*, in virtue of the logical orientation assumed by the phenomenology of this period. We were thus able to speak of these beginnings only as a residue revealed by the very demand for univocity.

It is quite different with the *Cartesian Meditations*, wherein phenomenology seeks to give an account not simply of the ideal meaning of well-formed expressions, but of the meaning of experience *as a whole*. So if *Auslegung* must play some part in this account, it will no longer be a limited one (limited, that is, to the extent that sense experience must be interpreted in order to serve as a basis for the apprehension of the 'generic'); rather, *Auslegung* will enter into problems of constitution *in their totality*.

That is indeed what happens. The concept of *Auslegung* – as has not, perhaps, been sufficiently recognised – intervenes in a decisive manner at the moment when the problematic reaches its most critical point. That is the point at which the egology is set up as the ultimate tribunal of meaning: 'the objective world which exists for me (*für mich*), which has existed and will exist for me, this objective world with all of its objects draws from me (*aus mir selbst*) all its meaning and all the validity of being which it has for me'.[10] The inclusion of all *Seinsgeltung* 'in' the *ego*, which is expressed in the reduction of the *für mich* to the *aus mir*, is finally achieved in the fourth *Cartesian Meditation*. This achievement is at once its culmination and its crisis.

Its culmination: in the sense that only the identification of phenomenology with egology secures the complete reduction of world-meaning to my *ego*. Egology alone satisfies the demand that objects are *for* me only if they draw *from* me all their meaning and all their validity of being.

Its crisis: in the sense that the status of the *alter ego* and, through it, of the very otherness of the world becomes entirely problematic.

Precisely at this point of culmination and crisis, the motif of *Auslegung* intervenes. In paragraph 33 we read: 'Since the monadically concrete ego includes also the whole of actual and potential conscious life, it is clear that the problem of *explicating (Auslegung) this monadic ego phenomenologically* (the problem of his constitution for himself) must include *all constitutional problems without exception*. Consequently the phenomenology of this *self-constitution* coincides with phenomenology as a whole' (*Hua* I 102–3; *CM* 68).

What does Husserl mean here by *Auslegung*, and what does he expect from it? To answer these questions, let us pass from the fourth to the fifth *Meditation*, situating ourselves at the heart of the paradox which would remain insoluble without recourse to *Auslegung*. Then, retracing our steps, we shall attempt to understand the strategic role of this concept in the transition from the fourth to the fifth *Meditation*.

The apparently insoluble paradox is this: on the one hand, the reduction of all meaning to the intentional life of the concrete *ego* implies that the other is constituted 'in me' and 'from me'; on the other hand, phenomenology must account for the originality of the other's experience, precisely insofar as it is the experience of someone other than me. The whole of the fifth *Meditation* is dominated by the tension between these two demands: to constitute the other *in me*, to constitute it as *other*. This formidable paradox was latent in the other four *Meditations*: already the 'thing' tore itself away from my life as something other than me, as my *vis-à-vis*, even if it was only an intentional synthesis, a presumed unity. However, the latent tension between the reductive and descriptive demands becomes an open conflict when the other is no longer a thing but another self, a self other than me. For although, absolutely speaking, the only subject is me, the other is not given simply as a psychophysical object, situated in nature; it is also a subject of experience in the same way as I am, and as such it perceives me as belonging to the world of its experience. Moreover, it is on the basis of this intersubjectivity that a 'common' nature and a 'common' cultural world are constituted. In this respect, the reduction to the sphere of belonging – a veritable reduction within a reduction – can be understood as the conquest of the paradox *qua* paradox: 'In this quite particular intentionality, there is constituted a new existential meaning that goes beyond (*überschreitet*) the being of my monadic *ego*; there is constituted an *ego*, not as "I myself", but as mirrored (*spiegelnden*) in my own *ego*, in my monad' (*Hua* i 125; *CM* 94).† Such is the paradox whereby another existence breaks away from my existence at the very moment when I posit the latter as unique.

The paradox is in no way mitigated by recourse to the notions of 'analogical apprehension' and 'pairing' (*Paarung*), so long as the role of *Auslegung* introduced by the fourth *Meditation* is not perceived. For to say that the other is 'appresented' and never properly 'presented' seems to be a way of identifying the difficulty rather than resolving it. To say that analogical apprehension is not reasoning by analogy but transference based directly on a pairing of my body here with that body there is to designate the point where the descriptive and constitutive demands intersect, giving a name to the mixture in which the paradox should be resolved. But what does this 'apperceptive transposition', this 'analogical apperception', really signify? If the *ego* and the *alter ego* are not coupled from the very beginning, they never will be. For this 'coupling' implies that the meaning of all my experience refers back to the meaning of the experience of the other. But if the coupling is not originally part of the constitution of the *ego* for itself, then the *ego*'s experience will not incorporate any reference to that of others. In fact, the most remarkable thing about the fifth *Meditation* is the many descriptions which explode idealism; for example, the concrete images of the coupling, or the discernment of an alien mental life on the basis of the consistency between signs, expressions, gestures and postures which fulfil the anticipation of another's lived experience, or the role of imagination in analogical apperception: I could be there if I could project myself . . .

In spite of these admirable descriptions, what remains enigmatic is how the *alter ego* can be both transcendent and an intentional modification of my monadic life: 'Thanks to the constitution of its meaning, the other appears necessarily in my primordial 'world', as an *intentional modification* of my self which is objectivated in the first instance . . . In other words, *another monad* is constituted, by appresentation, in mine' (*Hua* I 144; *CM* 115).† It is this enigma, this paradox, indeed this latent conflict between two projects – a project of describing transcendence and a project of constituting in immanence – that the recourse to *Auslegung* may be able to resolve.

So let us go back to the point where the fourth *Cartesian Meditation* defines the entire phenomenological enterprise in terms of *Auslegung*. Paragraph 41, which closes the fourth *Meditation*, expressly defines transcendental idealism as 'the "phenomenological self-explication" that went on in my ego' (*Hua* I 117; *CM* 84). The 'style' of the interpretation is characterised by the 'infinite work' involved in unfolding the horizons of present experiences. Phenomenology is a meditation 'indefinitely *pursued*', because reflection is overwhelmed by the *potential* meanings of one's own lived experience. The same theme reappears at the end of the fifth *Meditation*. Paragraph 59 is entitled 'Ontological explication and its place within constitutional transcendental phenomenology as a whole'. What Husserl calls 'ontological explication' consists in unfolding the layers of meaning (nature, animality, psychism, culture, personality), which together form the 'world as constituted meaning'. Explication is thus mid-way between a philosophy of construction and a philosophy of description. Against Hegelianism and its sequels, against all 'metaphysical construction', Husserl maintains that phenomenology does not 'create' but only 'finds' (*Hua* II 168). This is the hyper-empirical side of phenomenology; explication is an explication of experience: 'phenomenological explication does nothing – and this could not be over-emphasised – but explicate the meaning which the world has for us all, prior to any philosophy, and which is obviously conferred upon it by our experience. This meaning can be uncovered (*enthüllt*) by philosophy but never altered (*geändert*) by it; and in each present experience it is surrounded – for essential reasons and not as a result of our weakness – by horizons in need of clarification (*Klärung*)' (*Hua* I 177; *CM* 151).† However, in thus linking explication to the clarification of horizons, phenomenology seeks to go beyond a static description of experience, a mere geography of the layers of meaning. The processes of transferring from the self towards the other, then towards objective nature and finally towards history, realise a progressive constitution – indeed ultimately a 'universal genesis' – of what we naively experience as the 'life-world'.

It is this 'intentional explication' which encompasses the two demands that appeared to be in conflict throughout the fifth *Meditation*: on the one hand, respect for the alterity of others; on the other hand, anchoring this experience of transcendence in primordial experience. For *Auslegung* does nothing more than unfold the surplus of meaning which, in my experience, indicates the place for the other.

A less dichotomous reading of the fifth *Meditation* as a whole thus becomes possible. *Auslegung* is already at work in the reduction to the sphere of belonging. For the latter is not a given from which I could progress towards another given, which would be the other. Experience reduced to one's lived body is the result of an abstraction from everything which is 'foreign'; by this abstractive reduction, says Husserl, I 'bring to light my animate organism, reduced to my sphere of belonging' (*Hua* I 128; *CM* 97).† This *Herausstellung* [bringing out] signifies, it seems to me, that the primordial remains always the limit of a 'questioning back'; thanks to this *Rückfrage*, reflection glimpses, in the thickness of experience and through the successive layers of constitution, what Husserl calls a 'primal instituting' – an *Urstiftung* (*Hua* I 141; *CM* 111) – to which these layers refer. The primordial is thus the intentional limit of such a reference. So there is no need to search, under the title of 'sphere of belonging', for some sort of brute experience which would be preserved at the heart of my experience of culture, but rather for an antecedent which is never given in itself. Hence, in spite of its intuitive kernel, this experience remains an interpretation. 'My own too is discovered by explication and gets its original meaning by virtue thereof' (*Hua* I 132; *CM* 102).† What is one's own is revealed only as 'explicated experience' (*Hua* I 132; *CM* 102). Even better, it could be said that what is one's own and what is foreign are polarly constituted in the *same interpretation*.

Thus it is as *Auslegung* that the other is constituted both in me and as other. It is characteristic of experience in general, says paragraph 46, that it becomes a determined object only in 'interpreting itself by itself; it is thus realised only as pure explication' (*Hua* I 131; *CM* 101).† All determination is explication: 'This own-essential content is only generally and horizonally anticipated beforehand; it then becomes constituted originaliter – with the sense: internal, own-essential feature (specifically, part or property) – by explication' (*Hua* I 132; *CM* 101).

The paradox of a constitution which would be both constitution 'in me' and constitution of 'another' takes on a completely new significance if it is clarified by the role of explication. The other is included, not in my existence as given, but in the latter insofar as it is characterised by an 'open and infinite horizon' (*Hua* I 132; *CM* 102), a potentiality of meaning which I cannot master in a glance. I can indeed say, therefore, that the experience of others merely 'develops' my own identical being, but what it develops was already more than myself, since what I call here my own identical being is a potentiality of meaning which exceeds the gaze of reflection. The possibility of going beyond myself towards the other is inscribed in this horizonal structure which calls for 'explication', which calls, in the words of Husserl himself, for an 'explication of the horizons of my own being' (*Hua* I 132; *CM* 102).†

Husserl perceived the coincidence of intuition and explication, although he failed to draw all its consequences. All phenomenology is an explication of evidence and an evidence of explication. An evidence which is explicated, an explication which unfolds evidence: such is the phenomenological experience. It is in this sense that phenomenology can be realised only as hermeneutics.

But the truth of this proposition can be grasped only if, at the same time, the hermeneutical critique of Husserlian idealism is fully accepted. The second part of this essay thus refers back to the first: phenomenology and hermeneutics presuppose one another only if the idealism of Husserlian phenomenology succumbs to the critique of hermeneutics.

Part II

Studies in the theory of interpretation

4. The hermeneutical function of distanciation

In previous studies, I have described the background against which I shall try to elaborate the hermeneutical problem in a way that will be significant for the dialogue between hermeneutics and the semiological and exegetical disciplines. The description has led us to an antinomy which seems to me to be the mainspring of Gadamer's work, namely the opposition between alienating distanciation and belonging. This opposition is an antinomy because it establishes an untenable alternative: on the one hand, alienating distanciation is the attitude that renders possible the objectification which reigns in the human sciences; but on the other hand, this distanciation, which is the condition of the scientific status of the sciences, is at the same time the fall that destroys the fundamental and primordial relation whereby we belong to and participate in the historical reality which we claim to construct as an object. Whence the alternative underlying the very title of Gadamer's work *Truth and Method:* either we adopt the methodological attitude and lose the ontological density of the reality we study, or we adopt the attitude of truth and must then renounce the objectivity of the human sciences.

My own reflection stems from a rejection of this alternative and an attempt to overcome it. The first expression of this attempt consists in the choice of a dominant problematic which seems to me to escape from the alternative between alienating distanciation and participatory belonging. The dominant problematic is that of the text, which reintroduces a positive and, if I may say so, productive notion of distanciation. In my view, the text is much more than a particular case of intersubjective communication: it is the paradigm of distanciation in communication. As such, it displays a fundamental characteristic of the very historicity of human experience, namely that it is communication in and through distance.

In what follows, I shall elaborate the notion of the text in view of that to which it testifies, the positive and productive function of distanciation at the heart of the historicity of human experience. I propose to organise this problematic around five themes: (1) the realisation of language as *discourse;* (2) the realisation of discourse as a *structured work;* (3) the relation of *speaking to writing* in discourse and in the works of discourse; (4) the work of discourse as the *projection of a world;* (5) discourse and the work of discourse as the *mediation of self-understanding.* Taken together, these features constitute the criteria of textuality.

We shall see that the question of writing, when placed at the centre of this network of criteria, in no way constitutes the unique problematic of the text. The text cannot, therefore, be purely and simply identified with writing. There are several reasons for this. First, it is not writing as such which gives rise to the hermeneutical problem, but the dialectic of speaking and writing. Second, this dialectic is constructed upon a dialectic of distanciation which is more primitive than the opposition of writing to speaking and which is already part of oral discourse *qua* discourse; we must therefore search in discourse itself for the roots of all subsequent dialectics. Finally, between the realisation of language as discourse and the dialectic of speaking and writing, it seems necessary to insert the fundamental notion of the realisation of discourse as a structured work. It seems to me that the objectification of language in works of discourse constitutes the proximate condition of the inscription of discourse in writing; literature consists of written works, hence above all of works. But that is not all: the triad discourse–work–writing still only constitutes the tripod which supports the decisive problematic, that of the projection of a world, which I shall call the world of the work, and where I see the centre of gravity of the hermeneutical question. The whole preliminary discussion will serve only to prepare the way for the displacement of the problem of the text towards that of the *world* which it opens up. At the same time, the question of self-understanding, which had occupied the foreground in Romantic hermeneutics, is postponed until the end, appearing as a terminal point and not as an introductory theme or even less as the centre of gravity.

I. The realisation of language as discourse

Discourse, even in an oral form, displays a primitive type of distanciation which is the condition of possibility of all the characteristics we shall consider later. This primitive type of distanciation can be discussed under the heading of the dialectic of event and meaning.

Discourse is given as an event: something happens when someone speaks. The notion of discourse as event is essential when we take into consideration the passage from a linguistics of language or codes to a linguistics of discourse or messages. The distinction comes, as we know, from Ferdinand de Saussure[1] and Louis Hjelmslev;[2] the first distinguished 'language' [*langue*] and 'speech' [*parole*], the second 'schema' and 'use'. The theory of discourse draws all the epistemological consequences of this duality. Whereas structural linguistics simply places speech and use in parentheses, the theory of discourse removes the parentheses and proclaims the existence of two linguistics resting upon different principles. The French linguist Emile Benveniste[3] has gone the furthest in this direction. For him, the linguistics of discourse and the linguistics of language are constructed upon different units. If the 'sign' (phonological and lexical) is the basic unit of language, the 'sentence' is the basic unit of discourse. The linguistics of the sentence underlies the dialectic of event and meaning, which forms the starting point for our theory of the text.

What are we to understand by 'event'? To say that discourse is an event is to say, first, that discourse is realised temporally and in the present, whereas the system of language is virtual and outside of time. In this sense, we can speak with Benveniste of the 'instance of discourse', in order to designate the emergence of discourse itself as an event. Moreover, whereas language has no subject insofar as the question 'who speaks?' does not apply at this level, discourse refers back to its speaker by means of a complex set of indicators, such as personal pronouns. We can say, in this sense, that the instance of discourse is self-referential. The eventful character is now linked to the person who speaks; the event consists in the fact that someone speaks, someone expresses himself in taking up speech. Discourse is an event in yet a third way: the signs of language refer only to other signs in the interior of the same system so that language no more has a world than it has a time and a subject, whereas discourse is always about something. Discourse refers to a world which it claims to describe, express or represent. The event, in this third sense, is the advent of a world in language [*langage*] by means of discourse. Finally, while language is only a prior condition of communication for which it provides the codes, it is in discourse that all messages are exchanged. So discourse not only has a world, but it has an other, another person, an interlocutor to whom it is addressed. The event, in this last sense, is the temporal phenomenon of exchange, the establishment of a dialogue which can be started, continued or interrupted. All of these features, taken together, constitute discourse as an event. It is notable that they appear only in the realisation of language in discourse, in the actualisation of our linguistic competence in performance.

However, in thus accentuating the eventful character of discourse, we have brought out only one of the two constitutive poles of discourse. Now we must clarify the second pole, that of meaning. For it is the tension between the two poles which gives rise to the production of discourse as a work, the dialectic of speaking and writing, and all the other features of the text which enrich the notion of distanciation.

In order to introduce the dialectic of event and meaning, I propose to say that, if all discourse is realised as an event, all discourse is understood as meaning. What we wish to understand is not the fleeting event, but rather the meaning which endures. This point demands the greatest clarification, for it may seem that we are reverting from the linguistics of discourse to the linguistics of language. But that is not so; it is in the linguistics of discourse that event and meaning are articulated. This articulation is the core of the whole hermeneutical problem. Just as language, by being actualised in discourse, surpasses itself as system and realises itself as event, so too discourse, by entering the process of understanding, surpasses itself as event and becomes meaning. The surpassing of the event by the meaning is characteristic of discourse as such. It attests to the very intentionality of language, to the relation within the latter of the noema and the noesis. If language is a *meinen*, a meaningful intention, it is precisely in virtue of the surpassing of the event by the meaning. The very first distanciation is thus the distanciation of the saying in the said.

But what is said? To clarify more completely this problem, hermeneutics must appeal not only to linguistics – even when this is understood as the linguistics of discourse as opposed to the linguistics of language – but also to the theory of *speech-acts,* as found in the work of Austin[4] and Searle.[5] According to these authors, the act of discourse is constituted by a hierarchy of subordinate acts distributed on three levels: (1) the level of the locutionary or propositional act, the act *of* saying; (2) the level of the illocutionary act (or force), what we do *in* saying; (3) the level of the perlocutionary act, what we do *by the fact that* we speak. If I tell you to close the door, I do three things. First, I relate the action predicate (to close) to two variables (you and the door): this is the act of saying. Second, I tell you this with the force of an order rather than a statement, wish or promise: this is the illocutionary act. Finally, I can provoke certain consequences, such as fear, by the fact that I give you an order; hence discourse is a sort of stimulus which produces certain results: this is the perlocutionary act.

What are the implications of these distinctions for our problem of the intentional exteriorisation by which the event is surpassed in the meaning? The locutionary act is exteriorised in the sentence *qua* proposition. For it is as such and such proposition that the sentence can be identified and reidentified as the *same*. A sentence thus appears as an ut-terance (*Aus-sage*), capable of being conveyed to others with such and such a meaning. What is identified is the predicative structure itself, as the above example reveals. An action sentence can be identified, therefore, by its specific predicate (the action) and by its two variables (the agent and the object). The illocutionary act can also be exteriorised by means of grammatical paradigms (the moods: indicative, imperative, etc.) and other procedures which 'mark' the illocutionary force of a sentence and thus enable it to be identified and reidentified. It is true that, in oral discourse, the illocutionary force can be identified by gestures and gesticulations as well as by properly linguistic features; it is also true that the least articulated aspects of discourse, the aspects we call prosody, provide the most compelling indices. Nevertheless, the properly syntactic marks constitute a system of inscription which makes possible in principle the fixation by writing of these indications of illocutionary force. It must be conceded that the perlocutionary act, being primarily a characteristic of oral discourse, is the least inscribable element. But the perlocutionary action is also the least discursive aspect of discourse: it is discourse *qua* stimulus. Here discourse operates, not through the recognition of my intention by the interlocutor, but in an energetic mode, as it were, by direct influence upon the emotions and affective attitudes of the interlocutor. Thus the propositional act, the illocutionary force and the perlocutionary action are susceptible, in decreasing degrees, to the intentional exteriorisation which renders inscription by writing possible.

Thus, by the meaning of the act of discourse, or the *noema* of the *saying*, we must understand not only the correlate of the sentence, in the narrow sense of the propositional act, but also the correlate of the illocutionary force and even that of the perlocutionary action, insofar as these three aspects of the act of discourse are codified and regulated according to paradigms, and hence insofar as they can be identified and reidentified as having the same meaning. I therefore give the word 'meaning' a very broad connotation that covers all the aspects and levels

of the *intentional exteriorisation* which, in turn, renders possible the exteriorisation of discourse in writing and in the work.

II. Discourse as a work

I shall propose three distinctive features of the notion of a work. First,
a work is a sequence longer than the sentence; it raises a new problem
of understanding, relative to the finite and closed totality which constitutes the work as such. Second, the work is submitted to a form of
codification which is applied to the composition itself, and which transforms discourse into a story, a poem, an essay, etc. This codification is
known as a literary genre; a work, in other words, is characteristically
subsumed to a literary genre. Finally, a work is given a unique configuration which likens it to an individual and which may be called its
style.

Composition, belonging to a genre and individual style characterise
discourse as a work. The very word 'work' reveals the nature of these
new categories; they are categories of production and of labour. To impose a form upon material, to submit production to genres, to produce
an individual: these are so many ways of treating language as a material
to be worked upon and formed. Discourse thereby becomes the object
of a *praxis* and a *techne*. In this respect, there is not a sharp opposition
between mental and manual labour. We may recall what Aristotle says
about practice and production: 'All practice and all production concern
the individual. For it is not man that medicine cures, except by accident; rather it is Callias or Socrates or some other individual, thus designated, who at the same time happens to be a man' (*Metaphysics* A,
91a, a15). In a similar vein, G.-G. Granger writes in his *Essai d'une philosophie du style*: 'Practice is activity considered together with its complex context and in particular with the social conditions which give it
meaning in a world actually experienced.'[6] Labour is thus one, if not
the principal, structure of practice; it is 'practical activity objectifying
itself in works'.[7] In the same way, the literary work is the result of a
labour which organises language. In labouring upon discourse, man
effects the practical determination of a category of individuals: the
works of discourse. Here the notion of meaning receives a new specification, linking it to the level of the individual work. There is thus a
problem of the interpretation of works, a problem irreducible to the
step by step understanding of sentences. The phenomenon of the work
globally signifying *qua* work is underlined by the fact of style. The

problem of literature can then be situated within a general stylistics, conceived as a 'meditation on human works'[8] and specified by the notion of labour, for which it seeks the conditions of possibility: 'To investigate the most general conditions of inserting structures in individual practices would be the task of a stylistics.'[9]

In the light of these principles, what happens to the features of discourse outlined at the beginning of this study? Let us recall the initial paradox of event and meaning: discourse, we said, is realised as event but understood as meaning. How does the notion of work fit into this paradox? By introducing the categories of production and labour into the dimension of discourse, the notion of work appears as a practical mediation between the irrationality of the event and the rationality of meaning. The event is stylisation itself, but this stylisation is in dialectical relation with a complex, concrete situation presenting conflictual tendencies. Stylisation occurs at the heart of an experience which is already structured but which is nevertheless characterised by openings, possibilities, indeterminacies. To grasp a work as an event is to grasp the relation between the situation and the project in the process of restructuration. The work of stylisation takes the peculiar form of an interplay between an anterior situation which appears suddenly undone, unresolved, open, and a conduct or strategy which reorganises the residues left over from the anterior structuration. At the same time, the paradox of the fleeting event and the identifiable and repeatable meaning, which is at the origin of our meditation on distanciation in discourse, finds a remarkable mediation in the notion of work. The two aspects of event and meaning are drawn together by the notion of style. Style, we said, is expressed temporally as an individual work and in this respect concerns the irrational moment of taking a stand [*parti pris*], but its inscription in the materials of language give it the appearance of a sensible idea, a concrete universal, as W.K. Wimsatt says in *The Verbal Icon*.[10] A style is the promotion of a particular standpoint in a work which, by its singularity, illustrates and exalts the eventful character of discourse; but this event is not to be sought elsewhere than in the very form of the work. If the individual work cannot be grasped theoretically, it can be recognised as the singularity of a process, a construction, in response to a determinate situation.

The concept of the subject of discourse receives a new status when discourse becomes a work. The notion of style permits a new approach to the question of the subject of the literary work. The key is in the categories of production and labour; in this respect, the model of the artisan is particularly instructive (the stamp on furniture in the eighteenth century, the signature of the artist, etc.). For the concept of author, which qualifies that of the speaking subject on this level, appears as the correlate of the individuality of the work. The most striking proof is provided by the example which is least literary, namely the style of the construction of the mathematical object such as Granger describes it in the first part of his *Essai d'une philosophie du style*. Even the construction of an abstract model of phenomena, insofar as it is a practical activity immanent in a process of structuration, bears a proper name. A given mode of structuration necessarily appears to be chosen instead of some other mode. Since style is labour which individuates, that is, which produces an individual, so it designates retroactively its author. Thus the word 'author' belongs to stylistics. Author says more than speaker: the author is the artisan of a work of language. But the category of author is equally a category of interpretation, in the sense that it is contemporaneous with the meaning of the work as a whole. The singular configuration of the work and the singular configuration of the author are strictly correlative. Man individuates himself in producing individual works. The signature is the mark of this relation.

The most important consequence of introducing the category of work pertains to the notion of composition. For the work of discourse presents the characteristics of organisation and structure which enable structural methods to be applied to discourse itself, methods which were first successfully applied to linguistic entities shorter than the sentence in phonology and semantics. The objectification of discourse in the work and the structural character of composition, to which we shall add distanciation by writing, compel us to place in question the Diltheyan opposition between 'understanding' and 'explanation'. A new phase of hermeneutics is opened by the success of structural analysis; henceforth explanation is the obligatory path of understanding. This does not mean, I hasten to say, that explanation can eliminate understanding. The objectification of discourse in a structured work does not abolish the first and fundamental feature of discourse, namely that it is constituted by a series of sentences whereby someone says something to someone about something. Hermeneutics, I shall say, remains the art of discerning the discourse in the work; but this discourse is only given in and through the structures of the work. Thus interpretation is the reply to the fundamental distanciation constituted by the objectification of man in works of discourse, an objectification comparable to that expressed in the products of his labour and his art.

III. The relation of speaking and writing

What happens to discourse when it passes from speaking to writing? At first sight, writing seems only to introduce a purely external and material factor: fixation, which shelters the event of discourse from destruction. In fact, fixation is only the external appearance of a problem which is much more important, and which affects all the properties of discourse that we have enumerated above. To begin with, writing renders the text autonomous with respect to the intention of the author. What the text signifies no longer coincides with what the author meant; henceforth, textual meaning and psychological meaning have different destinies.

This first modality of autonomy encourages us to recognise a positive significance in *Verfremdung*, a significance which cannot be reduced to the nuance of decline which Gadamer tends to give to it. The autonomy of the text already contains the possibility that what Gadamer calls the 'matter' of the text may escape from the finite intentional horizon of its author; in other words, thanks to writing, the 'world' of the *text* may explode the world of the *author*.

What is true of the psychological conditions holds also for the sociological conditions of the production of the text. An essential characteristic of a literary work, and of a work of art in general, is that it transcends its own psycho-sociological conditions of production and thereby opens itself to an unlimited series of readings, themselves situated in different socio-cultural conditions. In short, the text must be able, from the sociological as well as the psychological point of view, to 'decontextualise' itself in such a way that it can be 'recontextualised' in a new situation – as accomplished, precisely, by the act of reading.

The emancipation with respect to the author has a parallel on the side of those who receive the text. In contrast to the dialogical situation, where the *vis-à-vis* is determined by the very situation of discourse, written discourse creates an audience which extends in principle to anyone who can read. The freeing of the written material with respect to the dialogical condition of discourse is the most significant effect of writing. It implies that the relation between writing and reading is no longer a particular case of the relation between speaking and hearing.

The first important hermeneutical consequence of the autonomy of the text is this: distanciation is not the product of methodology and hence something superfluous and parasitical; rather it is constitutive of the phenomenon of the text as writing. At the same time, it is the condition of interpretation; *Verfremdung* is not only what understanding must overcome, but also what conditions it. We are thus prepared to discover a relation between *objectification* and *interpretation* which is much less dichotomous, and consequently much more complementary, than that established by the Romantic tradition. The passage from speaking to writing affects discourse in several other ways. In particular, the functioning of reference is profoundly altered when it is no longer possible to identify the thing spoken about as part of the common situation of the interlocutors. We shall offer a separate analysis of this phenomenon under the title of 'the world of the text'.

IV. The world of the text

The feature which we have placed under this title is going to lead us further from the position of Romantic hermeneutics, including the work of Dilthey, as well as towards the antipodes of structuralism, which I confront here as the simple contrary of Romanticism.

We may recall that Romantic hermeneutics placed the emphasis on the expression of genius; to liken oneself to this genius, to render it contemporary, such was the task of hermeneutics. Dilthey, still close in this sense to Romantic hermeneutics, based his concept of interpretation on that of 'understanding', that is, on grasping an alien life which expresses itself through the objectifications of writing. Whence the psychologising and historicising character of Romantic and Diltheyan hermeneutics. This route is no longer open to us, once we take distanciation by writing and objectification by structure seriously. But is this to say that, renouncing any attempt to grasp the soul of an author, we shall restrict ourselves to reconstructing the structure of a work?

The answer to this question distances us as much from structuralism as from Romanticism. The principal task of hermeneutics eludes the alternative of genius or structure; I shall link it to the notion of 'the world of the text'. This notion extends what we earlier called the reference or denotation of discourse. Following Frege, we can distinguish between the *sense* and the *reference* of any proposition.[11] The sense is the ideal object which the proposition intends, and hence is purely immanent in discourse. The reference is the truth value of the proposition, its claim to reach reality. Reference thus distinguishes discourse from language [*langue*]; the latter has no relation with reality, its words returning to other words in the endless circle of the dictionary. Only discourse, we shall say, intends things, applies itself to reality, expresses the world.

The new question which arises is this: what happens to reference when discourse becomes a text? Here we find that writing, and above all the structure of the work, modify reference to the point of rendering it entirely problematic. In oral discourse, the problem is ultimately resolved by the ostensive function of discourse; in other words, reference is determined by the ability to point to a reality common to the interlocutors. If we cannot point to the thing about which we speak, at least we can situate it in relation to the unique spatio-temporal network which is shared by the interlocutors. It is the 'here' and 'now', determined by the situation of discourse, which provides the ultimate reference of all discourse. With writing, things already begin to change. For there is no longer a situation common to the writer and the reader, and the concrete conditions of the act of pointing no longer exist. This abolition of the ostensive character of reference is no doubt what makes possible the phenomenon we call 'literature', which may abolish all reference to a given reality. However, the abolition of ostensive reference is taken to its most extreme conditions only with the appearance of certain literary genres, which are generally linked to but not necessarily dependent upon writing. The role of most our literature is, it seems, to destroy the world. That is true of fictional literature – folktales, myths, novels, plays – but also of all literature which could be called poetic, where language seems to glorify itself at the expense of the referential function of ordinary discourse.

Nevertheless, there is no discourse so fictional that it does not connect up with reality. But such discourse refers to another level, more fundamental than that attained by the descriptive, constative, didactic discourse which we call ordinary language. My thesis here is that the abolition of a first order reference, an abolition effected by fiction and poetry, is the condition of possibility for the freeing of a second order reference, which reaches the world not only at the level of manipulable objects, but at the level that Husserl designated by the expression *Lebenswelt* [life-world] and Heidegger by the expression 'being-in-the-world'.

The unique referential dimension of the work of fiction and poetry raises, in my view, the most fundamental hermeneutical problem. If we can no longer define hermeneutics in terms of the search for the psychological intentions of another person which are concealed *behind* the text, and if we do not want to reduce interpretation to the dismantling of structures, then what remains to be interpreted? I shall say: to interpret is to explicate the type of being-in-the-world unfolded *in front of* the text.

Here we rejoin one of Heidegger's suggestions concerning the notion of *Verstehen*. Recall that, in *Being and Time*, the theory of 'understanding' is no longer tied to the understanding of others, but becomes a structure of being-in-the-world. More precisely, it is a structure which is explored after the examination of *Befindlichkeit* [state-of-mind]. The moment of 'understanding' corresponds dialectically to being in a situation: it is the projection of our ownmost possibilities at the very heart of the situations in which we find ourselves. I want to retain from this analysis the idea of 'the projection of our ownmost possibilities', applying it to the theory of the text. For what must be interpreted in a text is a *proposed world* which I could inhabit and wherein I could project one of my ownmost possibilities. That is what I call the world of the text, the world proper to *this* unique text.

The world of the text is therefore not the world of everyday language. In this sense, it constitutes a new sort of distanciation which could be called a distanciation of the real from itself. It is this distanciation which fiction introduces into our apprehension of reality. We said that narratives, folktales and poems are not without a referent; but this referent is discontinuous with that of everyday language. Through fiction and poetry, new possibilities of being-in-the-world are opened up within everyday reality. Fiction and poetry intend being, not under the modality of being-given, but under the modality of power-to-be. Everyday reality is thereby metamorphosed by what could be called the imaginative variations which literature carries out on the real.

I have shown elsewhere, with the example of metaphorical language,[12] that fiction is the privileged path for the redescription of reality; and that poetic language is *par excellence* that which effects what Aristotle, reflecting on tragedy, called the *mimesis* of reality. For tragedy imitates reality only because it recreates it by means of a *mythos*, a 'fable', which reaches the profoundest essence of reality.

Such is the third sort of *distanciation* which the hermeneutic experience must incorporate.

V. Self-understanding in front of the work

I should like to consider a fourth and final dimension of the notion of the text. I announced it in the introduction by saying that the text is the medium through which we understand ourselves. This fourth theme marks the appearance of the subjectivity of the reader. It extends the fundamental characteristic of all discourse whereby the latter is addressed to someone. But in contrast to dialogue, this *vis-à-vis* is not given in the situation of discourse; it is, if I may say so, created or instituted by the work itself. A work opens up its readers and thus creates its own subjective *vis-à-vis*.

It may be said that this problem is well known in traditional hermeneutics: it is the problem of the appropriation (*Aneignung*) of the text, its application (*Anwendung*) to the present situation of the reader. Indeed, I also understand it in this way; but I should like to underline how this theme is transformed when it is introduced *after* the preceding points.

To begin with, appropriation is dialectically linked to the distanciation characteristic of *writing*. Distanciation is not abolished by appropriation, but is rather the counterpart of it. Thanks to distanciation by writing, appropriation no longer has any trace of affective affinity with the intention of an author. Appropriation is quite the contrary of contemporaneousness and congeniality: it is understanding at and through distance.

In the second place, appropriation is dialectically linked to the objectification characteristic of the *work*. It is mediated by all the structural objectifications of the text; insofar as appropriation does not respond to the author, it responds to the sense. Perhaps it is at this level that the mediation effected by the text can be best understood. In contrast to the tradition of the *cogito* and to the pretension of the subject to know itself by immediate intuition, it must be said that we understand ourselves only by the long detour of the signs of humanity deposited in cultural works. What would we know of love and hate, of moral feelings and, in general, of all that we call the *self*, if these had not been brought to language and articulated by literature? Thus what seems most contrary to subjectivity, and what structural analysis discloses as the texture of the text, is the very *medium* within which we can understand ourselves.

Above all, the *vis-à-vis* of appropriation is what Gadamer calls 'the matter of the text' and what I call here 'the world of the work'. Ultimately, what I appropriate is a proposed world. The latter is not *behind* the text, as a hidden intention would be, but *in front of* it, as that which the work unfolds, discovers, reveals. Henceforth, to understand is *to understand oneself in front of the text*. It is not a question of imposing upon the text our finite capacity of understanding, but of exposing ourselves to the text and receiving from it an enlarged self, which would be the proposed existence corresponding in the most suitable way to the world proposed. So understanding is quite different from a constitution of which the subject would possess the key. In this respect, it would be more correct to say that the *self* is constituted by the 'matter' of the text.

It is undoubtedly necessary to go still further: just as the world of the text is real only insofar as it is imaginary, so too it must be said that the subjectivity of the reader comes to itself only insofar as it is placed in suspense, unrealised, potentialised. In other words, if fiction is a fundamental dimension of the reference of the text, it is no less a fundamental dimension of the subjectivity of the reader. As reader, I find myself only by losing myself. Reading introduces me into the imaginative variations of the *ego*. The metamorphosis of the world in play is also the playful metamorphosis of the *ego*.

If that is true, then the concept of 'appropriation', to the extent that it is directed against *Verfremdung*, demands an internal critique. For the metamorphosis of the *ego*, of which we have just spoken, implies a moment of distanciation in the relation of self to itself; hence understanding is as much disappropriation as appropriation. A critique of the illusions of the subject, in a Marxist or Freudian manner, therefore can and must be incorporated into self-understanding. The consequence for hermeneutics is important: we can no longer oppose hermeneutics and the critique of ideology. The critique of ideology is the necessary detour which self-understanding must take, if the latter is to be formed by the matter of the text and not by the prejudices of the reader.

Thus we must place at the very heart of self-understanding that dialectic of objectification and understanding which we first perceived at the level of the text, its structures, its sense and its reference. At all these levels of analysis, distanciation is the condition of understanding.

5. What is a text? Explanation and understanding

This essay will be devoted primarily to the debate between two fundamental attitudes which may be adopted in regard to a text. These two attitudes were summed up, in the period of Wilhelm Dilthey at the end of the last century, by the two words 'explanation' and 'interpretation'. For Dilthey, 'explanation' referred to the model of intelligibility borrowed from the natural sciences and applied to the historical disciplines by positivist schools; 'interpretation', on the other hand, was a derivative form of understanding, which Dilthey regarded as the fundamental attitude of the human sciences and as that which could alone preserve the fundamental difference between these sciences and the sciences of nature. Here I propose to examine the fate of this opposition in the light of conflicts between contemporary schools. For the notion of explanation has since been displaced, so that it derives no longer from the natural sciences but from properly linguistic models. As regards the concept of interpretation, it has undergone profound transformations which distance it from the psychological notion of understanding, in Dilthey's sense of the word. It is this new position of the problem, perhaps less contradictory and more fecund, which I should like to explore. But before unfolding the new concepts of explanation and understanding, I should like to pause at a preliminary question which in fact dominates the whole of our investigation. The question is this: what is a text?

I. What is a text?

Let us say that a text is any discourse fixed by writing. According to this definition, fixation by writing is constitutive of the text itself. But what is fixed by writing? We have said: any discourse. Is this to say that discourse had to be pronounced initially in a physical or mental form? that all writing was initially, at least in a potential way, speaking? In short, what is the relation of the text to speech?

To begin with, we are tempted to say that all writing is added to some anterior speech. For if by speech [*parole*] we understand, with Ferdinand de Saussure, the realisation of language [*langue*] in an event of discourse, the production of an individual utterance by an individual speaker, then each text is in the same position as speech with respect to language. Moreover, writing as an institution is subsequent to speech, and seems merely to fix in linear script all the articulations which have already appeared orally. The attention given almost exclusively to phonetic writings seems to confirm that writing adds nothing to the phenomenon of speech other than the fixation which enables it to be conserved. Whence the conviction that writing is fixed speech, that inscription, whether it be graphics or recording, is inscription of speech – an inscription which, thanks to the subsisting character of the engraving, guarantees the persistence of speech.

The psychological and sociological priority of speech over writing is not in question. It may be asked, however, whether the late appearance of writing has not provoked a radical change in our relation to the very statements of our discourse. For let us return to our definition: the text is a discourse fixed by writing. What is fixed by writing is thus a discourse which could be said, of course, but which is written precisely because it is not said. Fixation by writing takes the very place of speech, occurring at the site where speech could have emerged. This suggests that a text is really a text only when it is not restricted to transcribing an anterior speech, when instead it inscribes directly in written letters what the discourse means.

This idea of a direct relation between the meaning of the statement and writing can be supported by reflecting on the function of reading in relation to writing. Writing calls for reading in a way which will enable us shortly to introduce the concept of interpretation. For the moment, let us say that the reader takes the place of the interlocutor, just as writing takes the place of speaking and the speaker. The writing–reading relation is thus not a particular case of the speaking–answering relation. It is not a relation of interlocution, not an instance of dialogue. It does not suffice to say that reading is a dialogue with the author through his work, for the relation of the reader to the book is of a completely different nature. Dialogue is an exchange of questions and answers; there is no exchange of this sort between the writer and the reader. The writer does not respond to the reader. Rather, the book divides the act of writing and the act of reading into two sides, between which there is no communication. The reader is absent from the act of writing; the writer is absent from the act of reading. The text thus produces a double eclipse of the reader and the writer. It thereby replaces the relation of dialogue, which directly connects the voice of one to the hearing of the other.

The substitution of reading for a dialogue which has not occurred is so manifest that when we happen to encounter an author and to speak to him (about his book, for example), we experience a profound disruption of the peculiar relation that we have with the author in and through his work. Sometimes I like to say that to read a book is to consider its author as already dead and the book as posthumous. For it is when the author is dead that the relation to the book becomes complete and, as it were, intact. The author can no longer respond; it only remains to read his work.

The difference between the act of reading and the act of dialogue confirms our hypothesis that writing is a realisation comparable and parallel to speech, a realisation which takes the place of it and, as it were, intercepts it. Hence we could say that what comes to writing is discourse as intention-to-say and that writing is a direct inscription of this intention, even if, historically and psychologically, writing began with the graphic transcription of the signs of speech. This emancipation of writing, which places the latter at the site of speech, is the birth of the text.

Now, what happens to the statement itself when it is directly inscribed instead of being pronounced? The most striking characteristic has always been emphasised: writing preserves discourse and makes it an archive available for individual and collective memory. It may be added that the linearisation of symbols permits an analytic and distinctive translation of all the successive and discrete features of language and thereby increases its efficacy. Is that all? Preservation and increased efficacy still only characterise the transcription of oral language in graphic signs. The emancipation of the text from the oral situation entails a veritable upheaval in the relations between language and the world, as well as in the relation between language and the various subjectivities concerned (that of the author and that of the reader). We glimpsed something of this second upheaval in distinguishing reading from dialogue; we shall have to go still further, but this time beginning from the upheaval which the referential relation of language to the world undergoes when the text takes the place of speech.

What do we understand by the referential relation or referential function? In addressing himself to another speaker, the subject of discourse says something about something; that about which he speaks is the referent of his discourse. As is well known, this referential function is supported by the sentence, which is the first and the simplest unit of discourse. It is the sentence which intends to say something true or something real, at least in declarative discourse. The referential function is so important that it compensates, as it were, for another characteristic of language, namely the separation of signs from things. By means of the referential function, language 'pours back into the universe' (according to an expression of Gustave Guillaume) those signs which the symbolic function, at its birth, divorced from things. All discourse is, to some extent, thereby reconnected to the world. For if we did not speak of the world, of what should we speak?

When the text takes the place of speech, something important occurs. In speech, the interlocutors are present not only to one another, but also to the situation, the surroundings and the circumstantial milieu of discourse. It is in relation to this circumstantial milieu that discourse is fully meaningful; the return to reality is ultimately a return to this reality, which can be indicated 'around' the speakers, 'around', if we may say so, the instance of discourse itself. Language is, moreover, well equipped to secure this anchorage. Demonstratives, adverbs of time and place, personal pronouns, verbal tenses, and in general all the 'deictic' and 'ostensive' indicators serve to anchor discourse in the circumstantial reality which surrounds the instance of discourse. Thus, in living speech, the *ideal* sense of what is said turns towards the *real* reference, towards that 'about which' we speak. At the limit, this real reference tends to merge with an ostensive designation where speech rejoins the gesture of pointing. Sense fades into reference and the latter into the act of showing.

This is no longer the case when the text takes the place of speech. The movement of reference towards the act of showing is intercepted, at the same time as dialogue is interrupted by the text. I say intercepted and not suppressed; it is in this respect that I shall distance myself from what may be called henceforth the ideology of the absolute text. On the basis of the sound remarks which we have just made, this ideology proceeds, by an unwarranted hypostasis, through a course that is ultimately surreptitious. As we shall see, the text is not without reference; the task of reading, *qua* interpretation, will be precisely to fulfil the reference. The suspense which defers the reference merely leaves the text, as it were, 'in the air', outside or without a world. In virtue of this obliteration of the relation to the world, each text is free to enter into relation with all the other texts which come to take the place of the circumstantial reality referred to by living speech. This relation of text to text, within the effacement of the world about which we speak, engenders the quasi-world of texts or *literature.*

Such is the upheaval which affects discourse itself, when the movement of reference towards the act of showing is intercepted by the text. Words cease to efface themselves in front of things; written words become words for themselves.

The eclipse of the circumstantial world by the quasi-world of texts can be so complete that, in a civilisation of writing, the world itself is no longer what can be shown in speaking but is reduced to a kind of 'aura' which written works unfold. Thus we speak of the Greek world or the Byzantine world. This world can be called 'imaginary', in the sense that it is *represented* by writing in lieu of the world *presented* by speech; but this imaginary world is itself a creation of literature.

The upheaval in the relation between the text and its world is the key to the other upheaval of which we have already spoken, that which affects the relation of the text to the subjectivities of the author and the reader. We think that we know what the author of a text is because we derive the notion of the author from that of the speaker. The subject of speech, according to Benveniste, is what designates itself in saying 'I'. When the text takes the place of speech, there is no longer a speaker, at least in the sense of an immediate and direct self-designation of the one who speaks in the instance of discourse. This proximity of the speaking subject to his own speech is replaced by a complex relation of the author to the text, a relation which enables us to say that the author is instituted by the text, that he stands in the space of meaning traced and inscribed by writing. The text is the very place where the author appears. But does the author appear otherwise than as first reader? The distancing of the text from its author is already a phenomenon of the first reading which, in one move, poses the whole series of problems that we are now going to confront concerning the relations between explanation and interpretation. These relations arise at the time of reading.

II. Explanation or understanding?

As we shall see, the two attitudes which we have initially placed under the double title of explanation and interpretation will confront one another in the act of reading. This duality is first encountered in the work of Dilthey. For him, these distinctions constituted an alternative wherein one term necessarily excluded the other: either you 'explain' in the manner of the natural scientist, or you 'interpret' in the manner of the historian. This exclusive alternative will provide the point of departure for the discussion which follows. I propose to show that the concept of the text, such as we have formulated it in the first part of this essay, demands a renewal of the two notions of explanation and interpretation and, in virtue of this renewal, a less contradictory conception of their interrelation. Let us say straightaway that the discussion will be deliberately oriented towards the search for a strict complementarity and reciprocity between explanation and interpretation.

The initial opposition in Dilthey's work is not exactly between explanation and interpretation, but between explanation and understanding, interpretation being a particular province of understanding. We must therefore begin from the opposition between explanation and understanding. Now if this opposition is exclusive, it is because, in Dilthey's work, the two terms designate two spheres of reality which they serve to separate. These two spheres are those of the natural sciences and the human sciences. Nature is the region of objects offered to scientific observation, a region subsumed since Galileo to the enterprise of mathematisation and since John Stuart Mill to the canons of inductive logic. Mind is the region of psychological individualities, into which each mental life is capable of transposing itself. Understanding is such a transference into another mental life. To ask whether the human sciences can exist is thus to ask whether a scientific knowledge of individuals is possible, whether this understanding of the singular can be objective in its own way, whether it is susceptible of universal validity. Dilthey answered affirmatively, because inner life is given in external signs which can be perceived and understood as signs of another mental life: 'Understanding', he says in the famous article on 'The development of hermeneutics', 'is the process by which we come to know something of mental life through the perceptible signs which manifest it.'[1] This is the understanding of which interpretation is a particular province. Among the signs of another mental life, we have the 'manifestations fixed in a durable way', the 'human testimonies preserved by writing', the 'written monuments'. Interpretation is the art of understanding applied to such manifestations, to such testimonies, to such monuments, of which writing is the distinctive characteristic. Understanding, as the knowledge through signs of another mental life, thus provides the basis in the pair understanding–interpretation; the latter element supplies the degree of objectification, in virtue of the fixation and preservation which writing confers upon signs.

Although this distinction between explanation and understanding seems clear at first, it becomes increasingly obscure as soon as we ask ourselves about the conditions of scientificity of interpretation. Explanation has been expelled from the field of the human sciences; but the conflict reappears at the very heart of the concept of interpretation between, on the one hand, the intuitive and unverifiable character of the psychologising concept of understanding to which interpretation is subordinated, and on the other hand the demand for objectivity which belongs to the very notion of human science. The splitting of hermeneutics between its psychologising tendency and its search for a logic of interpretation ultimately calls into question the relation between understanding and interpretation. Is not interpretation a species of understanding which explodes the genre? Is not the specific difference, namely fixation by writing, more important here than the feature common to all signs, that of presenting inner life in an external form? What is more important: the inclusion of hermeneutics in the sphere of understanding or its difference therefrom? Schleiermacher, before Dilthey, had witnessed this internal splitting of the hermeneutical project and had overcome it through a happy marriage of *romantic genius* and *philological virtuosity*. With Dilthey, the epistemological demands are more pressing. Several generations separate him from the scholar of Romanticism, several generations well versed in epistemological reflection; the contradiction now explodes in full daylight. Listen to Dilthey commenting upon Schleiermacher: 'The ultimate aim of hermeneutics is to understand the author better than he understands himself.' So much for the psychology of understanding. Now for the logic of interpretation: 'The function of hermeneutics is to establish theoretically, against the constant intrusion of romantic whim and sceptical subjectivism into the domain of history, the universal validity of interpretation, upon which all certitude in history rests.'[2] Thus hermeneutics fulfils the aim of understanding only by extricating itself from the immediacy of understanding others – from, let us say, dialogical values. Understanding seeks to coincide with the inner life of the author, to liken itself to him (*sich gleichsetzen*), to reproduce (*nachbilden*) the creative processes which engendered the work. But the signs of this intention, of this creation, are to be found nowhere else than in what Schleiermacher called the 'exterior' and 'interior form' of the work, or again, the 'interconnection' (*Zusammenhang*) which makes it an organised whole. The last writings of Dilthey ('The construction of the historical world in the human sciences') further aggravated the tension. On the one hand, the objective side of the work was accentuated under the influence of Husserl's *Logical Investigations* (for Husserl, as we know, the 'meaning' of a statement constitutes an 'ideality' which exists neither in mundane reality nor in psychic reality: it is a pure unity of meaning without a real localisation). Hermeneutics similarly proceeds from the objectification of the creative energies of life in works which come in between the author and us; it is mental life itself, its creative dynamism, which calls for the mediation by 'meanings', 'values' or 'goals'. The scientific demand thus presses towards an ever greater depsychologisation of interpretation, of understanding itself and perhaps even of introspection, if it is true that memory itself follows the thread of meanings which are not themselves mental phenomena. The exteriorisation of life implies a more indirect and mediate characterisation of the interpretation of self and others. But it is a self and another, posed in psychological terms, that interpretation pursues; interpretation always aims at a reproduction, a *Nachbildung*, of lived experiences.

This intolerable tension, which the later Dilthey bears witness to, leads us to raise two questions which guide the following discussion: Must we not abandon once and for all the reference of interpretation to understanding and cease to make the interpretation of written monuments a particular case of understanding the external signs of an inner mental life? But if interpretation no longer seeks its norm of intelligibility in understanding others, then does not its relation to explanation, which we have set aside hitherto, now demand to be reconsidered?

III. The text and structural explanation

Let us begin again from our analysis of the text and from the autonomous status which we have granted it with respect to speech. What we have called the eclipse of the surrounding world by the quasi-world of texts engenders two possibilities. We can, as readers, remain in the suspense of the text, treating it as a worldless and authorless object; in this case, we explain the text in terms of its internal relations, its structure. On the other hand, we can lift the suspense and fulfil the text in speech, restoring it to living communication; in this case, we interpret the text. These two possibilities both belong to reading, and reading is the dialectic of these two attitudes.

Let us consider them separately, before exploring their articulation.

We can undertake a first type of reading which formally records, as it were, the text's interception of all the relations to a world that can be pointed out and to subjectivities that can converse. This transference into the 'place' – a place which is a non-place – constitutes a special project with respect to the text, that of prolonging the suspense concerning the referential relation to the world and to the speaking subject. By means of this special project, the reader decides to situate himself in the 'place of the text' and in the 'closure' of this place. On the basis of this choice, the text has no outside but only an inside; it has no transcendent aim, unlike a speech which is addressed to someone about something.

This project is not only possible but legitimate. For the constitution of the text as text and of the body of texts as literature justifies the interception of the double transcendence of discourse, towards the world and towards someone. Thus arises the possibility of an explanatory attitude in regard to the text.

In contrast to what Dilthey thought, this explanatory attitude is not borrowed from a field of knowledge and an epistemological model other than that of language itself. It is not a naturalistic model subsequently extended to the human sciences. The nature–mind opposition plays no role here at all. If there is some form of borrowing, it occurs within the same field, that of signs. For it is possible to treat the text according to the explanatory rules that linguistics successfully applies to the simple system of signs which constitute language [*langue*] as opposed to speech [*parole*]. As is well known, the language–speech distinction is the fundamental distinction which gives linguistics an homogenous object; speech belongs to physiology, psychology and sociology, whereas language, as rules of the game of which speech is the execution, belongs only to linguistics. As is equally well known, linguistics considers only systems of units devoid of proper meaning, each of which is defined only in terms of its difference from all of the others. These units, whether they be purely distinctive like those of phonological articulation or significant like those of lexical articulation, are oppositive units. The interplay of oppositions and their combinations within an inventory of discrete units is what defines the notion of structure in linguistics. This structural model furnishes the type of explanatory attitude which we are now going to see applied to the text.

Even before embarking upon this enterprise, it may be objected that the laws which are valid only for language as distinct from speech could not be applied to the text. Although the text is not speech, is it not, as it were, on the same side as speech in relation to language? Must not discourse, as a series of statements and ultimately of sentences, be opposed in an overall way to language? In comparison to the language–discourse distinction, is not the speaking–writing distinction secondary, such that speaking and writing occur together on the side of discourse? These remarks are perfectly legitimate and justify us in thinking that the structural model of explanation does not exhaust the field of possible attitudes which may be adopted in regard to a text. But before specifying the limits of this explanatory model, it is necessary to grasp its fruitfulness. The working hypothesis of any structural analysis of texts is this: in spite of the fact that writing is on the same side as speech in relation to language – namely, on the side of discourse – the specificity of writing in relation to speech is based on structural features which can be treated as analogues of language in discourse. This working hypothesis is perfectly legitimate; it amounts to saying that under certain conditions the larger units of language [*langage*], that is, the units of a higher order than the sentence, display organisations comparable to those of the smaller units of language, that is, the units which are of a lower order than the sentence and which belong to the domain of linguistics.

In *Structural Anthropology*, Claude Lévi-Strauss formulates this working hypothesis for one category of texts, the category of myths:

> Like every linguistic entity, myth is made up of constitutive units. These units imply the presence of those which normally enter into the structure of language, namely the phonemes, the morphemes and the semantemes. The constituent units of myth are in the same relation to semantemes as the latter are to morphemes, and as the latter in turn are to phonemes. Each form differs from that which precedes it by a higher degree of complexity. For this reason, we shall call the elements which properly pertain to myth (and which are the most complex of all): large constitutive units.[3]

By means of this working hypothesis, the large units which are minimally the size of the sentence, and which placed together constitute the narrative proper to the myth, can be treated according to the same rules that are applied to the smaller units familiar to linguistics. To indicate this analogy, Lévi-Strauss speaks of 'mythemes' in the same way that one speaks of phonemes, morphemes and semantemes. But in order to remain within the limits of the analogy between mythemes and the linguistic units of a lower level, the analysis of texts will have to proceed to the same sort of abstraction as that practised by the phonologist. For the latter, the phoneme is not a concrete sound, to be taken absolutely in its sonorous substance; it is a function defined by the commutative method and its oppositive value is determined by the relation to all other phonemes. In this sense it is not, as Saussure would say, a 'substance' but a 'form', an interplay of relations. Similarly, a mytheme is not one of the sentences of the myth but an oppositive value which is shared by several particular sentences, constituting, in the language of Lévi-Strauss, a 'bundle of relations'. 'Only in the form of combinations of such bundles do the constituent units acquire a signifying function.'[4] What is called here the 'signifying function' is not at all what the myth means, its philosophical or existential import, but rather the arrangement or disposition of mythemes, in short, the structure of the myth.

I should like to recall briefly the analysis which, according to this method, Lévi-Strauss offers of the Oedipus myth. He divides the sentences of the myth into four columns. In the first column he places all the sentences which speak of overrated blood relations (for example, Oedipus marries Jocasta, his mother; Antigone buries Polynices, her brother, in spite of the order forbidding it). In the second column, we find the same relation, but modified by the inverse sign: underrated or devalued blood relations (Oedipus kills his father, Laios; Eteocles kills his brother, Polynices). The third column concerns monsters and their destruction; the fourth groups together all those proper names whose meaning suggests a difficulty in walking straight (lame, clumsy, swollen foot). The comparison of the four columns reveals a correlation. Between the first and second columns we have blood relations overrated or underrated in turn; between the third and fourth we have an affirmation and then a negation of the autochtony of man. 'It follows that the fourth column is related to the third column as the first is to the second . . . ; the overrating of blood relations is to their underrating as the attempt to escape from autochtony is to the impossibility of succeeding in it.' The myth thus appears as a kind of logical instrument which brings together contradictions in order to overcome them: 'the impossibility of connecting the groups of relations is overcome (or, more exactly, replaced) by the assertion that two contradictory relations are identical, insofar as each is, like the other, self-contradictory'.[5] We shall return shortly to this conclusion; let us restrict ourselves here to stating it.

We can indeed say that we have thereby explained the myth, but not that we have interpreted it. We have brought out, by means of structural analysis, the logic of the operations which interconnect the packets of relations; this logic constitutes 'the structural law of the myth concerned'.[6] We shall not fail to notice that this law is, *par excellence,* the object of reading and not at all of speech, in the sense of a recitation whereby the power of the myth would be reactivated in a particular situation. Here the text is only a text and the reading inhabits it only as such, while its meaning for us remains in suspense, together with any realisation in present speech.

I have just taken an example from the domain of myths; I could take another from a nearby domain, that of folklore. This domain has been explored by the Russian formalists of the school of Propp and by the French specialists in the structural analysis of narratives, Roland Barthes and A.J. Greimas. In the work of these authors, we find the same postulates as those employed by Lévi-Strauss: the units above the sentence have the same composition as the units below the sentence; the sense of the narrative consists in the very arrangement of the elements, in the power of the whole to integrate the sub-units; and conversely, the sense of an element is its capacity to enter in relation with other elements and with the whole of the work. These postulates together define the closure of the narrative. The task of structural analysis will be to carry out the segmentation of the work (horizontal aspect), then to establish the various levels of integration of the parts in the whole (hierarchical aspect). Thus the units of action isolated by the analyst will not be psychological units capable of being experienced, nor will they be units of behaviour which could be subsumed to a behaviourist psychology. The extremities of these sequences are only the switching points of the narrative, such that if one element is changed, all the rest is different. Here we recognise the transposition of the method of commutation from the phonological level to the level of narrative units. The logic of action thus consists in an interconnected series of action kernels which together constitute the structural continuity of the narrative. The application of this technique ends up by 'dechronologising' the narrative, in a way that brings out the logic underlying narrative time. Ultimately the narrative would be reduced to a combination [combinatoire] of a few dramatic units (promising, betraying, hindering, aiding, etc.) which would be the paradigms of action. A sequence is thus a succession of nodes of action, each closing off an alternative opened up by the preceding one. Just as the elementary units are linked together, so too they fit into larger units; for example, an encounter is comprised of elementary actions like approaching, calling out, greeting, etc. To explain a narrative is to grasp this entanglement, this fleeting structure of interlaced actions.

Corresponding to the nexus of actions are relations of a similar nature between the 'actants' of the narrative. By that we understand, not at all the characters as psychological subjects endowed with their own existence, but rather the roles correlated with formalised actions. Actants are defined entirely by the predicates of action, by the semantic axes of the sentence and the narrative: the actant is the one by whom, to whom, with whom, . . . the action is done; it is the one who promises, who receives the promise, the giver, the receiver, etc. Structural analysis thus brings out a hierarchy of *actants* correlative to the hierarchy of *actions*.

The narrative remains to be assembled as a whole and put back into narrative communication. It is then a discourse which a narrator addresses to an audience. For structural analysis, however, the two interlocutors must be sought only in the text. The narrator is designated by the signs of narrativity, which belong to the very constitution of the narrative. Beyond the three levels of actions, actants and narration, there is nothing else that falls within the scope of the science of semiology. There is only the world of narrative users, which can eventually be dealt with by other semiological disciplines (those analysing social, economic and ideological systems); but these disciplines are no longer linguistic in nature. This transposition of a linguistic model to the theory of the narrative fully confirms our initial remark: today, explanation is no longer a concept borrowed from the natural sciences and transferred to the alien domain of written artefacts; rather, it stems from the very sphere of language, by analogical transference from the small units of language (phonemes and lexemes) to the units larger than the sentence, such as narratives, folklore and myth. Henceforth, interpretation – if it is still possible to give a sense to this notion – will no longer be confronted by a model external to the human sciences. It will, instead, be confronted by a model of intelligibility which belongs, from birth so to speak, to the domain of the human sciences, and indeed to a leading science in this domain: linguistics. Thus it will be upon the same terrain, within the same sphere of language [*langage*], that explanation and interpretation will enter into debate.

IV. Towards a new concept of interpretation

Let us consider now the other attitude that can be adopted in regard to the text, the attitude which we have called interpretation. We can introduce this attitude by initially opposing it to the preceding one, in a manner still close to that of Dilthey. But as we shall see, it will be necessary to proceed gradually to a more complementary and reciprocal relation between explanation and interpretation.

Let us begin once again from reading. Two ways of reading, we said, are offered to us. By reading we can prolong and reinforce the suspense which affects the text's reference to a surrounding world and to the audience of speaking subjects: that is the explanatory attitude. But we can also lift the suspense and fulfil the text in present speech. It is this second attitude which is the real aim of reading. For this attitude reveals the true nature of the suspense which intercepts the movement of the text towards meaning. The other attitude would not even be possible if it were not first apparent that the text, as writing, awaits and calls for a reading. If reading is possible, it is indeed because the text is not closed in on itself but opens out onto other things. To read is, on any hypothesis, to conjoin a new discourse to the discourse of the text. This conjunction of discourses reveals, in the very constitution of the text, an original capacity for renewal which is its open character. Interpretation is the concrete outcome of conjunction and renewal.

In the first instance, we shall be led to formulate the concept of interpretation in opposition to that of explanation. This will not distance us appreciably from Dilthey's position, except that the opposing concept of explanation has already gained strength by being derived from linguistics and semiology rather than being borrowed from the natural sciences.

According to this first sense, interpretation retains the feature of appropriation which was recognised by Schleiermacher, Dilthey and Bultmann. In fact, this sense will not be abandoned; it will only be mediated by explanation, instead of being opposed to it in an immediate and even naive way. By 'appropriation', I understand this: that the interpretation of a text culminates in the self-interpretation of a subject who thenceforth understands himself better, understands himself differently, or simply begins to understand himself. This culmination of the understanding of a text in self-understanding is characteristic of the kind of reflective philosophy which, on various occasions, I have called 'concrete reflection'. Here hermeneutics and reflective philosophy are correlative and reciprocal. On the one hand, self-understanding passes through the detour of understanding the cultural signs in which the self documents and forms itself. On the other hand, understanding the text is not an end in itself; it mediates the relation to himself of a subject who, in the short circuit of immediate reflection, does not find the meaning of his own life. Thus it must be said, with equal force, that reflection is nothing without the mediation of signs and works, and that explanation is nothing if it is not incorporated as an intermediary stage in the process of self-understanding. In short, in hermeneutical reflection – or in reflective hermeneutics – the constitution of the *self* is contemporaneous with the constitution of *meaning*.

The term 'appropriation' underlines two additional features. One of the aims of all hermeneutics is to struggle against cultural distance. This struggle can be understood in purely temporal terms as a struggle against secular estrangement, or in more genuinely hermeneutical terms as a struggle against the estrangement from meaning itself, that is, from the system of values upon which the text is based. In this sense, interpretation 'brings together', 'equalises', renders 'contemporary and similar', thus genuinely making one's *own* what was initially *alien*.

Above all, the characterisation of interpretation as appropriation is meant to underline the 'present' character of interpretation. Reading is like the execution of a musical score; it marks the realisation, the enactment, of the semantic possibilities of the text. This final feature is the most important because it is the condition of the other two (that is, of overcoming cultural distance and of fusing textual interpretation with self-interpretation). Indeed, the feature of realisation discloses a decisive aspect of reading, namely that it fulfils the discourse of the text in a dimension similar to that of speech. What is retained here from the notion of speech is not the fact that it is uttered but that it is an event, an instance of discourse, as Benveniste says. The sentences of a text signify *here and now*. The 'actualised' text finds a surrounding and an audience; it resumes the referential movement – intercepted and suspended – towards a world and towards subjects. This world is that of the reader, this subject is the reader himself. In interpretation, we shall say, reading becomes like speech. I do not say 'becomes speech', for reading is never equivalent to a spoken exchange, a dialogue. But reading culminates in a concrete act which is related to the text as speech is related to discourse, namely as event and instance of discourse. Initially the text had only a sense, that is, internal relations or a structure; now it has a meaning, that is, a realisation in the discourse of the reading subject. By virtue of its sense, the text had only a semiological dimension; now it has, by virtue of its meaning, a semantic dimension.

Let us pause here. Our discussion has reached a critical point where interpretation, understood as appropriation, still remains external to explanation in the sense of structural analysis. We continue to oppose them as if they were two attitudes between which it is necessary to choose. I should like now to go beyond this antithetical opposition and to bring out the articulation which would render structural analysis and hermeneutics complementary. For this it is important to show how each of the two attitudes which we have juxtaposed refers back, by means of its own peculiar features, to the other.

Consider again the examples of structural analysis which we have borrowed from the theory of myth and narrative. We tried to adhere to a notion of sense which would be strictly equivalent to the arrangement of the elements of a text, to the integration of the segments of action and the actants within the narrative treated as a whole closed in upon itself. In fact, no one stops at so formal a conception of sense. For example, what Lévi-Strauss calls a 'mytheme' – in his eyes, the constitutive unit of myth – is expressed in a sentence which has a specific meaning: Oedipus kills his father, Oedipus marries his mother, etc. Can it be said that structural explanation neutralises the specific meaning of sentences, retaining only their position in the myth? But the bundle of relations to which Lévi-Strauss reduces the mytheme is still of the order of the sentence; and the interplay of oppositions which is instituted at this very abstract level is equally of the order of the sentence and of meaning. If one speaks of 'overrated' or 'underrated blood relations', of the 'autochtony' or 'non-autochtony' of man, these relations can still be written in the form of a sentence: the blood relation is the highest of all, or the blood relation is not as high as the social relation, for example in the prohibition of incest, etc. Finally, the contradiction which the myth attempts to resolve, according to Lévi-Strauss, is itself stated in terms of meaningful relations. Lévi-Strauss admits this, in spite of himself, when he writes: 'The reason for these choices becomes clear if we recognise that mythical thought proceeds from the consciousness of certain oppositions and tends towards their progressive mediation';[7] and again, 'the myth is a kind of logical tool intended to effect a mediation between life and death'.[8] In the background of the myth there is a question which is highly significant, a question about life and death: 'Are we born from one or from two?' Even in its formalised version, 'Is the same born from the same or from the other?', this question expresses the anguish of origins: whence comes man? Is he born from the earth or from his parents? There would be no contradiction, nor any attempt to resolve contradiction, if there were not significant questions, meaningful propositions about the origin and the end of man. It is this function of myth as a narrative of origins that structural analysis seeks to place in parentheses. But such analysis does not succeed in eluding this function: it merely postpones it. Myth is not a logical operator between any propositions whatsoever, but involves propositions which point towards limit situations, towards the origin and the end, towards death, suffering and sexuality.

Far from dissolving this radical questioning, structural analysis reinstates it at a more radical level. Would not the function of structural analysis then be to impugn the surface semantics of the recounted myth in order to unveil a depth semantics which is, if I may say so, the living semantics of the myth? If that were not the function of structural analysis, then it would, in my opinion, be reduced to a sterile game, to a derisory combination [*combinatoire*] of elements, and myth would be deprived of the function which Lévi-Strauss himself recognises when he asserts that mythical thought arises from the awareness of certain oppositions and tends towards their progressive mediation. This awareness is a recognition of the *aporias* of human existence around which mythical thought gravitates. To eliminate this meaningful intention would be to reduce the theory of myth to a necrology of the meaningless discourses of mankind. If, on the contrary, we regard structural analysis as a stage – and a necessary one – between a naive and a critical interpretation, between a surface and a depth interpretation, then it seems possible to situate explanation and interpretation along a unique *hermeneutical arc* and to integrate the opposed attitudes of explanation and understanding within an overall conception of reading as the recovery of meaning.

We shall take another step in the direction of this reconciliation between explanation and interpretation if we now turn towards the second term of the initial contradiction. So far we have worked with a concept of interpretation which remains very subjective. To interpret, we said, is to appropriate *here and now* the intention of the text. In saying that, we remain enclosed within Dilthey's concept of understanding. Now what we have just said about the depth semantics unveiled by the structural analysis of the text invites us to say that the intended meaning of the text is not essentially the presumed intention of the author, the lived experience of the writer, but rather what the text means for whoever complies with its injunction. The text seeks to place us in its meaning, that is – according to another acceptation of the word *sens* – in the same direction. So if the intention is that of the text, and if this intention is the direction which it opens up for thought, then depth semantics must be understood in a fundamentally dynamic way. I shall therefore say: to explain is to bring out the structure, that is, the internal relations of dependence which constitute the statics of the text; to interpret is to follow the path of thought opened up by the text, to place oneself *en route* towards the *orient* of the text. We are invited by this remark to correct our initial concept of interpretation and to search – beyond a subjective process of interpretation as an act *on* the text – for an objective process of interpretation which would be the act *of* the text.

I shall borrow an example from a recent study which I made of the exegesis of the sacerdotal story of creation in Genesis 1–2, 4a.[9] This exegesis reveals, in the interior of the text, the interplay of two narratives: a *Tatbericht* in which creation is expressed as a narrative of action ('God made . . .'), and a *Wortbericht*, that is, a narrative of speech ('God said, and there was . . .'). The first narrative could be said to play the role of tradition and the second of interpretation. What is interesting here is that interpretation, before being the act of the exegete, is the act of the text. The relation between tradition and interpretation is a relation internal to the text; for the exegete, to interpret is to place himself in the meaning indicated by the relation of interpretation which the text itself supports.

This objective and, as it were, intra-textual concept of interpretation is by no means unusual. Indeed, it has a long history rivalling that of the concept of subjective interpretation which is linked, it will be recalled, to the problem of understanding others through the signs that others give of their conscious life. I would willingly connect this new concept of interpretation to that referred to in the title of Aristotle's treatise *On Interpretation*. Aristotle's *hermenetia*, in contrast to the hermeneutical technique of seers and oracles, is the very action of language on things. Interpretation, for Aristotle, is not what one does in a second language with regard to a first; rather, it is what the first language already does, by mediating through signs our relation to things. Hence interpretation is, according to the commentary of Boethius, the work of the *vox significativa per se ipsam aliquid significans, sive complexa, sive incomplexa*. Thus it is the noun, the verb, discourse in general, which interprets in the very process of signifying.

It is true that interpretation in Aristotle's sense does not exactly prepare the way for understanding the dynamic relation between several layers of meaning in the same text. For it presupposes a theory of speech and not a theory of the text: 'The sounds articulated by the voice are symbols of states of the soul, and written words are symbols of words uttered in speech' (*On Interpretation*, para. 1). Hence interpretation is confused with the semantic dimension of speech: interpretation is discourse itself, it is any discourse. Nevertheless, I retain from Aristotle the idea that interpretation is interpretation *by* language before being interpretation *of* language.

I would look in the work of Charles Sanders Peirce for a concept of interpretation which is closer to that required by an exegesis which relates interpretation to tradition in the very interior of a text. According to Peirce, the relation of a 'sign' to an 'object' is such that another relation, that between 'interpretant' and 'sign', can be grafted onto the first. What is important for us is that this relation between interpretant and sign is an open relation, in the sense that there is always another interpretant capable of mediating the first relation. G.-G. Granger explains this very well in his *Essai d'une philosophie du style:*

The interpretant which the sign evokes in the mind could not be the result of a pure and simple deduction which would extract from the sign something already contained therein . . . The interpretant is a commentary, a definition, a gloss on the sign in its relation to the object. The interpretant is itself symbolic expression. The sign–interpretant association, realised by whatever psychological processes, is rendered possible only by the community, more or less imperfect, of an experience between speaker and hearer . . . It is always an experience which can never be perfectly reduced to the idea or object of the sign of which, as we said, it is the structure. Whence the indefinite character of Peirce's series of interpretants.[10]

We must, of course, exercise a great deal of care in applying Peirce's concept of interpretant to the interpretation of texts. His interpretant is an interpretant of signs, whereas our interpretant is an interpretant of statements. But our use of the interpretant, transposed from small to large units, is neither more nor less analogical than the structuralist transfer of the laws of organisation from units of levels below the sentence to units of an order above or equal to the sentence. In the case of structuralism, it is the phonological structure of language which serves as the coding model of structures of higher articulation. In our case, it is a feature of lexical units which is transposed onto the plane of statements and texts. So if we are perfectly aware of the analogical character of the transposition, then we can say that the open series of interpretants, which is grafted onto the relation of a sign to an object, brings to light a triangular relation of object–sign–interpretant; and that the latter relation can serve as a model for another triangle which is constituted at the level of the text. In the new triangle, the object is the text itself; the sign is the depth semantics disclosed by structural analysis; and the series of interpretants is the chain of interpretations produced by the interpreting community and incorporated into the dynamics of the text, as the work of meaning upon itself. Within this chain, the first interpretants serve as tradition for the final interpretants, which are the interpretation in the true sense of the term.

Thus informed by the Aristotelian concept of interpretation and above all by Peirce's concept, we are in a position to 'depsychologise' as far as possible our notion of interpretation, and to connect it with the process which is at work in the text. Henceforth, for the exegete, to interpret is to place himself within the sense indicated by the relation of interpretation supported by the text.

The idea of interpretation as appropriation is not, for all that, eliminated; it is simply postponed until the termination of the process. It lies at the extremity of what we called above the *hermeneutical arc*: it is the final brace of the bridge, the anchorage of the arch in the ground of lived experience. But the entire theory of hermeneutics consists in mediating this interpretation-appropriation by the series of interpretants which belong to the work of the text upon itself. Appropriation loses its arbitrariness insofar as it is the recovery of that which is at work, in labour, within the text. What the interpreter says is a re-saying which reactivates what is said by the text.

At the end of our investigation, it seems that reading is the concrete act in which the destiny of the text is fulfilled. It is at the very heart of reading that explanation and interpretation are indefinitely opposed and reconciled.

6. Metaphor and the central problem of hermeneutics

It will be assumed here that the central problem of hermeneutics is that of interpretation. Not interpretation in any sense of the word, but interpretation determined in two ways: the first concerning its field of application, the second its epistemological specificity. As regards the first point, I shall say that there is a problem of interpretation because there are texts, written texts, the autonomy of which creates specific difficulties. By 'autonomy' I understand the independence of the text with respect to the intention of the author, the situation of the work and the original reader. The relevant problems are resolved in oral discourse by the kind of exchange or intercourse which we call dialogue or conversation. With written texts, discourse must speak by itself. Let us say, therefore, that there are problems of interpretation because the writing–reading relation is not a particular case of the speaking–hearing relation which we experience in the dialogical situation. Such is the most general feature of interpretation as regards its field of application.

Second, the concept of interpretation seems, at the epistemological level, to be opposed to the concept of explanation. Taken together, these concepts form a contrasting pair which has given rise to a great many disputes since the time of Schleiermacher and Dilthey. According to the tradition to which the latter authors belong, interpretation has certain subjective connotations, such as the implication of the reader in the processes of understanding and the reciprocity between interpretation of the text and self-interpretation. This reciprocity is known by the name of the hermeneutical circle; it entails a sharp opposition to the sort of objectivity and non-implication which is supposed to characterise the scientific explanation of things. Later I shall say to what extent we may be able to amend, indeed to reconstruct on a new basis, the opposition between interpretation and explanation. Whatever the outcome of the subsequent discussion may be, this schematic description of the concept of interpretation suffices for a provisional circumscription of the central problem of hermeneutics: the status of written texts *versus* spoken language, the status of interpretation *versus* explanation.

Now for the metaphor! The aim of this essay is to link up the problems raised in hermeneutics by the interpretation of texts and the problems raised in rhetoric, semantics, stylistics – or whatever the discipline concerned may be – by metaphor.

I. The text and metaphor as discourse

Our first task will be to find a common ground for the theory of the text and the theory of metaphor. This common ground has already received a name – discourse; it has yet to be given a status.

One thing is striking: the two sorts of entities that we are considering are of different lengths. In this respect, they can be compared to the sentence, which is the basic unit of discourse. A text can undoubtedly be reduced to a single sentence, as in proverbs or aphorisms; but texts have a maximum length which can extend from a paragraph to a chapter, a book, a collection of 'selected works' or even the corpus of the 'complete works' of an author. Let us use the term 'work' to describe the closed sequence of discourse which can be considered as a text. Whereas texts can be identified on the basis of their maximal length, metaphors can be identified on the basis of their minimal length, that of the word. Even if the rest of this discussion seeks to show that there is no metaphor – in the sense of a word taken metaphorically – in the absence of certain contexts, and consequently even if we are constrained by what follows to replace the notion of metaphor by that of the metaphorical statement which implies at least the length of the sentence, nevertheless the 'metaphorical twist' (to speak like Monroe Beardsley) is something which happens to the word. The change of meaning, which requires the full contribution of the context, affects the word. We can describe the word as having a 'metaphorical use' or a 'non-literal meaning'; the word is always the bearer of the 'emergent meaning' which specific contexts confer upon it. In this sense, Aristotle's definition of metaphor as the transposition of an unusual name (or word) is not invalidated by a theory emphasising the contextual action which creates the shift of meaning in the word. The word remains the 'focus', even if the focus requires the 'frame' of the sentence, to use the vocabulary of Max Black.

This first, altogether formal remark concerning the difference in length between the text and the metaphor, or better between the *work* and the *word*, is going to help us to elaborate our initial problem in a more precise way: to what extent can we treat the metaphor as a *work in miniature?* The answer to this question will then help us to pose the second: to what extent can the hermeneutical problems raised by the interpretation of texts be considered as a large-scale extension of the problems condensed in the explanation of a local metaphor in a given text?

Is a metaphor a work in miniature? Can a work, say a poem, be considered as a sustained or extended metaphor? The answer to this first question requires a prior elaboration of the general properties of discourse, if it is true that text and metaphor, work and word, fall within the same category of discourse. I shall not elaborate in detail the concept of discourse, restricting my analysis to the features which are necessary for the comparison between text and metaphor. It is remarkable that all of these features present themselves in the form of paradoxes, that is, apparent contradictions.

To begin with, all discourse is produced as an event; as such, it is the counterpart of language understood as code or system. Discourse *qua* event has a fleeting existence: it appears and disappears. But at the same time – and herein lies the paradox – it can be identified and re-identified as the same. This 'sameness' is what we call, in a broad sense, its meaning. All discourse, we shall say, is realised as event but understood as meaning. Soon we shall see in what sense the metaphor concentrates this double character of event and meaning.

The second pair of contrasting features stems from the fact that meaning is supported by a specific structure, that of the proposition, which envelops an internal opposition between a pole of singular identification (this man, this table, Monsieur Dupont, Paris) and a pole of general predication (humanity as a class, brightness as a property, equality as a relation, running as an action). Metaphor, we shall also see, rests upon this 'attribution' of characteristics to the 'principal subject' of a sentence.

The third pair of opposing features is the polarity, which discourse primarily in sentential form implies, between sense and reference. That is, discourse implies the possibility of distinguishing between *what* is said by the sentence as a whole and by the words which compose it on the one hand, and *that about which* something is said on the other. To speak is to say something about something. This polarity will play a decisive role in the second and third parts of this essay, where I shall try to connect the problem of explanation to the dimension of 'sense' or the immanent pattern of discourse, and the problems of interpretation to the dimension of 'reference', understood as the power of discourse to apply itself to an extra-linguistic reality about which it says what it says.

Fourth, discourse as an act can be considered from the viewpoint of the 'contents' of the propositional act (it predicates a certain characteristic of a certain subject), or from the viewpoint of what Austin called the 'force' of the complete act of discourse (the *speech-act* in his terminology). What is said of the subject is one thing; what I 'do' *in* saying it is another: I can make a mere description, or give an order, or formulate a wish, or give a warning, etc. Hence the polarity between the locutionary act (the act *of* saying) and the illocutionary act (what I do *in* saying). This polarity may seem less useful than the preceding ones, at least at the structural level of the metaphorical statement. Nevertheless, it will play a decisive role when we have to place the metaphor back in the concrete setting of, for example, a poem, an essay, or a work of fiction.

Before developing the dichotomy of sense and reference as the basis of the opposition between explanation and interpretation, let us introduce a final polarity which will play a decisive role in hermeneutical theory. Discourse has not merely one sort of reference but two: it is related to an extralinguistic reality, to the world or a world; and it refers equally to its own speaker, by means of specific procedures which function only in the sentence and hence in discourse – personal pronouns, verbal tenses, demonstratives, etc. In this way, language has both a reference to reality and a self-reference. It is the same entity – the sentence – which supports this double reference: intentional and reflexive, turned towards the thing and towards the self. In fact, we should speak of a triple reference, for discourse refers as much to the one to whom it is addressed as to its own speaker. The structure of personal pronouns similarly designates, as Benveniste taught, the triple reference: 'it' designates the reference to the thing, 'you' the reference to the one to whom the discourse is addressed, and 'I' the reference to the one who speaks. As we shall see later, this connection between the two and even the three directions of reference will provide us with the key to the hermeneutical circle and the basis for our reinterpretation of this circle.

I shall list the basic polarities of discourse in the following condensed fashion: event and meaning, singular identification and general predication, propositional act and illocutionary act, sense and reference, reference to reality and reference to interlocutors. In what sense can we now say that the text and metaphor both rest upon the sort of entity which we have just called discourse?

It is easy to show that all texts are discourses, since they stem from the smallest unit of discourse, the sentence. A text is at least a series of sentences. We shall see that it must be something more in order to be a work; but it is at least a set of sentences, and consequently a discourse. The connection between metaphor and discourse requires a special justification, precisely because the definition of metaphor as a transposition affecting names or words seems to place it in a category of entities smaller than the sentence. But the semantics of the word demonstrates very clearly that words acquire an actual meaning only in a sentence and that lexical entities – the words of the dictionary – have merely potential meanings in virtue of their potential uses in typical contexts. In this respect, the theory of polysemy is a good preparation for the theory of metaphor. At the lexical level, words (if indeed they can already be called that) have more than one meaning; it is only by a specific contextual action of sifting that they realise, in a given sentence, a part of their potential semantics and acquire what we call a determinate meaning. The contextual action which enables univocal discourse to be produced with polysemic words is the model for that other contextual action whereby we draw genuinely novel metaphorical effects from words whose meaning is already codified in the vocabulary. We are thus prepared to allow that even if the meaningful effect which we call metaphor is inscribed in the word, nevertheless the origin of this effect lies in a contextual action which places the semantic fields of several words in interaction.

As regards the metaphor itself, semantics shows with the same force that the metaphorical meaning of a word is nothing which can be found in the dictionary. In this sense, we can continue to oppose metaphorical meaning to literal meaning, if by the latter we understand *any* of the meanings that can be found among the partial meanings codified by the vocabulary. By literal meaning, therefore, we do not understand the supposedly original, fundamental, primitive or proper meaning of a word on the lexical plane; rather, literal meaning is the totality of the semantic field, the set of possible contextual uses which constitutes the polysemy of a word. So even if metaphorical meaning is something more and other than the actualisation of one of the possible meanings of a polysemic word (and all of the words in natural languages are polysemic), nevertheless this metaphorical use must be solely contextual, that is, a meaning which emerges as the unique and fleeting result of a certain contextual action. We are thus led to oppose contextual changes of meaning to the lexical changes which concern the diachronic aspect of language as code or system. Metaphor is one such contextual change of meaning.

In this respect, I am partially in agreement with the modern theory of metaphor, as elaborated in English by I.A. Richards, Max Black, Monroe Beardsley, Douglas Berggren, etc.[1] More precisely, I agree with these authors on the fundamental point: a word receives a metaphorical meaning in specific contexts, within which it is opposed to other words taken literally. The shift in meaning results primarily from a clash between literal meanings, which excludes the literal use of the word in question and provides clues for finding a new meaning capable of according with the context of the sentence and rendering the sentence meaningful therein. Consequently, I retain the following points from this recent history of the problem of metaphor: the replacement of the rhetorical theory of substitution by a properly semantic theory of the interaction between semantic fields; the decisive role of semantic clash leading to logical absurdity; the issuance of a particle of meaning which renders the sentence as a whole meaningful. We shall now see how this properly semantic theory – or the interaction theory – satisfies the principal characteristics which we have recognised in discourse.

To begin with, let us return to the contrast between event and meaning. In the metaphorical statement (we shall speak of metaphor as a sentence and no longer as a word), contextual action creates a new meaning which is indeed an event, since it exists only in this particular context; but at the same time, it can be repeated and hence identified as the same. Thus the innovation of an 'emergent meaning' (Beardsley) may be regarded as a linguistic creation; but if it is adopted by an influential part of the language community, it may become an everyday meaning and add to the polysemy of léxical entities, contributing thereby to the history of language as code or system. At this final stage, when the meaningful effect that we call metaphor has rejoined the change of meaning which augments polysemy, the metaphor is no longer living but dead. Only authentic, living metaphors are at the same time 'event' and 'meaning'.

Contextual action similarly requires our second polarity, that between singular identification and general predication. A metaphor is said of a 'principal subject'; as 'modifier' of this subject, it works like a kind of 'attribution'. All of the theories to which I have referred above rest upon this predicative structure, whether they oppose 'vehicle' to 'tenor' (Richards), 'frame' to 'focus' (Max Black), or 'modifier' to 'principal subject' (Beardsley).

To show that metaphor requires the polarity between sense and reference, we shall need a whole section of this essay; the same thing must be said of the polarity between reference to reality and reference to self. Later it will become clear why, at this stage, I am not in a position to say more about these polarities. We shall require the mediation of the theory of the text in order to discern the oppositions which do not appear so clearly within the narrow limits of a simple metaphorical statement.

Having thus delimited the field of comparison, we are ready to reply to the second question: to what extent can the explanation and interpretation of texts on the one hand, and the explanation and interpretation of metaphors on the other, be regarded as similar processes which are merely applied to two different strategic levels of discourse, the level of the work and that of the word?

II. From metaphor to the text: explanation

I propose to explore a working hypothesis which, to begin with, I shall simply state. From one point of view, the understanding of metaphor can serve as a guide to the understanding of longer texts, such as a literary work. This point of view is that of explanation; it concerns only that aspect of meaning which we have called the 'sense', that is, the immanent pattern of discourse. From another point of view, the understanding of a work taken as a whole gives the key to metaphor. This other point of view is that of interpretation proper; it develops the aspect of meaning which we have called 'reference', that is, the intentional orientation towards a world and the reflexive orientation towards a self. So if we apply explanation to 'sense', as the immanent pattern of the work, then we can reserve interpretation for the sort of inquiry concerned with the *power of a work* to project a world of its own and to set in motion the hermeneutical circle, which encompasses in its spiral both the apprehension of projected worlds and the advance of self-understanding in the presence of these new worlds. Our working hypothesis thus invites us to proceed from metaphor to text at the level of 'sense' and the explanation of 'sense', then from text to metaphor at the level of the reference of a work to a world and to a self, that is, at the level of interpretation proper.

What aspects of the explanation of metaphor can serve as a paradigm for the explanation of a text? These aspects are features of the explanatory process which could not appear so long as trivial examples of metaphor were considered, such as man is a wolf, a fox, a lion (if we read the best authors on metaphor, we observe interesting variations within the bestiary which provides them with examples!). With these examples, we elude the major difficulty, that of *identifying a meaning* which is *new*. The only way of achieving this identification is to construct a meaning which alone enables us to make sense of the sentence as a whole. For what do trivial metaphors rest upon? Max Black and Monroe Beardsley note that the meaning of a word does not depend merely on the semantic and syntactic rules which govern its literal use, but also on other rules (which are nevertheless rules) to which the members of a language community are 'committed' and which determine what Black calls the 'system of associated commonplaces' and Beardsley the 'potential range of connotations'. In the statement, 'man is a wolf' (the example favoured by Black!), the principal subject is qualified by one of the features of animal life which belongs to 'the lupine system of associated commonplaces'. The system of implications operates like a filter or screen; it does not merely select, but also accentuates new aspects of the principal subject.

What are we to think of this explanation in relation to our description of metaphor as a new meaning appearing in a new context? As I said above, I entirely agree with the 'interaction view' implied by this explanation; metaphor is more than a simple substitution whereby one word would replace a literal word, which an exhaustive paraphrase could restore to the same place. The algebraic sum of these two operations – substitution by the speaker and restoration by the author or reader – is equal to zero. No new meaning emerges and we learn nothing. As Black says, ' "interaction-metaphors" are not expendable . . . This use of a "subsidiary subject" to foster insight into a "principal subject" is a distinctive intellectual operation.' Hence interaction metaphors cannot be translated into direct language without 'a loss in cognitive content'.[2]

Although this account describes very well the meaningful effect of metaphor, we must ask whether, by simply adding the 'system of associated commonplaces' and cultural rules to the semantic polysemy of the word and semantic rules, this account does justice to the power of metaphor 'to inform and enlighten'. Is not the 'system of associated commonplaces' something dead or at least something already established? Of course, this system must intervene in some way or another, in order that contextual action may be regulated and that the construction of new meaning may obey some prescription. Black's theory reserves the possibility that 'metaphors can be supported by specially constructed systems of implications, as well as by accepted common-places'.[3] The problem is precisely that of these 'specially constructed systems of implications'. We must therefore pursue our investigation into the process of interaction itself, if we are to explain the case of new metaphors in new contexts.

Beardsley's theory of metaphor leads us a stage further in this direction. If, following him, we emphasise the role of logical absurdity or the clash between literal meanings within the same context, then we are ready to recognise the genuinely creative character of metaphorical meaning: 'In poetry, the principal tactic for obtaining this result is logical absurdity.'[4] Logical absurdity creates a situation in which we have the choice of either preserving the literal meaning of the subject and the modifier and hence concluding that the entire sentence is absurd, or attributing a new meaning to the modifier so that the sentence as a whole makes sense. We are now faced not only with 'self-contradictory' attribution, but with a 'meaningful self-contradictory' attribution. If I say 'man is a fox' (the fox has chased away the wolf!), I must slide from a literal to a metaphorical attribution if I want to save the sentence. But from where do we draw this new meaning?

As long as we ask this type of question – 'from where do we draw . . . ?' – we return to the same type of ineffectual answer. The 'potential range of connotations' says nothing more than the 'system of associated commonplaces'. Of course, we expand the notion of meaning by including 'secondary meanings', as connotations, within the perimeter of full meaning; but we continue to bind the creative process of metaphor to a non-creative aspect of language.

Is it sufficient to supplement this 'potential range of connotations', as Beardsley does in the 'revised verbal-opposition theory',[5] with the properties which do not yet belong to the range of connotations of my language? At first sight, this supplementation ameliorates the theory; as Beardsley forcefully says, 'metaphor transforms a *property* (actual or attributed) into a *sense*'.[6] This change is important, since it must now be said that metaphors do not merely actualise a potential connotation, but establish it 'as a staple one'; and further, 'some of [the object's] relevant properties can be given a new status as elements of verbal meaning'.[7]

However, to speak of properties of *things* (or *objects*), which are supposed not yet to have been signified, is to admit that the new, emergent meaning is not drawn from anywhere, at least not from anywhere in language (the property is an implication of things, not of words). To say that a metaphor is not drawn from anywhere is to recognise it for what it is: namely, a momentary creation of language, a semantic innovation which does not have a status in the language as something already established, whether as a designation or as a connotation.

It may be asked how we can speak of a semantic innovation, a semantic event, as a meaning capable of being identified and reidentified (that was the first criterion of discourse stated above). Only one answer remains possible: it is necessary to take the viewpoint of the hearer or the reader and to treat the novelty of the emergent meaning as the counterpart, on the author's side, of a construction on the side of the reader. Thus the process of explanation is the only access to the process of creation.

If we do not take this path, we do not really free ourselves from the theory of substitution; instead of substituting a literal meaning restored by paraphrase for the metaphorical expression, we substitute the system of connotations and commonplaces. This task must remain a preparatory one, enabling literary criticism to be reconnected to psychology and sociology. The decisive moment of explanation is the construction of a network of interactions which constitutes the context as actual and unique. In so doing, we direct our attention towards the semantic event which is produced at the point of intersection between several semantic fields. This construction is the means by which all of the words taken together make sense. Then and only then, the 'metaphorical twist' is both an event and a meaning, a meaningful event and an emergent meaning in language.

Such is the fundamental feature of explanation which makes metaphor a paradigm for the explanation of a literary work. We construct the meaning of a text in a manner similar to the way in which we make sense of all the terms of a metaphorical statement.

Why must we 'construct' the meaning of a text? First, because it is written: in the asymmetrical relation between the text and the reader, one of the partners speaks for both. Bringing a text to language is always something other than hearing someone and listening to his speech. Reading resembles instead the performance of a musical piece regulated by the written notations of the score. For the text is an autonomous space of meaning which is no longer animated by the intention of its author; the autonomy of the text, deprived of this essential support, hands writing over to the sole interpretation of the reader.

A second reason is that the text is not only something written but is a work, that is, a singular totality. As a totality, the literary work cannot be reduced to a sequence of sentences which are individually intelligible; rather, it is an architecture of themes and purposes which can be constructed in several ways. The relation of part to whole is ineluctably circular. The presupposition of a certain whole precedes the discernment of a determinate arrangement of parts; and it is by constructing the details that we build up the whole. Moreover, as the notion of singular totality suggests, a text is a kind of individual, like an animal or a work of art. Its singularity can be regained, therefore, only by progressively rectifying generic concepts which concern the class of texts, the literary genre and the various structures which intersect in this singular text. In short, understanding a work involves the sort of judgement which Kant explored in the third *Critique*.

What, then, can we say about this construction and this judgement? Here understanding a text, at the level of its articulation of sense, is strictly homologous to understanding a metaphorical statement. In both cases, it is a question of 'making sense', of producing the best overall intelligibility from an apparently discordant diversity. In both cases, the construction takes the form of a wager or guess. As Hirsch says in *Validity in Interpretation*, there are no rules for making good guesses, but there are methods for validating our guesses.[8] This dialectic between guessing and validating is the realisation at the textual level of the micro-dialectic at work in the resolution of the local enigmas of a text. In both cases, the procedures of validation have more affinity with a logic of probability than with a logic of empirical verification – more affinity, let us say, with a logic of uncertainty and qualitative probability. Validation, in this sense, is the concern of an argumentative discipline akin to the juridical procedures of legal interpretation.

We can now summarise the corresponding features which underlie the analogy between the explanation of metaphorical statements and that of a literary work as a whole. In both cases, the construction rests upon 'clues' contained in the text itself. A clue serves as a guide for a specific construction, in that it contains at once a permission and a prohibition; it excludes unsuitable constructions and allows those which give more meaning to the same words. Second, in both cases, one construction can be said to be more probable than another, but not more truthful. The more probable is that which, on the one hand, takes account of the greatest number of facts furnished by the text, including its potential connotations, and on the other hand, offers a qualitatively better convergence between the features which it takes into account. A mediocre explanation can be called narrow or forced.

Here I agree with Beardsley when he says that a good explanation satisfies two principles: the principle of congruence and that of plenitude. Until now, we have in fact spoken about the principle of congruence. The principle of plenitude will provide us with a transition to the third part of the essay. This principle may be stated as follows: 'All of the connotations which are suitable must be attributed; the poem means all that it can mean.' This principle leads us further than a mere concern with 'sense'; it already says something about reference, since it takes as a measure of plenitude the requirements stemming from an experience which demands to be said and to be equalled by the semantic density of the text. I shall say that the principle of plenitude is the corollary, at the level of meaning, of a principle of full expression which draws our investigation in a quite different direction.

A quotation from Humboldt will lead us to the threshold of this new field of investigation: 'Language as discourse (*Rede*) lies on the boundary between the expressible and the inexpressible. Its aim and its goal is to push back still further this boundary.' Interpretation, in its proper sense, similarly lies on this frontier.

III. From the text to metaphor: interpretation

At the level of interpretation proper, understanding the text provides the key to understanding metaphor. Why? Because certain features of discourse begin to play an explicit role only when discourse takes the form of a literary *work*. These features are the very ones which we have placed under the heading of reference and self-reference. It will be recalled that I opposed reference to sense, saying that sense is the 'what' and reference the 'about what' of discourse. Of course, these two features can be recognised in the smallest units of language as discourse, namely in sentences. The sentence is about a situation which it expresses, and it refers back to its speaker by means of the specific procedures that we have enumerated. But reference and self-reference do not give rise to perplexing problems so long as discourse has not become a text and has not taken the form of a work. What are these problems?

Let us begin once again from the difference between written and spoken languages. In spoken language, that to which a dialogue ultimately refers is the situation common to the interlocutors, that is, the aspects of reality which can be shown or pointed to; we then say that the reference is 'ostensive'. In written language, the reference is no longer ostensive; poems, essays, works of fiction speak of things, events, states of affairs and characters which are evoked but which are not there. And yet literary texts are about something. About what? I do not hesitate to say: about a world, which is the world of the work. Far from saying that the text is without a world, I shall say that only now does man have a world and not merely a situation, a *Welt* and not merely an *Umwelt*. In the same way that the text frees its meaning from the tutelage of mental intention, so too it frees its reference from the limits of ostensive reference. For us, the world is the totality of references opened up by texts. Thus we speak of the 'world' of Greece, not to indicate what the situations were for those who experienced them, but to designate the non-situational references which outlast the effacement of the first and which then offer themselves as possible modes of being, as possible symbolic dimensions of our being-in-the-world.

The nature of reference in the context of literary works has an important consequence for the concept of interpretation. It implies that the meaning of a text lies not behind the text but in front of it. The meaning is not something hidden but something disclosed. What gives rise to understanding is that which points towards a possible world, by means of the non-ostensive references of the text. Texts speak of possible worlds and of possible ways of orientating oneself in these worlds. In this way, disclosure plays the equivalent role for written texts as ostensive reference plays in spoken language. Interpretation thus becomes the apprehension of the proposed worlds which are opened up by the non-ostensive references of the text.

This concept of interpretation expresses a decisive shift of emphasis with respect to the Romantic tradition of hermeneutics. In that tradition, the emphasis was placed on the ability of the hearer or reader to transfer himself into the spiritual life of a speaker or writer. The emphasis, from now on, is less on the other as a spiritual entity than on the world which the work unfolds. To understand is to follow the dynamic of the work, its movement from what it says to that about which it speaks. Beyond my situation as reader, beyond the situation of the author, I offer myself to the possible mode of being-in-the-world which the text opens up and discloses to me. That is what Gadamer calls the 'fusion of horizons' (*Horizontverschmelzung*) in historical knowledge.

The shift of emphasis from understanding the other to understanding the world of his work entails a corresponding shift in the conception of the 'hermeneutical circle'. For the thinkers of Romanticism, the latter term meant that the understanding of a text cannot be an objective procedure, in the sense of scientific objectivity, but that it necessarily implies a pre-understanding, expressing the way in which the reader already understands himself and his work. Hence a sort of circularity is produced between understanding the text and self-understanding. Such is, in condensed terms, the principle of the hermeneutical circle. It is easy to see how thinkers trained in the tradition of logical empiricism could only reject, as utterly scandalous, the mere idea of a hermeneutical circle and consider it to be an outrageous violation of all the canons of verifiability.

For my part, I do not wish to conceal the fact that the hermeneutical circle remains an unavoidable structure of interpretation. An interpretation is not authentic unless it culminates in some form of appropriation (*Aneignung*), if by that term we understand the process by which one makes one's own (*eigen*) what was initially other or alien (*fremd*). But I believe that the hermeneutical circle is not correctly understood when it is presented, first, as a circle between two subjectivities, that of the reader and that of the author; and second, as the projection of the subjectivity of the reader into the reading itself.

Let us correct each of these assumptions in turn. What we make our own, what we appropriate for ourselves, is not an alien experience or a distant intention, but the horizon of a world towards which a work directs itself. The appropriation of the reference is no longer modelled on the fusion of consciousnesses, on empathy or sympathy. The emergence of the sense and the reference of a text in language is the coming to language of a world and not the recognition of another person. The second correction of the Romantic concept of interpretation results from the first. If appropriation is the counterpart of disclosure, then the role of subjectivity must not be described in terms of projection. I should prefer to say that the reader understands himself in front of the text, in front of the world of the work. To understand oneself in front of a text is quite the contrary of projecting oneself and one's own beliefs and prejudices; it is to let the work and its world enlarge the horizon of the understanding which I have of myself. [. . .] Thus the hermeneutical circle is not repudiated but displaced from a subjectivistic level to an ontological plane. The circle is between my mode of being – beyond the knowledge which I may have of it – and the mode opened up and disclosed by the text as the world of the work.

Such is the model of interpretation which I now propose to transfer from texts, as long sequences of discourse, to the metaphor, understood as 'a poem in miniature' (Beardsley). Of course, the metaphor is too short a discourse to unfold this dialectic between the disclosure of a world and the disclosure of oneself in front of that world. Nevertheless, this dialectic points to some features of metaphor which the modern theories cited so far do not seem to take into consideration, but which were not absent from the classical theory of metaphor.

Let us return to the theory of metaphor in Aristotle's *Poetics*. Metaphor is only one of the 'parts' (*mere*) of what Aristotle calls 'diction' (*lexis*). As such, it belongs to a group of discursive procedures – using unusual words, coining new words, abbreviating or extending words – which all depart from the common (*kurion*) use of words. Now what constitutes the unity of *lexis*? Only its function in poetry. *Lexis*, in turn, is one of the 'parts' (*mere*) of tragedy, taken as the paradigm of the poetic work. In the context of the *Poetics*, tragedy represents the level of the literary work as a whole. Tragedy, in the form of a poem, has sense and reference. In Aristotle's language, the 'sense' of tragedy is secured by what he calls the 'fable' (*mythos*). We can understand the latter as the sense of tragedy because Aristotle constantly emphasises its structural characteristics. The *mythos* must have unity and coherence; it must make of the represented actions something 'whole and complete'. The *mythos* is thus the principal 'part' of tragedy, its 'essence'. All the other parts of tragedy – the 'characters', the 'thoughts', the 'delivery', the 'production' – are linked to the myth as means or conditions, or as the performance of tragedy *qua* myth. We must draw the consequence that it is only in relation to the *mythos* of tragedy that its *lexis*, and hence metaphor, make sense. There is no local meaning of metaphor outside of the regional meaning secured by the *mythos* of tragedy.

If metaphor is linked to the 'sense' of tragedy by means of its *mythos*, it is also linked to the 'reference' of tragedy in virtue of its general aim, which Aristotle calls *mimesis*.

Why do poets write tragedies, elaborate fables, use 'unusual' words such as metaphors? Because tragedy itself is connected to a more fundamental human project, that of *imitating* human actions in a *poetic* way. With these two keywords – *mimesis* and *poiesis* – we reach the level which I have called the referential world of the work. Indeed we may say that the Aristotelian concept of *mimesis* already encompasses all of the paradoxes of reference. On the one hand, it expresses a world of human actions which is already there; tragedy is destined to express human reality, to express the tragedy of life. But on the other hand, *mimesis* does not mean the duplication of reality; *mimesis* is not a copy: *mimesis* is *poiesis,* that is, construction, creation. Aristotle gives at least two indications of this creative dimension of *mimesis.* First, the fable is an original, coherent construction which attests to the creative genius of the artist. Second, tragedy is an imitation of human actions which makes them appear better, higher, more noble than they are in reality. Could we not say that *mimesis* is the Greek term for what we have called the non-ostensive reference of the literary work, or in other words, the Greek term for the disclosure of a world?

If this is right, we are now in a position to say something about the *power* of metaphor. I speak now of power and no longer of structure or even of process. The power of metaphor stems from its connection, internal to the poetic work, with three features: first, with the other procedures of the *lexis;* second, with the *fable,* which is the essence of the work, its immanent sense; and third, with the intentionality of the work as a whole, that is, with its intention to represent human actions as higher than they are in reality – and therein lies the *mimesis.* In this sense, the power of the metaphor arises from the power of the poem as a totality.

Let us apply these remarks, borrowed from Aristotle's *Poetics,* to our own description of metaphor. Could we say that the feature of metaphor which we have placed above all others – its nascent or emergent character – is linked to the function of poetry as the creative imitation of reality? Why should we invent new meanings, meanings which exist only in the instant of discourse, if it were not to serve the *poiesis* in the *mimesis?* If it is true that the poem creates a world, then it requires a language which preserves and expresses its creative power in specific contexts. By taking the *poiesis* of the poem together with metaphor as emergent meaning, we shall give sense to both at the same time, to poetry and to metaphor.

Thus the theory of interpretation paves the way for an ultimate approximation to the power of the metaphor. The priority given to the interpretation of the text in this final stage of the analysis does not mean that the relation between the two is not reciprocal. The explanation of metaphor, as a local event in the text, contributes to the interpretation of the work as a whole. We could even say that if the interpretation of local metaphors is illuminated by the interpretation of the text as a whole and by the clarification of the kind of world which the work projects, then in turn the interpretation of the poem as a whole is controlled by the explanation of the metaphor as a local phenomenon of the text.

As an example of this reciprocal relation between the regional and local aspects of the text, I shall venture to mention a possible connection, implicit in Aristotle's *Poetics*, between what he says about *mimesis* on the one hand and metaphor on the other. *Mimesis*, as we have seen, makes human actions appear higher than they are in reality; and the function of metaphor is to transpose the meanings of ordinary language by way of unusual uses. Is there not a mutual and profound affinity between the project of making human actions appear better than they are and the special procedure of metaphor which raises language above itself?

Let us express this relation in more general terms. Why should we draw new meanings from our language if we have nothing new to say, no new world to project? The creations of language would be devoid of sense unless they served the general project of letting new worlds emerge by means of poetry . . .

Allow me to conclude in a way which would be consistent with a theory of interpretation which places the emphasis on 'opening up a world'. Our conclusion should also 'open up' some new perspectives, but on what? Perhaps on the old problem of the imagination which I have carefully put aside. Are we not ready to recognise in the power of imagination, no longer the faculty of deriving 'images' from our sensory experience, but the capacity for letting new worlds shape our understanding of ourselves? This power would not be conveyed by images, but by the emergent meanings in our language. Imagination would thus be treated as a dimension of language. In this way, a new link would appear between imagination and metaphor. We shall, for the time being, refrain from entering this half-open door.

7. Appropriation

This essay will attempt to explicate a key idea which governs the methodology of interpretation. It concerns the way in which a text is *addressed to* someone. Elsewhere[1] we have noted that the writing–reading relation is distinguished from the speaking–hearing relation not only in terms of the relation to the speaker, but also in terms of the relation to the audience. We have asked: for whom does one write? and we have answered: for anyone who can read. We have also spoken of the 'potentialisation' of the audience, which is no longer the partner in dialogue but the unknown reader that the text procures. The culmination of reading in a concrete reader who appropriates the meaning will thus constitute the theme of this essay.

It is obvious that we shall rediscover the old problem of the role of subjectivity in understanding and, therefore, the problem of the hermeneutical circle. But this problem is presented in new terms, as a result of the fact that it has been postponed for so long. Instead of considering it as the first problem, we have pushed it back to the end of our investigation. What we have said in other essays about the notion of interpretation is, in this respect, decisive. If it is true that interpretation concerns essentially the power of the work to disclose a world, then the relation of the reader to the text is essentially his relation to the kind of world which the text presents. The theory of appropriation which will now be sketched follows from the displacement undergone by the whole problematic of interpretation: it will be less an intersubjective relation of mutual understanding than a relation of apprehension applied to the world conveyed by the work. A new theory of subjectivity follows from this relation. In general we may say that appropriation is no longer to be understood in the tradition of philosophies of the subject, as a constitution of which the subject would possess the key. To understand is not to project oneself into the text; it is to receive an enlarged self from the apprehension of proposed worlds which are the genuine object of interpretation. Such is the general line of this essay, which will be pursued in detail as follows.

(1) To begin with, the necessity of the concept of appropriation will be shown. It will be introduced as the counterpart of a concept of distanciation which is linked to any objective and objectifying study of a text. Hence the first section: 'distanciation and appropriation'.

(2) Then we shall take up the relation between the concept of appropriation and that of the revelation of a world. Following Gadamer's analysis in *Truth and Method*, we shall introduce the theme of 'play'. This theme will serve to characterise the metamorphosis which, in the work of art, is undergone not only by reality but also by the author (writer and artist), and above all (since this is the point of our analysis) by the reader or the subject of appropriation. Appropriation will thus appear as the 'playful' transposition of the text, and play itself will appear as the modality appropriate to the reader *potentialis*, that is, to anyone who can read.

(3) Next we shall identify the illusions and errors which the concept of appropriation must overcome. Here the critique of the illusions of the subject will be the necessary path to the sound appreciation of the concept of appropriation. Appropriation will be the complement not only of the distanciation of the text, but also of the relinquishment of the self.

The conclusion will sketch the place of hermeneutic philosophy in relation to the reflective Kantian tradition on the one hand, and the speculative Hegelian tradition on the other. It will be shown why a hermeneutic philosophy must situate itself at an equal distance from both.

I. Distanciation and appropriation

The dialectic of distanciation and appropriation is the final figure which the dialectic of explanation and understanding must assume. It concerns the way in which the text is addressed to someone.

The potentialisation of the audience implies two ways of reconnecting the discourse of the reader to that of the writer. These possibilities pertain to the status of *history* in the whole process of interpretation. The general tendency of literary and biblical criticism since the mid-nineteenth century has been to link the contents of literary works, and in general of cultural documents, to the social conditions of the community in which these works were produced or to which they were directed. To explain a text was essentially to consider it as the expression of certain socio-cultural needs and as a response to certain perplexities localised in space and time. In contrast to this trend, which was subsequently called 'historicism', an alternative tendency arose, stemming from Frege and from the Husserl of the *Logical Investigations*. According to these thinkers, meaning (they were interested in the meaning of a proposition rather than that of a text) is not an idea which someone has in mind; it is not a mental content but an ideal object which can be identified and reidentified, by different individuals in different periods, as being one and the same object. By 'ideality', they understood that the meaning of a proposition is neither a physical nor a mental reality. In Frege's terms, *Sinn* is not *Vorstellung*, if *Vorstellung* (idea, representation) is the mental event linked to the actualisation of meaning by a given speaker in a given situation. The identity of 'sense' in the infinite series of its mental actualisations constitutes the ideal dimension of the proposition. In a similar way, Husserl described the contents of all intentional acts as the 'noematic' object, irreducible to the mental aspect of the acts themselves. The notion of ideal 'sense', borrowed from Frege, was thus extended by Husserl to all mental operations – not just logical acts but also perceptual acts, volitional acts, affective acts, etc. For a phenomenology 'turned towards the object', all intentional acts without exception must be described in terms of their noematic side, understood as the 'correlate' of the corresponding noetic acts.

The inversion in the theory of propositional acts has an important implication for hermeneutics, insofar as this discipline is conceived as the theory of the fixation of life expressions by writing. After 1900, Dilthey himself made a great effort to incorporate into his theory of meaning the kind of ideality which he found in Husserl's *Logical Investigations*. In Dilthey's later works, the interconnection (*Zusammenhang*) which gives a text, a work of art or a document its power to be understood by another and to be fixed by writing is somewhat similar to the ideality that Frege and Husserl discerned at the basis of all propositions. If this comparison holds, then the act of 'understanding' is less 'historical' and more 'logical' than the famous article of 1900 declares.[2] The whole theory of the 'human sciences' is affected by this important shift.

A comparable change in the domain of literary criticism, in America and on the Continent, can be related to the turn from history to logicity in the explanation of cultural expressions. A wave of 'anti-historicism' followed the earlier excesses of psychologism and sociologism. For this new attitude, a text is not primarily a message addressed to a specific range of readers; in this sense, it is not a segment of an historical chain. Insofar as it is a text, it is a kind of atemporal object which has, as it were, broken its moorings with all historical development. The rise to writing implies the 'suspension' of the historical process, the transference of discourse to a sphere of ideality which permits an indefinite expansion of the sphere of communication.

I must say that I take this 'anti-historicist' trend into account and that I accept its principal presupposition concerning the objectivity of meanings in general. It is because I concur with the project and the method of this sort of literary criticism that I am ready to define, in new terms, the dialectic between explanation and understanding which results from the recognition of the specificity of the literary object.

Let us develop this new dialectic: the objectification of meaning is a necessary mediation between the writer and the reader. But as mediation, it calls for a complementary act of a more existential character which I shall call the appropriation of meaning. 'Appropriation' is my translation of the German term *Aneignung*. *Aneignen* means 'to make one's own' what was initially 'alien'. According to the intention of the word, the aim of all hermeneutics is to struggle against cultural distance and historical alienation. Interpretation brings together, equalises, renders contemporary and similar. This goal is attained only insofar as interpretation actualises the meaning of the text for the present reader. Appropriation is the concept which is suitable for the actualisation of meaning as addressed to someone. It takes the place of the answer in the dialogical situation, in the same way that 'revelation' or 'disclosure' takes the place of ostensive reference in the dialogical situation. The interpretation is complete when the reading releases something like an event, an event of discourse, an event in the present time. As appropriation, the interpretation becomes an event. Appropriation is thus a dialectical concept: the counterpart of the timeless distanciation implied by any literary or textual criticism of an anti-historicist character.

II. 'Play' as the mode of being of appropriation

The following theme was suggested by reading Gadamer;[3] but it is also called for by the theory of the *heuristic fiction*. I should like to show that it is not only reality which is metamorphosed by the heuristic fiction, but also the author and the reader. Thus the metamorphosis of the reading subject results initially from the metamorphosis of the world, and then from the metamorphosis of the author.

1. The heuristic fiction as play

Gadamer develops his conception of play in the course of a meditation on the work of art. This meditation is wholly directed against the subjectivism of the aesthetic consciousness which stems from the Kantian theory of the 'judgement of taste', itself linked to the theory of 'reflecting judgement'. Play is not determined by the consciousness which plays; play has its own way of being. Play is an experience which transforms those who participate in it. It seems that the subject of aesthetic experience is not the player himself, but rather what 'takes place' in play. In a similar way we speak of the play of waves, of light, of parts of a machine and even of words. We play with a project, with an idea; we can equally 'be played'. What is essential is the 'to and fro' (Hin und Her) of play. Play is thereby close to dance, which is a movement that carries away the dancer. Thus we say that the part 'is played', or again that something 'is in play' between . . . All of these expressions betray that play is something other than the activity of a subject. The to and fro of play occurs as if by itself, that is, without effort or applied intention. This 'in-itself' of play is such that, even in solitary play, there must be something with which or against which one plays (with luck as one's partner in times of success!). In this risk of an unknown partner lies the 'charm' of play. Whoever plays is also played: the rules of the game impose themselves upon the player, prescribing the to and fro and delimiting the field where everything 'is played'. Hence play shatters the seriousness of a utilitarian preoccupation where the self-presence of the subject is too secure. In play, subjectivity forgets itself; in seriousness, subjectivity is regained.

In what respects does this analysis, which we have briefly recalled, clarify our problem of hermeneutic understanding? In the first place, the presentation of a world in a work of art, and in general in a work of discourse, is a playful presentation. Worlds are proposed in the mode of play. The analysis of play thus enables us to recover in a new way the dialectic between the suspension of didactic reference and the manifestation of another sort of reference, beyond the epoché of the former. Play displays the same dialectic, developing a serious side of its own – what Gadamer calls 'presentation' (Darstellung). In play, nothing is serious, but something is presented, produced, given in representation. There is thus an interesting relation between play and the presentation of a world. This relation is, moreover, absolutely reciprocal: on the one hand, the presentation of the world in a poem is a heuristic fiction and in this sense 'playful'; but on the other hand, all play reveals something true, precisely because it is play. To play, says Gadamer, is to play at something. In entering a game we hand ourselves over, we abandon ourselves to the space of meaning which holds sway over the reader.

In play there occurs what Gadamer calls a 'metamorphosis' (*Verwandlung*), that is, both an imaginary transposition marked by the reign of 'figures' (*Gebilde*), *and* the transformation of everything into its true being. Everyday reality is abolished and yet everyone becomes himself. Thus the child who disguises himself as another expresses his profoundest truth. The player is metamorphosed 'in the true'; in playful representation, 'what is emerges'. But 'what is' is no longer what we call everyday reality; or rather, reality truly becomes reality, that is, something which comprises a future horizon of undecided possibilities, something to fear or to hope for, something unsettled. Art only abolishes non-metamorphosed reality. Whence the true *mimesis:* a metamorphosis according to the truth. In this sense, we shall speak of recognition rather than cognition. In a theatrical representation, we recognise characters and roles. Therein lies the paradox: the most imaginary creation elicits recognition. 'As recognised, the presented being is what is retained in its essence, what is detached from its haphazard aspects',[4] stripped of all that is fortuitous and accidental. This is the sense in which Aristotle could dare to say that poetry (he was thinking of tragedy) is more philosophical than history. For poetry proceeds to the essential, whereas history remains content with the anecdotal. Such is the significant link between fiction, figuration and recognition of the essential.

2. The author as playful figure

A second implication emerges which is no less interesting than the first. It is not only the presentation of the world which is 'playful', but also the position of the author who 'puts himself on stage' and hence gives himself in representation. Is this not the key to what we have called the potentialisation of the reader? Is he not also 'metamorphosed' by the play upon the world which unfolds in the work of art? The hypothesis of a playful relation between the author and his work is supported by diverse analyses which come from quite a different perspective, in particular from German and Anglo-Saxon literary criticism.[5] The discussion in this critical literature was polarised, above all, by the problem of the relation between the novelist and his characters. The term 'point of view' was used to describe the various possible solutions contributed by novelists of the past to this difficult problem: a total view of the characters by an omniscient author, the identification with one of the characters through whose eyes the author sees everything that is shown, the annihilation of the author in a story which tells itself all alone, and so on.

How can this debate be clarified by our earlier reflections on play? The very fact that there have been numerous solutions to this technical problem results, in my opinion, from the playful character of the relation itself. The author is rendered fictitious; and the different modalities of the relation of author to narration are like so many rules of this playful relation. The solutions classified by Norman Friedman and F.K. Stanzel may be reconsidered from this point of view.[6] That these solutions constitute so many fictions of the author seems to me confirmed by the remark of one of the critics: 'The author can, to a certain extent, choose to disguise himself, but he can never choose to disappear.'[7] To disguise oneself, to assume different 'voices', is this not to play?

For their part the French, more affected by the structuralist concern to cut the links between the text and the author, emphasise the non-coincidence of the 'psychological' author and the 'narrator', where the latter is 'marked' by the signs of the narrator in the text. But this non-coincidence cannot imply the elimination of the author; just as Benveniste spoke of split reference with respect to poetic language, so too we must introduce the idea of a 'split speaker'. This splitting marks the irruption of the playful relation into the very subjectivity of the author. We are no longer very far from Dilthey when he speaks of 'the position of the poet's imagination before the world of experiences'.[8] In the same sense, Wolfgang Kayser speaks of the 'mythical creator' in order to designate the situation of the narrator. The narrator is the one who abstracts from his personality so that a voice other than his is heard. Thus the very disappearance of the subject is still an imaginative variation of the writer's *ego*. The imaginative variation then consists in being part of the narrative, in disguising oneself according to the narrative. In any case, it is still a matter of a role assumed by the narrator. For the omniscient narrator is just as much a fiction of the subject as the narrator identified with a character or as the narrator dispersed among the characters who appear to speak and to act all alone. The omniscient narrator is also an 'autonomous figure created by the author in the same way as the characters';[9] even more so if the narrator is identified with a character or hidden behind all. The objective and Olympian narrator may well disappear: play is displaced towards the partial and restricted viewpoints of the characters; or, as in *The Sorrows of Young Werther*, it is hidden in an imaginary character inserted between the character and ourselves, such that this third person is sensed to have put together the words of the poor Werther, addressing us in the preface and engaging us in a pseudo-dialogue.

It makes little difference, therefore, whether a text is written in third or in first person. In every case, the distanciation is the same and the variety of solutions proves that we have not gone beyond rule-governed play. Thus the novelist may change his perspective and become suddenly omniscient when he reads the thoughts of his characters. So while it is true to say that the narrator is never the author, nevertheless the narrator is always the one who is metamorphosed in a fictional character which is the author. Even the death of the author is a game that the author plays. In all cases he remains, according to Kayser's expression, a 'creator of the universe'.[10]

3. The reader as playful figure

It is now possible to transfer the remarks on the author to the reader, and to treat the reader in turn as a fictive or playful figure. For the author's subjectivity, submitted to imaginative variations, becomes a model offered by the narrator to the subjectivity of his reader. The reader as well is invited to undergo an imaginative variation of his *ego*. When the fictive author of the preface of *Werther* addresses us, 'and you, good soul . . .', this 'you' is not the prosaic man who knows that Werther did not exist, but is the 'me' who believes in fiction. As Kayser says, 'the reader is a fictive creation, a role which we can assume in order to look at ourselves'.[11] In this sense we may speak of metamorphosis, as Gadamer speaks of the metamorphosis of reality in play. The reader is this imaginary 'me', created by the poem and participating in the poetic universe.

We may still speak of a relation of congeniality, but it is exercised from the playful author to the playful reader. For the work itself has constructed the reader in his role. So the congeniality does not signify anything other than the double metamorphosis of the author and the reader: 'Assuming the role of reader corresponds to the mysterious meta-morphosis which the audience undergoes in the theatre when the lights go out and the curtains are drawn.'[12]

It is easy, therefore, to generalise beyond the novel or the story: even when we read a philosophical work, it is always a question of entering into an alien work, of divesting oneself of the earlier 'me' in order to receive, as in play, the self conferred by the work itself.

III. The illusions of the subject

The concept of appropriation has hardly been introduced when it be-comes the victim of errors linked to the primacy of the subject in mod-ern philosophy, insofar as the latter originates in the writings of Des-cartes, Kant and Husserl. The role of the subject seems to imply that appropriation is a form of the constitution of objectivity in and by the subject. This inference results in a series of errors about the very mean-ing of appropriation. The first of these errors is a surreptitious return to the Romantic pretension of recovering, by congenial coincidence, the genius of the author: from genius to genius! Another error is to con-ceive of appropriation in terms of the primacy of the original audience with which one seeks to coincide: to discover to whom a text was ad-dressed and to identify oneself with that original audience, such would be the task of hermeneutics. Or more bluntly, appropriation would con-sist in subsuming interpretation to the finite capacities of understand-ing of the present reader.

This way of conceiving of appropriation, ensnared in these various errors, is responsible for the distrust which scientific minds display to-wards hermeneutics, understood as a form of subjectivism or of subjec-tivist existentialism. Even Heidegger has been read this way: his 'pre-understanding' (*Vorverständnis*) is taken as indistinguishable from a simple projection of the prejudices of the reader into his reading. The same could be said of Bultmann's hermeneutical circle: 'to believe in order to understand', is this not to project the reading self into the text read?

Here I shall say that the notion of subject must be submitted to a critique parallel to that which the theory of metaphor exercises on the notion of object. In fact, it is the same philosophical error which must be taken by its two extremities: objectivity as confronting the subject, the subject as reigning over objectivity.

At this stage, everything gained from the critique of the illusions of the subject must be integrated into hermeneutics. This critique, which I see conducted in either a Freudian or a Marxist tradition, constitutes the modern form of the critique of 'prejudice'.

According to the Marxist tradition, the critique of the subject is one aspect of the general theory of ideology. Our understanding is based on prejudices which are linked to our position in the relations of force of society, a position which is partially unknown to us. Moreover, we are propelled to act by hidden interests. Whence the falsification of reality. Thus the critique of 'false consciousness' becomes an integral part of hermeneutics. Here I see the place for a necessary dialogue between hermeneutics and the theory of ideology as developed, for instance, by Habermas.[13]

According to the Freudian tradition, the critique of the subject is one part of the critique of 'illusions'. Here I am interested in psychoanalysis, not as a grid for reading a text, but as the self-criticism of the reader, as the purification of the act of appropriation. In *Freud and Philosophy*, I spoke of an effect of self-analysis which I called the relinquishment of the subject. As Freud said, the subject is not master in his own house. This critique is addressed to what could be called the 'narcissism of the reader': to find only oneself in a text, to impose and rediscover oneself.

Relinquishment is a fundamental moment of appropriation and distinguishes it from any form of 'taking possession'. Appropriation is also and primarily a 'letting-go'. Reading is an appropriation-divestiture. How can this letting-go, this relinquishment, be incorporated into appropriation? Essentially by linking appropriation to the revelatory power of the text which we have described as its referential dimension. It is in allowing itself to be carried off towards the reference of the text that the *ego* divests itself of itself. [. . .]

The link between appropriation and revelation is, in my view, the cornerstone of a hermeneutics which seeks both to overcome the failures of historicism and to remain faithful to the original intention of Schleiermacher's hermeneutics. To understand an author better than he understood himself is to unfold the revelatory power implicit in his discourse, beyond the limited horizon of his own existential situation.

On this basis, it is possible to refute fallacious views about the concept of interpretation. In the first place, appropriation does not imply any direct congeniality of one soul with another. Nothing is less intersubjective or dialogical than the encounter with a text; what Gadamer

calls the 'fusion of horizons' expresses the convergence of the *world* horizons of the writer and the reader. The ideality of the text remains the
mediator in this process of the fusion of horizons.

According to another fallacious view, the hermeneutical task would
be governed by the original audience's understanding of the text. As
Gadamer has firmly demonstrated, this is a complete mistake: the Letters of Saint Paul are no less addressed to me than to the Romans, the
Galatians, the Corinthians, etc. Only dialogue has a 'you', whose identification proceeds from the dialogue itself. If the meaning of a text is
open to anyone who can read, then it is the omni-temporality of meaning which opens it to unknown readers; and the historicity of reading
is the counterpart of this specific omni-temporality. From the moment
that the text escapes from its author and from his situation, it also escapes from its original audience. Hence it can procure new readers for
itself.

According to a third fallacious view, the appropriation of the meaning of a text would subsume interpretation to the finite capacities of
understanding of a present reader. The English and French translation
of *Aneignung* by 'appropriation' reinforces this suspicion. Do we not
place the meaning of the text under the domination of the subject who
interprets? This objection can be dismissed by observing that what is
'made our own' is not something mental, not the intention of another
subject, nor some design supposedly hidden behind the text; rather, it
is the projection of a world, the proposal of a mode of being-in-the-
world, which the text discloses in front of itself by means of its non-
ostensive references. Far from saying that a subject, who already masters his own being-in-the-world, projects the *a priori* of his own understanding and interpolates this *a priori* in the text, I shall say that appropriation is the process by which the revelation of new modes of
being – or, if you prefer Wittgenstein to Heidegger, new 'forms of
life' – *gives* the subject new capacities for knowing himself. If the reference of a text is the projection of a world, then it is not in the first
instance the reader who projects himself. The reader is rather broad-
ened in his capacity to project himself by receiving a new mode of
being from the text itself.

Thus appropriation ceases to appear as a kind of possession, as a way
of taking hold of . . . It implies instead a moment of dispossession of
the narcissistic *ego*. This process of dispossession is the work of the sort
of universality and atemporality implied by the explanatory procedures. Only the interpretation which satisfies the injunction of the text,

which follows the 'arrow' of meaning and endeavours to 'think in accordance with' it, engenders a new *self*-understanding. By the expression '*self*-understanding', I should like to contrast the *self* which emerges from the understanding of the text to the *ego* which claims to precede this understanding. It is the text, with its universal power of unveiling, which gives a *self* to the *ego*.

It would require, at the end of this excursion, a long explanation in order to situate hermeneutic philosophy in relation to the reflective Kantian tradition on the one hand, and the speculative Hegelian tradition on the other. We shall restrict ourselves here to offering a few remarks in support of the thesis that hermeneutic philosophy must place itself at equal distance from both traditions, accepting as much from one tradition as from the other but opposing each with equal force.

By its concern to secure the link between understanding meaning and self-understanding, hermeneutic philosophy is a continuation of reflective philosophy. But the critique of the illusions of the subject and the permanent recourse to the great detour of signs distances it decisively from the primacy of the *cogito*. Above all, the subordination of the theme of appropriation to that of manifestation turns more towards a hermeneutics of the *I am* than a hermeneutics of the *I think*.[14]

It may be thought that what distances hermeneutic philosophy from reflective philosophy brings it nearer to speculative philosophy. That is largely true. Thus Gadamer can say that his hermeneutics revives Hegel insofar as it breaks with Schleiermacher. Fundamentally, the concept of manifestation of a world, around which all other hermeneutical concepts are organised, is closer to the idea of the 'self-presentation' (*Selbstdarstellung*) of the true, following the preface to *The Phenomenology of Mind*, than to the Husserlian idea of constitution. But the permanent return of this self-presentation to the event of speech in which, *ultimately*, interpretation is accomplished signifies that philosophy mourns the loss of absolute knowledge. It is because absolute knowledge is impossible that the conflict of interpretations is insurmountable and inescapable.

Between absolute knowledge and hermeneutics, it is necessary to choose.

Part III

Studies in the philosophy of social science

8. The model of the text: meaningful action considered as a text

My aim in this essay is to test an hypothesis which I shall expound briefly.

I assume that the primary sense of the word 'hermeneutics' concerns the rules required for the interpretation of the written documents of our culture. In assuming this starting point I am remaining faithful to the concept of *Auslegung* as it was stated by Wilhelm Dilthey; whereas *Verstehen* (understanding, comprehension) relies on the recognition of what a foreign subject means or intends on the basis of all kinds of signs in which psychic life expresses itself (*Lebensäusserungen*), *Auslegung* (interpretation, exegesis) implies something more specific: it covers only a limited category of signs, those which are fixed by writing, including all the sorts of documents and monuments which entail a fixation similar to writing.

Now my hypothesis is this: if there are specific problems which are raised by the interpretation of texts because they are texts and not spoken language, and if these problems are the ones which constitute hermeneutics as such, then the human sciences may be said to be hermeneutical (1) inasmuch as their *object* displays some of the features constitutive of a text as text, and (2) inasmuch as their *methodology* develops the same kind of procedures as those of *Auslegung* or text-interpretation.

Hence the two questions to which my essay will be devoted are: (1) To what extent may we consider the notion of text as a good paradigm for the so-called object of the social sciences? (2) To what extent may we use the methodology of text-interpretation as a paradigm for interpretation in general in the field of the human sciences?

I. The paradigm of text

In order to justify the distinction between spoken and written language, I want to introduce a preliminary concept, that of *discourse*. It is as discourse that language is either spoken or written.

Now what is discourse? We shall not seek the answer from the logicians, not even from the exponents of linguistic analysis, but from the linguists themselves. Discourse is the counterpart of what linguists call language-systems or linguistic codes. Discourse is language-event or linguistic usage. [. . .]

If the sign (phonological or lexical) is the basic unit of language, the sentence is the basic unit of discourse. Therefore it is the linguistics of the sentence which supports the theory of speech as an event. I shall retain four traits from this linguistics of the sentence which will help me to elaborate the hermeneutics of the event and of discourse.

First trait: Discourse is always realised temporally and in the present, whereas the language system is virtual and outside of time. Emile Benveniste calls this the 'instance of discourse'.

Second trait: Whereas language lacks a subject – in the sense that the question 'Who is speaking?' does not apply at its level – discourse refers back to its speaker by means of a complex set of indicators such as the personal pronouns. We shall say that the 'instance of discourse' is self-referential.

Third trait: Whereas the signs in language only refer to other signs within the same system, and whereas language therefore lacks a world just as it lacks temporality and subjectivity, discourse is always about something. It refers to a world which it claims to describe, to express, or to represent. It is in discourse that the symbolic function of language is actualised.

Fourth trait: Whereas language is only the condition for communication for which it provides the codes, it is in discourse that all messages are exchanged. In this sense, discourse alone has not only a world, but an other, another person, an interlocutor to whom it is addressed.

These four traits taken together constitute speech as an event. [. . .] Let us see how differently these four traits are actualised in spoken and written language.

(1) Discourse, as we said, only exists as a temporal and present instance of discourse. This first trait is realised differently in living speech and in writing. In living speech, the instance of discourse has the character of a fleeting event. The event appears and disappears. This is why there is a problem of fixation, of inscription. What we want to fix is what disappears. If, by extension, we can say that one fixes language – inscription of the alphabet, lexical inscription, syntactical inscription – it is for the sake of that which alone has to be fixed, discourse. Only discourse is to be fixed, because discourse disappears.

The atemporal system neither appears nor disappears; it does not happen. Here is the place to recall the myth in Plato's *Phaedo*. Writing was given to men to 'come to the rescue' of the 'weakness of discourse', a weakness which was that of the event. The gift of the *grammata* – of that 'external' thing, of those 'external marks', of that materialising alienation – was just that of a 'remedy' brought to our memory. The Egyptian king of Thebes could well respond to the god Theuth that writing was a false remedy in that it replaced true reminiscence by material conservation, and real wisdom by the semblance of knowing. This inscription, in spite of its perils, is discourse's destination. What in effect does writing fix? Not the event of speaking, but the 'said' of speaking, where we understand by the 'said' of speaking that intentional exteriorisation constitutive of the aim of discourse thanks to which the *sagen* – the saying – wants to become *Aus-sage* – the enunciation, the enunciated. In short, what we write, what we inscribe, is the *noema* of the speaking. It is the meaning of the speech event, not the event as event.

What, in effect, does writing fix? If it is not the speech *event*, it is speech itself insofar as it is *said*. But what is said?

Here I should like to propose that hermeneutics has to appeal not only to linguistics (linguistics of discourse versus linguistics of language) as it does above, but also to the theory of the speech-act such as we find it in Austin and Searle. The act of speaking, according to these authors, is constituted by a hierarchy of subordinate acts which are distributed on three levels: (1) the level of the locutionary or propositional act, the act *of* saying; (2) the level of the illocutionary act or force, that which we do *in* saying; and (3) the level of the perlocutionary act, that which we do *by* saying. [. . .]

What is the implication of these distinctions for our problem of the intentional exteriorisation by which the event surpasses itself in the meaning and lends itself to material fixation? The locutionary act exteriorises itself in the sentence. The sentence can in effect be identified and reidentified as being the same sentence. A sentence becomes an utterance (*Aus-sage*) and thus is transferred to others as being such-and-such a sentence with such-and-such a meaning. But the illocutionary act can also be exteriorised through grammatical paradigms (indicative, imperative, and subjunctive modes, and other procedures expressive of the illocutionary force) which permit its identification and reidentification. Certainly, in spoken discourse, the illocutionary force leans upon mimicry and gestural elements and upon the non-articulated aspects of discourse, what we call prosody. In this sense, the illocutionary force is less completely inscribed in grammar than is the propositional meaning. In every case, its inscription in a syntactic articulation is itself gathered up in specific paradigms which in principle make possible fixation by writing. Without a doubt we must concede that the perlocutionary act is the least inscribable aspect of discourse and that by preference it characterises spoken language. But the perlocutionary action is precisely what is the least discourse in discourse. It is the discourse as stimulus. It acts, not by my interlocutor's recognition of my intention, but sort of energetically, by direct influence upon the emotions and the affective dispositions. Thus the propositional act, the illocutionary force, and the perlocutionary action are apt, in a decreasing order, for the intentional exteriorisation which makes inscription in writing possible.

Therefore it is necessary to understand by the meaning of the speech-act, or by the noema of the saying, not only the sentence, in the narrow sense of the propositional act, but also the illocutionary force and even the perlocutionary action in the measure that these three aspects of the speech-act are codified, gathered into paradigms, and where, consequently, they can be identified and reidentified as having the same meaning. Therefore I am here giving the word 'meaning' a very large acceptation which covers all the aspects and levels of the intentional exteriorisation that makes the inscription of discourse possible.

The destiny of the other three traits of discourse in passing from discourse to writing will permit us to make more precise the meaning of this elevation of saying to what is said.

(2) In discourse, we said – and this was the second differential trait of discourse in relation to language – the sentence designates its speaker by diverse indicators of subjectivity and personality. In spoken discourse, this reference by discourse to the speaking subject presents a character of immediacy that we can explain in the following way. The subjective intention of the speaking subject and the meaning of the discourse overlap each other in such a way that it is the same thing to understand what the speaker means and what his discourse means. The ambiguity of the French expression *vouloir-dire*, the German *meinen*, and the English 'to mean', attests to this overlapping. It is almost the same thing to ask 'What do you mean?' and 'What does that mean?' With written discourse, the author's intention and the meaning of the text cease to coincide. This dissociation of the verbal meaning of the text and the mental intention is what is really at stake in the inscription

of discourse. Not that we can conceive of a text without an author; the tie between the speaker and the discourse is not abolished, but distended and complicated. The dissociation of the meaning and the intention is still an adventure of the reference of discourse to the speaking subject. But the text's career escapes the finite horizon lived by its author. What the text says now matters more than what the author meant to say, and every exegesis unfolds its procedures within the circumference of a meaning that has broken its moorings to the psychology of its author. Using Plato's expression again, written discourse cannot be 'rescued' by all the processes by which spoken discourse supports itself in order to be understood – intonation, delivery, mimicry, gestures. In this sense, the inscription in 'external marks' which first appeared to alienate discourse, marks the actual spirituality of discourse. Henceforth, only the meaning 'rescues' the meaning, without the contribution of the physical and psychological presence of the author. But to say that the meaning rescues the meaning is to say that only interpretation is the 'remedy' for the weakness of discourse which its author can no longer 'save'.

(3) The event is surpassed by the meaning a third time. Discourse, we said, is what refers to the world, to *a* world. In spoken discourse this means that what the dialogue ultimately refers to is the *situation* common to the interlocutors. This situation in a way surrounds the dialogue, and its landmarks can all be shown by a gesture, or by pointing a finger, or designated in an ostensive manner by the discourse itself through the oblique reference of those other indicators which are the demonstratives, the adverbs of time and place, and the tense of the verb. In oral discourse, we are saying, reference is *ostensive*. What happens to it in written discourse? Are we saying that the text no longer has a reference? This would be to confound reference and monstration, world and situation. Discourse cannot fail to be about something. In saying this, I am separating myself from any ideology of an absolute text. Only a few sophisticated texts satisfy this ideal of a text without reference. They are texts where the play of the signifier breaks away from the signified. But this new form is only valuable as an exception and cannot give the key to all other texts which in one manner or another speak about the world. But what then is the subject of texts when nothing can be shown? Far from saying that the text is then without a world, I shall now say without paradox that only man *has a world* and not just a situation. In the same manner that the text frees its meaning from the tutelage of the mental intention, it frees its reference from the

limits of ostensive reference. For us, the world is the ensemble of references opened up by the texts. Thus we speak about the 'world' of
Greece, not to designate any more what were the situations for those
who lived them, but to designate the non-situational references which
outlive the effacement of the first and which henceforth are offered as
possible modes of being, as symbolic dimensions of our being-in-the-
world. For me, this is the referent of all literature; no longer the *Umwelt*
of the ostensive references of dialogue, but the *Welt* projected by the
non-ostensive references of every text that we have read, understood,
and loved. To understand a text is at the same time to light up our own
situation, or, if you will, to interpolate among the predicates of our
situation all the significations which make a *Welt* of our *Umwelt*. It is
this enlarging of the *Umwelt* into the *Welt* which permits us to speak of
the references *opened up* by the text – it would be better to say that the
references *open up* the world. Here again the spirituality of discourse
manifests itself through writing, which frees us from the visibility and
limitation of situations by opening up a world for us, that is, new dimensions of our being-in-the-world.

In this sense, Heidegger rightly says – in his analysis of *verstehen* in
Being and Time – that what we understand first in a discourse is not
another person, but a project, that is, the outline of a new being-in-the-
world. Only writing, in freeing itself, not only from its author, but from
the narrowness of the dialogical situation, reveals this destination of
discourse as projecting a world.

In thus tying reference to the projection of a world, it is not only
Heidegger whom we rediscover, but Wilhelm von Humboldt for whom
the great justification of language is to establish the relation of man to
the world. If you suppress this referential function, only an absurd
game of errant signifiers remains.

(4) But it is perhaps with the fourth trait that the accomplishment of
discourse in writing is most exemplary. Only discourse, not language,
is addressed to someone. This is the foundation of communication. But
it is one thing for discourse to be addressed to an interlocutor equally
present to the discourse situation, and another to be addressed, as is
the case in virtually every piece of writing, to whoever knows how to
read. The narrowness of the dialogical relation explodes. Instead of
being addressed just to you, the second person, what is written is addressed to the audience that it creates itself. This, again, marks the spirituality of writing, the counterpart of its materiality and of the aliena-

tion which it imposes upon discourse. The *vis-à-vis* of the written is just whoever knows how to read. The co-presence of subjects in dialogue ceases to be the model for every 'understanding'. The relation writing–reading ceases to be a particular case of the relation speaking–hearing. But at the same time, discourse is revealed as discourse in the universality of its address. In escaping the momentary character of the event, the bounds lived by the author, and the narrowness of ostensive reference, discourse escapes the limits of being face to face. It no longer has a visible auditor. An unknown, invisible reader has become the unprivileged addressee of the discourse.

To what extent may we say that the object of the human sciences conforms to the paradigm of the text? Max Weber defines this object as *sinnhaft orientiertes Verhalten*, as meaningfully oriented behaviour. To what extent may we replace the predicate 'meaningfully oriented' by what I should like to call *readability-characters* derived from the preceding theory of the text?

Let us try to apply our four criteria of what a text is to the concept of meaningful action.

1. The fixation of action

Meaningful action is an object for science only under the condition of a kind of objectification which is equivalent to the fixation of a discourse by writing. This trait presupposes a simple way to help us at this stage of our analysis. In the same way that interlocution is overcome in writing, interaction is overcome in numerous situations in which we treat action as a fixed text. These situations are overlooked in a theory of action for which the discourse of action is itself a part of the situation of transaction which flows from one agent to another, exactly as spoken language is caught in the process of interlocution, or, if we may use the term, of translocution. This is why the understanding of action at the prescientific level is only 'knowledge without observation', or as E. Anscombe says, 'practical knowledge' in the sense of 'knowing how' as opposed to 'knowing that'. But this understanding is not yet an *interpretation* in the strong sense which deserves to be called scientific interpretation.

My claim is that action itself, action as meaningful, may become an object of science, without losing its character of meaningfulness, through a kind of objectification similar to the fixation which occurs in writing. By this objectification, action is no longer a transaction to which the discourse of action would still belong. It constitutes a delineated pattern which has to be interpreted according to its inner connections.

This objectification is made *possible* by some inner traits of the action which are similar to the structure of the speech-act and which make doing a kind of utterance. In the same way as the fixation by writing is made possible by a dialectic of intentional exteriorisation immanent to the speech-act itself, a similar dialectic within the process of transaction prepares the detachment of the *meaning* of the action from the *event* of the action.

First an action has the structure of a locutionary act. It has a *propositional* content which can be identified and reidentified as the same. This 'propositional' structure of the action has been clearly and demonstratively expounded by Anthony Kenny in *Action, Emotion and Will*.[1] The verbs of action constitute a specific class of predicates which are similar to relations and which, like relations, are irreducible to all the kinds of predicates which may follow the copula 'is'. The class of action predicates, in its turn, is irreducible to the relations and constitutes a specific set of predicates. Among other traits, the verbs of action allow a plurality of 'arguments' capable of complementing the verb, ranging from no argument (Plato taught) to an indeterminate number of arguments (Brutus killed Caesar in the Curia, on the Ides of March, with a . . . , with the help of . . .). This variable polydicity of the predicative structure of the action-sentences is typical of the propositional structure of action. Another trait which is important for the transposition of the concept of fixation from the sphere of discourse to the sphere of action concerns the ontological status of the 'complements' of the verbs of action. Whereas relations hold between terms equally existing (or non-existing), certain verbs of action have a topical subject which is identified as existing and to which the sentence refers, and complements which do not exist. Such is the case with the 'mental acts' (to believe, to think, to will, to imagine, etc.).

Anthony Kenny describes some other traits of the propositional structure of actions derived from the description of the functioning of the verbs of action. For example, the distinction between states, activities, and performances can be stated according to the behaviour of the tenses of the verbs of action which fix some specific temporal traits of the action itself. The distinction between the formal and the material object of an action (let us say the difference between the notion of all inflammable things and this letter which I am now burning) belongs to the logic of action as mirrored in the grammar of the verbs of action. Such, roughly described, is the propositional content of action which gives a basis to a dialectic of *event* and *meaning* similar to that of the speech-act. I should like to speak here of the noematic structure of action. It is this noematic structure which may be fixed and detached from the process of interaction and become an object to interpret.

Moreover, this noema has not only a propositional content, but also presents 'illocutionary' traits very similar to those of the complete speech-act. The different classes of performative acts of discourse described by Austin at the end of *How to do Things with Words* may be taken as paradigms not only for the speech-acts themselves, but for the actions which fulfil the corresponding speech-acts.[2] A typology of action, following the model of illocutionary acts, is therefore possible. Not only a typology, but a criteriology, inasmuch as each type implies *rules,* more precisely 'constitutive rules' which, according to Searle in *Speech Acts,* allow the construction of 'ideal models' similar to the 'ideal types' of Max Weber.[3] For example, to understand what a promise is, we have to understand what the 'essential condition' is according to which a given action 'counts as' a promise. Searle's 'essential condition' is not far from what Husserl called *Sinngehalt,* which covers both the 'matter' (propositional content) and the 'quality' (the illocutionary force).

We may now say that an action, like a speech-act, may be identified not only according to its propositional content, but also according to its illocutionary force. Both constitute its 'sense-content'. Like the speech-act, the action-event (if we may coin this analogical expression) develops a similar dialectic between its temporal status as an appearing and disappearing event, and its logical status as having such-and-such identifiable meaning or 'sense-content'. But if the 'sense-content' is what makes possible the 'inscription' of the action-event, what makes it real? In other words, what corresponds to writing in the field of action?

Let us return to the paradigm of the speech-act. What is fixed by writing, we said, is the noema of the speaking, the saying as *said*. To what extent may we say that what is *done* is inscribed? Certain metaphors may be helpful at this point. We say that such-and-such event *left its mark* on its time. We speak of marking events. Are not there 'marks' on time, the kind of thing which calls for a reading, rather than for a hearing? But what is meant by this metaphor of the printed mark?

The three other criteria of the text will help us to make the nature of this fixation more precise.

2. The autonomisation of action

In the same way that a text is detached from its author, an action is detached from its agent and develops consequences of its own. This autonomisation of human action constitutes the *social* dimension of action. An action is a social phenomenon not only because it is done by several agents in such a way that the role of each of them cannot be distinguished from the role of the others, but also because our deeds escape us and have effects which we did not intend. One of the meanings of the notion of 'inscription' appears here. The kind of distance which we found between the intention of the speaker and the verbal meaning of a text occurs also between the agent and its action. It is this distance which makes the ascription of responsibility a specific problem. We do not ask, who smiled? who raised his hand? The doer is present to his doing in the same way as the speaker is present to his speech. With simple actions like those which require no previous action in order to be done, the meaning (noema) and the intention (noesis) coincide or overlap. With complex actions some segments are so remote from the initial simple segments, which can be said to express the intention of the doer, that the ascription of these actions or action-segments constitutes a problem as difficult to solve as that of authorship in some cases of literary criticism. The assignation of an author becomes a mediate inference well known to the historian who tries to isolate the role of an historical character in the course of events.

We just used the expression 'the course of events'. Could we not say that what we call the course of events plays the role of the material thing which 'rescues' the vanishing discourse when it is written? As we said in a metaphorical way, some actions are events which imprint their mark on their time. But on what did they imprint their mark? Is it not in something spatial that discourse is inscribed? How could an event be printed on something temporal? Social time, however, is not only something which flees; it is also the place of durable effects, of persisting patterns. An action leaves a 'trace', it makes its 'mark' when it contributes to the emergence of such patterns which become the *documents* of human action.

Another metaphor may help us to delineate this phenomenon of the social 'imprint': the metaphor of the 'record' or of the 'registration'. Joel

Feinberg, in *Reason and Responsibility*, introduces this metaphor in another context, that of responsibility, in order to show how an action may be submitted to blame. Only actions, he says, which can be 'registered' for further notice, placed as an entry on somebody's 'record', can be blamed.[4] And when there are no formal records (such as those which are kept by institutions like employment offices, schools, banks, and the police), there is still an informal analogue of these formal records which we call reputation and which constitutes a basis for blaming. I should like to apply this interesting metaphor of a record and reputation to something other than the quasi-judicial situations of blaming, charging, crediting, or punishing. Could we not say that history is itself the record of human action? History is this quasi-'thing' *on* which human action leaves a 'trace', puts its mark. Hence the possibility of 'archives'. Before the archives which are intentionally written down by the memorialists, there is this continuous process of 'recording' human action which is history itself as the sum of 'marks', the fate of which escapes the control of individual actors. Henceforth history may appear as an autonomous entity, as a play with players who do not know the plot. This hypostasis of history may be denounced as a fallacy, but this fallacy is well entrenched in the process by which human action becomes social action when written down in the archives of history. Thanks to this sedimentation in social time, human deeds become 'institutions', in the sense that their meaning no longer coincides with the logical intentions of the actors. The meaning may be 'depsychologised' to the point where the *meaning* resides in the work itself. In the words of P. Winch, in *The Idea of a Social Science*, the object of the social sciences is a 'rule-governed behaviour'.[5] But this rule is not superimposed; it is the meaning as articulated from within these sedimented or instituted works.

Such is the kind of 'objectivity' which proceeds from the 'social fixation' of meaningful behaviour.

3. Relevance and importance

According to our third criterion of what a text is, we could say that a meaningful action is an action the *importance* of which goes 'beyond' its *relevance* to its initial situation. This new trait is very similar to the way in which a text breaks the ties of discourse to all the ostensive references. As a result of this emancipation from the situational context, discourse can develop non-ostensive references which we called a 'world', in the sense in which we speak of the Greek 'world', not in the cosmological sense of the word, but as an ontological dimension. What would correspond in the field of action to the non-ostensive references of a text?

We opposed, in introducing the present analysis, the *importance* of an action to its *relevance* as regards the situation to which it wanted to respond. An important action, we could say, develops meanings which can be actualised or fulfilled in situations other than the one in which this action occurred. To say the same thing in different words, the meaning of an important event exceeds, overcomes, transcends, the social conditions of its production and may be re-enacted in new social contexts. Its importance is its durable relevance and, in some cases, its omni-temporal relevance.

This third trait has important implications as regards the relation between cultural phenomena and their social conditions. Is it not a fundamental trait of the great works of culture to overcome the conditions of their social production, in the same way as a text develops new references and constitutes new 'worlds'? It is in this sense that Hegel spoke, in *The Philosophy of Right,* of the institutions (in the largest sense of the word) which 'actualise' freedom as a *second nature* in accordance with freedom. This 'realm of actual freedom' is constituted by the deeds and works capable of receiving relevance in new historical situations. If this is true, this way of overcoming one's own conditions of production is the key to the puzzling problem raised by Marxism concerning the status of the 'superstructures'. The autonomy of superstructures as regards their relation to their own infrastructures has its paradigm in the non-ostensive references of a text. A work does not only mirror its time, but it opens up a world which it bears within itself.

4. Human action as an 'open work'

Finally, according to our fourth criterion of the text as text, the meaning of human action is also something which is *addressed* to an indefinite range of possible 'readers'. The judges are not the contemporaries, but, as Hegel said, history itself. *Weltgeschichte ist Weltgericht.* That means that, like a text, human action is an open work, the meaning of which is 'in suspense'. It is because it 'opens up' new references and receives fresh relevance from them, that human deeds are also waiting for fresh interpretations which decide their meaning. All significant events and deeds are, in this way, opened to this kind of practical interpretation through present *praxis.* Human action, too, is opened to anybody who *can read.* In the same way that the meaning of an event is the sense of its forthcoming interpretations, the interpretation by the contemporaries has no particular privilege in this process.

This dialectic between the work and its interpretations will be the topic of the *methodology* of interpretation that we shall now consider.

II. The paradigm of text-interpretation

I want now to show the fruitfulness of this analogy of the text at the level of methodology.

The main implication of our paradigm, as concerns the methods of the social sciences, is that it offers a fresh approach to the question of the relation between *erklären* (explanation) and *verstehen* (understanding, comprehension) in the human sciences. As is well known, Dilthey gave this relation the meaning of a dichotomy. For him, any model of explanation is borrowed from a different region of knowledge, that of the natural sciences with their inductive logic. Thereafter, the autonomy of the so-called *Geisteswissenschaften* is preserved only by recognising the irreducible factor of understanding a foreign psychic life on the basis of the signs in which this life is immediately exteriorised. But if *verstehen* is separated from *erklären* by this logical gap, how can the human sciences be scientific at all? Dilthey kept wrestling with this paradox. He discovered more and more clearly, mainly after having read Husserl's *Logical Investigations*, that the *Geisteswissenschaften* are sciences inasmuch as the expressions of life undergo a kind of objectification which makes possible a scientific approach somewhat similar to that of the natural sciences, in spite of the logical gap between *Natur* and *Geist*, factual knowledge and knowledge by signs. In this way the mediation offered by these objectifications appeared to be more important, for a scientific purpose, than the immediate meaningfulness of the expressions of life for everyday transactions.

My own interrogation starts from this last perplexity in Dilthey's thought. And my hypothesis is that the kind of objectification implied in the status of discourse as text provides a better answer to the problem raised by Dilthey. This answer relies on the dialectical character of the relation between *erklären* and *verstehen* as it is displayed in reading. Our task therefore will be to show to what extent the paradigm of reading, which is the counterpart of the paradigm of writing, provides a solution for the methodological paradox of the human sciences.

The dialectic involved in reading expresses the originality of the relation between writing and reading and its irreducibility to the dialogical situation based on the immediate reciprocity between speaking and hearing. There is a dialectic between explaining and comprehending *because* the writing–reading situation develops a problematic of its own which is not merely an extension of the speaking–hearing situation constitutive of dialogue.

It is here, therefore, that our hermeneutics is most critical as regards the Romantic tradition in hermeneutics which took the dialogical situation as the standard for the hermeneutical operation applied to the text. My contention is that it is this operation, on the contrary, which reveals the meaning of what is already hermeneutical in dialogical understanding. So if the dialogical relation does not provide us with the paradigm of reading, we have to build it as an original paradigm, as a paradigm of its own.

This paradigm draws its main features from the status of the text itself as characterised by (1) the fixation of the meaning, (2) its dissociation from the mental intention of the author, (3) the display of non-ostensive references, and (4) the universal range of its addressees. These four traits taken together constitute the 'objectivity' of the text. From this 'objectivity' derives a possibility of *explaining* which is not derived in any way from another field, that of natural events, but which is congenial to this kind of objectivity. Therefore there is no transfer from one region of reality to another – let us say, from the sphere of facts to the sphere of signs. It is within the same sphere of signs that the process of objectification takes place and gives rise to explanatory procedures. And it is within the same sphere of signs that explanation and comprehension are confronted.

I propose that we consider this dialectic in two different ways: (1) as proceeding from comprehension to explanation, and (2) as proceeding from explanation to comprehension. The exchange and the reciprocity between both procedures will provide us with a good approximation of the dialectical character of the relation. At the end of each half of this demonstration I shall try to indicate briefly the possible extension of the paradigm of reading to the whole sphere of the human sciences.

1. From understanding to explanation
This first dialectic – or rather this first figure of a unique dialectic – may be conveniently introduced by our contention that to understand a text is not to rejoin the author. The disjunction of the meaning and the intention creates an absolutely original situation which engenders the dialectic of *erklären* and *verstehen*. If the objective meaning is something

other than the subjective intention of the author, it may be construed in various ways. The problem of the right understanding can no longer be solved by a simple return to the alleged intention of the author.

This construction necessarily takes the form of a process. As Hirsch says in his book *Validity in Interpretation,* there are no rules for making good guesses. But there are methods for validating guesses.[6] This dialectic between guessing and validating constitutes one figure of our dialectic between comprehension and explanation.

In this dialectic both terms are decisive. Guessing corresponds to what Schleiermacher called the 'divinatory', validation to what he called the 'grammatical'. My contribution to the theory of this dialectic will be to link it more tightly to the theory of the text and text-reading.

Why do we need an art of guessing? Why do we have to 'construe' the meaning? Not only – as I tried to say a few years ago – because language is metaphorical and because the double meaning of metaphorical language requires an art of deciphering which tends to unfold the several layers of meaning. The case of the metaphor is only a particular case for a general theory of hermeneutics. In more general terms, a text has to be construed because it is not a mere sequence of sentences, all on an equal footing and separately understandable. A text is a whole, a totality. The relation between whole and parts – as in a work of art or in an animal – requires a specific kind of 'judgement' for which Kant gave the theory in the third *Critique*. Correctly, the whole appears as a hierarchy of topics, or primary and subordinate topics. The reconstruction of the text as a whole necessarily has a circular character, in the sense that the presupposition of a certain kind of whole is implied in the recognition of the parts. And reciprocally, it is in construing the details that we construe the whole. There is no necessity and no evidence concerning what is important and what is unimportant, what is essential and what is unessential. The judgement of importance is a guess.

To put the difficulty in other terms, if a text is a whole, it is once more an individual like an animal or a work of art. As an individual it can only be reached by a process of narrowing the scope of generic concepts concerning the literary genre, the class of text to which this text belongs, the structures of different kinds which intersect in this text. The localisation and the individualisation of this unique text is still a guess.

Still another way of expressing the same enigma is that as an individual the text may be reached from different sides. Like a cube, or a volume in space, the text presents a 'relief'. Its different topics are not at the same altitude. Therefore the reconstruction of the whole has a perspectivist aspect similar to that of perception. It is always possible to relate the same sentence in different ways to this or that sentence considered as the cornerstone of the text. A specific kind of onesidedness is implied in the act of reading. This onesidedness confirms the guess character of interpretation.

For all these reasons there is a problem of interpretation not so much because of the incommunicability of the psychic experience of the author, but because of the very nature of the verbal intention of the text. This intention is something other than the sum of the individual meanings of the individual sentences. A text is more than a linear succession of sentences. It is a cumulative, holistic process. This specific structure of the text cannot be derived from that of the sentence. Therefore the kind of plurivocity which belongs to texts as texts is something other than the polysemy of individual words in ordinary language and the ambiguity of individual sentences. This plurivocity is typical of the text considered as a whole, open to several readings and to several constructions.

As concerns the procedures of validation by which we test our guesses, I agree with Hirsch that they are closer to a logic of probability than to a logic of empirical verification. To show that an interpretation is more probable in the light of what is known is something other than showing that a conclusion is true. In this sense, validation is not verification. Validation is an argumentative discipline comparable to the juridical procedures of legal interpretation. It is a logic of uncertainty and of qualitative probability. In this sense we may give an acceptable sense to the opposition between *Geisteswissenschaften* and *Naturwissenschaften* without conceding anything to the alleged dogma of the ineffability of the individual. The method of conveyance of indices, typical of the logic of subjective probability, gives a firm basis for a science of the individual deserving the name of science. A text is a quasi-individual, and the validation of an interpretation applied to it may be said, with complete legitimacy, to give a scientific knowledge of the text.

Such is the balance between the genius of guessing and the scientific character of validation which constitutes the modern complement of the dialectic between *verstehen* and *erklären*.

At the same time, we are prepared to give an acceptable meaning to the famous concept of a *hermeneutical circle*. Guess and validation are in a sense circularly related as subjective and objective approaches to the text. But this circle is not a vicious circularity. It would be a cage if we were unable to escape the kind of 'self-confirmability' which, according to Hirsch,[7] threatens this relation between guess and validation. To the procedures of validation also belong procedures of invalidation similar to the criteria of falsifiability emphasised by Karl Popper in his *Logic of Scientific Discovery*.[8] The role of falsification is played here by the conflict between competing interpretations. An interpretation must not only be probable, but more probable than another. There are criteria of relative superiority which may easily be derived from the logic of subjective probability.

In conclusion, if it is true that there is always more than one way of construing a text, it is not true that all interpretations are equal and may be assimilated to so-called 'rules of thumb'. The text is a limited field of possible constructions. The logic of validation allows us to move between the two limits of dogmatism and scepticism. It is always possible to argue for or against an interpretation, to confront interpretations, to arbitrate between them, and to seek for an agreement, even if this agreement remains beyond our reach.

To what extent is this dialectic between guessing and validating paradigmatic for the whole field of the human sciences?

That the meaning of human actions, of historical events, and of social phenomena may be *construed* in several different ways is well known by all experts in the human sciences. What is less known and understood is that this methodological perplexity is founded in the nature of the object itself and, moreover, that it does not condemn the scientist to oscillate between dogmatism and scepticism. As the logic of text-interpretation suggests, there is a *specific plurivocity* belonging to the meaning of human action. Human action, too, is a limited field of possible constructions.

A trait of human action which has not yet been emphasised in the preceding analysis may provide an interesting link between the specific plurivocity of the text and the analogical plurivocity of human action. This trait concerns the relation between the purposive and the motivational dimensions of action. As many philosophers in the new field of action theory have shown, the purposive character of an action is fully recognised when the answer to the question 'what' is explained in terms of an answer to the question 'why'. I *understand* what you intended to do, if you are able to *explain* to me why you did such-and-such an action. Now, what kinds of answer to the question 'why' make sense? Only those answers which afford a motive understood as a reason for . . . and not as a cause. And what is a reason for . . . which is not a cause? It is, in the terms of E. Anscombe and A.I. Melden, an expression, or a phrase, which allows us to consider the action *as* this or that.[9] If you tell me that you did this or that because of jealousy or in a spirit of revenge, you are asking me to put your action in the light of this category of feelings or dispositions. By the same token, you claim to make sense of your action. You claim to make it understandable for others and for yourself. This attempt is particularly helpful when applied to what Anscombe calls the 'desirability-character' of wanting. Wants and beliefs have the character not only of being *forces* which make people act in such-and-such ways, but of making sense as a result of the apparent good which is the correlate of their desirability-character. I may have to answer the question, *as* what do you want this? On the basis of these desirability-characters and the apparent good which corresponds to them, it is possible to *argue* about the meaning of an action, to argue for or against this or that interpretation. In this way the account of motives already foreshadows a logic of argumentation procedures. Could we not say that what can be (and must be) *construed* in human action is the motivational basis of this action, i.e., the set of desirability-characters which may explain it? And could we not say that the process of *arguing* linked to the explanation of action by its motives unfolds a kind of plurivocity which makes action similar to a text?

What seems to legitimate this extension from guessing the meaning of a text to guessing the meaning of an action is that in arguing about the meaning of an action I put my wants and my beliefs at a distance and submit them to a concrete dialectic of confrontation with opposite points of view. This way of putting my action at a distance in order to make sense of my own motives paves the way for the kind of distanciation which occurs with what we called the social *inscription* of human action and to which we applied the metaphor of the 'record'. The same actions which may be put into 'records' and henceforth 'recorded' may also be *explained* in different ways according to the multivocity of the arguments applied to their motivational background.

If we are correct in extending to action the concept of 'guess' which we took as a synonym for *verstehen*, we may also extend to the field of action the concept of 'validation' in which we saw an equivalent of *erklären*. Here, too, the modern theory of action provides us with an intermediary link between the procedures of literary criticism and those of the social sciences. Some thinkers have tried to elucidate the way in which we *impute* actions to agents in the light of the juridical procedures by which a judge or a tribunal validates a decision concerning a contract or a crime. In a famous article, 'The ascription of responsibility and rights', H.L.A. Hart shows in a very convincing way that juridical reasoning does not at all consist in applying general laws to particular cases, but each time in construing uniquely referring decisions.[10] These decisions terminate a careful refutation of the excuses and defences which could 'defeat' the claim or the accusation. In saying that human actions are fundamentally 'defeasible' and that juridical reasoning is an argumentative process which comes to grips with the different ways of 'defeating' a claim or an accusation, Hart has paved the way for a general theory of validation in which juridical reasoning would be the fundamental link between validation in literary criticism and validation in the social sciences. The intermediary function of juridical reasoning clearly shows that the procedures of validation have a polemical character. In front of the court, the plurivocity common to texts and to actions is exhibited in the form of a conflict of interpretations, and the final interpretation appears as a verdict to which it is possible to make appeal. Like legal utterances, all interpretations in the field of literary criticism and in the social sciences may be challenged, and the question 'what can defeat a claim' is common to all argumentative situations. Only in the tribunal is there a moment when the procedures of appeal are exhausted. But it is because the decision of the judge is implemented by the force of public power. Neither in literary criticism, nor in the social sciences, is there such a last word. Or, if there is any, we call that violence.

2. From explanation to understanding

The same dialectic between comprehension and explanation may receive a new meaning if taken in the reverse way, from explanation to understanding. This new *Gestalt* of the dialectic proceeds from the nature of the referential function of the text. This referential function, as we said, exceeds the mere ostensive designation of the situation common to both speaker and hearer in the dialogical situation. This abstraction from the surrounding world gives rise to two opposite attitudes. As readers, we may either remain in a kind of state of suspense as regards any kind of referred-to world, or we may actualise the potential non-ostensive references of the text in a new situation, that of the reader. In the first case, we treat the text as a worldless entity; in the second, we create a new ostensive reference through the kind of 'execution' which the art of reading implies. These two possibilities are equally entailed by the act of reading, conceived as their dialectical interplay.

The first way of reading is exemplified today by the different *structural* schools of literary criticism. Their approach is not only possible, but legitimate. It proceeds from the suspension, the *epoché*, of the ostensive reference. To read, in this way, means to prolong this suspension of the ostensive reference to the world and to transfer oneself into the 'place' where the text stands, within the 'enclosure' of this worldless place. According to this choice, the text no longer has an outside, it has only an inside. Once more, the very constitution of the text as text and of the system of texts as literature justifies this conversion of the literary thing into a closed system of signs, analogous to the kind of closed system which phonology discovered at the root of all discourse, and which de Saussure called *la langue*. Literature, according to this working hypothesis, becomes an *analogon* of *la langue*.

On the basis of this abstraction, a new kind of explanatory attitude may be extended to the literary object, which, contrary to the expectation of Dilthey, is no longer borrowed from the natural sciences, i.e., from an area of knowledge alien to language itself. The opposition between *Natur* and *Geist* is no longer operative here. If some model is borrowed, it comes from the same field, from the semiological field. It is henceforth possible to treat texts according to the elementary rules which linguistics successfully applied to the elementary systems of signs that underlie the use of language. We have learned from the Geneva school, the Prague school, and the Danish school, that it is always possible to abstract *systems* from *processes* and to relate these systems – whether phonological, lexical, or syntactical – to units which are merely defined by their opposition to other units of the same system. This interplay of merely distinctive entities within finite sets of such units defines the notion of structure in linguistics.

It is this structural model which is now applied to *texts*, i.e., to sequences of signs longer than the sentence, which is the last kind of unit that linguistics takes into account. In his *Structural Anthropology*, Claude Lévi-Strauss formulates this working hypothesis in regard to one category of texts, that of myths.[11]

By means of this working hypothesis, the large units which are at least the same size as the sentence and which, put together, form the narrative proper of the myth, will be able to be treated according to the same rules as the smallest units known to linguistics. [. . . In this way,] we can indeed say that we have explained a myth, but not that we have interpreted it. We can, by means of structural analysis, bring out the logic of it, the operations which relate the 'bundles of relations' among themselves. This logic constitutes 'the structural law of the myth under consideration'.[12] This law is pre-eminently an object of reading and not at all of speaking, in the sense of a recitation where the power of the myth would be re-enacted in a particular situation. Here the text is only a text, thanks to the suspension of its meaning for us, to the postponement of all actualisation by present speech.

I want now to show in what way 'explanation' (*erklären*) requires 'understanding' (*verstehen*) and brings forth in a new way the inner dialectic which constitutes 'interpretation' as a whole.

As a matter of fact, nobody stops with a conception of myths and of narratives as formal as this algebra of constitutive units. This can be shown in different ways. First, even in the most formalised presentation of myths by Lévi-Strauss, the units which he calls 'mythemes' are still expressed as sentences which bear meaning and reference. Can anyone say that their meaning as such is neutralised when they enter into the 'bundle of relations' which alone is taken into account by the 'logic' of the myth? Even this bundle of relations, in its turn, must be written in the form of a sentence. Finally, the kind of language-game which the whole system of oppositions and combinations embodies, would lack any kind of significance if the oppositions themselves, which, according to Lévi-Strauss, the myth tends to mediate, were not meaningful oppositions concerning birth and death, blindness and lucidity, sexuality and truth. Beside these existential conflicts there would be no contradictions to overcome, no logical function of the myth as an attempt to solve these contradictions. Structural analysis does not exclude, but presupposes, the opposite hypothesis concerning the myth, i.e., that it has a meaning as a narrative of origins. Structural analysis merely represses this function. But it cannot suppress it. The myth would not even function as a logical operator if the propositions which it combines did not point toward boundary situations. Structural analysis, far from getting rid of this radical questioning, restores it at a level of higher radicality.

If this is true, could we not say that the function of structural analysis is to lead from a surface semantics, that of the narrated myth, to a depth semantics, that of the boundary situations which constitute the ultimate 'referent' of the myth?

I really believe that if such were not the function of structural analysis, it would be reduced to a sterile game, a divisive algebra, and even the myth would be bereaved of the function which Lévi-Strauss himself assigns to it, that of making men aware of certain oppositions and of tending toward their progressive mediation. To eliminate this reference to the *aporias* of existence around which mythic thought gravitates would be to reduce the theory of myth to the necrology of the meaningless discourses of mankind. If, on the contrary, we consider structural analysis as a stage – and a necessary one – between a naive interpretation and a critical interpretation, between a surface interpretation and a depth interpretation, then it would be possible to locate explanation and understanding at two different stages of a unique *hermeneutical arc*. It is this depth semantics which constitutes the genuine object of understanding and which requires a specific affinity between the reader and the kind of things the text is *about*.

But we must not be misled by this notion of personal affinity. The depth semantics of the text is not what the author intended to say, but what the text is about, i.e., the non-ostensive reference of the text. And the non-ostensive reference of the text is the kind of world opened up by the depth semantics of the text. Therefore what we want to understand is not something hidden behind the text, but something disclosed in front of it. What has to be understood is not the initial situation of discourse, but what points toward a possible world. Understanding has less than ever to do with the author and his situation. It wants to grasp the proposed worlds opened up by the references of the text. To understand a text is to follow its movement from sense to reference, from what it says, to what it talks about. In this process the *mediating* role played by structural analysis constitutes both the justification of this objective approach and the rectification of the subjective approach. We are definitely prevented from identifying understanding with some kind of intuitive grasping of the intention underlying the text. What we have said about the depth semantics which structural analysis yields invites us rather to think of the sense of the text as an injunction starting from the text, as a new way of looking at things, as an injunction to think in a certain manner. [. . .]

This second figure or *Gestalt* of the dialectic between explanation and comprehension has a strong paradigmatic character which holds for the whole field of the human sciences. I want to emphasise three points.

First, the structural model, taken as a paradigm for explanation, may be extended beyond textual entities to all social phenomena because it is not limited in its application to linguistic signs, but applies to all kinds of signs which are analogous to linguistic signs. The intermedi-

ary link between the model of the text and social phenomena is constituted by the notion of semiological systems. A linguistic system, from
the point of view of semiology, is only a species within the semiotic
genre, although this species has the privilege of being a paradigm for
the other species of the genre. We can say therefore that a structural
model of explanation can be generalised as far as all social phenomena
which may be said to have a semiological character, i.e., as far as it is
possible to define the typical relations of a semiological system at their
level: the general relation between code and message, relations among
the specific units of the code, the relation between signifier and signified, the typical relation within and among social messages, the structure of communication as an exchange of messages, etc. Inasmuch as
the semiological model holds, the semiotic or symbolic function, i.e.,
the function of substituting signs for things and of representing things
by the means of signs, appears to be more than a mere effect in social
life. It is its very foundation. We should have to say, according to this
generalised function of the semiotic, not only that the symbolic function is social, but that social reality is fundamentally symbolic.

If we follow this suggestion, then the kind of explanation which is
implied by the structural model appears to be quite different from the
classical causal model, especially if causation is interpreted in Humean
terms as a regular sequence of antecedents and consequents with no
inner logical connection between them. Structural systems imply relations of a quite different kind, correlative rather than sequential or con-
secutive. If this is true, the classical debate about motives and causes
which has plagued the theory of action these last decades loses its importance. If the search for correlations within semiotic systems is the
main task of explanation, then we have to reformulate the problem of
motivation in social groups in new terms. But it is not the aim of this
essay to develop this implication.

Secondly, the second paradigmatic factor in our previous concept of
text-interpretation proceeds from the role which we assigned to depth
semantics *between* structural analysis and appropriation. This mediating function of depth semantics must not be overlooked, since the appropriation's losing its psychological and subjective character and receiving a genuine epistemological function depends on it.

Is there something similar to the depth semantics of a text in social
phenomena? I should tend to say that the search for correlations within
and between social phenomena treated as semiotic entities would lose
importance and interest if it did not yield *something like* a depth seman-

tics. In the same way as language-games are forms of life, according to the famous aphorism of Wittgenstein, social structures are also attempts to cope with existential perplexities, human predicaments and deep-rooted conflicts. In this sense, these structures, too, have a referential dimension. They point toward the *aporias* of social existence, the same *aporias* around which mythical thought gravitates. And this analogical function of reference develops traits very similar to what we called the non-ostensive reference of a text, i.e., the display of a *Welt* which is no longer an *Umwelt*, the projection of a world which is more than a situation. May we not say that in social science, too, we proceed from naive interpretations to critical interpretations, from surface interpretations to depth interpretations *through* structural analysis? But it is depth interpretation which gives meaning to the whole process.

This last remark leads us to our third and last point. If we follow the paradigm of the dialectic between explanation and understanding to its end, we must say that the meaningful patterns which a depth interpretation wants to grasp cannot be understood without a kind of personal commitment similar to that of the reader who grasps the depth semantics of the text and makes it his 'own'. Everybody knows the objection which an extension of the concept of appropriation to the social sciences is exposed to. Does it not legitimate the intrusion of personal prejudices, of subjective bias into the field of scientific inquiry? Does it not introduce all the paradoxes of the hermeneutical circle into the human sciences? In other words, does not the paradigm of disclosure *plus* appropriation destroy the very concept of a human science? The way in which we introduced this pair of terms within the framework of text-interpretation provides us not only with a paradigmatic problem, but with a paradigmatic solution. This solution is not to deny the role of personal commitment in understanding human phenomena, but to qualify it.

As the model of text-interpretation shows, understanding has nothing to do with an *immediate* grasping of a foreign psychic life or with an *emotional* identification with a mental intention. Understanding is entirely *mediated* by the whole of explanatory procedures which precede it and accompany it. The counterpart of this personal appropriation is not something which can be *felt*, it is the dynamic meaning released by the explanation which we identified earlier with the reference of the text, i.e., its power of disclosing a world.

The paradigmatic character of text-interpretation must be applied down to this ultimate implication. This means that the conditions of an authentic appropriation, as they were displayed in relation to texts, are themselves paradigmatic. Therefore we are not allowed to exclude the final act of personal commitment from the whole of objective and explanatory procedures which mediate it.

This qualification of the notion of personal commitment does not eliminate the 'hermeneutical circle'. This circle remains an insuperable structure of knowledge when it is applied to human things, but this qualification prevents it from becoming a vicious circle.

Ultimately, the correlation between explanation and understanding, between understanding and explanation, is the 'hermeneutical circle'.

9. Science and ideology

Allow me to honour the memory of the Angelic Doctor [St Thomas Aquinas] by placing the present study under the patronage of what he called the Philosopher. In the prologue to the *Nicomachean Ethics*, we read this:

> Our discussion will be adequate if it has as much clearness as the subject-matter admits of, for precision is not to be sought for alike in all discussions, any more than in all the products of the crafts. Now fine and just matters, which politics investigates, admit of much variety and fluctuation of opinion, so that they may be thought to exist only by convention, and not by nature . . . We must be content, then, in speaking of such subjects and with such premises to indicate the truth roughly and in outline . . . In the same spirit, therefore, should each type of statement be *received;* for it is the mark of an educated man to look for precision in each class of things just so far as the nature of the subject admits . . . And so the man who has been educated in a subject is a good judge of that subject, and the man who has received an all-round education is a good judge in general. (1094 b 11–1095 a 2)

Why did I quote this text? Not for the luxury of epigraph and exordium, but for the very discipline of reasoning itself. For I propose to show that, if the properly Aristotelian thesis of the plurality of levels of scientificity is maintained, then the phenomenon of ideology is susceptible of a relatively positive assessment. Aristotle tells us several things: that politics has to deal with variable and unstable matters, and that here reasoning begins from facts which are generally, but not always, true; that it is the cultivated man and not the specialist who is judge in these matters; that it is therefore necessary to be content with showing the truth in a rough and approximate way (or, according to the above translation, 'roughly and in outline'); finally, that this is so because the problem is of a practical nature.

The text has cautionary value at the threshold of our inquiry. For it can guard us from the numerous snares which the subject of ideology sets for us (a subject, it may be said in passing, which I would not have chosen spontaneously, but which I have received and accepted in the form of a challenge). I have just spoken of numerous snares. They are of two kinds and their identification will introduce the first two, properly critical parts of my presentation.

What is in question, to begin with, is the initial definition of the phenomenon. Here there are already several snares. The first is to assume as self-evident an analysis in terms of social classes. That today this assumption seems natural to us is an indication of the deep influence of Marxism on the problem of ideology, even if it was Napoleon who first used this term as a weapon of war (something, as we shall see, which should not perhaps be completely forgotten). To begin by accepting the analysis in terms of social classes is at the same time to seal oneself in a sterile polemic for or against Marxism. What we need today is a thought which is free from any process of intimidation, a thought which would have the audacity and the capacity to *cross* Marx, without either following or fighting him. Merleau-Ponty, I think, speaks somewhere of an a-Marxist thought; that is also what I seek to practise. But in order to avoid this first snare, it is necessary to avoid a second, that of initially defining ideology in terms of its justificatory function not only for a class, but for a *dominant* class. It is necessary, it seems to me, to escape from the fascination exercised by the problem of domination, in order to consider the broader phenomenon of social integration, of which domination is a dimension but not the unique and essential condition. If it is taken for granted that ideology is a function of domination, then it is assumed uncritically that ideology is an essentially negative phenomenon, the cousin of error and falsehood, the brother of illusion. The contemporary literature on the subject no longer even examines the idea, which has become entirely natural, that ideology is a *false* representation propagated by a person or a group, and that the function of this representation is to conceal a common membership among individuals which the propagator has an interest in not recognising. Consequently, if this problematic of interested and unconscious distortion is to be neither eluded nor assumed, then it is necessary, it seems to me, to loosen the link between the theory of ideology and the strategy of suspicion, leaving it to be shown, by description and analysis, why the phenomenon of ideology calls for the riposte of suspicion.

This first questioning of the accepted ideas incorporated in the initial definition of the phenomenon is closely connected with a second, which concerns the epistemological status of the theory of ideology. My theme, ideology and truth, pertains more precisely to this second line of interrogation. A series of snares also awaits us here. It is, to begin with, too quickly assumed that the man of suspicion is himself unscathed by the defects which he denounces; ideology is the thought of my adversary, the thought of the *other*. *He* does not know it, but *I* do. The question, however, is whether there exists a point of view on action which is capable of extricating itself from the ideological condition of knowledge engaged in praxis. Conjoined with this claim is another: not only, it is said, does there exist a non-ideological place, but this place is that of a *science*, comparable to Euclid's geometry and to the physics and cosmology of Galileo and Newton. It is remarkable that this claim, particularly alive among the most Eleatic of Marxists, is exactly the claim which Aristotle condemned among the Platonists of his time in ethical and political matters, and to which he opposed the pluralism of methods and degrees of rigour and truth. We have fresh reasons to justify this pluralism, reasons which stem from the modern reflection on the properly historical condition of understanding history. This simple remark, which anticipates a whole development, forewarns us that the nature of the relation between science and ideology depends as much on the meaning that is given to science in practical and political matters as on the meaning which is given to ideology itself.

The two lines of discussion will converge towards a question which is, as it were, the question of confidence; this will be the object of my third section. If there is no science capable of extricating itself from the ideological condition of practical knowledge, is it necessary to renounce purely and simply the opposition between science and ideology? Despite the very strong reasons which militate in this direction, I shall try to save the opposition, but without formulating it in terms of an alternative and a disjunction. I shall try thereby to give a more modest meaning – a meaning less pre-emptive and less pretentious – to the notion of a *critique of ideology*, placing the latter within the framework of an interpretation which knows itself to be historically situated, but which strives to introduce so far as it can a factor of distanciation into the work that we constantly resume in order to reinterpret our cultural heritage.

Such is the horizon of this essay: only the search for an intimately dialectical relation between science and ideology seems to me compatible with the degree of truth which, as Aristotle tells us, can be claimed in practical and political matters.

I. Search for criteria of the ideological phenomenon

The level at which I shall attempt to describe the ideological phenomenon will therefore not be, to begin with, that of an analysis in terms of social classes. I propose to arrive at the concept of ideology which corresponds to this analysis, rather than starting from it. This will be my way of 'crossing' Marxism. I shall do it in three stages.

My point of departure is provided by the Weberian analysis of the concepts of social action and social relation. There is social action, for Max Weber, when human behaviour is meaningful for individual agents and when the behaviour of one is oriented towards that of the other. The notion of social relation adds to this double phenomenon of meaningful action and mutual orientation the idea of the stability and predictability of a system of meanings. It is at this level of the meaningful, mutually oriented and socially integrated character of action that the ideological phenomenon appears in all its originality. It is linked to the necessity for a social group to give itself an image of itself, to represent and to realise itself, in the theatrical sense of the word. Therein lies the first feature from which I wish to begin.

Why is it so? Jacques Ellul, in an article which strongly impressed and inspired me,[1] considers as primitive in this regard the relation that an historical community sustains with respect to the founding act which established it: the American Declaration of Independence, the French Revolution, the October Revolution, etc. Ideology is a function of the distance that separates the social memory from an inaugural event which must nevertheless be repeated. Its role is not only to diffuse the conviction beyond the circle of founding fathers, so as to make it the creed of the entire group; its role is also to perpetuate the initial energy beyond the period of effervescence. It is into this gap, characteristic of all situations *après coup*, that the images and interpretations intervene. A founding act can be revived and reactualised only in an interpretation which models it retroactively, through a representation of itself. Perhaps no social group could exist without this indirect relation to its own inaugural event. The ideological phenomenon thus begins very early: for domestication by memory is accompanied not only by consensus, but also by convention and rationalisation. At this point, ideology has ceased to be mobilising in order to become justificatory; or rather, it continues to be mobilising only insofar as it is justificatory.

Whence the second feature which characterises ideology at this first level: its dynamism. Ideology falls within what could be called a theory of social motivation; it is to social praxis what a motive is to an individual project. A motive is both something that justifies and something that carries along. In the same way, ideology argues; it is animated by the will to show that the group which professes it is right to be what it is. But an argument against ideology must not be drawn too quickly from this. For its mediating role remains irreplaceable, as attested to by the fact that ideology is always more than a *reflection*, is always also a *justification and project*. This 'generative' character of ideology is expressed in the second-order foundational power that it exercises with respect to enterprises and institutions, which receive from it the belief in the just and necessary character of the instituted action.

How does ideology preserve its dynamism? Here a third feature suggests itself: all ideology is simplifying and schematic. It is a grid or code for giving an overall view, not only of the group, but also of history and, ultimately, of the world. The 'codified' character of ideology is inherent in its justificatory function; its transformative capacity is preserved only on condition that the ideas which it conveys become opinions, that thought loses rigour in order to enhance its social efficacy, as if ideology alone could mediate not only the memory of founding acts, but systems of thought themselves. Hence anything can become ideological: ethics, religion, philosophy. 'This mutation of a system of thought into a system of belief', says Ellul, *is* the ideological phenomenon.[2] The idealisation of the image which a group forms of itself is only a corollary of this schematisation. For it is through an idealised image that a group represents its own existence, and it is this image which, in turn, reinforces the interpretative code. The phenomena of ritualisation and stereotype thus appear with the first celebrations of the founding events. A vocabulary is already born and with it an order of 'correct denominations', the reign of the *isms*. Ideology is *par excellence* the reign of the *isms:* liberalism, socialism. Perhaps there are *isms* for speculative thought itself only by assimilation to this level of discourse: spiritualism, materialism . . .

This third feature concerns what I shall call the doxic character of ideology. The epistemological level of ideology is that of opinion, of the Greek *doxa;* or, if you prefer Freudian terminology, it is the moment of rationalisation. Hence ideology is readily expressed in maxims, in slogans, in lapidary formulas. Hence also nothing is closer to rhetoric – the art of the probable and the persuasive – than ideology. This *rapprochement* suggests that social cohesion can be unquestioningly secured only if the doxic threshold which corresponds to the average cultural level of the group concerned is not surpassed. But once again, one must not be too quick to denounce the fraud: schematism, idealisation and rhetoric are the prices to be paid for the social efficacy of ideas.

With the fourth feature, the negative characteristics generally associated with ideology begin to take shape. However, this feature is not ignominious in itself. It consists in the fact that the interpretative code of an ideology is something *in which* men live and think, rather than a conception *that* they pose. In other words, an ideology is operative and not thematic. It operates behind our backs, rather than appearing as a theme before our eyes. We think from it rather than about it. Thus arises the possibility of dissimulation, of distortion, which since Marx has been associated with the idea of an inverted image of our own position in society. It is perhaps impossible for an individual, and still more for a group, to thematise everything, to pose everything as an object of thought. This impossibility – to which I shall return at greater length in criticising the idea of *total* reflection – makes ideology by nature an uncritical instance. It seems that the non-transparence of our cultural codes is a condition for the production of social messages.

The fifth feature complicates and aggravates the non-reflective and non-transparent status of ideology. I am thinking of the inertia, the lag, which appears to characterise the ideological phenomenon. This feature seems to be the specifically temporal aspect of ideology. It signifies that what is new can be accommodated only in terms of the typical, itself stemming from the sedimentation of social experience. This is where the function of dissimulation can come in. It occurs in particular with respect to realities actually experienced by the group, but unassimilable through the principal schema. Every group displays traits of orthodoxy, of intolerance to marginality. Perhaps a radically pluralist, radically permissive society is not possible. Somewhere there is the intolerable; and from the latter, intolerance springs. The intolerable begins when novelty seriously threatens the possibility for the group to recognise and re-discover itself. This feature appears to contradict the first function of ideology, which is to prolong the shock wave of the founding act. But the initial energy has a limited capacity; it obeys the law of attrition.

Ideology is both an effect of and resistance to attrition. This paradox is inscribed in the initial function of ideology, which is to perpetuate a founding act in the mode of 'representation'. Hence ideology is both interpretation of the real and obturation of the possible. All interpretation takes place in a limited field; but ideology effects a narrowing of the field in relation to the possibilities of interpretation which characterised the original momentum of the event. In this sense we may speak of ideological closure, indeed of ideological blindness. But even when the phenomenon veers towards the pathological, it conserves something of its initial function. It is impossible for consciousness to develop otherwise than through an ideological code. Ideology is thus affected by the schematisation which ineluctably accompanies it; and in modifying itself in this way, it undergoes sedimentation, even though facts and situations change. It is this paradox which leads us to the threshold of the much emphasised function of *dissimulation*.

Here our analysis reaches the second concept of ideology. It seems to me that the function of dissimulation fully prevails when there is a conjunction between the general function of *integration*, which we have considered until now, and the particular function of *domination*, which is linked to the hierarchical aspects of social organisation.

I was concerned to place the analysis of the second concept of ideology after the preceding one, to arrive at the second concept rather than begin from it. For it is necessary to have understood the other functions of ideology in order to understand the crystallisation of the phenomenon in face of the problem of authority. What ideology interprets and justifies is, above all, the relation to the system of authority. To explain this phenomenon, I shall refer again to the well-known analyses of Max Weber concerning authority and domination. All authority, he observes, seeks to legitimate itself, and political systems are distinguished according to their type of legitimation. Now it appears that if every claim to legitimacy is correlative with a belief on the part of individuals in this legitimacy, then the relation between the claim issued by the authority and the belief which responds to it is essentially asymmetrical. I shall say that there is always more in the claim which comes from the authority than in the belief which is returned to it. I see therein an irreducible phenomenon of surplus-value, if by that we understand the excess of the demand for legitimation in relation to the offer of belief. Perhaps this is the real surplus-value: all authority demands more than our belief can bear, in the double sense of supplying and supporting. Ideology asserts itself as the transmitter of surplus-value and, at the same time, as the justificatory system of domination.

This second concept of ideology is closely interwoven with the first, insofar as the phenomenon of authority is itself coextensive with the constitution of a group. The founding act of a group, which is represented ideologically, is political in its essence. As Eric Weil has always taught, an historical community becomes a political reality only when it becomes capable of decision; whence arises the phenomenon of domination. Ideology-dissimulation thus interacts with all the other features of ideology-integration, in particular with the characteristic of non-transparence which is tied to the mediating function of ideology. We have learned from Weber that there is no fully transparent legitimation. Even without assimilating all authority to the charismatic form, we can see that there is an essential opacity to the phenomenon of authority; we do not desire it but desire *within* it. Finally, no phenomenon confirms so completely the inertia of ideology than the phenomenon of authority and domination. I have always been intrigued and disturbed by what I shall willingly call the stagnation of politics. Each power imitates and repeats an anterior power: every prince wants to be Caesar, every Caesar wants to be Alexander, every Alexander wants to Hellenise an oriental despot.

So it is when the mediating role of ideology encounters the phenomenon of domination that the distorting and dissimulating character of ideology comes to the fore. But precisely insofar as the integration of a group never simply amounts to the phenomenon of authority and domination, so too the features of ideology which we have related to its mediating role do not fully pass into the function of dissimulation, to which ideology is too often reduced.

We are now at the threshold of the third concept of ideology, the properly Marxist concept. I should like to show that by integrating it with the preceding two concepts, it takes on its contours and its depth. What does it offer which is new? Essentially the idea of a distortion, of a deformation by *inversion*. 'If in all ideology', writes Marx, 'men and their circumstances appear upside-down as in a *camera obscura*, this phenomenon arises just as much from their historical life-process as the inversion of objects on the retina does from their physical life-process.'[3] For the moment I shall disregard the metaphorical character of the expression to which I shall return in the second part of the essay. What interests me here is the new descriptive content. The crucial point is that ideology is defined both by its function and by its content. If there is inversion, it is because a certain human production is, as such, inversion. This content, for Marx who here follows Feuerbach, is religion, which is not an example of ideology but ideology *par excellence*. For it is religion which effects the inversion of heaven and earth and makes men stand on their head. In terms of this model, Marx tries to grasp the general process by which the activity of real life ceases to be the base and is replaced by what men say, imagine and represent. Ideology is the error which makes us take the image for the real, the reflection for the original.

As we see, the description is supported by the genealogical critique of productions which proceed from the real towards the imaginary, a critique which, in turn, effects an inversion of the inversion. So the description is not innocent: it takes for granted Feuerbach's reduction of all German idealism and all philosophy to religion, and of religion to an inverted reflection. Not that Marx simply repeated Feuerbach, since he supplemented the reduction in ideas with the reduction in practice, destined to revolutionise the basis of ideology.

My problem at this level is to grasp the descriptive potential brought to light by this genealogy, which we shall soon interrogate from the point of view of its claims to scientificity. To begin with, it seems to me that what Marx has provided is a *specification* of the concept of ideology, which presupposes the two other concepts analysed above. For how could illusions and fantasies have any historical efficacy if ideology did not have a mediating role incorporated in the most elementary social bond, as the latter's symbolic constitution in the sense of Mauss and Lévi-Strauss? Hence we cannot speak of a pre-ideological or non-ideological activity. Moreover, we could not understand how an inverted representation of reality could serve the interests of a dominant class unless the relation between domination and ideology were more primitive than the analysis in terms of social classes and capable of surviving the latter. What Marx offers that is new stands out against this prior backcloth of a symbolic constitution of the social bond in general and the authority relation in particular; and what he adds is the idea that the justificatory function of ideology is preferentially applied to the relation of domination stemming from the division into social classes and the class struggle. We are indebted to him for this specific thematic of the functioning of ideology in connection with the dominant position of a class. But I shall try to show that his specific contribution cannot be fully recognised unless his analysis is freed from a fundamental narrowness, which can be overcome only if the Marxist concept is related to the more encompassing notion of ideology. The fundamental limitation of the Marxist concept does not derive from its link with the idea of a dominant class, that is, from its function, but rather from the definition in terms of a specific content: religion. This limitation is the heritage of Feuerbach, as the fourth thesis on Feuerbach attests. The

Marxist thesis potentially extends much further than its application to religion in the phase of early capitalism, an application which seems to me – it may be said in passing – perfectly well-founded, even if religion constitutes its authentic meaning in another sphere of experience and discourse. The Marxist thesis applies in principle to any system of thought which has the same function: that is what Horkheimer, Adorno, Marcuse, Habermas and the other members of the Frankfurt School have clearly seen. Science and technology as well, at a certain phase of history, can play the role of ideology. The ideological function must therefore be detached from the ideological content. That religion lends itself to this function, reversing the relation of heaven and earth, signifies that it is no longer religion, that is, the insertion of the Word in the world, but rather the *inverted image of life*. Then it is nothing more than the ideology denounced by Marx. But the same thing can happen, and undoubtedly does happen, to science and technology, as soon as their claim to scientificity masks their justificatory function with regard to the military-industrial system of advanced capitalism.

In this way, the conjunction of the Marxist criterion with the other criteria of ideology can liberate the critical potential of this criterion and eventually turn it against the ideological uses of Marxism which I shall examine in a moment. But these secondary consequences must not obscure the fundamental thesis which dominates this first part, namely that ideology is an unsurpassable phenomenon of social existence, insofar as social reality always has a symbolic constitution and incorporates an interpretation, in images and representations, of the social bond itself.

Our second problem is thereby posed in all of its acuteness: what is the epistemological status of a discourse on ideology? Does there exist a non-ideological place, from which it is possible to speak scientifically about ideology?

II. Social sciences and ideology

All of the current quarrels over ideology begin from the implicit or explicit repudiation of Aristotle's contention concerning the rough and schematic character of argumentation in the sciences which he subsumed under the name of politics, and which have been successively called: moral sciences, *Geisteswissenschaften*, human sciences, social sciences, critical social sciences, and finally the critique of ideology developed by the Frankfurt School. The thing that strikes me in the contemporary discussions is not only – not so much – what is said about ideology, but the claim to say it from a non-ideological place called science. Consequently, everything that is said about ideology is dictated by what is presumed to be science and to which ideology is opposed. In my opinion, the two terms in the science–ideology antithesis must together be placed in question. If ideology loses its mediating role and retains only its role as the mystifier of false consciousness, it is because it has been coupled with a science itself defined by its non-ideological status. Now the question is: does such a science exist? I shall distinguish two stages in the discussion, according to whether the word 'science' is taken in a positivist or a non-positivist sense.

Let us begin with the positivist sense. My thesis here is that this is the only sense which would allow the science–ideology opposition to be given a clear and sharp meaning, but that unfortunately social science, at least at the level of general theories where the discussion takes place, does not satisfy the positive criteria of scientificity. Only by becoming positive was the mathematical physics of Galileo able irrevocably to expurgate the *impetus* of pre-Galilean physics, and was the astronomy of Kepler, Copernicus and Newton able to terminate the career of Ptolemaic astronomy. General social theory would be in the same relation with ideology if it could satisfy the same criteria of positive science. In fact, however, the epistemological weakness of general social theory is proportional to the force with which it denounces ideology. For nowhere does social theory rise to a status of scientificity which would entitle it to use, in a pre-emptive way, the term 'epistemological break' to mark its distance from ideology. As Maurice Lagueux, a young philosopher from Quebec, recently wrote in a remarkable essay, we consider scientific only those intellectual results which '*both* provide a satisfying explanation of phenomena which hitherto remain unintelligible (at the superficial level where accounts are vainly sought), *and* successfully resist attempts at falsification to which they are systematically and rigorously submitted (verification in the Popperian sense of non-falsification)'.[4] The important point is not the separate formulation of these two criteria, but rather their combined functioning. A theory can be powerfully explanatory and weakly supported by rigorous attempts at falsification. It is this coincidence of two criteria which disqualifies, and perhaps always will disqualify, general theories in the social sciences. Such theories are either unifying and unverified, or partial and well verified as in demography and other theoretical domains which have a mathematical or statistical basis but which, for this very reason, renounce any ambition to be integrative. In general it is the proponents of the unifying and unverified theories who denounce with the most arrogance the ideology of their adversaries. Here I should like to dismantle some of the traps into which it is very easy to fall.

One common argument is to say that ideology is a surface discourse which remains unaware of its own real motivations. The argument becomes even more impressive when the unconscious character of these real motivations is contrasted with the merely conscious character of public or official motivations. Now it is important to see that to propound something as real, even if unconscious, is not in itself a guarantee of scientificity. The change of plane from the illusory to the real, from consciousness to the unconscious, certainly has considerable explanatory power. But it is this very explanatory power which constitutes an epistemological trap. For the change of plane immediately gives a great intellectual satisfaction, leading us to believe that the opening of the unconscious field and the transfer of explanatory discourse into this field constitute by themselves, and as such, an operation of scientificity.

We are reinforced in this epistemological naivety by the conviction that in transferring explanation from the plane of conscious rationalisations to that of unconscious reality, we have reduced the element of subjectivity in explanation. And indeed if we compare the Marxism of Althusser with the sociology of Max Weber, we see that explanation in terms of the subjective motivations of social agents is replaced by the consideration of structural totalities in which subjectivity has been eliminated. But this elimination of subjectivity on the side of historical agents in no way guarantees that the practising sociologist has himself risen to a subjectless discourse. The epistemological trap is set therein. By a semantic confusion, which is a veritable sophism, explanation in terms of structures rather than subjectivities is construed as a discourse which would be conducted by no specific subject. At the same time, vigilance in the order of verification and falsification is weakened. The trap is all the more formidable in that ultimately the satisfaction obtained in the sphere of rationalisation operates as an obstacle and a mask with respect to the demand for verification. Yet it is precisely that which the theory denounces as ideology: a rationalisation which screens reality.

Diverse tactics have been employed to conceal the epistemological weaknesses of this position; I shall mention only two. On the one hand, a reinforcement of the formal apparatus is sought as a compensation for

the lack of empirical verifications. But that again is only a way of rein-
forcing the explanatory criterion at the expense of the verificationist
criterion. Moreover, I am inclined to think that, pushed back onto the
plane of formalism, a demystifying thought like Marx's would lose its
trump card. Is not its principal reproach to contemporary economic
thought precisely that the latter is reduced to constructing 'models devoid of all real density'?[5]

On the other hand, a mutual reinforcement of several critical disciplines is sought as a compensation for the epistemological inadequacies
of each; thus we witness a kind of crossing between the social theory of
ideology and psychoanalysis. This crossing appears as a chiasmus
where it is supposed that what is alleged but poorly verified in one
discipline is better verified in the other. Just as this crossing seems to
me interesting and decisive in the non-positivist perspective which I
shall discuss later, so too its effects are negative with respect to the
criteria of explanation and falsification discussed so far. Indeed, I would
be tempted to say that what is gained on one side is lost on the other.
For the price to be paid for the mutual reinforcement of the explanatory
power of the two theories is a proportional weakening of the 'character
of precision and decidability'[6] in the description of facts which could
settle a conflict between opposing hypotheses.

The result of this first phase of the discussion is that social theory is
far from possessing the authority which enabled astronomy to demar-
cate itself from astrology or chemistry from alchemy, and which would
entitle social theory to denounce the positions that it judged ideological.

The discussion is not, however, closed for all that. It could be objected that the above argument has imposed upon social theory criteria
which do not suit it, and that the argument itself remains imprisoned
within a positivist conception of social science. I quite agree with this
objection, and I am prepared to search for other criteria of scientificity
for social theory. But then we must be fully aware of what we are doing.
For abandoning the positivist criteria entails *ipso facto* the abandonment of a purely disjunctive conception of the relation between science
and ideology. We cannot play and win on two tables at once; we cannot
abandon the positivist model of science in order to give an acceptable
meaning to the idea of social theory, and at the same time take advantage of this model in order to institute an epistemological break between science and ideology. That is, unfortunately, what happens all
too often in the contemporary discourses on ideology.

So let us explore this second route, reserving for later the question of what new relation can be uncovered between science and ideology once the positivist criteria of social theory have been surpassed.

The second meaning that can be given to the term 'science' in its relation to ideology is a *critical* meaning. This designation accords with the request of the left Hegelians who, modifying the Kantian notion of critique, demanded a truly critical critique. Marx himself, even in the phase which today is said to come after the epistemological break of 1847, does not hesitate to give *Capital* the sub-title, 'A Critique of Political Economy'. The following question is posed: can social theory conceived as critique rise to an entirely non-ideological status, according to its own criteria of ideology? I see three difficulties here, of which the third will concern me particularly, for it is upon its resolution that the possibility of giving an acceptable meaning to the science–ideology dialectic depends.

The first difficulty which I see is this: in giving critique the status of a *combatant* science, how can one avoid surrendering it to the quasi-pathological phenomena denounced in the adversary's camp? When I speak of a combatant science, I am thinking especially of the Leninist interpretation of Marxism, revived with vigour by Althusser in his essay on *Lenin and Philosophy*. Althusser jointly maintains two theses: on the one hand, that Marxism represents the third great and radical break in the history of thought, the first being the birth of geometry with Euclid and the second the birth of mathematical physics with Galileo; in the same way, Marx carved out a new continent named History. So be it – even if History as knowledge and self-knowledge had other ancestors. What creates the difficulty is the simultaneous claim to draw what Lenin called the party line between this science and bourgeois science, and hence to conceive a 'partisan' science, in the strong sense of the word. Therein lies the danger that Marxist science transforms itself into ideology according to its own criteria. In this regard, the subsequent fate of Marxism confirms the most sober fears. Thus, to cite only one example, the analysis into social classes, and especially the thesis that there are fundamentally only two classes, after having been an extremely fruitful working hypothesis, becomes a dogma which hinders fresh attempts to analyse the new social stratifications of advanced industrial societies, or the class formations in a new sense of the term in socialist societies, not to mention the phenomenon of nationalism which lends itself with difficulty to an analysis in terms of social classes.

The creation of an official doctrine by the party provokes another phenomenon of ideology, more serious than this blindness to reality. Just as religion is accused of having justified the power of the dominant class, so too Marxism functions as a system of justification for the power of the party as the *avant-garde* of the working class and for the power of the ruling group within the party. This justificatory function with respect to the power of a dominant group explains why the sclerosis of Marxism provides the most striking example of ideology in modern times. The paradox is that Marxism after Marx is the most extraordinary exemplification of his own conception of ideology as the sustained expression of the relation to reality and as the occultation of that relation. At this point it may be of some significance to recall that it was Napoleon who transformed the honourable terms of 'ideology' and 'ideologue' into terms of polemic and abuse.

These severe remarks do not imply that Marxism is false. Quite the contrary, they imply that the critical function of Marxism can be liberated and manifested only if the use of Marx's work is completely dissociated from the exercise of power and authority and from judgements of orthodoxy; only if his analyses are submitted to the test of a direct application to the modern economy, as they were by Marx to the economy of the mid-nineteenth century; only if Marxism becomes one working tool among others; in short, only if Marx's *Capital* rejoins Nietzsche's *Zarathustra*, which the latter author described as 'a book for no one and for everyone'.

The second difficulty concerns the obstacles which confront an explanation in non-ideological terms of the formation of ideologies. We shall see that my remarks connect up with those of Jacques Taminiaux, although I shall not go so far as to place Marx in the tradition of ontotheology; the words 'origin', 'end' and 'subject' have such polysemy, and receive such different contextual meanings, that I hesitate to make these assimilations. Rather I shall insist, in accordance with an earlier remark left in suspense, on the mediating role exercised by the Hegelian and Feuerbachian concepts in the Marxist conceptualisation. Of course, Marx adds to the Feuerbachian critique, but he remains under its influence when he speaks of ideology. The whole of German philosophy first had to be conceived as a commentary on religion and the latter as an inversion of the relation between heaven and earth, in order that critique could in turn be presented as an inversion of the inversion. Now it is striking that Marx found it very difficult to think of this relation in anything other than metaphorical terms: the metaphor of the inversion of the retinal image, the metaphor of head and feet, of ground and sky, of reflection and echo, the metaphor of sublimation in the chemical sense of the word, that is, of the volatisation of a solid body in an ethereal residue, the metaphor of fixation in clouds . . . As Sarah Kofman notes in an essay[7] marked by the influence of Derrida, these metaphors remain caught in a network of specular images and in a system of oppositions, theory/practice, real/imaginary, light/obscurity, which attest to the metaphysical character of the conception of ideology as inversion of an inversion. Can it be said that after the epistemological break, ideology will no longer be thought ideologically? The text of *Capital* on the fetishism of commodities leaves little hope in this respect; the phantasmagorical form which the value relation assumes when the products of labour become commodities remains an enigma which does not explain the religious illusion but rests upon it, at least in an analogical way. In the end, religion – the master form of ideology – provides more than an analogy: it remains the 'secret' of the commodity itself. As Sarah Kofman says, the fetishism of commodities is not 'the reflection of real relations but that of a world already transformed, enchanted. Reflection of reflection, phantasm of phantasm.'[8] This failure to think of the production of illusion in non-metaphorical terms expresses in a reverse manner – we are in the inversion of the inversion! – the difficulty emphasised by Aristotle of thinking about participation in the Platonic sense. Aristotle said that the latter is only metaphor and empty discourse. In the case of ideology, participation functions in reverse, not from the idea to its shadow, but from the thing to its reflection. But it is the same difficulty.

The reason for the failure can be elucidated by our very first analysis. If it is true that the images which a social group forms of itself are interpretations which belong immediately to the constitution of the social bond, if, in other words, the social bond is itself symbolic, then it is absolutely futile to seek to derive the images from something prior which would be reality, real activity, the process of real life, of which there would be secondary reflections and echoes. A non-ideological discourse on ideology here comes up against the impossibility of reaching a social reality prior to symbolisation. This difficulty confirms me in the view that the phenomenon of inversion cannot be taken as the starting point for an account of ideology, but that the former must be conceived as a specification of a much more fundamental phenomenon which pertains to the representation of the social bond in the after-event of its symbolic constitution. Travesty is a second episode of symbolisation. Whence, in my opinion, the failure of any attempt to define a social reality which would be initially transparent and then obscured, and which could be grasped in its original transparence, short of the idealising reflection. What seems to me much more fecund in Marx's work is the idea that the transparence is not behind us, at the origin, but in front of us, at the end of an historical process which is perhaps interminable. But then we must have the courage to conclude that the separation of science and ideology is itself a limiting idea, the limit of an internal work of differentiation, and that we do not currently have at our disposal a non-ideological notion of the genesis of ideology.

The most fundamental difficulty has, however, not yet been discussed. It concerns the impossibility of exercising a critique which would be absolutely radical – impossible, because a radically critical consciousness would require a *total* reflection. Allow me to develop this argument with some care, for although it does not bear upon those works of social science which make no claim to total theory, it does affect any social theory with totalising pretensions, Marxism included.

To elaborate my argument, I shall consider the two models of explanation distinguished by Jean Ladrière,[9] models which one could readily discover at work in the two fundamental forms of the contemporary interpretation of Marxism itself. I wish to show that the presupposition of a total reflection is equally ineluctable in both models. 'Two models of explanation may be put forward', says Ladrière, 'explanation in terms of projects or explanation in terms of systems.'[10] The first model obviously includes the interpretative sociology of Max Weber, but also the Marxism of Gramsci, Lukács, Ernst Bloch and Goldmann. Now this model makes it extremely difficult to adhere to the position of 'value neutrality' proclaimed by Max Weber.[11] Explanation in terms of projects is necessarily an explanation in which the theoretician implicates himself, hence requiring that he clarify his own situation and his own project in relation to that situation. It is here that the unstated presupposition of total reflection intervenes.

Does the second model of explanation escape from this presupposition? It may seem so at first glance: since there is no claim to explain action in terms of projects, there is no need to elucidate completely the nature of the project and hence to effect a total reflection. But the implication of the knower in his instrument of interpretation is no less ineluctable when the systematic explanation seeks to be total. As Ladrière shows, the critical point of systems theory concerns the necessity of elaborating a theory relative to the evolution of systems. 'Here', he notes, 'one might be influenced by theories of physical or biological systems (using a cybernetic model for instance); or one might rely on philosophical (accordingly, non-scientific) theories – e.g. a dialectical philosophy.'[12] Along either route, the demand for completeness corresponds to that of total reflection in the case of explanation in terms of projects. A whole philosophy is tacitly implied, 'according to which there effectively exists at any one time a viewpoint of the totality and according to which, moreover, this viewpoint can be made explicit and described in an appropriate discourse. Once again, we are obliged to invoke a discourse of another type.'[13]

Thus explanation in terms of systems is no better off than explanation in terms of projects. Explanation in terms of projects could abstract history from every ideological condition only by tacitly presupposing that a total reflection can be carried out. Explanation in terms of systems similarly presupposes, although in a different way, that the knower can rise to a viewpoint which is capable of expressing the totality, and which is equivalent to total reflection on the other hypothesis. Such is the fundamental reason why social theory cannot entirely free itself from the ideological condition: it can neither carry out a total reflection, nor rise to a point of view capable of expressing the totality, and hence cannot abstract itself from the ideological mediation to which the other members of the social group are subsumed.

III. The dialectic of science and ideology

The question which in the introduction I called 'the question of confidence' henceforth appears in these terms: what can be made of the opposition – poorly thought out and perhaps unthinkable – between science and ideology? Must it be purely and simply renounced? I admit that I have often been very close to thinking so when reflecting on this puzzling issue. Simply to renounce it, however, would be to lose the benefit of a tension which can be reduced neither to a comfortable antithesis nor to a confusing *mélange*.

Perhaps it is necessary first, however, to come close to the point of non-distinction, in a step which may have great therapeutic value. That is the benefit which I drew from rereading the already old and unjustly forgotten – at least on this continent – work of Karl Mannheim, written in German in 1929 and entitled *Ideology and Utopia*.[14] The virtue of this book is to have drawn all the consequences from the discovery of the *recurrent* character of the accusation of ideology, and to have pursued to the end the backlash of ideology upon the position of whoever seeks to apply the ideological critique to the other.

Mannheim credits Marxism with the discovery that ideology is not a local error, explicable psychologically, but a structure of thought assignable to a group, a class, a nation. But he then reproaches Marxism for having stopped half-way and for not applying the manoeuvre of distrust and suspicion to itself. According to Mannheim, it is no longer up to Marxism to stop the chain reaction, because the fundamental phenomenon of the disintegration of cultural and spiritual unity sets each discourse at odds with every other. But what happens when we thus move from restricted to generalised suspicion? Mannheim replies: we have moved from a combatant to a peaceful science, namely to the sociology of knowledge, founded by Troeltsch, Max Weber and Max Scheler. What was a weapon of the proletariat becomes a method of research aiming to bring to light the social conditioning of all thought.

Mannheim thereby generalises the concept of ideology. For him, ideologies are defined essentially by their non-congruence, their discordance with regard to social reality. They differ from utopias only in secondary features. Ideologies are, for the most part, professed by the ruling class and denounced by under-privileged classes; utopias are generally supported by the rising classes. Ideologies look backwards, utopias look forwards. Ideologies accommodate themselves to a reality which they justify and dissimulate; utopias directly attack and explode reality. These oppositions between ideology and utopia are certainly considerable, but they are never decisive and total, as we see in Marx himself, who classes utopian socialism among ideological phantasms. Moreover, only subsequent history decides whether a utopia was what it claimed to be, namely a new vision capable of changing the course of history. But above all, the opposition between ideology and utopia cannot be total because both stand out against a common background of non-congruence (behind or ahead) in relation to a concept of reality which itself is revealed only in effective practice. Action is possible only if such a gap does not preclude the continuous adaptation of man to a reality constantly in flux.

Let us accept as a working hypothesis this generalised concept of ideology, coupled in a complex way with the concept of utopia which is sometimes one of its species, sometimes of an opposed genre. My question – the troubling question – is this: from what place does the investigator speak in a generalised theory of ideology? It must be admitted that this place does not exist. And it exists even less than in a restricted theory of ideology, where only the other's thought is ideological. This time the knower knows that he is also immersed in ideology. In this respect, Mannheim's debate with himself is exemplary for its unlimited intellectual honesty. For Mannheim knows that the Weberian claim to a value-free sociology is a deceptive lure. It is only a stage, even if a necessary stage: 'What is needed', he writes,

is a continual readiness to recognize that every point of view is particular to a certain definite situation, and to find out through analysis of what this particularity consists. A clear and explicit avowal of the implicit metaphysical presuppositions which underlie and make possible empirical knowledge will do more for the clarification and advancement of research than a verbal denial of the existence of these presuppositions accompanied by their surreptitious admission through the back door. (*IU* 80)

But to leave the matter there is to lapse into full relativism, into complete historicism, and research itself is killed; for as Mannheim notes, without presuppositions no questions can be asked, and without questions no hypotheses can be formulated and hence nothing any longer can be investigated. This is the case for the investigator as well as for societies themselves. Ideologies are gaps or discordances in relation to the real course of things, but the death of ideologies would be the most sterile of lucidities; for a social group without ideology and utopia would be without a plan, without a distance from itself, without a self-representation. It would be a society without a global project, consigned to a history fragmented into events which are all equal and insignificant.

How then can we make presuppositions, when we know that everything is relative? How can we take a decision which is not a mere toss of the dice, a logical bid for power, a movement of pure fideism? I have already said that Mannheim struggles with this difficulty with exemplary courage of thought. He seeks, at any price, to distinguish relationism from relativism. But at what price? At the price of an impossible demand: to situate all partial ideologies within a total vision which assigns them a relative meaning; and thus, to move from the non-evaluative conception of the pure observer to an evaluative conception which dares to say that one ideology is congruent and another is not. Once again we are led back to the impossible request for total knowledge: 'To provide modern man with a revised view of the *total* historical process' (*IU* 69).† Relationism and relativism are thus divided by a disgraced Hegelianism. 'The task', says Mannheim, 'is to discover, through changes of norms and institutions, a system whose unity and meaning it is incumbent upon us to understand' (*IU* 81);† and further on: 'to discover in the totality of the historical complex the role, significance, and meaning of each element. It is with this type of sociological approach to history that we identify ourselves' (*IU* 83).

Such is the price that must be paid so that the investigator can escape from scepticism and cynicism, and can evaluate the present in order to say: these ideas are valid in the given situation, these others form an obstacle to lucidity and change. But to administer this criterion of accommodation to a given situation, the thinker must have completed his scientific inquiry. For to measure distortions against reality, it is necessary to know social reality in its entirety; and it is precisely at the end of the inquiry that the very meaning of reality is determined: 'the attempt to escape ideological and utopian distortions is, in the last analysis, a quest for reality' (*IU* 87). Once again we are spinning in circles, as with Marx who said that the reality to which ideological illusion is initially opposed will be known only in the end, when the ideologies have been practically dissolved. Here as well, everything is circular: 'Only when we are thoroughly aware of the limited scope of every point of view are we on the road to the sought-for comprehension of the whole' (*IU* 93). But the inverse is no less constraining: 'a total view implies both the assimilation and transcendence of the limitations of particular points of view' (*IU* 94).

Thus Mannheim places himself under the interminable obligation of conquering historicism through its own excesses, leading it from a partial to a total historicism. In this respect, it is not insignificant that Mannheim is interested at the same time in the social problem of the intelligentsia. For the synthesis of points of view presupposes a social carrier, which cannot be a middle class but must be a stratum relatively unclassed, not firmly situated in the social order. Such is the relatively unattached intelligentsia of Alfred Weber, the *freischwebende Intelligenz*. Thus the theory of ideology falls back upon the utopia of a 'mind totally clarified from the sociological point of view' (*IU* 175).†

It must be admitted that the task of a total synthesis is impossible. So are we returned, without any progress of thought, to the critique of total reflection? Do we emerge simply defeated from this exhausting struggle with the ideological conditions of every point of view? Must we renounce any judgement of truth on ideology? I do not think so. As I have said, I regard Mannheim's position as a turning point from which we can glimpse the direction of a viable solution.

The elements of a solution seem to me to be contained in a discourse of a *hermeneutical* character on the conditions of all *historical* understanding. Here I rejoin, by the long detour of a discussion on the conditions of possibility of knowledge about ideology, the analyses which I offered in an earlier study.[15] There I took up, under Gadamer's guidance, a reflection of a Heideggerian type, in order to address myself to the central phenomenon of pre-understanding, the ontological structure of which precedes and commands all the properly epistemological difficulties that the social sciences encounter under the names of prejudice, ideology and the hermeneutical circle. These epistemological difficulties – although diverse and irreducible to one another – have the same origin. They stem from the very structure of a being which is never in the sovereign position of a subject capable of distancing itself from the totality of its conditionings. In the present essay, however, I did not want to allow myself the facility of a discourse which would immediately situate itself in an ontology of pre-understanding, in order to pass judgement from above on the quandaries of the theory of ideology. I have preferred the long and difficult route of an epistemological reflection on the conditions of possibility of knowledge about ideology, and in general on the conditions of validation of explanatory discourse in the social sciences. I have thus tried to rediscover from within, through the failure of the project of total reflection or of total knowledge of ideological differences, the necessity of another type of discourse, that of the hermeneutics of historical understanding.

Here I shall not pursue the analysis of this other discourse. I shall restrict myself, by way of conclusion, to formulating a few propositions which may be able to give an acceptable meaning to the science–ideology couple.

First proposition: all objectifying knowledge about our position in society, in a social class, in a cultural tradition and in history is preceded by a relation of *belonging* upon which we can never entirely reflect. Before any critical distance, we belong to a history, to a class, to a nation, to a culture, to one or several traditions. In accepting this belonging which precedes and supports us, we accept the very first role of ideology, that which we have described as the mediating function of the image, the self-representation. Through the mediating function, we also participate in the other functions of ideology, those of dissimulation and distortion. But we now know that the ontological condition of pre-understanding excludes the total reflection which would put us in the advantageous position of non-ideological knowledge.

Second proposition: if objectifying knowledge is always secondary to the relation of belonging, it can nevertheless be constituted in a *relative autonomy*. For the critical moment which constitutes it is fundamentally possible in virtue of the factor of *distanciation* which is part of the relation of historicity. This theme is not made explicit by Heidegger himself, but he points to its place when he declares:

In the circle of understanding . . . is hidden a positive possibility of the most primordial kind of knowing. We genuinely take hold of this possibility only when, in our explication (*Auslegung*), we have understood that our first, last, and constant task is never to allow our fore-having, fore-sight, and fore-conception to be presented to us by fancies (*Einfälle*) and popular conceptions, but rather to make the scientific theme secure by working out these anticipations in terms of the things themselves.[16]

Thereby the necessity is posed in principle of including the critical instance in the movement of return towards the very structure of the pre-understanding which constitutes us and which we are. A critical distinction between pre-understanding and prejudice is thus required by the hermeneutics of pre-understanding. It is this theme, barely sketched by Heidegger and possibly smothered by the very radicality of his enterprise, that Gadamer has carried a little further, without perhaps giving it the emphasis which it deserves. He has, however, put his finger on the central problem of distanciation, which is not only temporal distance, as in the interpretation of texts and monuments from the past, but positive distancing; a *consciousness exposed to the efficacy of history* can understand only under the condition of distance. I have tried, in turn, to push further in the same direction. The mediation by texts has, in my view, an exemplary value. To understand a saying is firstly to confront it as something said, to receive it in its textual form, detached from its author; this distancing is intimately part of any reading whereby the matter of the text is rendered near only in and through a distance. In my opinion, this hermeneutics of the text, upon which I have sought to reflect, contains crucial indications for a just reception of the critique of ideology. For all distancing is, as Mannheim, generalising Marx, has taught us, a self-distancing, a distanciation of the self from itself. Thus the critique of ideology can be and must be assumed in a work of self-understanding, a work which organically implies a critique of the illusions of the subject. Such is my second proposition: distanciation, dialectically opposed to belonging, is the condition of possibility of the critique of ideology, not outside or against hermeneutics, but within hermeneutics.

Third proposition: if the critique of ideology can partially free itself from its initial anchorage in pre-understanding, if it can thus organise itself in knowledge and enter into the movement of what Jean Ladrière characterises as the passage to theory, nevertheless this knowledge cannot become total. It is condemned to remain partial, fragmentary, insular knowledge; its *non-completeness* is hermeneutically founded in the original and unsurpassable condition which makes distanciation itself a moment of belonging. Forgetting this absolutely insurmountable condition is the source of all the equally insurmountable obstacles which are connected with the reappearance of ideology on the level of the knowledge of ideology. The theory of ideology is here subsumed to an epistemological constraint of non-completeness and *non-totalisation*, which has its hermeneutical justification in the very condition of understanding.

In this respect, I accept Habermas's thesis that all knowledge is supported by an interest, and that the critical theory of ideology is itself supported by an interest in emancipation, that is, in unrestricted and unconstrained communication. But it must be seen that this interest functions as an ideology or a utopia; and we do not know which of the two, since only subsequent history will decide between sterile and creative discordances. It is necessary to keep in mind, not only the indistinctly ideological or utopian character of the interest which supports the critique of ideology, but also and even more that this interest is organically linked to the other interests which the theory describes elsewhere: the interest in material domination and manipulation applied to things and to men, and the interest in historical communication pursued through the understanding of cultural heritages. So the interest in emancipation never effects a total division in the system of interests, a division capable of introducing a clean epistemological break at the level of knowledge.

Such, then, is my third proposition: the critique of ideology, supported by a specific interest, never breaks its links to the basis of belonging. To forget this primordial tie is to enter into the illusion of a critical theory elevated to the rank of absolute knowledge.

My fourth and final proposition will be straightforward deontology. It concerns the *correct usage* of the critique of ideology. From the whole of this meditation it follows that the critique of ideology is a task which must always be begun, but which in principle can never be completed. Knowledge is always in the process of tearing itself away from ideology, but ideology always remains the grid, the code of interpretation, in virtue of which we are not unattached intellectuals but remain supported by what Hegel called the 'ethical substance', *Sittlichkeit*. I describe my fourth proposition as deontological: for nothing is more necessary today than to renounce the arrogance of critique and to carry on with patience the endless work of distancing and renewing our historical substance.

10. The question of proof in Freud's psychoanalytic writings

The question of proof in psychoanalysis is as old as psychoanalysis itself. The 1895 'Project' aims at being a project of scientific psychology. *The Interpretation of Dreams* purports to be a science and not a fantastic construction, a 'fine fairy tale', to use Krafft-Ebing's remark, hurled at Freud at the close of one public presentation. Each of Freud's didactic works – the *Introductory Lectures*, the *New Introductory Lectures*, and the *Outline* – represents a new effort to communicate to the layman the conviction that psychoanalysis is genuinely related to what is intelligible and what claims to be true. And yet, psychoanalysis has never quite succeeded in stating how its assertions are justified, how its interpretations are authenticated, how its theory is verified. This relative failure of psychoanalysis to be recognised as a science results, I think, from a failure to ask certain preliminary questions to which I devote the first two parts of my essay; the third part is an attempt to reply directly to the original question.

I. The criteria for 'facts' in psychoanalysis

The first question concerns what is relevant as a *fact* in psychoanalysis. We may begin by noting that traditional discussions about the epistemological status of analytic theory take it for granted that theories consist of propositions whose role is to systematise, explain, and predict phenomena comparable to those which verify or falsify theories in the natural sciences or in human sciences which, like academic psychology, themselves adopt the epistemology of the natural sciences. Even when we are not dealing with a narrow empiricism which does not require a theory to be directly validated by observables, we nevertheless continue to ask the same questions we would put to an observational science. In this way, we ask by what specific procedures psychoanalysis connects this or that theoretical notion to definite and unambiguous facts. However indirect the verification process may be, definitions must become operational, that is, they must be shown to generate procedures for verification and falsification. And this is precisely what is in question: what in psychoanalysis merits being considered as a verifiable fact?

My thesis is that psychoanalytic theory – in a certain sense which will be described in the second part of this essay – is the codification of what takes place in the analytic situation and, more precisely, in the analytic relationship. It is there that something happens which merits being called the *analytic experience*. In other words, the equivalent of what the epistemology of logical empiricism calls 'observables' is to be sought first in the analytic situation, in the analytic relationship.

Our first task, therefore, will be to show in what way the analytic relationship brings about a selection among the facts that are likely to be taken into account by the theory. I propose four criteria of this process of selection as useful for our discussion.

First criterion: To begin, there enters into the field of investigation and treatment only that part of experience which is capable of *being said*. There is no need to insist here on the *talk-cure* character of psychoanalysis. This restriction of language is first of all an inherent restriction on the analytic technique; it is the particular context of uninvolvement with reality belonging to the analytic situation that forces desire to speak, to pass through the defile of words, excluding substitute satisfactions as well as any regression toward acting out. This screening through speech in the analytic situation also functions as a criterion for what will be held to be the object of this science: not instinct as a physiological phenomenon, not even desire as energy, but desire as a meaning capable of being deciphered, translated, and interpreted. Hence the theory necessarily has to account for what we may call the semantic dimension of desire.

We can already see the misunderstanding that prevails in ordinary epistemological discussions: facts in psychoanalysis are in no way facts of observable behaviour. They are 'reports'. We know dreams only as told upon awakening; and even symptoms, although they are partially observable, enter into the field of analysis only in relation to other factors verbalised in the 'report'. It is this selective restriction which forces us to situate the facts of psychoanalysis inside a sphere of motivation and meaning.

Second criterion: The analytic situation singles out not only what is sayable, but what is said *to another person*. Here again, the epistemological criterion is guided by something absolutely central to the ana-

lytic technique. The transference stage, in this regard, is highly significant, for we might be tempted to confine the discussion of transference
to the sphere of psychoanalytic technique and thereby overlook its
epistemological implications in our search for relevant criteria. To see
this, let us consider just one text crucial for analytic technique, the 1914
essay entitled 'Remembering, repeating, and working through'.[1]

In this essay Freud begins with the precise moment in the cure when
the memory of traumatic events is replaced by the compulsion to repeat
which blocks remembering. Focusing on the relation between this compulsion to repeat, resistance, and transference, he writes, 'The greater
the resistance, the more extensively will acting out (repetition) replace
remembering.' And he adds, 'the patient repeats instead of remembering and repeats under the conditions of resistance' (*SE* 12:151). Then he
introduces transference, which he describes as 'the main instrument
. . . for curbing the patient's compulsion to repeat and for turning it
into a motive for remembering' (*SE* 12:154). Why does transference
have this effect? The reply leads to epistemological considerations directly grafted onto what appears to be a strictly technical matter. If the
resistance can be cleared away and remembering made free to occur, it
is because the transference constitutes something like 'a playground in
which [the patient's compulsion to repeat] is allowed to expand in almost complete freedom' (*SE* 12:154). Extending this analogy of the playground, Freud more specifically says: 'The transference thus creates an
intermediate region between illness and real life through which the
transition from one to the other is made' (*SE* 12:154).

It is this notion of transference as a 'playground' or 'intermediate region' that guides my remarks on the second criterion for what is psychoanalytically relevant as a fact. *In this 'playground', this 'intermediate
region', in effect, we can read the relationship with the other as constituting
an erotic demand addressed to another person.* It is in this regard that
'transference' has its place not only in a study of analytic technique, but
also in an epistemological inquiry about criteria. It reveals this constitutive trait of human desire: not only is it able to be spoken, to be
brought to language, but it is addressed to another; more specifically,
it is addressed to another desire which is capable of denying its request. What is thereby singled out or sifted out from human experience
is the immediately intersubjective dimension of desire.

We should therefore not overlook the fact that if we speak of objects,
of 'wish objects' – and we cannot fail to speak of them in such contexts
as the object-choice, the lost object, and the substitute object, which we

shall return to below – this object is another desire. In other words, the relationship to the other is not something added onto desire. And in this respect Freud's discovery of the Oedipus complex in the course of his self-analysis is to be included within the very structure of desire seen as a triangular structure bringing into play two sexes and three persons. It follows from this that what the theory will articulate as symbolic castration is not an additional, extrinsic factor, but something which attests to the initial relation of desire to an agency of prohibition and imposition of standards lived out in fantasies by the child as a paternal threat directed against his sexual activities. Therefore, from the outset, all that might be considered a solipsism of desire is eliminated, in spite of what a definition of desire simply in terms of energy as tension and release might lead us to believe. The mediation of the other is constitutive of human desire as addressed to . . . This other can be someone who responds or who refuses to respond, someone who gratifies, or someone who threatens. He may be, above all, real or a fantasy, present or lost, a source of anguish, or the object of a successful mourning. Through transference, psychoanalysis controls and examines these alternative possibilities by transposing the drama involving several actors which generated the neurotic situation onto a sort of miniature artificial stage. Thus it is analytic experience itself that forces the theory to include intersubjectivity within the very constitution of the libido and to conceive of it less as a need than as an other-directed wish.

Third criterion: The third criterion introduced by the analytic situation concerns the coherence and the resistance of certain manifestations of the unconscious which led Freud to speak of *'psychical reality'* in contrast to material reality. It is the distinctive traits of this psychical reality which are psychoanalytically relevant. And this criterion is paradoxical to the extent that what common sense sets in opposition to reality is what constitutes this psychical reality.

In 1917, for example, Freud writes, 'phantasies possess *psychical* as contrasted with *material* reality . . . ; *in the world of the neuroses it is psychical reality which is the decisive kind'* (SE 15–16:368). Symptoms and fantasies 'abstract from the object and thus renounce every relation with external reality'. He then goes on to refer to infantile scenes which themselves 'are not always true'. This is an especially important admission when we remember how difficult it was for Freud to give up his initial hypothesis of the father's real seduction of the child. More than fifteen years later he remarked how disturbing this discovery remained for him. What is so disturbing about it? Precisely that it is not clinically relevant whether the infantile scenes are true or false. And it does not matter, therefore, from an epistemological point of view either. This is what is expressed by the phrase 'psychical reality'.

What is important here is that it is the analytic experience itself that necessitates the use of 'psychical reality' to designate certain productions which fall under the opposition of the imaginary and the real, not just according to common sense, but also, in a way, in apparent contradiction to the fundamental opposition in psychoanalysis between the pleasure principle to which the fantasy affixes itself and the reality principle. This is why this concept meets resistance not only as induced by common sense or the attitude formed by the observational sciences, but also from psychoanalytic theory itself and its tenacious dichotomy between the imaginary and the real.

The epistemological consequences of this paradox from analytic experience are considerable: while academic psychology does not question the difference between the real and the imaginary, inasmuch as its theoretical entities are all said to refer to observable facts and ultimately to real movements in space and time, psychoanalysis deals with psychical reality and not with material reality. So the criterion for this reality is no longer that it is observable, but that it presents a coherence and a resistance comparable to that of material reality.

The range of phenomena satisfying this criterion is wide. Fantasies deriving from infantile scenes (observing the parents' sexual relations, seduction, and above all castration) constitute the paradigmatic case to the extent that, in spite of their fragile basis in the real history of the subject, they present a highly structured organisation and are inscribed in scenarios which are both typical and limited in number.

The notion of psychical reality is not exhausted by that of fantasy understood in terms of such archaic scenarios, however. The imaginary, in a broader sense, covers all the kinds of mediations implied in the unfolding of desire.

Close to the infantile scene, for example, we may put the whole domain of abandoned objects which continue to be represented as fantasies. Freud introduces this notion in connection with the problem of symptom formation. Objects abandoned by the libido provide the missing link between the libido and its points of fixation in the symptom.

And from the notion of abandoned objects the transition to that of the substituted object, which places us at the very heart of the analytic experience, is easy. The *Three Essays on the Theory of Sexuality* start from the variability of the object in contrast to the stability of the aim or goal of the libido and derive from this the substitutability of love objects. And in *Instincts and their Vicissitudes*, Freud goes on to construe on this basis, in a systematic fashion, the typical configurations arising from the criss-crossing of substitutions – through inversion, reversal, etc., the *ego* is capable of putting itself in the place of the object, as in the case of narcissism.

Substitutability, in turn, is the key to still another set of phenomena central to the analytic experience. From the time of *The Interpretation of Dreams*, Freud perceived the remarkable feature of dreams that they could be substituted for a myth, a folktale theme, or for a symptom, a hallucination, or an illusion. In effect, the entire reality of these psychic formations consists in the thematic unity which serves as a basis for the interplay of their substitutions. Their reality is their meaning, and their meaning is their capability of mutually replacing one another. It is in this sense that the notions of the lost object and the substitute object – cardinal notions for analytic experience – deserve to occupy a key position in the epistemological discussion as well. Put quite simply, they forbid our speaking of a 'fact' in psychoanalysis in the same way as in the observational sciences.

I do not want to leave this criterion of psychical reality without adding a final link to the chain of examples which has led us from fantasy to the lost object, then to the substitute object. This final link will assure us that the entire chain is placed fully within analytic experience. This example is the work of mourning.

Mourning, as such, is a remarkable case of reacting to the loss of an object (*SE* 14:243). It is, of course, reality which imposes the work of mourning, but a reality which includes the loss of the object, therefore a reality signified as the verdict of absence. Consequently, mourning consists in 'the step by step realization of each of the orders proclaimed by reality'. But this realisation consists precisely in the interiorisation of the lost object, concerning which Freud says, 'its existence continues psychically'.

If I conclude this examination of the criterion of psychical reality with the work of mourning, it is not only to emphasise the wide range of phenomena arising out of the abandonment of the object, but to show at what point the phenomenon of mourning is close to the very core of psychoanalysis. Psychoanalysis begins by acknowledging the fantasy as the paradigm of what, for it, represents psychical reality, but it continues by means of a labour that may itself be understood as a work of mourning, that is, as an internalisation of the lost objects of instinctual desires. Far from restricting itself to vanquishing the fantasy to the benefit of reality, the cure also recovers it as fantasy in order to situate it, without confusing it with what is real, on the level of the imaginary. This kinship between the cure and the work of mourning confirms, if any further confirmation is required, that it is the analytic experience which requires that we add the reference to fantasies to the two preceding criteria; for what has been said (the first criterion) and what is demanded of the other person (the second criterion) bear the mark of the particular imaginary formations which Freud brings together under the term *phantasieren*. It follows that what is relevant for the analyst is not observable facts or observable reactions to environmental variables, but the meaning which the same events that the behavioural psychologist considers as an observer assume for a subject. I shall venture to say, in summation, that *what is psychoanalytically relevant is what a subject makes of his fantasies.*

Fourth criterion: The analytic situation selects from a subject's experience what is capable of entering into a story or narrative. In this sense, 'case histories' as histories constitute the primary texts of psychoanalysis. This 'narrative' character of the psychoanalytic experience is never directly discussed by Freud, at least to my knowledge. But he refers to it indirectly in his considerations about memory. We may recall the famous declaration in *Studies on Hysteria* that 'hysterical patients suffer principally from reminiscences'. Of course memories will appear to be merely screen-memories and fantasies rather than real memories when Freud seeks the real origin of neurotic suffering, but such fantasies in turn will always be considered in their relation to forgetting and remembering due to their relation to resistance and the connection between resistance and repetition. Remembering, then, is what has to replace repetition. The struggle against resistance – which Freud calls 'working through' – has no other aim than to reopen the path of memory.

But what is it to remember? It is not just to recall certain isolated events, but to become capable of forming meaningful sequences and ordered connections. In short, it is to be able to constitute one's own existence in the form of a story where a memory as such is only a fragment of the story. It is the narrative structure of such life stories that makes a case a case history.

That such an ordering of one's life episodes in the form of a story

constitutes a kind of work – and even a 'working through' – is attested
by the role of one fundamental phenomenon of fantasy life, namely the
after-the-event phenomenon (*Nachträglichkeit*) which Lacan has
brought out so well.[2] It is the fact that 'expressions, impressions, mne-
sic traces, are recast later in function of new experience, of the access to
a new stage of development and that they may assume, not only a new
meaning, but a new efficiency'.[3] Before raising a theoretical problem,
this phenomenon is implied in the work of psychoanalysis itself. It is
in the process of working through just mentioned that Freud discovers
that the subject's history does not conform to a linear determinism
which would place the present in the firm grasp of the past in a univocal
fashion. On the contrary, recovering traumatic events through the work
of analysis reveals that at the time they were experiences that could not
be fully integrated in a meaningful context. It is only the arrival of new
events and new situations that precipitates the subsequent reworking
of these earlier events. Thus in the 'Wolf Man', it is a second sexually
significant scene which after the event confers upon the first scene its
effectiveness. And generally speaking, numerous repressed memories
only become traumas after the event. It is a question of more than just
a delay or a deferred action. Here we see that we are far removed from
the notion of a memory which would simply reproduce real events in a
sort of perception of the past; this is instead a work which goes over
and over extremely complex structuralisations. It is this work of memory that is implied, among other things, by the notion of the story or
narrative structure of existence.

For the fourth time, then, a vicissitude of the analytic experience reveals a pertinent trait of what, psychoanalytically, counts as a 'fact'.

II. Investigatory procedure, method of treatment and theoretical terms

The second preliminary question concerning proof in psychoanalysis is
that of the nature of the *relation* which can be found between theory
and what counts as a fact in psychoanalysis.

From the perspective of operational analysis, the theoretical terms of
an observational science must be capable of being connected to observables by way of rules of interpretation or translation which assure the
indirect verification of these terms. The question here is to know
whether the operative procedures which allow the transition from the
level of theoretical entities to that of facts have the same structure and

the same meaning in psychoanalysis as in the observational sciences. To reply to this question, I should like to return to one of Freud's statements which deals precisely with the epistemological status of theory in psychoanalysis. We read that 'Psychoanalysis is the name (1) of a procedure for the investigation of mental processes . . . (2) of a method (based upon that investigation) for the treatment of neurotic disorders and (3) of a collection of psychological information obtained along those lines, which is gradually being accumulated into a new scientific discipline' (*SE* 18:235). It is this triangular relation between a procedure of investigation, a method of treatment and a theory which will hold our attention because it takes the place of the theory–fact relation in the observational sciences. Not only does psychoanalysis deal with 'facts' of a special nature, as has just been stated, but what takes the place of the operative procedures at work in the natural sciences is a unique type of relation between the investigatory procedure and the method of treatment. It is this relation that mediates between the theory and the facts.

Now, before anything can be said about the role of the third term, theory, in relation to the other two terms, the relation between the investigatory procedure and the method of treatment is itself not easy to grasp. Broadly speaking, we may say that the investigatory procedure tends to give preference to relations of *meaning* between mental productions, while the method of treatment tends to give preference to relations of *force* between systems. The function of the theory will be precisely to integrate these two aspects of psychical reality.

The investigatory procedure has, in effect, a strong affinity with the disciplines of textual interpretation. We read, for example:

The aim which I have set before myself is to show that dreams are capable of being interpreted . . . My presumption that dreams can be interpreted at once puts me in opposition to the ruling theory of dreams and in fact to every theory of dreams with the exception of Scherner's; for 'interpreting' a dream implies assigning a 'meaning' to it – that is, replacing it by something which fits into the chain of our mental acts as a link having a validity and importance equal to the rest. (*SE* 4–5:96)

In this regard, interpretation is often compared to the translation from one language into another or to the solution of a rebus (see, for example, *SE* 4–5:277–8; *SE* 13:176; *SE* 14:166; *SE* 23:236). Freud never doubted that however inaccessible the unconscious might be it still participates in the same psychic structures as does consciousness. It is this common structure which allows us 'to interpolate' unconscious acts into the text of conscious acts. This trait belonging to the method of investigation coheres with the criteria for 'facts' in psychoanalysis discussed above, in particular with the criteria of sayability and substitutability. If the investigatory procedure may be applied to both neurotic symptoms and dreams, it may be done because 'dream-formation (*Traumbildung*) and symptom-formation (*Symptombildung*) are homogeneous and substitutable' (*SE* 4–5:605–8). This was recognised as early as 1893, where the 'Preliminary communication' already treats the relation between the determining cause and the hysterical symptom as a 'symbolic tie', akin to the dream process. *This deep kinship among all the compromise formations allows us to speak of the psyche as a text to be deciphered.*

This broadly inclusive notion of a text encompasses the profound unity not only of dreams and symptoms, but of these two taken together with daydreams, myths, folktales, sayings, proverbs, puns, and jokes. And the gradual extension of this method of investigation is assured by the special kinship that exists between, on the one hand, the group of fantasies referred to earlier as infantile scenes (classed in *The Interpretation of Dreams* along with typical dreams: dreams of nudity, of death of someone dear, etc.), and, on the other hand, the most highly organised and most permanent mythical structures of humanity. Under the same investigatory procedure comes most notably the 'textual' structure common to the Oedipus complex discovered by Freud in his self-analysis and the Greek tragedy of Oedipus carried down to us in literature. There is thus a correspondence between the extension of the investigatory procedure and what could be termed *the space of fantasy in general,* in which psychic productions as diverse as daydreams, children's games, psychological novels, and other poetic creations are set out. In the same way, the psychic conflicts portrayed in stone by Michaelangelo's Moses lend themselves to interpretation by virtue of the figurable and substitutable nature of all the sign systems which are included within the same investigatory procedure.

But if we were only to follow the suggestion of the concepts of the text and interpretation, we would arrive at an entirely erroneous notion of psychoanalysis. Psychoanalysis would be purely and simply subsumed under the aegis of the historico-hermeneutical sciences, alongside philology and exegesis. And we would overlook the very features of interpretation that are grasped only when the investigatory procedure is joined to the method of treatment. The meaning of the symptom and of the dream are so difficult to decipher, because of the interposed distortion mechanisms between the manifest and the hidden meaning – the mechanisms Freud listed under the term dream work.

This 'distortion' is indeed a strange sort of phenomenon, and Freud employs all sorts of quasi-physical metaphors to render this transformation, which he says, 'does not think, calculate, or judge in any way at all' (SE 4–5:507). Condensation and displacement are quasi-physical metaphors for the dream work. But it is the central metaphor of *repression* that orders all the others to the point of becoming a theoretical concept whose metaphorical origin is forgotten (as, moreover, is that of the concept of distortion itself, which literally signifies a violent displacement as well as a deformation). And the semi-metaphor of regression belongs to the same cycle.

Another quasi-physical metaphor of equal importance is that of *cathexis,* concerning which Freud does not conceal the kinship with the operation of a capitalist entrepreneur who invests his money in something. This metaphor allows regression to acquire not only a topographic signification, but also a dynamic one, to the extent that regression to an image proceeds from 'changes in the cathexes of energy attaching to the different systems' (SE 4–5:543). This play of metaphors becomes extremely complex because Freud goes on to interweave textual metaphors (translation, substitution, overdetermination, etc.) and energy metaphors, producing mixed metaphors such as disguise, censorship, etc.

Now, why does Freud get himself into such difficult straits with concepts which remain semi-metaphors and, in particular, with inconsistent metaphors which tend toward the polarity of, on the one hand, the *textual* concept of translation and, on the other hand, the *mechanical* concept of compromise, itself understood in the sense of a result of various forces interacting? I suggest that it is the conjunction of the investigatory procedure with the method of treatment that compels the theory to operate in this way, using semi-metaphorical concepts which lack coherence.

I should like to pause here to consider the word 'treatment', which we earlier distinguished from the method of investigation. The notion of a method of treatment must be understood in a sense that extends far beyond its strictly medical sense of 'cure', to designate the whole analytic procedure insofar as analysis itself is a sort of work. This work is both the inverse of what we just described as the dream work and the correlative of what earlier was termed the work of mourning. To the question of how analysis is a work, Freud gives a constant reply: Psychoanalysis is essentially *a struggle against resistances.* And it is this notion of resistance that prevents us from identifying the investigatory procedure with a simple interpretation, with an entirely intellectual understanding of the meaning of symptoms. Interpretation, seen as translation or a deciphering, as the substitution of an intelligible meaning for an absurd one, is only the intellectual segment of the analytic procedure. Even transference (which appeared earlier as an intersubjective criterion of desire) must be treated as one aspect of the handling of resistances (as is apparent in 'Remembering, repeating and working through'). Hence the three themes of compulsion to repeat, transference, and resistance are found to be connected at the level of analytic praxis.

What does this mean for our epistemological inquiry? Essentially the following: the pair formed by the investigatory procedure and the method of treatment takes exactly the same place as the operative procedures in the observational sciences which connect the level of theoretical entities to that of observable data. This pair constitutes the specific mediation between theory and fact in psychoanalysis. And this mediation operates in the following manner: by coordinating interpretation and the handling of resistances, analytic praxis calls for a theory in which the psyche will be represented both as a text to be interpreted and as a system of forces to be manipulated. In other words, it is the complex character of actual practice which requires the theory to overcome the apparent contradiction between the metaphor of the *text* to be interpreted and that of the *forces* to be regulated; in short, practice forces us to think of meaning and force together in a comprehensive theory. It is through the practical coordination of interpretation and the handling of resistances that the theory is given the task of forming a model capable of articulating the facts acknowledged as relevant in analytic experience. It is in this way that the relation between the investigatory procedure and the method of treatment constitutes the necessary mediation between theory and facts.

Now, does psychoanalysis possess a *theory* that satisfies these requirements? It seems to me that Freud's metapsychology should be examined in the light of the questions just raised. If Freud's metapsychology has been turned into a fetish by some and scorned as marginal by others, it is because it was treated as an independent construction. Too many epistemological works examine the great theoretical texts outside the total context of experience and practice. Isolated in this way, the body of doctrine can only lead to premature and truncated evaluations. The theory must therefore be relativised, by which I mean it must be placed back into the complex network of relations that encompass it.

For my part, I should like to submit two theses, apparently opposed to each other, but which, taken together in their unstable equilibrium, attempt to consider Freud's theoretical work as the imperfect yet indispensable starting point for any reformation of this theory.

On the one hand, I am prepared to acknowledge that Freud's theoretical model (or models) is (or are) not adequate to analytic experience and practice as these are formulated in his other writings (the case histories, the writings on technique, and on applied psychoanalysis). More specifically, Freud's metapsychology does not succeed in codifying and integrating into a single unified structure meaning and force, textual interpretation, and the handling of resistances.

In the first place, Freud always tends to reverse the relations between theory, on the one hand, and experience and practice, on the other, and to reconstruct the work of interpretation on the basis of theoretical models that have become autonomous. He thus loses sight of the fact that the language of the theory is narrower than that in which the technique is described. Next, he tends to construct his theoretical models in the positivist, naturalistic, and materialist spirit of the sciences of his day. Many texts assert the exclusive kinship of psychoanalysis with the natural sciences and even with physics, or announce that in the future psychoanalysis will be replaced by a more refined pharmacology.

In this respect, Habermas is correct in speaking of the 'self-misunderstanding of psychoanalysis as a natural science'.[4] According to Habermas, technique and experience call for a structural model which is betrayed by the preferred model of energy distribution. This latter model is superimposed upon analytic experience, ignoring its derivation from the work of reconstructing an individual history on the basis of scattered fragments. Most seriously, this model is in many ways antecedent to analytic experience, as we see in the 'Project', and it imposes its reference system on this experience: quantifiable energy, stimulation, tension, discharge, inhibitions, cathexis, etc. Even when the psychical apparatus includes only 'psychical localities' which are not anatomically localisable, the spatial arrangement and the temporal sequence of the systems continue to lend support to the energy-distribution model. The great article on 'The unconscious' is the principal witness to its sovereignty.

What is lost from sight in a model like this, however, is the very specificity of the psychoanalytic 'fact', with its fourfold nature of being able to be said, to be addressed to another person, to be fantasised, figured, or symbolised, and to be recounted in the story of a life. This set of criteria requires that elements be introduced at the theoretical level in a suitable manner so that they are capable of accounting for what occurs in the analytic relation. This is why I can adopt up to a certain point the suggestions Habermas offers in light of the work of Lorenzer.[5]

These authors assume as their frame of reference the symbolising process at work in human communication and in human interaction generally. The disturbances that give rise to psychoanalytic interventions are then considered as the pathology of our linguistic competence and are placed alongside the distortions uncovered, on another level, by the Marxist and post-Marxist critique of ideology. Psychoanalysis and the critique of ideology, in effect, share a common obligation to explain and interpret these distortions, which are not accidental, but systematic in the sense that they are organised systematically in the text of interhuman communication. These distortions are the occasion of a subject's self-misunderstanding. In order to account for this, we need a theory that is not limited to restoring the integral, unmutilated, and unfalsified text, but one that takes as its object the very mechanisms that distort the text. And this explains why, in turn, the interpretative decoding of symptoms and dreams goes beyond a simply philological hermeneutics, insofar as it is the very meaning of the mechanisms distorting the texts that requires explanation. This is also why the economic metaphors (resistance, repression, compromise, etc.) cannot be replaced by the philological metaphors (text, meaning, interpretation, etc.).

But the opposite is no less true: neither can the economic metaphors replace their complements. They cannot lose their metaphorical character and set themselves up as an energic theory to be taken literally. It is basically against this reduction to the literal nature of the energy-distribution model that our authors formulate their own theories in terms of communication and symbolic interaction. According to these alternative models, the mechanisms of the unconscious are no longer held to be things, they are 'split-off symbols', 'delinguisticised' or 'de-grammaticised motives'. Like banishment or political ostracism, repression banishes a part of language from the public sphere of communication and condemns it to the exile of a 'privatised' language. This is how mental functioning simulates a natural process. But only to the extent that it has been objectified and reified. If we forget that this reification results from a process of desymbolisation, hence from *a specific self-alienation*, we end up constructing a model wherein the unconscious is literally a thing. But at the same time, we are then unable to understand how resymbolisation is possible, that is, how analytic experience itself is possible. We can understand this only if we interpret the phenomena revealed by this experience in terms of *communication disturbances*, and analytic experience as a reappropriation that *inverts the process of splitting off symbols*.

To the extent that I take up this critique of the energic model of Freudian metapsychology, I accept classing psychoanalysis along with the critical social sciences, which are guided by the interest in emancipation and motivated in the final analysis by the wish to recover the force of *Selbstreflexion*.

Yet, in return, I would not want this *rapprochement* with the critical social sciences and this ultimate reference to self-reflection to go beyond the goal of placing the theory back into the complex network of psychoanalytic experience and practice. This is why I want to defend with equal vigour the complementary thesis, which holds that we must always start from the Freudian system in spite of its faults, even – I would venture to say – because of its deficiencies. Indeed, as Habermas himself has remarked, the self-misunderstanding of psychoanalysis is not entirely unfounded. The economic model, in particular, preserves something essential, which a theorising introduced from outside the system is always in danger of losing sight of, namely, that man's alienation from himself is such that mental functioning does actually resemble the functioning of a thing. This simulation keeps psychoanalysis from constituting itself as a province of the exegetical disciplines applied to texts – as a hermeneutics, in other words – and requires that psychoanalysis include in the process of self-understanding operations that were originally reserved for the natural sciences.

This requirement may be illustrated through a brief critique of those efforts at reformulating the theory which immediately exclude in principle this simulation of the thing. I am thinking here especially of those reformulations which borrow from phenomenology, from ordinary language analysis, or from linguistics. All these reformulations omit the task of integrating an explanatory stage into the process of desymbolisation and resymbolisation.

I shall limit myself here to those efforts which arise from consideration of the semantics of action in the school of linguistic analysis.[6] Under the name of the philosophy of action, an autonomous discipline has been constituted, one influenced by Austin, Wittgenstein, and the philosophy of ordinary language, which assigns itself the task of describing the logic implicit in our discourse on action when it uses terms designating actions, intentions, motives, individual or collective agents, etc. Some of the analysts who practise this discipline – although less numerous today, it is true, and subjected to increasingly rigorous criticism by other semanticists – have maintained that discourse on action brings into play criteria of intelligibility distinct from and different from the criteria for physical movement or observable behaviour. One of the implications of this dichotomy between the two 'language-games' of action and movement bears directly on the point at issue in our discussion: according to these analysts, our motives for acting can in no way be assimilated to the causes by which we explain natural events. Motives are reasons for our action, while causes are the constant antecedents of other events from which they are logically distinct.

Can psychoanalytic theory be reformulated on the basis of this distinction? Some authors have thought so and have interpreted psychoanalysis as an extension of the vocabulary of action (intention, motives, etc.) beyond the sphere where we are aware of what we do. Psychoanalysis, according to this interpretation, adds nothing to ordinary conceptuality except the use of the same concepts of ordinary language in a new domain characterised as 'unconscious'. In this way, for example, it is said of the Rat Man that he experienced a feeling of hostility toward his father without being aware of it. Understanding this assertion rests on the ordinary meaning we give to this sort of hostility in situations where the agent is able to recognise such a feeling as his own. The only novelty here is the use of clauses such as 'without being aware', 'unknowingly', 'unconsciously', etc.

In a sense this is true. Freud himself declares that in the unconscious we do find representations and affects to which we can give the same name as their conscious counterparts and which lack only the property of being conscious. But what is completely omitted in this reformulation is the very paradox of psychoanalytic theory, namely, that it is the becoming unconscious as such that requires a specific explanation so that the kinship of meaning between conscious and unconscious contents may be recognised. Now, the explanatory schema capable of accounting for the mechanisms of exclusion, banishment, reification, etc. completely challenges the separation of the domains of action and movement, along with the dichotomy between motive and cause. And in this regard, Michael Sherwood's demonstration in the critical part of *The Logic of Explanation in Psychoanalysis* is entirely convincing.[7] What is remarkable about psychoanalytic explanation is that it brings into view motives which are causes and which require an explanation of their autonomous functioning. Besides, Freud could not oppose motive to cause by giving motives the sense of 'reason for', inasmuch as rationalisation (a term he borrowed from Ernest Jones) is itself a process that calls for an explanation and, by this very fact, does not permit us to accept an alleged reason as the true one.

As a result, Freud is correct in completely ignoring the distinction between motive and cause and in making even its theoretical formulation impossible. In many ways his explanation refers to 'causally relevant' factors, whether this is in terms of the initial phenomenon (e.g., the *origin* of a neurosis), the intermediate stages (e.g., the *genesis* of a symptom, of a libidinal structure), its *function* (e.g., compromise formation), or, finally, its *'significance'* (e.g., substitution or symbolic value). These are the four modes of explanation retained by Sherwood, not only in Freud, but in general as well. Freud's use of the idea of cause and of causal explanation is perhaps both complex and flexible – Sherwood quotes[8] a text from Freud which also distinguishes between preconditions, specific causes, and concurrent causes – but he leaves no room for an opposition between cause and motive. All that is important to him is to explain through one or another of the explanatory modes just mentioned, or through an 'overdetermined' use of several of them, what in behaviour are 'the incongruities' in relation to the expected course of a human agent's action.

It is the attempt to reduce these 'incongruities' that forbids distinguishing between motives and causes because it calls for an *explanation* by means of causes in order to reach an *understanding* in terms of motives. And this is what I try to express in my own terms by saying that the facts of psychoanalysis arise both from the category of the text, and hence of meaning, and from the categories of energy and resistance, and hence of force. To say, for example, that a feeling is unconscious is not just to say that it resembles conscious motives occurring in other circumstances; rather it is to say that it is to be inserted as a causally relevant factor in order to explain the incongruities of an act of behaviour, and that this explanation is itself a causally relevant factor in the work – the working through – of analysis.

From this brief discussion it follows that psychoanalytic theory cannot be reformulated from the outside, on the basis of an alien conceptuality, without mistaking the initial situation in psychoanalysis, namely, that the human psyche under certain conditions of self-alienation is unable to understand itself by simply expanding its immediate interpretative capacities, but instead requires that the hermeneutics of self-understanding take the detour of causal explanation.

If Freud's economic model can therefore legitimately be accused of generating misunderstanding concerning the relation between theory and the analytic situation, it must also be said with equal force and in the opposite direction, that a model of understanding – be it phenomenological, linguistic, or symbolic – that does not integrate some explanatory segment, some economic phase, misunderstands the very facts that are brought to light by analytic experience.

This is why today we can neither be satisfied with the Freudian metapsychology, nor find another starting point to rectify and enrich the theoretical model to the extent that it is true that 'the misunderstanding of psychoanalysis as a natural science is not without basis'.

III. Truth and verification

Having considered two preliminary questions of the criteria that determine what counts as a *fact* in psychoanalysis, and of the relation which is established between the theory and analytic experience through the *double mediation* of the investigatory procedure and the method of treatment, I shall now attempt to deal directly with the specific question of proof in Freud's psychoanalytic writings.

To inquire about proof in psychoanalysis is to ask two separate questions: (1) What truth claim is made by the statements of psychoanalysis? and (2) What sort of verification or falsification are these statements capable of?

What truth claim is made by psychoanalytic statements? This question is not only one of degree, but also of the nature of truth; not only a question of quantity, but also of the quality of truth. Or to put it another way, the degree of exactitude that can be expected of psychoanalytic statements depends on the sort of truth that can be expected in this domain. For lack of an exact view of the qualitative diversity of the types of truth in relation to the types of facts, verificational criteria appropriate to the sciences, in which facts are empirically given to one or more external observers, have been repeatedly applied to psychoanalysis. The conclusion has then been either that psychoanalysis does not in any way satisfy these criteria or that it satisfies them only if they are weakened. Now, the question is not how to use strict criteria loosely and so place psychoanalysis higher or lower on a single scale of verifiability (and undoubtedly quite low on the scale), but how to specify the truth claim appropriate to the facts in the psychoanalytic domain.

Let us return to our enumeration of the criteria for facts in psychoanalysis and ask ourselves what sort of adequation of statements is appropriate to them.

First, if analytic experience is desire coming to discourse, the sort of truth that best answers to it is that of a saying-true rather than a being-true. This saying-true is negatively intended in the characterisation of the mechanisms of distortion as disguise, falsification, illusion, and in general as forms of misunderstanding. Truth here is closer to that of Greek tragedy than to that of modern physics. *Pathei-mathos*, learn through suffering, says the chorus in Aeschylus's *Agamemnon*. And what, indeed, is truth for Oedipus, if not the recognition of himself as one who has already killed his father and married his mother? Recognition is accepting instead of denigrating and accusing oneself, and this is the truth befitting saying-true, according to Sophocles.

This movement from misunderstanding to recognition is also the standard itinerary of analytic experience, and it designates what might be called the veracity threshold of truth in psychoanalysis.[9] And with certain reservations, which will be introduced below, we may say along with Habermas that this sort of truth involves, above all, the subject's capacity of *Selbstreflexion*. The truth claim of psychoanalysis is primarily its claim to increase this capacity by helping the subject to overcome the distortions which are the source of self-misunderstanding.

Second, if the analytic situation elicits – principally by means of transference – what is said *to the other*, the truth claim of psychoanalysis can legitimately be placed within the field of intersubjective communication. Everything Freud says about self-misunderstanding can in fact be carried over into misunderstanding the other. All his analyses concerning the object choice, the lost object, substitutions for the lost object, mourning, and melancholia suggest that the place of misunderstanding is the other person.

This second feature of the truth claim of psychoanalytic statements is thereby characterised in a negative manner, namely, that of pursuing self-recognition through the restoration and extension of the symbolic process in the public sphere of communication. In this sense, psychoanalysis pursues in its own way the project of recognition that Hegel placed at the summit of ethical life in his Jena philosophy. This thesis will seem less banal if we see its critical point in relation to the danger of manipulation, which seems to me implicit in any reduction of the historical sphere of communication to the empirical sphere of observable facts. If it is true that the sphere of empirically verifiable statements coincides with what governs our interest for control and domination, then reducing the historical to the empirical would entail the danger of placing the order of symbolic communication under the same system for controlling results as our instrumental action. This warning is not empty in light of a certain tendency of psychoanalysis to take the process of self-recognition and of recognising the other as an 'adjustment' to the objective conditions of a society which is itself diseased.

With the third criterion for psychoanalytic facts, we encounter the major difficulty facing the truth claims of psychoanalysis. We concluded from the study of the third criterion that what is psychoanalytically relevant is what a subject makes of his fantasies. What becomes of the truth claim of psychoanalysis when it is set within the framework of a more positive recognition of fantasy than Freud himself allowed? By losing its reference to actual reality and by giving wider rein to the liberation of fantasising, to emotional development, and to enjoyment than Freud wanted to do, are we not breaking the bond between veracity and truth? This is undoubtedly so. Nevertheless, I think that there is still something to be sought in the truth claim made from the perspective of the proper use of fantasies. I base this thinking on Freud himself. In 'The dissolution of the Oedipus complex' and 'Analysis, terminable and interminable', there arises the notion that the analytic cure may be understood as a work of mourning, which, far from striking down the fantasy, recovers it as a fantasy in order to situate it clearly with the real on the plane of the imaginary in the strong sense of *Einbildungskraft* used by Kant and the great post-Kantians. And in the same sense, I suggested in *Freud and Philosophy* that analytic experience aims at articulating several prime signifiers of existence (phallus, father, mother, death, etc.) in order to make their structuring function appear.[10] Here the truth claim would concern the passage from the fantasy as alienating to the symbolic as founding both individual and collective identity.[11]

The fourth criterion for psychoanalytic facts – the criterion of narrativity – will perhaps rid us of some of the difficulties raised by the preceding criterion. One could, in effect, raise the objection to the preceding analysis that by introducing something like a 'reasoned mythology' in the recognition process – self-recognition as well as the recognition of the other – we also introduce fiction into the circumference of truth.

How can *Dichtung und Wahrheit* be reconciled, to borrow Goethe's title? If we remember that fiction is pretending and that pretending is doing, are we not substituting doing-true, i.e., make-believe, for saying-true? Perhaps. But are not saying-true and doing-true reconciled in the idea of constructing or reconstructing a *coherent story or account* from the tattered remains of our experience? Let us follow this pathway opened up by the narrative character of psychoanalytic facts. Here the truth claim is tied to what Sherwood calls the 'narrative commitment of psychoanalytic explanation'. It seems to me that this author has shown in a clearly relevant manner that ultimately what is at issue in psychoanalysis is giving 'a single extended explanation of an individual patient's entire case history'.[12] Hence to explain here is to reorganise facts into a meaningful whole which constitutes a single and continuous history (even if it does not cover an entire life span).

I think it is wise to approach things in this way, for the narrative interest or involvement at issue here has no parallel in an observational science where we speak of 'cases' but not of 'case histories'. The psychoanalytic explanation of a case is a narrative explanation in the sense that the generalisations or law-like statements which are implied by the explanatory segments referred to in the second part of our study contribute to the *understandable narrative* toward which each individual case study leads. If we stated earlier that causal connections are explanatory segments in a process of understanding, even of self-reflection in Habermas's sense, this is because understanding is narrative and because the partial explanatory segments of this or that fragment of behaviour are integrated in a narrative structure. So the validation of analytic statements draws its specific nature from this ultimate reference to a *narrative commitment* in the name of which we try to integrate isolated or alien phenomena in 'a single unified process or sequence of events'.[13]

We are thus invited to reflect upon the concept of narrative intelligibility which psychoanalysis has in common with the historical sciences. Now it is difficult to define this concept inasmuch as the criteria for adequation are difficult to handle on this level. Indeed, it is precisely in psychoanalysis that reduction of the 'incongruities' raises the question of knowing what is meant by an intelligible account. A history that would remain inconsistent, incoherent, or incomplete would clearly resemble what we know of the course of life in ordinary experience, namely, that a human life as a whole remains strange, disconnected, incomplete, and fragmented.

We might be tempted therefore to give up any attempt to tie a truth claim to the idea of the intelligible accounts of an existence. But I do not think it would be correct to give in to this epistemological defeatism, for we would thereby turn psychoanalytic statements into the rhetoric of persuasion under the pretext that it is the account's acceptability to the patient that is therapeutically effective. Then, besides the renewed suspicion of suggestion by the analyst – which Freud never ceased to combat – a more serious suspicion is insinuated, namely, that the criterion of therapeutic success is exclusively the patient's ability to adapt to a given social milieu. And this suspicion leads in turn to the suspicion that the psychoanalyst finally represents, with regard to the patient, only the point of view of society, and that he imposes this on his patient by subtly involving him in a strategy of capitulation to which he alone holds the key. This is why we must not give up our efforts to link a truth claim with the narrativity criterion, even if this claim is validated on a basis other than that of narrativity itself. In other words, we must maintain the critical dimension of narrativity, which is just that of self-recognition, of recognition of the other, and of recognition of the fantasy. We may even say, then, that the patient is both the actor and the critic of a history which he is at first unable to recount. The problem of recognising oneself is the problem of recovering the ability to recount one's own history, to continue endlessly to give the form of a story to reflections on oneself. And working through is nothing other than this continuous narration.

We can now turn to the second half of our question: what sort of verification or falsification are the statements of psychoanalysis capable of? To ask about the procedures of verification and falsification is to ask which *means of proof* are appropriate to the truth claims of psychoanalysis. My thesis here is as follows: *if the ultimate truth claim resides in the case histories, the means of proof reside in the articulation of the entire network: theory, hermeneutics, therapeutics, and narration.*

The preceding discussion on narrativity is a good introduction to this final stage of our investigation. We have assumed that all truth claims of psychoanalysis are ultimately summed up in the narrative structure of psychoanalytic facts. But it does not follow that the means of proof are contained in the narrative structure itself; and the question remains whether the means of proof relevant to narrative explanation are not carried by the non-narrative statements of psychoanalysis.

To prove this point it will suffice to think about what makes a narration an explanation in the psychoanalytic sense of the term. It is the possibility of inserting several stages of causal explanation into the process of self-understanding in narrative terms. And it is this explanatory detour that entails recourse to non-narrative means of proof. These are spread over three levels: (1) the level of generalisations resulting from comparison with the rest of the clinical explanation; (2) the level of lawlike propositions applied to typical segments of behaviour (symptoms, for example) which are, as Sherwood has shown, themselves divided into explanations in terms of origin, explanations in terms of genesis, others in terms of function, and still others in terms of significance; finally (3) the level of *very general hypotheses* concerning the functioning of the psychic apparatus, which could be considered as axiomatic. This last level is divided into the topography, the theory of agencies, and the successive theories of instinctual drives, including the death instinct. Generalisations, laws, and axioms, therefore, constitute the non-narrative structure of psychoanalytic explanation.

At its first level, that of generalisations, this non-narrative structure of explanation is already present in the ordinary explanations of individual behaviour; alleged motives – for example, hate or jealousy – are not particular events, but classes of inclinations under which a particular action is placed in order to make it intelligible. To say that someone acted out of jealousy is to invoke in the case of his particular action a feature which is grasped from the outset as repeatable and common to an indeterminate variety of individuals. Such a motive draws its explanatory value from its power to place a particular action in a meaningful context characterised from the start by a certain universality of significance. So to explain is to characterise a given action by ascribing to it as its cause a motive which exemplifies a class. This is all the more true when we are dealing not with classes of motives, identifiable as the general features of human experience, but with fantasies which present organised, stable, and eminently typical scenes, or with stages – oral, anal, genital, etc. – which themselves are also typical organisations of libidinal development. And taking the next step, we are ready to understand that excommunication, on the basis of which an unconscious ensemble is autonomously structured, tends to produce the stereotyped incongruities which are the very object of analytic explanation.

The transition from generalities to lawlike statements broadly corresponds to the explanation not only in terms of unconscious motives but in terms of the mechanisms of distortion which render the motivational process unrecognisable. And above these lawlike statements we still have the propositions concerning the theoretical entities posed by psychoanalysis; these statements constitute the metapsychology as such, which can be considered from the point of view of the structure of these statements as the metalanguage of psychoanalysis – all that can be said regarding instinct, the representatives of instinct, the destiny of instinct, etc. At this level, every narrative feature, by which I mean the reference to a case history, is erased, at least at the manifest level of the statements.

This style of explanation has as its consequence that, in Freud, what Sherwood calls *narrative commitment* and *explanatory commitment* continually split apart, only to merge together again in the case histories – again we must note that even in the case histories, including the 'Rat Man', Freud juxtaposes the case study as such and theoretical considerations. In the other writings, which are far more numerous, however, they diverge again. We could even say that in these writings the relation between 'narrative commitment' and 'explanatory commitment' is reversed. Thus, case histories constitute just one pole of a very wide range of writings for which the essays on metapsychology constitute the other pole, which is basically non-narrative.

Such is the way in which it may be said that in psychoanalysis the means of proof reside in the very articulation of the entire network constituted by the theory, the interpretative procedures, the therapeutic treatment, and the narrative structure of the analytic experience.

I am not unaware that this assertion leads to the most formidable objection of all against psychoanalysis, namely, that these statements are irrefutable and therefore unverifiable if the theory, method, treatment, and interpretation of a particular case are all to be verified at once. If this entire investigation of mine does nothing more than formulate this objection correctly and assemble the means to reply to it, it will have attained its goal.

I shall leave aside the crude form of this objection, namely, that the analyst *suggests* to his patient that he accept the interpretation which verifies the theory. I am taking for granted the replies which Freud opposes to this accusation of suggestibility. They are worth what the measures taken at the level of the professional code and the analytic technique itself against the suspicion of suggestion are worth. I grant that these measures define a good analyst and that there are good analysts.

It is more interesting to take Freud at his word and to contend with a subtler form of the accusation of self-confirmation, that is, that validation in psychoanalysis is condemned to remain circular since everything is verified at once. It is all the more important to consider this argument since the notion of a circle is not foreign to all the historico-interpretative disciplines, in which a 'case' is not only an example to be placed under a law, but something which possesses its own dramatic structure which makes it a 'case history'. The problem, Heidegger says with reference to the hermeneutic circle, is not avoiding the circle but properly entering into it. This means: taking measures so that the circle is not a vicious circle. Now a circle is vicious if it takes the form of begging the question, that is, if the verification in each of the areas considered is the condition for verification in another area. The circle of verification will not be vicious, however, if validation proceeds in a cumulative fashion through the mutual reinforcement of criteria which taken in isolation would not be decisive, but whose convergence makes them plausible and, in the best cases, probable and even convincing.

I shall say, therefore, that the validation apt to confirm the truth claim belonging to the domain of psychoanalytic facts is an extremely complex process which is based on the synergy of partial and heterogeneous criteria. If we take as our guideline the idea of a constellation formed by the theory, the investigatory procedure, the treatment technique, and the reconstruction of a case history, we can then say the following: (1) a good psychoanalytic explanation must be coherent with the theory, or, if one prefers, it must conform to Freud's psychoanalytic system, or to the system by which this or that school claiming his name is identified – recall, however, that I have limited my consideration in this essay to Freud's writings.

This first criterion is not peculiar to psychoanalysis. In every field of inquiry, explanation establishes a connection of this kind between a theoretical apparatus of concepts and an array of facts relevant to this theoretical style. In this sense, all explanations are limited by their own conceptual framework. Their validity extends as far as the correlation between theory and facts works. For the same reason, any theory is questionable. A new theory is required, as Kuhn has argued,[14] as soon as new facts are recognised which can no longer be 'covered' by the ruling paradigm. And something like this is happening today in psychoanalysis, perhaps. The theoretical model of energy distribution appears more and more inadequate, but no alternative model seems to be powerful enough to 'cover' all the accepted facts relevant to psychoanalysis or their paradoxical nature.

(2) A good psychoanalytic explanation must satisfy the universalis-

able rules set up by the procedures of interpretation for the sake of decoding the text of the unconscious. This second criterion is relatively independent of the preceding one to the extent that it relies on the *inner* consistency of the new text substituted by means of translation for the unreadable text of symptoms and dreams. In this respect, the model of the rebus is quite appropriate. It shows that the character of intelligibility of the substituted text resides in its capacity to take into account as many scattered elements as possible from those provided by the analytic process itself, especially as a result of the technique of free association.

A corollary of this second criterion deserves attention. It concerns the expansion of the procedures of interpretation beyond the native domain of psychoanalysis, i.e., symptoms and dreams, along the analogical lines that connect tales, puns, jokes, etc. to the first analogon of this series, the dream. A new kind of coherence is implied here which concerns not only the inner intelligibility of the translated text, but also the analogy of structure which obtains between all the members of the series of psychic productions. This second criterion of validation may be formulated accordingly in two complementary ways as a criterion of intratextual consistency and a criterion of intertextual consistency. The second formulation may even be the more decisive one to the extent that the universalisation of the rules of decoding relies on the soundness of the analogical extrapolation from symptoms and dreams to other cultural expressions. At the same time, the merely analogical character of this extrapolation reminds us of the problematic value of this means of proof. But even the limitation resulting from the analogical structure of this criterion of validation proceeds from structural reasons distinct from those which impose a limitation on the first criterion. The second criterion is not only relatively independent of the first one, but it may correct and even shatter it, inasmuch as it is under the guidance of these procedures of investigation that new facts are released which may defeat the claim of the theoretical framework to 'cover' them. This is what happens, for example, to the energy-distribution model when it is confronted with the facts yielded by the procedures of interpretation in conjunction with the methods of treatment.

(3) A good psychoanalytic explanation must be satisfactory in economic terms; in other words, it must be able to be incorporated into the work of the analysand, into his 'working through', and so become a therapeutic factor of amelioration. This third criterion, too, is relatively independent of the first one since it implies something which

happens to the analysand under the condition of his own 'work' (hence the substitution of the term analysand for that of patient and even of client). And it is relatively independent of the second one, to the extent that an interpretation which is only understood, i.e., intellectually grasped, remains ineffective and may even be harmful so long as a new pattern of energies has not emerged from the 'handling' of resistances. The therapeutic success resulting from this new energetical configuration constitutes in this way an autonomous criterion of validation.

(4) Finally, a good psychoanalytic explanation must raise a particular case history to the sort of narrative intelligibility we ordinarily expect from a story. This fourth criterion should not be overemphasised as would be the case in a purely 'narrative' account of psychoanalytic theory. But the relative autonomy of this criterion must not be overlooked either, because narrative intelligibility implies something more than the subjective acceptability of one's own life story. It comes to terms with the general condition of acceptability that we apply when we read any story, be it historical or fictional. In the terms of W.B. Gallie, a story has to be 'followable', and in this sense, 'self-explanatory'.[15] We interpolate explanation when the narrative process is blocked and in order to 'follow-further'. These explanations are acceptable to the extent that they may be grafted upon the archetypes of storytelling which have been culturally developed and which rule our actual competence to follow new stories. Here psychoanalysis is not an exception. Psychoanalytic reports are kinds of biographies and autobiographies whose literary history is a part of the long tradition emerging from the oral epic tradition of the Greeks, the Celts, and the Germans. It is this whole tradition of storytelling that provides a relative autonomy to the criterion of narrative intelligibility as regards, not only the consistency of the interpretative procedures, but also the efficacy of the change in the balance of libidinal energies.

Consequently, when these criteria of validation do not derive from one another, but mutually reinforce one another, they constitute the proof apparatus in psychoanalysis. It may be granted that this apparatus is extremely complex, very difficult to handle, and highly problematical. But it can at least be assumed that this cumulative character of the validation criteria is the only one suited to both the criteria for psychoanalytic facts that specify the truth claim in psychoanalysis and the complex relations between the theory, the investigatory procedure, and the method of treatment that govern the means of proof in psychoanalysis.

11. The narrative function

The aim of this essay is to sketch a general theory of narrative discourse which encompasses both the 'true' narrative of the historians and the 'fictional' narratives of storytellers, playwrights and novelists. What is at stake is the possibility of delimiting the act of narrating which is common to these two narrative types. To use Wittgenstein's vocabulary, if narrating is a unique 'language-game', and if a language-game 'is part of an activity or a form of life', then we must ask to which form of life narrative discourse as a whole is bound. That is what I call 'to inquire into the narrative function'.

The inquiry may be pursued at two different but interconnected levels: the level of *sense* and the level of *reference*. At the first level, the problem is whether history and fiction have a *common structure*, that is, a common way of ordering sentences on the properly discursive plane. This first analysis has and must retain a formal character. At the second level, the problem is whether, in spite of the evident differences in the way that history and fiction are related to 'reality' – in whatever sense of the word – they refer nonetheless, each in its own way, to the same fundamental feature of our individual and social existence. This feature is characterised in very different philosophies by the term 'historicity', which signifies the fundamental and radical fact that we make history, that we are immersed in history, that we are historical beings. The ultimate problem is thus to show in what way history and fiction contribute, in virtue of their common narrative structure, to the description and redescription of our historical condition. In a word, what is ultimately at stake in our inquiry is the correlation, or better the mutual belonging, between narrativity and historicity.

I. The structural unity of historical and fictional narratives

It should not be assumed that the structural unity of historical and fictional narratives is easier to establish than their common reference or, as I shall say later, than their reference *crossing* upon our historicity. Indeed, the very concept of narrativity poses difficulties. On the side of history, it has been forcefully denied that history is in the last instance narrative in character; and equally, on the side of fiction, it has been denied that the chronological dimension of the narrative is irreducible. So the first paradox we encounter is that narrativity, supposedly common to historical and fictional narratives, must be independently established on each side of the line which divides the two narrative genres.

1. History as narrative

I shall begin by defending the thesis of the irreducibly narrative character of history. The resistance to this thesis rests upon the epistemological arguments of English-speaking authors and upon the arguments of historians in France.

In analytical philosophy, the misrecognition of the irreducibly narrative character of history goes back to the arguments of Carl Hempel in his famous article, 'The function of general laws in history'.[1] This article, it is true, does not bear directly upon the narrative aspect of history, which was not the key issue at the time. The central thesis is rather that general laws have a wholly analogous function in history and in the natural sciences. But the exclusion of the narrative specificity of history is implicitly contained in the thesis that historical explanation does not differ from physical explanation, where the latter concerns events such as a change of physical state, the bursting of a reservoir, an earthquake, etc. The argument is as follows: any singular event can be deduced from two premises. The first describes the initial conditions: antecedent events, prevailing conditions, etc. The second asserts a regularity, a universal hypothesis which, when verified, merits the name of law. If the two premises can be properly established, then the event under consideration can be logically deduced and is said thereby to be explained. It is true that history does not seem to accord entirely with this model. But that only proves that history has not yet risen to the nomological level of the sciences, either because the regularities upon which it bases its explanatory claim are not explicitly formulated, or because these regularities are pseudo-laws borrowed from common sense or from non-scientific psychology – one could even say that it is because these regularities stem from manifest prejudices, as in the case of the magical or mystical conception of the course of nature or history. The only attenuation which Hempel's intransigent thesis tolerates is that, in the best cases, history only rests upon 'explanatory sketches'.

These sketches are regularities which, while not satisfying the criteria of a verified law, nevertheless point in the direction where more specific regularities could be discovered; they also prescribe the measures to take and the stages to go through in order to satisfy the model of scientific explanation.

Thus nothing in the construction of the Hempelian model seems to concern the narrative nature of history. In its first phase, the discussion was focused on the discrepancies between the work of the historian and the model which was imposed upon it. In reflecting on this discrepancy, the question of the irreducibly narrative structure of history arose as a counter-example to the model. For all the critics of the Hempelian model agree that laws do not function in the same way in history as in the natural sciences. The historian does not establish laws, he uses them. Hence these laws can remain implicit and can belong to heterogeneous levels of regularity and universality, according to the anticipations of the reader, who does not approach the historical text with a unique, monolithic model of explanation in mind. If that is so, it is because historical explanation – however structurally related it may be to explanation in the natural sciences – performs a different function. It is, as it were, interpolated in a type of discourse which already has a narrative form.

From the outset, the Hempelian-type analysis suffers from the failure to take into consideration the initial distinction between a physical event which simply occurs, and an event which has already received its historical status from the fact that it has been recounted in chronicles, in legendary stories, in memories, etc. Hempel's analysis depends upon a neutral concept, that of 'singular statements asserting the occurrence of unique events at specific places and times', or that of an 'account of individual events that have occurred once and only once'.[2] The historical event, thus torn from its initial setting, has lost its specificity in order to conform with a general concept of event, itself deprived of any particular relation to the act of narrating. So if we take account of the fact that historical events derive their historical status not only from their articulation in singular statements, but also from the position of these singular statements in configurations of a certain sort which properly constitute a narrative, then what we must place at the centre of the epistemological discussion is no longer the *nature* of historical explanation but its *function*. One may very well grant that the nature of explanation is the same in history as in the natural sciences and that there is no basis at this level to oppose understanding and explanation. The question is not whether the structure of explanation is different, but rather in what sort of discourse this explanatory structure functions.

2. *The concept of plot*

At this point, it is necessary to introduce the decisive concept of *plot.* To be historical, I shall say, an event must be more than a singular occurrence: it must be defined in terms of its contribution to the development of a plot. This concept, let us say straightaway, will provide the link between the history of the historians and fictional narratives.

What is a plot? The phenomenology of the act of following a story, as elaborated by W.B. Gallie in *Philosophy and Historical Understanding,*[3] will serve as our point of departure. Let us say, to begin with, that a story describes a sequence of actions and experiences of a certain number of characters, whether real or imaginary. These characters are represented in situations which change or to the changes of which they react. These changes, in turn, reveal hidden aspects of the situation and the characters, giving rise to a new predicament which calls for thought or action or both. The response to this predicament brings the story to its conclusion.

Accordingly, to follow a story is to understand the successive actions, thoughts and feelings as displaying a particular *directedness.* By this I mean that we are pushed along by the development and that we respond to this thrust with expectations concerning the outcome and culmination of the process. In this sense, the 'conclusion' of the story is the pole of attraction of the whole process. But a narrative conclusion can be neither deduced nor predicted. There is no story unless our attention is held in suspense by a thousand contingencies. Hence we must follow the story to its conclusion. So rather than being *predictable,* a conclusion must be *acceptable.* Looking back from the conclusion towards the episodes which led up to it, we must be able to say that this end required those events and that chain of action. But this retrospective glance is made possible by the teleologically guided movement of our expectations when we follow the story. Such is the paradox of the contingency, 'acceptable after all', which characterises the understanding of any story.

Gallie's thesis is that 'history is a species of the genus story'. As a story, history is about 'some major achievement or failure of men living and working together, in societies or nations or any other lastingly organized groups'.[4] Hence, in spite of their critical relation to the traditional narrative, those histories which deal with the unification or disintegration of an empire, with the rise and fall of a class, a social movement, a religious sect or a literary style *are narratives*. Reading such histories depends on our ability to follow stories. If history is thus rooted in our ability to follow a story, then the distinctive features of historical explanation must be regarded as developments at the service of the capacity of the basic story to be followed. In other words, *explanations have no other function than to help the reader to follow further*. The function of the generalisations which the historian asks us to accept is to facilitate the process of following the story, when the latter is interrupted or obscured. Explanations must therefore be woven into the narrative tissue.

Consideration of some anti-narrative arguments directed against an epistemology of history based on the phenomenology of following a story will enable us to take the remaining decisive step towards narrative structure and thus to bridge the gulf between historical and fictional narrative. Philosophers like Gallie, Dray and Danto have been reproached for subsuming history to a type of narrative which is too dependent on chronological order, on the blind complexity of the present as it is experienced, and finally on the point of view of historical agents immersed in their prejudices. The response to this objection will provide us with the opportunity to specify more precisely the epistemological structure of the notion of plot.

To begin with, in contrast to the view that a story is necessarily bound to a strictly chronological order, it must be said that any narrative combines, in varying proportions, two dimensions: a chronological dimension and a non-chronological dimension. The first may be called the 'episodic dimension' of the narrative. Within the art of following a story, this dimension is expressed in the expectation of contingencies which affect the story's development; hence it gives rise to questions such as: and so? and then? what happened next? what was the outcome? etc. But the activity of narrating does not consist simply in adding episodes to one another; it also constructs meaningful totalities out of scattered events. This aspect of the art of narrating is reflected, on the side of following a story, in the attempt to 'grasp together' successive events. The art of narrating, as well as the corresponding art of following a story, therefore require that we are able *to extract a configuration from a succession*. This 'configurational' operation, to use an expression of Louis Mink,[5] constitutes the second dimension of the narrative activity. This dimension is completely overlooked by the anti-narrative authors, who tend to divest the narrative activity of its complexity and above all of its power to combine sequences and configurations. Indeed, this structure is so paradoxical that every narrative can be conceived in terms of the competition between its episodic dimension and its configurational dimension, between sequence and figure. This complex structure implies that the most humble narrative is always more than a chronological series of events and, in turn, that the configurational dimension cannot eclipse the episodic dimension without abolishing the narrative structure itself. This second aspect of the problem will occupy us shortly when we discuss the structuralist claim to 'de-chronologise' narratives; for the moment, I am concerned only with the first aspect. If it has been possible to graft historical inquiry onto the narrative activity, it is because the configurational dimension, present both in the art of narrating and the art of following a story, has already paved the way for the investigation of meaningful totalities. This activity does not break radically with the narrative activity, insofar as the latter already combines the chronological order and the configurational order.

The full recognition of the continuity between narrative and history presupposes, however, that we dispense with the two other assumptions: that the art of narrating is necessarily linked to the blind complexity of the present as it is experienced by the authors themselves, and that this art is subsumed to the interpretation which the agents themselves give of their actions.

In contrast to these assumptions, Mink observes that, in grasping together events in configurational acts, the narrative operation has the character of a judgement and more precisely of a reflective judgement in the Kantian sense of the term. To narrate and to follow a story is already to 'reflect upon' events with the aim of encompassing them in successive totalities.

For the same reason, it is false to maintain that narratives restrict the hearer or reader to the perspective within which the agents consider their action. The notion of reflective judgement upon events includes the concept of 'point of view'. This aspect will be justified more completely in the analysis of fictional narratives. But here we may affirm that the narrative art characteristically links a story to a narrator. This relation envelops the whole range of possible attitudes which the narrator may display towards his story. These attitudes constitute what Scholes and Kellogg call 'point of view in narrative'. They write: 'In the relationship between the teller and the tale, and that other relationship between the teller and the audience, lies the essence of the narrative art. The narrative situation is thus ineluctably ironical.'[6] This *narrative distance* renders possible the emergence of a new kind of narrator which the authors call *histor,* whose authority derives from the documents which he reads and no longer from the tradition that he receives. The shift from the 'singer of tales' to the *histor* as inquirer cannot be disputed. But the shift takes place within the very concept of 'point of view' which characterises the narrator as such and which must be placed on the same level as the configurational and reflective nature of the narrative act.

The consequence of this continuity between story and history is that the explanatory procedures of scientific history cannot replace a prior narrative but function in conjunction with it, insofar as they are grafted onto its configurational structure.

II. Fictional narrative and the plot

The task now is to defend the specific character of plot at the level of the fictional narrative. We continue, therefore, to place in parentheses the differences which separate true history from fictional stories as regards their referential mode, that is, their different ways of relating to the world of action, of being *about* this world.

Especially in the case of fictional narratives, this inquiry into sense at the exclusion of reference deserves the name of *structural analysis.* Hence I give priority in this section to the exposition of French structuralism. This priority is all the more justified in that this school has produced its most convincing results in the narrative sphere. That will not prevent us, when we criticise this model of analysis, from appealing to English-speaking authors in order to re-establish the primacy of plot over structure.

In general, it may be said that structural analysis tends to reduce the role of plot to a secondary function of figuration in relation to underlying logical structures and the transformations of these structures. Plot is thus assigned to the level of manifestation in contrast to the level of deep grammar, which consists only of structures and their transformations.

This situation is reminiscent of the Hempelian model in the sphere of historical knowledge and the primacy which this model accords to universal laws of explanation. But the elimination of plot is effected more radically in structuralism. The epistemology of history dismissed plot because it is too dependent on chronology. Structuralism, in relegating plot to the level of surface structures, divests it completely of its master role in the narrative.

Let us briefly recall, to begin with, the reasons which have been adduced for the change of level characteristic of all structural analyses. The first argument – the fundamental one – is that a semiotics of the narrative must replace the *inductive* method by a purely *deductive* procedure, on the basis of models constructed in a quasi-axiomatic way; for the almost infinite variety of narrative expressions (oral, written, graphic, gestural) and of narrative classes (myths, folklore, legends, novels, epics, tragedies, drama, films, comic strips, etc.) renders the inductive method impracticable.[7] Linguistics paves the way for this methodological inversion by favouring *codes* and their finite lists of basic units over the infinite number of *messages* that a speaker can produce on the basis of these codes. Linguistics shows, moreover, that the systematic organisation of these basic units can also be mastered by establishing the rules of their combination and transformation which generate all the internal relations of the system. Under these conditions, a structure can be defined as a closed set of internal relations between a finite number of units. The immanence of the relations, that is, the system's indifference to extra-linguistic reality, is an important corollary of the rule of closure which characterises a structure.

As is well known, structural principles were first applied with the greatest success to phonology, and then to lexical semantics and to syntactic rules. The structural analysis of the narrative may be regarded as one attempt to extend or transpose this model of linguistic entities beyond the level of the *sentence*, which is the ultimate entity for the linguist. What we find beyond the sentence is *discourse* in the proper sense of the word, that is, a sequence of sentences presenting their own rules of composition (taking charge of this ordered aspect of discourse was, for a long time, the heritage of classical rhetoric). The narrative is one of the largest classes of discourse, that is, of sequences of sentences subsumed to a certain order.

The extension of the semiotic model to the narrative is the source of the general tendency of structural analysis to 'de-chronologise' the narrative, that is, to reduce its temporal aspects to underlying formal properties. In other words, structural analysis can be characterised in terms of the systematic project of coordinating and subordinating every syntagmatic aspect of the narrative to a paradigmatic aspect.

Let us underline once again the irony of the situation: whereas the tendency of many historians or epistemologists of history was to overestimate the chronological and sequential character of the narrative and to draw from that an argument against the narrative character of history, the tendency of structuralist literary criticism is, on the contrary, to assign the chronological aspect of the narrative to the mere surface structure and to recognise nothing but 'achronic' features in the deep structure. This ironic situation, with its unexpected inversions, suggests that what is at stake in both the theory of history and the theory of fictional narrative is the connection within the notion of plot between figure and sequence, configuration and succession. In the preceding section, our strategy was to accentuate the configurational dimension which was overlooked by the anti-narrative arguments in the theory of historical knowledge; now our strategy will be to underline the irreducibly sequential element of the narrative which a structuralist analysis would like to abolish or repress.

As a paradigmatic example, I shall consider the first model proposed by Greimas in *Sémantique structurale*.[8] I shall leave aside Vladimir Propp's analysis in *Morphology of the Folktale,* in spite of the pioneering role of this work in the domain of narrative semiotics. For Propp was the first to have the idea of reducing the innumerable episodes of the Russian folktale to variations on one unique narrative type. The latter contains only thirty-one basic narrative segments, which Propp calls 'functions', and seven basic roles, which will become Greimas's 'actants'. I leave this analysis aside because Propp's chain of thirty-one functions still preserves the character of temporal sequence. The form of the folktale is one unique tale, governed by a rigid interconnection between functions placed in an irreversible order. The storyteller always follows the same route because there is only one, that of *the* 'Russian folktale'. But this form is not transposable, for example, to the tales of Grimm or of Andersen, still less to narrative structures more removed from the Russian folktale and from the form of the folktale in general.

For this reason, Propp's successors have tried to move a step beyond the sequential appearance which he preserved and to construct a model which is as independent as possible of the chronological order. Such is the option embraced by the French structuralists of Greimas's school. Their aim is to elaborate a syntax of mutual relations between typical roles defined at the level of deep structures and to establish as systematically as possible the rules of transformation of these fundamental relations. The question which concerns us is how far the chronological sequence of the narrative, which remained fundamental in Propp's chain of functions, can be replaced by an 'achronic structure', that is, a structure characterised by non-successive relations. Reciprocally, the problem is to determine what remains properly diachronic in the model. Indeed, the 'narrative' quality of the model itself ultimately rests upon this residue. For could there be a narrative which did not say: and then . . . ? and so . . . ? Could a model be narrative if it did not account for, at the very level of the deep structure, this diachronic dimension?

In order to escape from temporal constraints, Greimas reverses Propp's order of analysis, proceeding directly to the inventory of roles or actants and returning, at a second stage of the analysis, to the inventory of functions or of basic segments of action. The narrative will thus be defined initially by its actantial structure: 'A limited number of actantial terms suffices to account for the organisation of a micro-universe.'[9] This actantial structure is obtained by a mutual adjustment between an *a priori* matrix stemming from syntactic considerations, and an *a posteriori* structure derived inductively by comparison between several *corpora* (in addition to Propp's, that of Etienne Souriau in his work on *Les Deux Cent Mille Situations dramatiques*).

The mutual adjustment attains equilibrium in a model of six roles resting on three pairs of actantial categories, each of which constitutes a binary opposition. The first category opposes subject to object: it has a syntactic basis in the form 'A desires B'; and moreover, it derives from the inventories. For the latter confirm that the transitive or teleological relation operates in the sphere of desire: the hero sets out to find the person sought (Propp). The second actantial category rests on the relation of communication: an addressee is opposed to an addressor. Here again the basis is syntactic: every message links together a sender and a receiver. We also find Propp's sender (king or proxy of the hero) and receiver fused in the hero himself. The third axis is pragmatic: it opposes the helper to the opponent. This axis is composed of either the relation of desire or the relation of communication, both of which can be helped or hindered. Greimas admits that the syntactic basis is less evident here, although certain adverbs (willingly, nevertheless), certain circumstantial participles or the aspects of the verb in certain languages take the place of the syntactic basis. In short, the model combines three relations – the relation of desire, of communication and of action – resting each on a binary opposition.

On the basis of this actantial model of three relations and six places, Greimas attempts to reformulate Propp's functions by ordering them into systematic pairs on a binary model: prohibition *vs* violation. Then he applies laws of transformation to these simple relations. At this point, Greimas formulates the major proposition which will give rise to the second model in *Du sens* (1970). Outside of any syntagmatic context, all the transformations which result from one semic category taken alone can be characterised as forms of conjunction and disjunction. Hence an attempt will be made to replace the inventory of functions with identities to be conjoined and oppositions to be disjoined. For instance, in the pair 'prohibition *vs* violation', prohibition is the negative transformation of the injunction or the mandate. The counterpart of the mandate is the acceptance, the relation mandate–acceptance constituting the establishment of the contract. By a simple opposition of the type 's *vs* non-s', we obtain prohibition as the negative form of mandate, violation as the negative form of acceptance. This system of double opposition thus puts four functions into place by simple confirmation. The narrative as a whole appears at the syntagmatic level as a process which unfolds itself from the rupture of the contract to the restoration of the broken contract. Step by step, all the other of Propp's functions must be reformulated in accordance with the rules of transformation. Thus the test [*épreuve*], the syntagmatic character of which is evident, can be rewritten according to a logical schema on the basis of the double opposition 'injunction *vs* acceptance'/'confrontation *vs* success', from which follows the reception of the helper in the 'qualifying test', the liquidation of the lack in the 'principal test', the recognition in the 'glorifying test'. Finally, all the dramatic processes of the narrative can be interpreted as the inversion of an initial situation, roughly described as the rupture of an order, for the sake of a terminal situation which is conceived as the restoration of order.

The point of departure for my discussion of Greimas's model was the resistance offered by certain irreducibly temporal factors to the enterprise of de-chronologisation. The recognition of the irreducible temporality of the narrative must eventually lead us to call into question some of the basic hypotheses.

The difficulty is clearly concentrated in the notion of test, the significance of which has been brought out strikingly by the analysis. Greimas himself acknowledges this: 'the whole narrative would be reduced to this simple structure if there did not remain a diachronic residue, under the form of a functional pair, confrontation *vs* success . . . , which cannot be transformed into an elementary semic category'; and again, 'the test could thus be considered as the irreducible kernel which accounts for the definition of the narrative as diachrony'.[10] The pair 'confrontation–success', constitutive of the test, is incorporated in turn in a larger sequence – the quest – the diachronic character of which is insurmountable. Consequently, the diachronic element does not seem to be simply a residue of structural analysis: the whole movement from contract to conflict, from alienation to the restoration of order, is *successive by nature*. And it is successive in several ways. The split between the contract and the conflict expresses the temporal character that Augustin, following Plotinus, described as *distentio*, translating the Greek *diastasis*. Moreover, all the episodic elements of the narrative tend to postpone the *dénouement* by introducing delay, detour and suspense, all of which imply what could be called a strategy of procrastination. Further, the unfolding of the action implies alternatives, bifurcations, hence contingent connections, which create the feeling of surprise, essential to the interest taken by the hearer or the reader of the narrative. Finally, the unforeseeable outcome of the quest in terms of success or failure fills the entire story with a general air of uncertainty, which characterises the action as a whole precisely *qua* quest. In this sense, the quest renders possible the plot, that is, the disposition of events capable of being 'grasped together'. The quest is the mainspring of the story, separating and reuniting the lack and the suppression of the lack. The quest is truly the crux of the process without which nothing would happen. *Hence the diachronic reading of the narrative cannot be absorbed into the achronic reading,* according to the atemporal model constructed by the analysis. I shall say that it is this irreducible chronological factor which narrativises the plot itself.

If that is so, the plot cannot be a mere surface manifestation – a mere 'placarding', as Greimas says at one point[11] – of the transformations implied by the model. What is missing from the operations of conjunction and opposition is precisely the *diastasis* of time. Thus the mediation effected by the narrative cannot be of a mere logical order: the transformation of the terms is properly historical.

This critique leads us to question the basic hypothesis: namely that, for want of being able to proceed inductively and thereby risking an infinite enumeration, it is necessary to proceed deductively on the basis of a constructed model. From this quasi-axiomatic assertion derives the methodological rule according to which the deep grammar must not contain any chronological element, as well as its consequence: the retreat of the plot to the surface level of manifestation. We may ask whether it is not this very order of precedence between the deep level and the level of manifestation which must be reversed, and whether the logical structure of the deep level is not merely the ideal projection of an eminently temporalising operation which unfolds first at the level of the narrative. But in order to effect this reversal, what must be questioned first is the initial alternative from which everything follows: for want of being able to proceed inductively, it is necessary to proceed deductively.

To conclude this discussion, I should like to suggest a solution which would escape the alleged alternative. If we adopt a more genetic approach to the question of 'the nature of narrative' (the title of an important work by Robert Scholes and Robert Kellogg), it seems to me that certain recurrent configurations can be seen to emerge from the tradition to which the art of narrating belongs. Here it is necessary, I believe, to emphasise the concept of tradition. If it is possible to write a book on 'the nature of narrative', it is because there is a narrative tradition and because this tradition transmits sedimented forms. Thus Scholes and Kellogg show first how narratives, in their written form, are rooted in an ancient heritage magnificently described by Albert Lord in his classic work *The Singer of Tales*. Then the authors proceed to describe 'the classical heritage of modern narrative', beginning in these terms: 'The literature of Greece and Rome is still of interest to us in the twentieth century . . . The classical literatures provide us with prototypes of virtually all later narrative forms and with paradigms of the processes which govern their interaction and evolution.'[12] This methodological proposition is of considerable importance, for it suggests that the structures of narrative can be uncovered only at the end of a long association with the narrative tradition as a whole. This tradition suggests that the analysis be organised in terms of 'such general and continuing aspects of narrative as meaning, character, plot, and point of view'.[13] In turn, it is the general and continuing aspects which allow one to speak of 'prototypes of form' (by that the authors mean the typical forms of narrative in the West, from the time of the epic and its Semitic, Greek, Celtic, Germanic, etc. varieties up to the modern novel) and of 'processual paradigms' (for example, those which govern the intersections between the kinds of 'empirical' narrative and the kinds of fictional narrative; or within the empirical domain, between biography, chronicle and history on the one hand, and confession and autobiography on the other; or in a more striking way, between the great historical works of the nineteenth century and the great novels of the same period).

The idea that the narrative structures are borne by the tradition of narrative has similarly given rise to an enterprise which, at first sight, displays a certain kinship with the project of French structuralists, yet which does not break its close links to the whole narrative tradition of the West. I am thinking here of the 'archetypal criticism' developed by Northrop Frye in the third essay of his *Anatomy of Criticism*. Its taxonomic appearance, its organisation into classes and sub-classes and its impressive ramifications make it seem more like a formalist reconstruction than a structural construction. But the difference between archetypal criticism and structural analysis consists precisely in the difference of method between an *a priori* construction of narrative models and a schematism provided by familiarity with the narrative tradition. What Frye calls an 'archetype' is not a nontemporal structure; it is the product of the conventionalisation of art and the sedimentation of these conventions. Each poem, newly brought into existence, emerges in a prior world of works: 'Poetry', he says, 'can only be made out of other poems; novels out of other novels. Literature shapes itself.'[14] Thanks to its conventionalised status, art is fundamentally communicable. The archetypes of this criticism are thus nothing other than communicable units, that is, the nuclei of recurrent images.

From this hasty comparison between the initial project of an *a priori* logic of narrative structures and the kind of archetypal criticism developed by Frye, I shall draw the following suggestion: could it not be said that the recurrent forms of the narrative tradition constitute the schematism of the impossible logic of narrative structures? Is it not this schematism which displays in a primordial way the basic modalities of the countless combinations between configuration and sequence in narrative art? Everything happens as if the free play of the imagination of mankind in its best storytellers had spontaneously created the intelligible forms on which our reflective judgement can in turn be applied, without having to impose upon itself the impossible task of constructing *a priori* the matrix of all possible stories. If that is the case, we could then paraphrase Kant's famous formula about schematism and say: the narrative schematism 'is an art hidden in the depths of the human soul, and it will always be difficult to extract the true mechanism from nature in order to lay it open before our eyes'.

III. Narrativity and historicity

The two separate analyses which we have just made of the role of plot in historical narrative and fictional narrative suggest the idea of a family resemblance at the level of sense or structure between these two narrative types. In this respect, we may justly speak of narration as a unique language-game. The question now is in what sense 'speaking this language' is at the same time 'part of an activity or a form of life' which we conventionally call *historicity*. To ask this question is to inquire into the unity of reference which might correspond to the unity of sense in the narrative genre. For as long as the referential dimension of narrative discourse has not been established, the structural unity of the narrative genre remains problematic, contingent and, at most, factual. But what link can there be between narrativity and historicity?

This is the time to remind ourselves that in most European languages, the term 'history' has an intriguing ambiguity, meaning both what really happens and the narrative of those events. Now this ambiguity seems to hide more than a mere coincidence or a deplorable confusion. Our languages most probably preserve (and indicate) by means of this overdetermination of words – *Geschichte, histoire,* history, etc. – a certain mutual belonging between the act of narrating (or writing) history and the fact of being in history, between *doing* history and *being* historical. In other words, *the form of life to which narrative discourse belongs is our historical condition itself.* To show this will be to resolve the problem of the referential dimension of historical discourse as a whole.

The task is not, however, as easy as it may appear. For on first approach, the narrative genre, which displayed a certain unity at the level of sense or structure, seems to lose all unity at the level of reference and to split into two radically distinct types: the 'true' narrative (or, as Scholes and Kellogg say, the 'empirical' narrative) and the fictional narrative. Not only do these two types of narrative appear to be without a common referent, but only the first seems to refer to anything at all. For only *history* can claim to speak about events which really happened, about the real action of men in the past. Documents and archives are the material sources of proof, of 'evidence', for an investigation which proceeds through such sources towards historical reality. Narrative fiction, on the other hand, ignores this burden of proof. Its characters, events, situations and plots are *imaginary*. So it is utterly mistaken to search for the reality represented in stories, for example to try to recognise real Acheans through the heroes of the *Iliad*. On first approach, therefore, narrative discourse seems to have a unity of structure and hence of sense, but no unity of reference. History speaks of the real as past; stories speak of the unreal as fictional. Or to use the terminology familiar to the analytic philosophy of neo-positivist origins, a break concerning truth claims separates 'empirical narratives' from 'fictional narratives'.

So if we wish to demonstrate that the narrative genre as a whole refers to historicity as a whole, it is necessary to shatter the appearance of asymmetry between true narrative and fictional narrative at the level of reference. In other words, it must be shown that all narratives make, in a certain sense, a referential claim.

The argument divides into three steps. (1) It is necessary to establish that there is more *fiction in history* than the positivist conception of history admits. (2) Then it must be shown that fiction in general, and narrative fiction in particular, are more *mimetic* than the same positivism allows. (3) These two prior points being granted, I shall suggest that the references of empirical narrative and fictional narrative *cross upon* what I provisionally called historicity or the historical condition of man. The concept of *crossed reference* provides, in my view, the key to the fundamental relation between narrativity and historicity. It is this relation which, in the final instance, constitutes the hermeneutical theme of the narrative function. In other words, historicity is the form of life correlative to the language-game of narrating.

1. History as a literary 'artefact'

The way has been paved for the explicit recognition of the fictional dimension of history by the whole critique of positivist epistemology in history, exemplified in France by Seignobos and others. For positivism, the task of history is to uncover the facts which are, as it were, buried in documents, just like, as Leibniz would have said, the statue of Hercules was lying dormant in the veins of marble. Against the positivist conception of the historical fact, more recent epistemology emphasises the 'imaginative reconstruction' which characterises the work of the historian. It may be noted that the expression comes from Collingwood who, more than any other author, stressed that historical knowledge was concerned with the reactivation of the past. Collingwood's critique here converges with that of the French epistemologists most influenced by German neo-Kantianism, from the seminal work of Raymond Aron, *Introduction to the Philosophy of History*, through Henri Marrou's *The Meaning of History* to Paul Veyne's *Comment on écrit l'histoire*. For this school of thought, a gulf separates what has really happened from what we know historically. The real event thus retreats to the position of the thing-in-itself, assuming the function of a limit concept in relation to our reconstructions.

However, the decisive step was taken when categories stemming from literary criticism, and more precisely from the semiotics of the narrative, were transferred to the field of history. History could then be explicitly treated as a 'literary artefact',[15] and the writing of history began to be reinterpreted according to categories which were variously called 'semiotic', 'symbolic' and 'poetic'. In this respect, the most influential works were Auerbach's *Mimesis*, Northrop Frye's *Anatomy of Criticism* and Kenneth Burke's *A Grammar of Motives*, to which we may add the critique of the visual arts in Gombrich's *Art and Illusion* and the general theory of symbolic representation in Nelson Goodman's *Languages of Art*. These works have given rise to a general concept of the *fictional representation of reality*, the horizon of which is sufficiently broad to encompass both the writing of history and fiction, whether the latter be literary, pictorial or plastic.

We find in the work of Hayden White a good illustration of this 'poetic' approach to the writing of history. It is true that his study entitled *The Historical Imagination in Nineteenth Century Europe* – described by the author as 'metahistory' – concerns only the great historians of the nineteenth century, who were also great writers and the contemporaries of the great nineteenth-century novelists. It would remain to be shown that contemporary historians, whose university status makes them more concerned to present themselves as 'scientific' rather than 'literary', lend themselves to the same analysis. Nevertheless, what seems to me to be of general significance in White's study is his attempt to establish, initially at the level of plot, the correlation between works of fiction and works of history. He borrows from Northrop Frye the notion of 'emplotment' and its four fundamental types, romance, tragedy, comedy and satire; this notion constitutes, in White's view, more than a secondary artifice of literary presentation. It determines a first level of explanation, 'explanation by emplotment', in the sense that the events begin to be explained when they are transformed *into* a story by emplotment. A similar argument can be found in Paul Veyne's *Comment on écrit l'histoire*: in the chaos of facts, the historian determines the plots, or as Raymond Aron says in his review of Veyne's book, traces the itineraries. But White does not leave it there. He sees that in the work of historians as writers, a whole hierarchy of organising schemes is grafted onto the notion of emplotment. The first schemes involve explanation by formal argument, whether these invoke the laws required by the Hempelian model or the laws alleged by the Marxist dialectic. The second schemes are closer to the great 'World Hypotheses' (in Stephan Pepper's sense)[16] of an epoch: formism, organicism, mechanism, contextualism. The last are similar to mobilising schemes of action, such as ideology and utopia, dealt with here on the basis of Karl Mannheim's categories (anarchism, conservatism, radicalism, liberalism). It is the complex totality of these organising schemes, from emplotment to the ideological implications, which constitute the historical imagination.

Two misunderstandings must be avoided. The first would consist in restricting the procedures described here (or similar procedures) to a merely didactic role, as an aspect of writing extrinsic to historical research proper. The second would be to conceive this 'fictional' representation of reality as excluding rules of 'evidence' which history shares with other sciences (even though documentary evidence may be of a peculiar character). To counter the first misunderstanding, I shall maintain that the three or four levels of conceptualisation relevant to a 'poetics of history' are intrinsic to historical understanding as such. By these procedures, events are properly transformed *into* history; and if one says that emplotment, for example, only concerns writing, then one forgets that history is writing (Italian historians speak of historiography). Paul Veyne entitled his book *Comment on écrit l'histoire*. In reply to the second misunderstanding, I should like to emphasise that however fictional the historical text may be, it claims nevertheless to be a representation *of* reality. In other words, history is both a literary *artefact* (and in this sense a fiction) and a representation of *reality*. It is a literary artefact insofar as, in the manner of all literary texts, it tends to assume the status of a self-sufficient system of symbols. It is a representation of reality insofar as the world that it depicts – and which is the 'world of the work' – claims to hold for real events in the real world.

2. Fiction as 'mimesis'

The view that fiction and representation of reality do not exclude one another must now be established through a direct examination of fictional narrative. This is the second step of my argument. There is, we said, more fiction in the historical work than positivist epistemology would like. But in addition, fictional narrative is more mimetic than the same epistemology would wish. If I use the word 'mimetic' here, it is

in order to evoke straightaway the paradigm of this conjunction between fiction and representation of the real. The paradigm is that of
Aristotle in the *Poetics*. In discussing tragedy – which for him is *poiesis
par excellence* – he sees no difficulty in saying, on the one hand, that
the essence of *poiesis* is the *mythos* of the tragic poem (*mythos* meaning
speech, fable and plot together) and, on the other hand, that the aim of
the poem is the *mimesis* of human action. We thus rediscover, with the
mythos of Aristotle's *Poetics*, what is essential in our concept of plot in
history: union of contingency and consecution, of chronology and configuration, of sequence and consequence.

However, we stumble upon an intolerable paradox if, in thus linking
plot and *mimesis*, we translate the latter term as 'imitation', in the sense
of copying some already existing model. Aristotle had in mind a completely different kind of imitation, a creative imitation. In the first
place, imitation is the concept which distinguishes the human arts from
those of nature. There is *mimesis* only where there is 'doing' or 'activity';
and poetic 'activity' consists precisely in the construction of plots.
Moreover, what *mimesis* imitates is not the effectivity of events but their
logical structure, their meaning. *Mimesis* is so little a reduplication of
reality that tragedy 'seeks to represent men as better (*beltiones*) than
they are in reality' (*Poetics*, 1448a, 17–18). Tragic *mimesis* reactivates
reality – in this case, human action – but in accordance with its mag-
nifien essential features. *Mimesis*, in this sense, is a kind of metaphor
of reality. Like metaphor, it places before the eyes, it shows by 'signifying the thing in activity' (*Poetics*, 1448a, 24). The effect here is similar
to that in painting which, on the basis of an artificial alphabet of lines
and colours, produces what François Dagognet calls, in *Ecriture et icon-
ographie*, an 'iconic augmentation' of the real. Fictional narrative as well
is an iconic augmentation of the human world of action.

I should like now to take this conjunction between *mythos* and *mimesis* in Aristotle's *Poetics* as the paradigm of the referential claim which
seems to me appropriate to fictions in general. The recognition of this
referential claim is often hindered by the prejudices which still dominate in the domain of the theory of the imagination. According to these
prejudices, the image is only a mental thing, a thing in the mind; moreover, it is only the copy or replica of a pregiven reality, which becomes
the indirect referent of the mental image. Against the first prejudice, it
must be re-emphasised that the image is not enclosed within the mind,
that it has a distinctive intentionality, namely to offer a model for *per-
ceiving things differently*, the paradigm of a new vision. Against the second prejudice, it must be said that fiction is not an instance of repro-

ductive imagination, but of *productive imagination*. As such, it refers to reality not in order to copy it, but in order to prescribe a new reading. I shall say, with Nelson Goodman in *Languages of Art*, that all symbolic systems make and remake reality (the first chapter of this book is entitled 'Reality remade'). In this sense, all symbolic systems have a cognitive value: they make reality appear in such and such a way.

With these prejudices put aside, the idea of a productive or creative reference loses its paradoxical appearance. As Goodman says, fictions – or in his language, symbolic systems – 'reorganize the world in terms of works and works in terms of the world'.[17] This is the case with aesthetic icons, but also with epistemological models and political utopias. All deploy this organising power because they have a signifying dimension, because they are forged through labour and *savoir-faire*, and because they generate new grids for reading experience or for producing it. It will be observed that these are the three features already encountered in the Aristotelian concept of *mythos*: saying, doing, emplotment.

The application of this general theory of fiction to narrative fiction is all the easier since the paradigm of poetics in Aristotle's work is already of a narrative order, whether it be tragic drama or the epic. It will thus suffice to generalise the Aristotelian theory of drama to all narrative fictions, on the basis of what has just been said of fictions in general.

As with any poetic work, narrative fiction arises from an *epoché* of the ordinary world of human action and of its description in ordinary discourse. Whence the appearance, which narrative fiction like any poetic work gives, of being closed in on itself. So the poetic function seems to be the inverse of the referential function, as a famous analysis by Roman Jakobson suggests. But as I tried to show in *The Rule of Metaphor*, this suspension of the relation to the world is only the negative counterpart of a more fundamental relation which is precisely that of productive reference. Description, I shall say, must be suspended for redescription to be deployed. Hence I shall characterise the reference of fictional narrative – in the same way as that of any poem – as *split or cleft reference*, by which I understand a way of relating to things which envelops, as a negative condition, the suspension of the referential claim of ordinary language.

3. Narrativity and historicity

This twofold preparatory analysis – of history as fiction and of fiction as *mimesis* – brings us to the threshold of the third proposition, namely that the references of 'true history' and 'fictional history' *cross* upon the basic historicity of human experience. This proposition does not cancel out the difference between the respective referential modes of history and fiction: the *indirect* reference of the first 'through' traces, documents and archives, the *split* reference of the second by suspension of the reference of ordinary language. Not only does this proposition not cancel out the difference, but it makes it function as a difference. How?

A meditation on historicity of a more ontological than epistemological character, one which I cannot develop here, would bring out features in the historical condition itself which demand that the historicity of human experience can be brought to language only as narrativity, and moreover that this narrativity itself can be articulated only by the crossed interplay of the two narrative modes. For historicity comes to language only so far as we tell stories or tell history. In a word, if our historical condition requires nothing less than the conjunction of two narrative genres, it is because of the very nature of our experience of *being* historical. In this experience, the subject–object relation is, as it were, undermined. We are members of the field of historicity as storytellers, as novelists, as historians. *We belong to history before telling stories or writing history.* The game of telling is included in the reality told. That is undoubtedly why, as we have already said, the word 'history' preserves in many languages the rich ambiguity of designating both the course of recounted events and the narrative that we construct. For they belong together. To use Gadamer's complex expression, the history that we recount or write belongs to the 'effective history' of the things that have happened, to the *Wirkungsgeschichte* of historicity itself.

The intimate involvement of the act of narrating in the historical experience itself may explain why the mutual interplay of two narrative genres and two referential modes is required in order to articulate this experience. It is only insofar as each narrative mode shares in some way the intentionality of the other that their references can cross upon historicity; and it is in the exchange between history and fiction, between their opposed referential modes, that *our historicity is brought to language.*

The intersection of intentionalities may appear more clearly if we pass from the consideration of procedures and methods to an inquiry into the interests underlying the two narrative modes. (I use 'interest' in Kant's sense when he juxtaposes the various interests of reason involved in the theses and antitheses of his antinomies.) Here interest is much more than a psychological factor: it designates the teleological horizon which orientates a cognitive activity.

If we inquire into the interests which animate historical research, we obtain, it seems to me, an answer much more complex than that which results from a consideration of methodology in an abstract state. For the historian's interest in 'facts' seems to be coupled with a more deeply anchored interest which could be called, following Habermas, an interest in communication. Our ultimate interest in doing history is to enlarge our sphere of communication. This interest expresses the situation of the historian as a member belonging to the field which he studies. Consequently, any procedure of objectification, distanciation, doubt, suspicion – in sum, everything which makes history a form of research and inquiry – is abstracted from the interest in communication. It is the interest in communication which secures the link between the intentionality of historical knowledge and the intentionality of fiction. How? In at least two ways.

First, the interest operates as a factor of selection of what seems important to a particular historian. The latter retains from the past only what, in his estimation, should not be forgotten, what is memorable in the strict sense. Now what is most worthy of being retained in our memories if not the values which governed the actions of individuals, the life of institutions, the struggles of the past? Thanks to the objective work of the historian, these values are added to the collective wealth of mankind.

However, this way of resurrecting the forgotten requires as its counterpart the capacity to suspend our own prejudices, our own convictions, our own point of view, ultimately to put into parentheses our own desires. In virtue of this *epoché*, the otherness of the other is preserved in its difference and history can be, according to Paul Veyne's phrase, the 'inventory of differences'. Whence the dialectic between the alien and the familiar, the far and the near, at the very heart of the interest in communication.

This dialectic is what places history in the neighbourhood of fiction. For to recognise the values of the past in their *differences* with respect to our values is already to open up the real towards the possible. The 'true' histories of the past uncover the buried potentialities of the present. Croce said that there is only a history of the present. That is true, provided we add: *there is only a history of the potentialities of the present.* History, in this sense, explores the field of 'imaginative' variations which surround the present and the real that we take for granted in everyday life. Such is the way in which history, precisely because it seeks to be objective, partakes of fiction.

But the reverse is no less true: fictional narrative also shares something of the realist intention of history. Everything we have said about the mimetic dimension of fiction enables us to conclude that, by its mimetic intention, *the world of fiction leads us to the heart of the real world of action*. Aristotle already said, in the form of a paradox, that 'poetry is more philosophical . . . than history' (*Poetics*, 1451b, 5–6). He meant that history, insofar as it remains tied to the contingent, to the anecdotal – which is perhaps less true of history today – misses what is essential, whereas poetry, not being subsumed to the real event, proceeds directly to the universal, that is, to what a certain type of man would probably or necessarily do in a certain type of situation.

Could we not say, in conclusion, that by opening us to what is different, history opens us to the possible, whereas fiction, by opening us to the unreal, leads us to what is essential in reality?

Notes

Editor's introduction

1 For a short history of hermeneutics from classical Greece until the nineteenth century, see W. Dilthey, 'The development of hermeneutics', in *Selected Writings*, edited and translated by H.P. Rickman (Cambridge: Cambridge University Press, 1976), pp. 246–63. A survey of developments from the nineteenth century until the present day may be found in Ricoeur's essay on 'The task of hermeneutics', in this volume, pp. 43–62. For an introduction to some of the key figures in modern hermeneutics, see Richard E. Palmer, *Hermeneutics: Interpretation Theory in Schleiermacher, Dilthey, Heidegger, and Gadamer* (Evanston: Northwestern University Press, 1969).

2 For a detailed discussion of Ricoeur's work in the 1950s and 1960s, see Don Ihde, *Hermeneutic Phenomenology: The Philosophy of Paul Ricoeur* (Evanston: Northwestern University Press, 1971). A review of Ricoeur's contributions to educational and theological issues may be found in Michel Philibert, *Ricoeur ou la liberté selon l'espérance* (Paris: Seghers, 1971).

3 See my *Critical Hermeneutics: A Study in the Thought of Paul Ricoeur and Jürgen Habermas* (Cambridge: Cambridge University Press, 1981).

4 Paul Ricoeur, *Husserl: An Analysis of His Phenomenology*, translated by Edward G. Ballard and Lester E. Embree (Evanston: Northwestern University Press, 1967), p. 215.

5 Paul Ricoeur, *Freedom and Nature: The Voluntary and the Involuntary*, translated by Erazim V. Kohák (Evanston: Northwestern University Press, 1966), p. 486.

6 Paul Ricoeur, *Fallible Man*, translated by Charles Kelbley (Chicago: Henry Regnery, 1965), p. xvi.

7 Paul Ricoeur, 'The hermeneutics of symbols and philosophical reflection: I', translated by Denis Savage, in *The Conflict of Interpretations: Essays in Hermeneutics*, edited by Don Ihde (Evanston: Northwestern University Press, 1974), p. 299.

8 Paul Ricoeur, *Freud and Philosophy: An Essay on Interpretation*, translated by Denis Savage (New Haven: Yale University Press, 1970), pp. 26–7.

9 Paul Ricoeur, 'The question of the subject: the challenge of semiology', translated by Kathleen McLaughlin, in *The Conflict of Interpretations*, p. 263.

10 Paul Ricoeur, *Freud and Philosophy*, p. 375.

11 Ibid., p. 419.

12 Paul Ricoeur, 'The question of the subject', p. 250.

13 Paul Ricoeur, 'Structure and hermeneutics', translated by Kathleen McLaughlin, in *The Conflict of Interpretations*, p. 40.

14 Paul Ricoeur, 'Structure, word, event', translated by Robert Sweeney, in *The Conflict of Interpretations*, p. 84.
15 Paul Ricoeur, 'Structure and hermeneutics', p. 51.
16 Paul Ricoeur, 'Structure, word, event', p. 86.
17 Paul Ricoeur, 'The hermeneutical function of distanciation', in this volume, p. 134.
18 Paul Ricoeur, 'Creativity in language', translated by David Pellauer, in *The Philosophy of Paul Ricoeur: An Anthology of His Work*, edited by Charles E. Reagan and David Stewart (Boston: Beacon Press, 1978), p. 125.
19 Paul Ricoeur, *The Rule of Metaphor: Multi-Disciplinary Studies of the Creation of Meaning in Language*, translated by Robert Czerny (London: Routledge and Kegan Paul, 1978), pp. 156–7.
20 Paul Ricoeur, 'The hermeneutical function of distanciation', p. 136.
21 Ibid., p. 139.
22 Paul Ricoeur, 'The model of the text: meaningful action considered as a text', in this volume, p. 211.
23 Paul Ricoeur, 'What is a text? Explanation and understanding', in this volume, p. 161.
24 Paul Ricoeur, 'The model of the text', p. 209.
25 Paul Ricoeur, 'Explanation and understanding: on some remarkable connections among the theory of the text, theory of action, and theory of history', translated by Charles E. Reagan and David Stewart, in *The Philosophy of Paul Ricoeur*, p. 161 (translation modified).
26 Paul Ricoeur, 'History and hermeneutics', translated by David Pellauer, *Journal of Philosophy*, 73 (1976), p. 692.
27 Paul Ricoeur, 'The narrative function', in this volume, p. 295.
28 Paul Ricoeur, *Freud and Philosophy*, p. 46.
29 Paul Ricoeur, 'The question of the subject', p. 243.
30 Paul Ricoeur, 'Appropriation', in this volume, p. 185.
31 Paul Ricoeur, 'Existence and hermeneutics', translated by Kathleen McLaughlin, in *The Conflict of Interpretations*, p. 11.

1. The task of hermeneutics

1 See 'The hermeneutical function of distanciation', in this volume.
2 Cf. W. Dilthey, 'Origine et développement de l'herméneutique' (1900) in *Le Monde de l'Esprit* I (Paris: Aubier, 1947), especially pp. 319–22, 333 [English translation: 'The development of hermeneutics' in *Selected Writings*, edited and translated by H.P. Rickman (Cambridge: Cambridge University Press, 1976)].
3 F. Schleiermacher, *Hermeneutik und Kritik*, volume VII of *Sämmtliche Werke*, edited by F. Lucke (Berlin: G. Reimer, 1938), secs. 15–16; see also Hans-Georg Gadamer, *Wahrheit und Methode* (Tübingen: J.C.B. Mohr, 1960; hereafter cited in the text as *WM*), p. 173 [English translation: *Truth and Method* (London: Sheed and Ward, 1975; hereafter cited in the text as *TM*), p. 163].
4 F. Schleiermacher, *Hermeneutik*, edited by H. Kimmerle (Heidelberg: Carl Winter, 1959), p. 56.
5 This edition appeared in the *Abhandlungen der Heidelberger Akademie der Wissenschaften, Phil.-hist. Klasse*, 2 (1959).
6 Cf. *Abhandlungen gelesen in der Königlichen Akademie der Wissenschaften*, in

Schleiermachers Werke ɪ, edited by O. Braum and J. Bauer (Leipzig: F. Erkardt, 1911), pp. 374ff.

7 W. Dilthey, 'The development of hermeneutics', p. 260.†

8 Cf. F. Mussner, *Histoire de l'herméneutique de Schleiermacher à nos jours*, translated from German by T. Nieberding and M. Massart (Paris: Cerf, 1972), pp. 27–30.

9 Martin Heidegger, *Sein und Zeit* (Tübingen: Max Niemeyer, 1927; hereafter cited in the text as *SZ*), pp. 2, 5ff. [English translation: *Being and Time*, translated by John Macquarrie and Edward Robinson (Oxford: Basil Blackwell, 1978; hereafter cited in the text as *BT*), pp. 21, 25ff.].

2. Hermeneutics and the critique of ideology

1 Here roughly is the history of the debate. In 1965 the second edition of Hans-Georg Gadamer's *Wahrheit und Methode* (Tübingen: J.C.B. Mohr; hereafter cited in the text as *WM*) appeared, published for the first time in 1960. [English translation: *Truth and Method*] (London: Sheed and Ward, 1975; hereafter cited in the text as *TM*).] This edition contains a preface which replies to a first group of critics. Habermas launched an initial attack in 1967 in *Zur Logik der Sozialwissenschaften* (Frankfurt: Suhrkamp), an attack directed against the section of *Wahrheit und Methode* on which we shall concentrate, namely the rehabilitation of prejudice, authority and tradition, and the famous theory of the 'historical-effective consciousness'. The same year Gadamer published, in *Kleine Schriften* ɪ (Tübingen: J.C.B. Mohr), a lecture from 1965 entitled 'Der Universalität des hermeneutischen Problems' [English translation: 'The universality of the hermeneutical problem', translated by David E. Linge, in *Philosophical Hermeneutics* (Berkeley: University of California Press, 1976)] as well as another essay, 'Rhetorik, Hermeneutik und Ideologiekritik'. Habermas replied in a long essay, 'Der Universalitätsanspruch der Hermeneutik', published in the *Festschrift* in honour of Gadamer entitled *Hermeneutik und Dialektik* ɪ (Tübingen: J.C.B. Mohr, 1970). (The latter two essays are reprinted in a collection edited by Habermas and others entitled *Hermeneutik und Ideologiekritik* (Frankfurt: Suhrkamp, 1971).) But the principal work of Habermas which we shall consider is called *Erkenntnis und Interesse* (Frankfurt: Suhrkamp, 1968) [English translation: *Knowledge and Human Interests*, translated by Jeremy J. Shapiro (London: Heinemann, 1972)]; it contains in the appendix an important exposition of principles and methods published in 1965 as 'A general perspective'. His conception of the contemporary form of ideology is found in 'Technik und Wissenschaft als "Ideologie" ', offered to Herbert Marcuse on his seventieth birthday in 1968 [English translation: 'Technology and science as "ideology" ', translated by Jeremy J. Shapiro, in *Toward a Rational Society* (London: Heinemann, 1971)].

2 Hans-Georg Gadamer, *Hermeneutik und Ideologiekritik*, p. 57.

3 Ibid.

4 Martin Heidegger, *Sein und Zeit* (Tübingen: Max Niemeyer, 1927; hereafter cited in the text as *SZ*) [English translation: *Being and Time*, translated by John Macquarrie and Edward Robinson (Oxford: Basil Blackwell, 1978; hereafter cited in the text as *BT*)].

5 Hans-Georg Gadamer, *Kleine Schriften* ɪ, p. 158.

6 Ibid., p. 101 [*Philosophical Hermeneutics*, pp. 3–4].
7 Ibid., p. 104 [p. 7].
8 Ibid., p. 107 [p. 11].
9 Jürgen Habermas, *Knowledge and Human Interests*, p. 9.
10 Ibid., p. 309.
11 Cf. *Hermeneutik und Ideologiekritik*, pp. 120ff.
12 Ibid., p. 149.

3. Phenomenology and hermeneutics

1 This essay reflects the changes of method implied by my own evolution, from an eidetic phenomenology in *Freedom and Nature* (1950), to *Freud and Philosophy* (1965) and *The Conflict of Interpretations* (1969).
2 The 'Nachwort' first appeared in the *Jahrbuch für Philosophie und phänomenologische Forschung* (1930); it was subsequently published in *Husserliana* v, edited by H.L. van Breda (The Hague: Martinus Nijhoff, 1952; hereafter cited in the text as *Hua* v), pp. 138–62.
3 The word 'verliert' reappears three times: *Hua* v 145.
4 Martin Heidegger, *Sein und Zeit* (Tübingen: Max Niemeyer, 1927; hereafter cited in the text as *SZ*), p. 149 [English translation: *Being and Time*, translated by John Macquarrie and Edward Robinson (Oxford: Basil Blackwell, 1978; hereafter cited in the text as *BT*), p. 189].
5 Hans-Georg Gadamer, *Wahrheit und Methode* (Tübingen: J.C.B. Mohr, 1960; hereafter cited in the text as *WM*), pp. 250ff. [English translation: *Truth and Method* (London: Sheed and Ward, 1975; hereafter cited in the text as *TM*), pp. 235ff.].
6 See 'Hermeneutics and the critique of ideology', in this volume.
7 Martin Heidegger, 'Hegels Begriff der Erfahrung' in *Holzwege* (Frankfurt: Vittoria Klostermann, 1950) [English translation: *Hegel's Concept of Experience* (New York: Harper and Row, 1970)].
8 Jean-Paul Sartre, 'Une idée fondamentale de la phénoménologie de Husserl: l'intentionnalité' in *Situations 1* (Paris: Gallimard, 1947) [English translation: 'Intentionality: a fundamental idea of Husserl's phenomenology', translated by Joseph P. Fell, *Journal of the British Society for Phenomenology*, 1, no. 2 (1970), pp. 4–5].
9 Edmund Husserl, *Logische Untersuchungen* ii (Tübingen: Max Niemeyer, 1900; hereafter cited in the text as *LU* ii), pp. 61ff. [English translation: *Logical Investigations* i, translated by J.N. Findlay (London: Routledge and Kegan Paul, 1970; hereafter cited in the text as *LI* i), pp. 299ff.].
10 Edmund Husserl, *Cartesianische Meditationen* in *Husserliana* i, edited by S. Strasser (The Hague: Martinus Nijhoff, 1950; hereafter cited in the text as *Hua* i), p. 30 [English translation: *Cartesian Meditations: An Introduction to Phenomenology*, translated by Dorion Cairns (The Hague: Martinus Nijhoff, 1960; hereafter cited in the text as *CM*), p. 99].

4. The hermeneutical function of distanciation

1 Ferdinand de Saussure, *Cours de linguistique générale* (Paris: Edition critique T. de Mauro, 1973), pp. 30ff., 36ff., 112, 227 [English translation: *Course in*

General Linguistics, translated by Wade Baskin (London: Fontana/Collins, 1974), pp. 13ff., 17ff., 77, 165].

2 Louis Hjelmslev, *Essais linguistiques* (Copenhague: Cercle linguistique de Copenhague, 1959).

3 Emile Benveniste, *Problèmes de linguistique générale* (Paris: Gallimard, 1966) [English translation: *Problems in General Linguistics*, translated by Mary Elizabeth Meek (Florida: University of Miami Press, 1971)].

4 J.L. Austin, *How to do Things with Words* (Oxford: Oxford University Press, 1962).

5 John R. Searle, *Speech Acts: An Essay in the Philosophy of Language* (Cambridge: Cambridge University Press, 1969).

6 G.-G. Granger, *Essai d'une philosophie du style* (Paris: A. Colin, 1968), p. 6.

7 Ibid.

8 Ibid., p. 11.

9 Ibid., p. 12.

10 W.K. Wimsatt, *The Verbal Icon: Studies in the Meaning of Poetry* (Kentucky: University of Kentucky Press, 1954).

11 G. Frege, 'On sense and reference' in *Translations from the Philosophical Writings of Gottlob Frege*, edited by Peter Geach and Max Black (Oxford: Basil Blackwell, 1960).

12 See 'Metaphor and the central problem of hermeneutics', in this volume.

5. What is a text? Explanation and understanding

1 W. Dilthey, 'Origine et développement de l'herméneutique' (1900) in *Le Monde de l'Esprit* I (Paris: Aubier, 1947), p. 320 [English translation: 'The development of hermeneutics' in *Selected Writings*, edited and translated by H.P. Rickman (Cambridge: Cambridge University Press, 1976), p. 248].†

2 Ibid., p. 333 [pp. 259–60].†

3 Claude Lévi-Strauss, *Anthropologie structurale* (Paris: Plon, 1958) p. 233 [English translation: *Structural Anthropology*, translated by Claire Jacobson and Brooke Grundfest Schoepf (Harmondsworth: Penguin Books, 1968), pp. 210–11].†

4 Ibid., p. 234 [p. 211].†

5 Ibid., p. 239 [p. 216].†

6 Ibid., p. 241 [p. 217].†

7 Ibid., p. 248 [p. 224].†

8 Ibid., p. 243 [p. 220].†

9 See Paul Ricoeur, 'Sur l'exégèse de Genèse 1, 1–2, 4a' in Roland Barthes et al., *Exégèse et herméneutique* (Paris: Seuil, 1971), pp. 67–84.

10 G.-G. Granger, *Essai d'une philosophie du style* (Paris: A. Colin, 1968), p. 115.

6. Metaphor and the central problem of hermeneutics

1 On this subject, see: I.A. Richards, *The Philosophy of Rhetoric* (New York: Oxford University Press, 1936); Max Black, *Models and Metaphors* (Ithaca: Cornell University Press, 1962); Monroe Beardsley, *Aesthetics* (New York: Harcourt, Brace and World, 1958), and 'The metaphorical twist', *Philosophy and Phenomenological Research*, 20 (1962), pp. 293–307; Douglas Berggren,

'The use and abuse of metaphor, I and II', *Review of Metaphysics*, 16 (1962), pp. 237–58, and 16 (1963), pp. 450–72.
2 *Models and Metaphors*, p. 46.
3 Ibid., p. 43; see condition 4 in his summary, p. 44.
4 *Aesthetics*, p. 138.
5 Cf. 'The metaphorical twist'.
6 Ibid., p. 302.
7 Ibid.
8 Cf. Eric D. Hirsch, Jr, *Validity in Interpretation* (New Haven: Yale University Press, 1967), chapter 5.

7. Appropriation

1 See 'The hermeneutical function of distanciation', in this volume.
2 W. Dilthey, 'Origine et développement de l'herméneutique' (1900) in *Le Monde de l'Esprit* I (Paris: Aubier, 1947) [English translation: 'The development of hermeneutics' in *Selected Writings*, edited and translated by H.P. Rickman (Cambridge: Cambridge University Press, 1976)].
3 Hans-Georg Gadamer, *Wahrheit und Methode* (Tübingen: J.C.B. Mohr, 1960) [English translation: *Truth and Method* (London: Sheed and Ward, 1975)].
4 Ibid., p. 109 [p. 102].†
5 See F. van Rossum-Guyon, 'Point de vue ou perspective narrative'; Wolfgang Kayser, 'Qui raconte le roman?'; and Wayne C. Booth, 'Distance et point de vue'; all in *Poétique*, IV (1970). In France a related problem was posed by J. Pouillon in his work *Temps et roman* (Paris: Gallimard, 1946).
6 Cf. F. van Rossum-Guyon, 'Point de vue ou perspective narrative', pp. 481–2 and 485–90.
7 W.C. Booth, quoted in F. van Rossum-Guyon, ibid., p. 482.
8 W. Dilthey, quoted in F. van Rossum-Guyon, ibid., p. 486.
9 F.K. Stanzel, quoted in F. van Rossum-Guyon, ibid., p. 490.
10 Wolfgang Kayser, 'Qui raconte le roman?', p. 510.
11 Ibid., p. 502.
12 Ibid., p. 510.
13 See 'Hermeneutics and the critique of ideology', in this volume.
14 See Paul Ricoeur, 'The question of the subject: the challenge of semiology', translated by Kathleen McLaughlin, in *The Conflict of Interpretations: Essays in Hermeneutics*, edited by Don Ihde (Evanston: Northwestern University Press, 1974), pp. 236–66.

8. The model of the text

1 Anthony Kenny, *Action, Emotion and Will* (London: Routledge and Kegan Paul, 1963).
2 J.L. Austin, *How to do Things with Words* (Oxford: Oxford University Press, 1962).
3 John R. Searle, *Speech Acts: An Essay in the Philosophy of Language* (Cambridge: Cambridge University Press, 1969), p. 56.
4 Joel Feinberg, *Reason and Responsibility* (Belmont, Calif.: Dickenson, 1965).
5 Peter Winch, *The Idea of a Social Science and its Relation to Philosophy* (London: Routledge and Kegan Paul, 1958).

6 Eric D. Hirsch, Jr, *Validity in Interpretation* (New Haven: Yale University Press, 1967), p. 25: 'The act of understanding is at first a genial (or a mistaken) guess and there are no methods for making guesses, no rules for generating insights; the methodological activity of interpretation commences when we begin to test and criticize our guesses'; and further: 'A mute symbolism may be construed in several ways.'

7 Ibid., pp. 164ff.

8 Karl Popper, *The Logic of Scientific Discovery* (New York: Basic Books, 1959).

9 G.E.M. Anscombe, *Intention* (Oxford: Basil Blackwell, 1972); A.I. Melden, *Free Action* (London: Routledge and Kegan Paul, 1961).

10 H.L.A. Hart, 'The ascription of responsibility and rights', *Proceedings of the Aristotelian Society*, 49 (1948), pp. 171–94.

11 Claude Lévi-Strauss, *Anthropologie structurale* (Paris: Plon, 1958) [English translation: *Structural Anthropology*, translated by Claire Jacobson and Brooke Grundfest Schoepf (Harmondsworth: Penguin Books, 1968)].

12 Ibid., p. 241 [p. 217].†

9. Science and ideology

1 Jacques Ellul, 'Le rôle médiateur de l'idéologie', in *Démythisation et idéologie*, edited by E. Castelli (Paris: Aubier, 1973), pp. 335–54.

2 Ibid., p. 351.

3 Karl Marx and Frederick Engels, *The German Ideology*, edited by C.J. Arthur (London: Lawrence and Wishart, 1970), p. 47.

4 Maurice Lagueux, 'L'usage abusif du rapport science/idéologie', *Culture et langage* (Montreal: Cahiers du Québec, 1973), p. 202.

5 Ibid., p. 219.

6 Ibid., p. 217.

7 Sarah Kofman, *Camera Obscura. De l'idéologie* (Paris: Galilée, 1973).

8 Ibid., p. 25.

9 Jean Ladrière, 'Signes et concepts en science' in *L'Articulation du sens* (Paris: Cerf, 1970), pp. 40–50 [English translation: 'Signs and concepts in science' in *Language and Belief*, translated by Garrett Barden (Dublin: Gill and Macmillan, 1972), pp. 17–43].

10 Ibid., p. 42 [p. 34].

11 Max Weber, 'The meaning of "ethical neutrality" in sociology and economics' in *The Methodology of the Social Sciences*, translated and edited by Edward A. Shils and Henry A. Finch (Glencoe: The Free Press, 1949), pp. 1–49.

12 *L'Articulation du sens*, p. 42 [*Language and Belief*, p. 35].

13 Ibid., p. 43 [p. 36].†

14 Karl Mannheim, *Ideologie und Utopie* (Bonn: F. Cohen, 1929) [English translation: *Ideology and Utopia*, translated by Louis Wirth and Edward Shils (London: Routledge and Kegan Paul, 1936; hereafter cited in the text as *IU*)].

15 See 'Hermeneutics and the critique of ideology', in this volume.

16 Martin Heidegger, *Sein und Zeit* (Tübingen: Max Niemeyer, 1927), p. 153 [English translation: *Being and Time*, translated by John Macquarrie and Edward Robinson (Oxford: Basil Blackwell, 1978), p. 195].†

10. The question of proof in Freud's writings

1 All references to Freud's writings are to the *Standard Edition*, 24 volumes (London: Hogarth Press, 1953–), hereafter cited in the text as *SE*, followed by the volume number and the page number.

2 Jacques Lacan, *Ecrits* (Paris: Seuil, 1966), pp. 256, 839.

3 Jean Laplanche and J.-B. Pontalis, *Vocabulaire de la psychanalyse* (Paris: Presses Universitaires de France, 1967), p. 33.

4 Jürgen Habermas, *Knowledge and Human Interests*, translated by Jeremy J. Shapiro (London: Heinemann, 1972), p. 247.

5 Alfred Lorenzer, *Über den Gegenstand der Psychoanalyse* (Frankfurt: Suhrkamp, 1973).

6 For a discussion of the phenomenological interpretation at length, see Paul Ricoeur, *Freud and Philosophy: An Essay on Interpretation*, translated by Denis Savage (New Haven: Yale University Press, 1970); for a discussion of the properly linguistic formulations, see Paul Ricoeur, 'Language and image in psychoanalysis' in *Psychiatry and the Humanities* III, edited by Joseph H. Smith (New Haven: Yale University Press, 1978).

7 Michael Sherwood, *The Logic of Explanation in Psychoanalysis* (New York: Academic Press, 1969).

8 Ibid., p. 172.

9 See Paul Ricoeur, 'Psychiatry and moral values', in *American Handbook of Psychiatry* I, edited by S. Arieti et al. (New York: Basic Books, 1974).

10 *Freud and Philosophy*, pp. 372–3.

11 See Paul Ricoeur, 'Fatherhood: From phantasm to symbol', translated by Robert Sweeney, in *The Conflict of Interpretations: Essays in Hermeneutics*, edited by Don Ihde (Evanston: Northwestern University Press, 1974).

12 *The Logic of Explanation in Psychoanalysis*, p. 4.

13 Ibid., p. 169.

14 Thomas Kuhn, *The Structure of Scientific Revolutions* (Chicago: University of Chicago Press, 1962).

15 W.B. Gallie, *Philosophy and Historical Understanding* (New York: Schocken Books, 1964).

11. The narrative function

1 Carl Hempel, 'The function of general laws in history' in *Aspects of Scientific Explanation and Other Essays in the Philosophy of Science* (New York: The Free Press, 1942), pp. 231–43.

2 Charles Frankel, 'Explanation and interpretation in history' in *Theories of History*, edited by Patrick Gardner (New York: The Free Press, 1959), pp. 409, 410.

3 W.B. Gallie, *Philosophy and Historical Understanding* (New York: Schocken Books, 1964).

4 Ibid., p. 66.

5 Louis O. Mink, 'History and fiction as modes of comprehension' in *New Directions in Literary History*, edited by Ralph Cohen (Baltimore: Johns Hopkins University Press, 1974), p. 117.

6 Robert E. Scholes and Robert Kellogg, *The Nature of Narrative* (New York: Oxford University Press, 1966), p. 240.

7 Cf. Roland Barthes, 'Introduction à l'analyse structurale du récit', *Communications*, 8 (1966), pp. 1–27 [English translation: 'Introduction to the structural analysis of narratives', in *Image-Music-Text*, edited and translated by Stephen Heath (London: Fontana/Collins, 1977), pp. 79–124].

8 A.J. Greimas, *Sémantique structurale: recherche de méthode* (Paris: Librarie Larousse, 1966). Cf. Corina Galland, 'Introduction à la méthode de A.J. Greimas', *Etudes théologiques et religieuses*, 48 (1973), pp. 35–48.

9 A.J. Greimas, *Sémantique structurale*, p. 176.

10 Ibid., p. 205.

11 Ibid., p. 206.

12 Robert E. Scholes and Robert Kellogg, *The Nature of Narrative*, p. 57.

13 Ibid., p. 81.

14 Northrop Frye, *Anatomy of Criticism* (Princeton: Princeton University Press, 1957), p. 97.

15 Hayden White, 'The historical text as literary artefact', *Clio*, 3 (1974), pp. 277–303.

16 Stephan C. Pepper, *World Hypotheses: A Study in Evidence* (Berkeley: University of California Press, 1942).

17 Nelson Goodman, *Languages of Art: An Approach to a Theory of Symbols* (Indianapolis: Bobbs-Merrill, 1969), p. 241.

Select bibliography

The bibliography is divided into two parts. The first part lists Ricoeur's major books and collections of essays, as well as those articles which are relevant to the issues discussed in this volume. The second part mentions some of the secondary literature on Ricoeur.

Writings by Paul Ricoeur

The following list is not exhaustive. For a full bibliography of Ricoeur's writings up to 1972, see:

Vansina, Dirk F. 'Bibliographie de Paul Ricoeur (jusqu'au 30 juin 1962)', *Revue philosophique de Louvain*, 60 (1962), pp. 394–413.

'Bibliographie de Paul Ricoeur, compléments (jusqu'à la fin de 1967)', *Revue philosophique de Louvain*, 66 (1968), pp. 85–101.

'Bibliographie de Paul Ricoeur, compléments (jusqu'à la fin de 1972)', *Revue philosophique de Louvain*, 72 (1974), pp. 156–81.

An abridged and updated version of this bibliography may be found on pages 180–94 of:

Reagan, Charles E., ed. *Studies in the Philosophy of Paul Ricoeur*. Athens, Ohio: Ohio University Press, 1979.

Books

The books in this section are listed according to the order in which they first appeared. If an item originally published in French has been translated into English, then only the English edition is cited; the original date of publication is given in square brackets.

Gabriel Marcel et Karl Jaspers: Philosophie du mystère et philosophie du paradoxe. Paris: Temps présent, 1947.

Karl Jaspers et la philosophie de l'existence (with Mikel Dufrenne). Paris: Seuil, 1947.

Freedom and Nature: The Voluntary and the Involuntary, tr. Erazim V. Kohák. Evanston: Northwestern University Press, 1966 [1950].

History and Truth, tr. Charles A. Kelbley. Evanston: Northwestern University Press, 1965 [1955].

Fallible Man, tr. Charles A. Kelbley. Chicago: Henry Regnery, 1965 [1960].

The Symbolism of Evil, tr. Emerson Buchanan. New York: Harper and Row, 1967 [1960].

Freud and Philosophy: An Essay on Interpretation, tr. Denis Savage. New Haven: Yale University Press, 1970 [1965].

Husserl: An Analysis of His Phenomenology, tr. E.G. Ballard and L.E. Embree. Evanston: Northwestern University Press, 1967.

The Conflict of Interpretations: Essays in Hermeneutics, ed. Don Ihde, tr. Willis Domingo et al. Evanston: Northwestern University Press, 1974 [1969].

Political and Social Essays, ed. David Stewart and Joseph Bien, tr. Donald Siewert et al. Athens, Ohio: Ohio University Press, 1974.

The Rule of Metaphor: Multi-Disciplinary Studies of the Creation of Meaning in Language, tr. Robert Czerny. London: Routledge and Kegan Paul, 1978 [1975].

Interpretation Theory: Discourse and the Surplus of Meaning. Fort Worth: Texas Christian University Press, 1976.

The Philosophy of Paul Ricoeur: An Anthology of His Work, ed. Charles E. Reagan and David Stewart. Boston: Beacon Press, 1978.

Articles

The articles in this section, all of which appeared during the last fifteen years, are listed in alphabetical order. If the article has been published in English, then only the English version is cited.

'Biblical hermeneutics', *Semeia*, 4 (1975), pp. 29–148.

'Can there be a scientific concept of ideology?', in *Phenomenology and the Social Sciences: A Dialogue*, ed. Joseph Bien, pp. 44–59. The Hague: Martinus Nijhoff, 1978.

'Hegel and Husserl on intersubjectivity', in *Reason, Action, and Experience: Essays in Honor of Raymond Klibansky*, ed. Helmut Kohlenberger, pp. 13–29. Hamburg: Felix Meiner, 1979.

'History and hermeneutics', *Journal of Philosophy*, 73 (1976), pp. 683–94.

'Husserl and Wittgenstein on language', in *Phenomenology and Existentialism*, ed. E.N. Lee and M. Mandelbaum, pp. 207–17. Baltimore: Johns Hopkins University Press, 1967.

'Ideology and utopia as cultural imagination', *Philosophic Exchange*, 2 (summer 1976), pp. 17–30.

'Imagination in discourse and in action', in *Analecta Husserliana*, vol. 7, ed. Anna-Teresa Tymieniecka, pp. 3–22. Dordrecht: D. Reidel, 1978.

'Language and image in psychoanalysis', in *Psychiatry and the Humanities*, vol. 3, ed. Joseph H. Smith, pp. 293–324. New Haven: Yale University Press, 1978.

'New developments in phenomenology in France: the phenomenology of language', *Social Research*, 34 (1967), pp. 1–30.

'Phenomenology and the social sciences', *Annals of Phenomenological Sociology* (1977), pp. 145–59.

'Phenomenology of freedom', in *Phenomenology and Philosophical Understanding*, ed. Edo Pivčević, pp. 173–94. Cambridge: Cambridge University Press, 1975.

'Philosophie et langage', *Revue philosophique de la France et de l'Etranger*, 4 (1978), pp. 449–63.

'Psychoanalysis and the work of art', in *Psychiatry and the Humanities*, vol. 1, ed. Joseph H. Smith, pp. 3–33. New Haven: Yale University Press, 1976.

'Schleiermacher's hermeneutics', *Monist*, 60 (1977), pp. 181–97.

'The function of fiction in shaping reality', *Man and World*, 12 (1979), pp. 123–41.

'The metaphorical process as cognition, imagination, and feeling', *Critical Inquiry*, 5 (1978), pp. 143–59.
'Writing as a problem for literary criticism and philosophical hermeneutics', *Philosophic Exchange*, 2 (summer 1977), pp. 3–15.

Secondary literature

The following list mentions book-length studies or collections of studies on Ricoeur's work. The items are listed in alphabetical order. For a more extensive bibliography of the secondary literature, see:
Lapointe, François H. 'Paul Ricoeur and his critics: a bibliographic essay', in *Studies in the Philosophy of Paul Ricoeur*, ed. Charles E. Reagan, pp. 164–77. Athens, Ohio: Ohio University Press, 1979.

Bourgeois, Patrick L. *Extension of Ricoeur's Hermeneutic*. The Hague: Martinus Nijhoff, 1973.
Ihde, Don. *Hermeneutic Phenomenology: The Philosophy of Paul Ricoeur*. Evanston: Northwestern University Press, 1971.
Madison, Gary B., ed. *Sens et existence: en hommage à Paul Ricoeur*. Paris: Seuil, 1975.
Philibert, Michel. *Paul Ricoeur ou la liberté selon l'espérance*. Paris: Seghers, 1971.
Rasmussen, David. *Mythic-Symbolic Language and Philosophical Anthropology*. The Hague: Martinus Nijhoff, 1971.
Reagan, Charles E., ed. *Studies in the Philosophy of Paul Ricoeur*. Athens, Ohio: Ohio University Press, 1979.
Thompson, John B. *Critical Hermeneutics: A Study in the Thought of Paul Ricoeur and Jürgen Habermas*. Cambridge: Cambridge University Press, 1981.

Index